Developing Power in Reading

Fifth Edition

Betty D. Roe

Elinor P. Ross

Tennessee Technological University

KENDALL/HUNT PUBLISHING COMPANY
2460 Kerper Boulevard P.O. Box 539 Dubuque, Iowa 52004-0539

Large cover photograph courtesy of ALLSTOCK.

Smaller cover photographs courtesy of Nancy Ann Dawe.

Photographs on pages viii, 16, 48, 82, 100, 114, 160, 194, 238, 262, 292, and 318 by Michael H. Roe

CONTENTS

9

Application of Reading/Study Skills to Content Areas 239

10

Rate 263

11

Functional and Recreational Reading 293

12

Professional Reading 319

Appendix 345

Index 411

PREFACE

This book provides a balanced program covering major reading strategies necessary for developing power in reading, such as study skills, vocabulary, general comprehension, critical reading, content area reading, rate, functional reading, recreational reading, and professional reading. Ways to improve strategies and exercises for practicing strategies are provided in each chapter.

This book can be used profitably in several possible ways.

1. As a basic textbook in a college reading improvement course. (See the *Instructor's Manual* for two possible plans for use of the book—one for use in a quarter system and the other for use in a semester system.)

2. For selected studies, assigned by a teacher or counselor in a student's areas of weakness.

3. As a basis for a performance contractual system. (When a contractual system is used, each chapter could serve as the nucleus of one or more projects.)

4. As an independent study tool in situations in which students plan their own programs based on recognized needs. (The answers to the exercises are provided in an Answer Key found in the *Instructor's Manual*. Instructors may wish to duplicate this key for use by students in an independent study program.)

In using this textbook, students should first read the explanatory material on each topic. Then they should complete the related exercises. When using this textbook for a generalized independent study program, each student should choose a rate exercise (found in the Appendix) to complete each week in order to practice rate skills. The first rate exercise is the easiest, and the exercises become more difficult as the exercise numbers increase, so a student may wish to begin with lower-numbered exercises and work up to higher-numbered exercises. Of course, individual factors such as background experiences or interests may make later exercises easier for certain individuals. Progress in rate should be recorded on the charts in the Appendix.

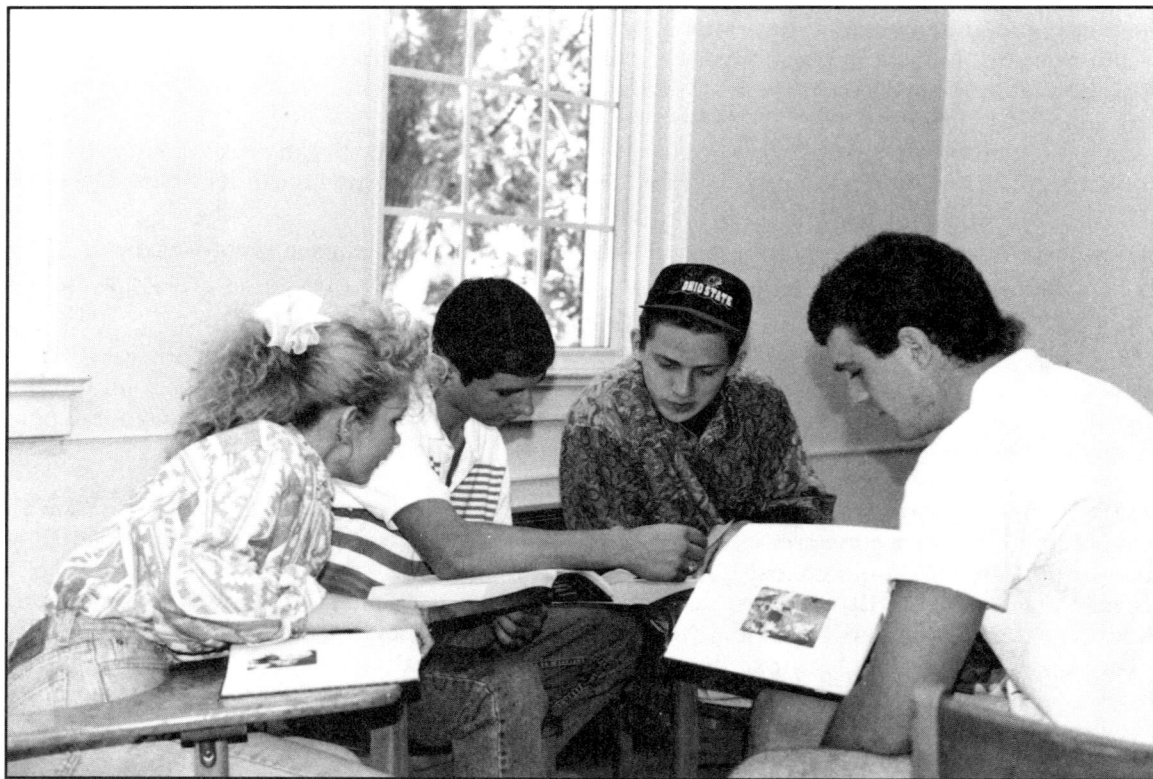

1 Self-Awareness

A few entering freshmen arrived early for class. As they waited, Fran looked tentatively around the group and began, "I really don't know what to expect. I've been out of school so long, but I've finally got my last child in school. I guess it's now or never. My husband took off, and I refuse to spend the rest of my life working for fast food places."

Mark said, "I really want to get into the courses that I'll need for pharmacy school—but I suppose it's a good idea to brush up on study skills and reading before I begin them. I hear those courses can be pretty rough."

"I'm here because I want to build bridges," added Lee. "I've *always* wanted to build bridges. I've been out of school seven years, saving money to get to college. I'm keeping my job part time while I take courses. I hope I can manage both."

Hestitatingly, Carlos admitted, "Nobody in my family has ever gone to college. I'm not sure what *I'm* doing here! But I got a grant that pays my tuition, and my high school counselor told me to give it a try. Maybe I can get to be a teacher—you know, help little kids learn. I'd really like to do that."

"It doesn't sound like it's going to be easy for any of us," Fran commented.

Glancing quickly around the group, Mark agreed. "You're right about that. It's going to be tough to keep up, but I suppose this course is a good place to start."

"The first thing I've got to do is learn how to study," said Carlos. "I never was much good at reading and writing and studying. I'm counting on this course to get me off to a good start."

"What do you know about this course?" Lee asked Fran.

"I think it's supposed to help us do better in our main courses—you know, so we can study better and understand more of what we read. I hope so because I can't afford to fail any courses."

"It looks like we get to make some choices about what work we do in here," added Carlos. "What do you think you need most, Mark?"

"For me, it's understanding what I read. I've always had trouble with making sense out of the words on the page."

"That looks like the teacher coming now," said Lee. "Let's get together after class and talk some more. I know I can use some help getting started."

Introduction

You have been going to school for many years now, and you are probably somewhat aware of your study habits, learning style, thought patterns, and attitudes as a student. When you understand yourself and how you learn—or fail to learn—you are taking an important step toward succeeding in college. This chapter should help you see your present strengths and weaknesses as a student and help you discover more effective strategies than those you use now.

The first activity is completing the Self-Awareness Inventory, SA Exercise 1. By causing you to think about your reactions to different situations, this inventory should help you become more aware of your learning strategies. When you complete the inventory, read the analysis that follows.

SA Exercise 1

Choose the answer that is *usually* true for you, even though more than one answer might be appropriate sometimes. Write the letter in the space.

Self-Awareness Inventory

_____ 1. When taking notes from a lecture, I usually
    a. try to write down everything.
    b. randomly select some of the ideas.
    c. identify and write down the important points.

_____ 2. When studying for an exam from my class notes, I usually find the notes
    a. incomprehensible.
    b. incomplete.
    c. adequate.

_____ 3. When I study, I usually
    a. need to get up and get supplies (dictionary, paper, pencil, etc.) frequently.
    b. have everything I need but get up because I'm restless.
    c. get down to work without frequent breaks because I have everything I need.

_____ 4. If I don't understand something, I usually
    a. avoid it, hoping I'll get by.
    b. ask someone about it.
    c. try to figure it out.

_____ 5. When I read a chapter in my textbook, I usually
    a. read it straight through, giving equal attention to each word.
    b. skip through it and read the parts that interest me.
    c. try to pick out the major points.

_____ 6. When I come to illustrations or other graphic aids in the textbook, I usually
  a. skip over them.
  b. glance at them casually.
  c. try to relate them to the narrative portion of the text.

_____ 7. When I try to remember material for an exam, I usually
  a. rely on memory tricks.
  b. make silly associations.
  c. relate new material to what I already know.

_____ 8. I prepare for exams by
  a. cramming the night before the exam.
  b. completing each assignment when it is due.
  c. completing assignments when due and reviewing periodically.

_____ 9. On an exam, I usually
  a. answer each question as I come to it.
  b. concentrate on the most difficult questions.
  c. work quickly through the exam, answering questions I'm sure of first.

_____ 10. When taking a test, the questions are usually
  a. a complete surprise.
  b. some that I expected and others that I did not anticipate.
  c. about what I expected them to be.

_____ 11. If I want to find a specific topic in my book, I am likely to
  a. flip through the pages hunting for it randomly.
  b. look in the table of contents.
  c. look in the index.

_____ 12. When I go to the library, I
  a. seldom know how to find what I need.
  b. usually ask for help in locating materials.
  c. usually find what I want.

_____ 13. When I need to study but I'm tempted to do something else, I usually
  a. give in to temptation.
  b. compromise—do a little of both.
  c. study.

_____ 14. I work best when
  a. someone tells me exactly what to do and checks up on me.
  b. I follow the same plan for every assignment.
  c. I work at my own pace and in my own way.

_____ 15. When the teacher calls on me unexpectedly during class, I usually
     a. guess at the answer.
     b. go blank.
     c. give the right answer.

_____ 16. When studying for an exam, I usually
     a. run out of time.
     b. have time left over.
     c. have about the right amount of time.

_____ 17. If I want to get good grades, I have to
     a. study nearly all the time.
     b. give up my social life.
     c. carefully balance my time between studying and extracurricular activities.

_____ 18. If I have a term paper to write, I
     a. wait until the last minute.
     b. am not sure how to proceed.
     c. organize the assignment and meet self-imposed deadlines.

_____ 19. When I think about my course work, I generally feel
     a. that it is a waste of time.
     b. discouraged and depressed.
     c. that I am learning something worthwhile.

_____ 20. When the teacher assigns homework, I usually
     a. try to get out of doing it.
     b. resent the assignment but do it anyway.
     c. do it because it will probably help me learn what I need to know.

_____ 21. When it's time to go to class, I usually
     a. dread going.
     b. go because attendance is required.
     c. go to learn something.

_____ 22. When I don't understand an assignment, I'm likely to
     a. not do it.
     b. do it any way I can.
     c. ask for clarification.

The a. responses indicate poor approaches to learning, while the c. answers indicate good approaches to learning. The b. answers are not necessarily good or bad indicators. If you marked ten or more a. responses, you will need to work hard to develop more positive approaches to learning. If ten or more of your responses are c., you have already developed some effective learning strategies.

The questions in the Inventory are divided into the following categories: 1–4, study skills; 5–6, textbook reading; 7–10, exams; 11–12, reference skills; 13–14, self-discipline; 15–16, stress; 17–19, time management; and 20–23, attitude. The b. choice of 3 and the c. choice of 17 are also related to self-discipline. The b. choices for 4 and 12 and the c. choice for 22 deal with asking for help, often a good strategy to follow when you are unsure of yourself. Now, look back at the Inventory and see if you can identify your strong and weak areas.

Metacognition

If you were able to answer the questions on the Self-Awareness Inventory easily, you know yourself pretty well. Understanding how you study and what you know is part of a process called metacognition, which is the ability to think about and control your own thinking.

Good students use metacognitive strategies intuitively while they read. Such strategies include

1. setting purposes for reading,
2. sifting through the material to find what is important,
3. checking frequently to make sure you are comprehending,
4. varying your rate according to your purposes and the difficulty of the material,
5. applying corrective techniques when unable to comprehend, and
6. evaluating comprehension through self-questioning and review.

Poor readers, on the other hand, do not usually apply this mental assessment of how well they are learning. Instead, they are likely to simply move their eyes over the pages without constantly checking their understanding of the material and without applying corrective strategies.

If you find that you are not understanding what you read, here are some corrective strategies that might help.

1. Think about what you already know about a subject and relate it to what you are reading.
2. Look for the headings, italicized words, introductory statements, and other clues to meaning. See how the material fits into an organizational pattern or framework.
3. Ask yourself what you think the author is trying to say and what you are trying to find out.
4. Slow down. You may be covering the material too rapidly and skipping over some important information.
5. Reread. Go back to where you began having difficulty and reread that part.
6. Check difficult vocabulary. Use context clues (meanings of surrounding words) or look up words in the dictionary if you are not certain of the meanings of key words.
7. Write down what you think are the key points; organize the main ideas so that they make sense to you. When you write and read these points, you may see the logic of the passage.
8. For clarification, check other sources that contain similar information (encyclopedias, comparable textbooks, specialized books on the topic from the library, and audiovisual media).

As you continue with this chapter and the next, learn as much as you can about how you think and how you study. When you know your own thought processes and study habits, you should be able to overcome weaknesses and develop more effective metacognitive strategies.

Attitude

Nothing is more important to your success in school than your attitude. Your attitude toward this reading improvement course will determine what you gain from it. If you are indifferent about improving your reading and only care about getting course credit, you may be able to complete the minimum requirements with little effort, but you will probably get little benefit from the course. On the other hand, if you are serious about improving your reading ability, you will need to work through the exercises carefully, putting forth the effort that will help you really increase your reading skills.

Being aware of your attitude may help you understand why you are or are not learning as well as you should be. People with negative attitudes often have difficulty because they don't really believe in what they are doing. Those with positive attitudes, on the other hand, are determined to do well and really believe they will succeed. A positive attitude can often overcome such handicaps as inadequate preparation for higher education and limited intelligence. The student who is determined to succeed will persist until the goal is reached.

In Table 1 there are two lists of attitudes you may have. The statements in the first list indicate positive attitudes toward learning, while those in the second list are negative. Check those statements in both lists that pertain to you. When you have finished, count the responses in each column to see if you have a basically positive or negative attitude.

Table 1

Attitude Checklist			
✔	*Positive*	✔	*Negative*
	1. I am attending school because I want to be here. 2. I feel that advanced education will help me have a good life. 3. Going to school is worth the sacrifices I must make. 4. My school work gets top priority. 5. I never miss class without a good reason. 6. I want to learn all I can while I'm here. 7. When I'm interested in learning something, I often do more than the assigned work. 8. I believe most teachers are interested in helping me learn.		1. I do as little as I can to get by. 2. I'm here because I don't know what else I want to do. 3. I often wonder if advanced education is worth the financial investment. 4. I rarely see the relevance between my courses and what I want to do with my life. 5. I resent the time I have to spend studying. 6. Most teachers do as little as possible and don't really care if I learn anything. 7. I cut class whenever I think I can get away with it. 8. I expect to drop out before I graduate.

If most of your checks are in the negative column, you may want to reconsider continuing with your education. If you checked mostly positive statements, you are off to a good start!

Learning Style

You have your own learning style, or overall pattern of behavior that determines how you learn best. In other words, there are certain ways and certain conditions in which you learn best. Your learning style is unique, but others may share many of the traits that make up your style. It may vary in different circumstances, and it may change as you grow older. Throughout your life, however, it will remain relatively stable.

Learning styles have cognitive, affective, and physiological aspects.[1] Cognitive aspects pertain to how people acquire knowledge or approach learning tasks. They involve ways in which people discover, process, and retrieve information. For instance, one person might consistently try to solve a problem by first analyzing its parts, while another might instead look first at the overall issue.

Affective aspects of your learning style are related to your emotions and attitudes. They include such personal traits as determination, sense of responsibility, willingness to take risks, interests, and motivation. For example, you may be motivated to do something for your own satisfaction, or you may be motivated only if someone offers you a reward for doing it.

Your sensory perception is a major aspect of your physiological learning style. In other words, do you learn better by listening (auditory) or by reading (visual)? Another physiological aspect is the time of day when your energy level is high and you are receptive to learning. Such environmental factors as noise level, light, and temperature also affect your ability to learn.

You should know your learning style for two reasons. First, you can set conditions in which you will learn best by observing your particular characteristics. Second, you can make some adjustments in your learning style if you need to do so. For instance, although you are a ''night person,'' you may find that you have to take an 8:00 A.M. class. Therefore, you will need to make some adjustments, perhaps by getting up early, taking a shower, eating a good breakfast, and getting to class a little early.

The first step in becoming aware of the traits that make up your learning style is to make a personal assessment. You can do this by completing the Learning Style Inventory which follows. Your answers might vary depending on the circumstances, but choose the answer that is typical of your behavior. When you finish the Inventory, write a summary in two or three sentences of your individual learning style.

SA Exercise 2

Write the letter of the *best* answer in the space.

Learning Style Inventory

_____ 1. I study best when I'm working
  a. alone.
  b. with a friend.
  c. in a group.

_____ 2. My energy level is highest
    a. early in the morning.
    b. in mid-afternoon.
    c. late at night.

_____ 3. I concentrate best
    a. in total silence.
    b. with the radio or television on.
    c. with normal noise and confusion around me.

_____ 4. I learn best if I
    a. highlight or underline important material in the text.
    b. say or read important points aloud.
    c. write important information in my own words.

_____ 5. I study best when I'm
    a. reclining in bed.
    b. sitting at a table or desk.
    c. relaxing in a comfortable chair.

_____ 6. I learn best when I study
    a. in long blocks of time.
    b. in several short blocks of time with short breaks.
    c. in no set pattern.

_____ 7. I study best when the room is
    a. warm and cozy.
    b. a little cool.
    c. about normal temperature.

_____ 8. I usually work best
    a. with dim lighting.
    b. with bright lights all around me.
    c. with normal lighting.

_____ 9. After studying a long time, I find I relax best by
    a. reading something light.
    b. exercising.
    c. visiting with friends.

_____ 10. I function best if I
    a. get eight or more hours of sleep a night.
    b. get only a few hours of sleep and nap occasionally during the day.
    c. vary the amount of sleep I get in relation to my activities.

_____ 11. I work best
    a. under pressure.
    b. when relaxed.

_____ 12. I can handle well
   a. only one thing at a time.
   b. many projects simultaneously.

Summary of my learning style:

Stress

You are constantly in situations that might cause stress. Being aware of potentially stressful situations and knowing how to deal with them can help make you a well-adjusted individual.

You experience stress when you feel mental or emotional tension. You may become tense when a teacher announces a pop quiz or when your name is called in class. Everyone is under stress at one time or another, but people experience different levels of stress and react differently to stressful situations. You cannot completely eliminate stress from your life, nor would you want to. Without some stress, you would be unable to perform at your best.

Normal indications of being under stress include having clammy palms, getting headaches, grinding your teeth, biting your fingernails, not sleeping well, breaking into a cold sweat, turning red, and developing a rapid heartbeat. A combination of these symptoms is sometimes referred to as ''stage fright.'' Everyone feels this way sometimes—you are not alone.

When you are in school, a number of factors may cause you to experience stress or anxiety. Some of these factors are misgivings about your career decision, concern about your finances, worry about not living up to expectations, doubts about your ability to do well academically, and uneasiness about your social life.

Your reaction to stressful situations has a lot to do with your ability to succeed. You can either let stress overcome you, or you can learn to deal with it. First, take preventive measures, such as getting enough sleep, exercising, and eating nourishing meals. Next, following these guidelines can help you avoid feeling tense.

1. Stop worrying. Worry won't solve your problem. Maybe nothing will happen, but, if it does, then take steps immediately to correct the situation.
2. Learn to relax. Take a break in what you are doing by stretching, taking a walk, or eating an apple. No one should work all the time.
3. Have realistic expectations for yourself. Aim high as you set your goals, but not so high that the goals are unattainable.
4. Look forward to something. When you have a lot of work to do, think ahead to a time when you can take a trip, be with people you enjoy, or do whatever you would like to do.

5. Set priorities. Don't try to do everything at once. Make a list of things to do and arrange them in order of their importance.

6. Have a sense of humor. Laughter is the enemy of stress. Seeing the funny side of a situation keeps you from feeling tense.

7. Concentrate on the good things. Think about your accomplishments, your lucky breaks, and the people who care about you.

It is important to consider how you manage your own stress during class and class-related activities. The table below suggests some pointers for reducing—not eliminating—stress in typical academic situations.

Table 2

Reducing Stress in Academic Situations	
If you have to give a presentation in class . . .	Know your topic well, but don't try to memorize your talk.
	Take a deep breath before you begin.
	Dress well so that you feel good about your appearance.
	Remember that the class is made up of individuals whom you could talk to easily on a one-to-one basis.
If you are taking a final exam . . .	Get to class a little early.
	Depending on your learning style, either look over your notes one more time or relax and talk to a classmate about something else.
	Bring adequate supplies—two sharpened pencils with erasers, a pen, a bluebook, a calculator, or whatever you will need. Know that you have studied as well as you could.
If you feel there is a personality conflict between you and the teacher . . .	Always be prepared for class by completing assignments carefully.
	Observe the interactions between the teacher and successful students; then base your behavior on the actions of these students.
	Try to analyze the problem and take steps to correct it.
If you have to write a term paper . . .	Choose your topic as soon as you can so you can begin thinking about it.
	Think of the term paper as a series of short, related assignments so you won't be overwhelmed by it.
	Set and observe deadlines for completing each of the short "assignments."
	Plan to finish early in case something else demands your attention just before the due date.

One way to learn to deal constructively with stress is to analyze your own behavior in stressful situations. What is your normal reaction? Is there a better way to react? What might you do next time? Then, if a similar situation occurs, you will be better prepared to deal with it. Use the form shown in SA Exercise 3 to keep track of the frequency of your stressful situations, your reaction to each situation, and ways to avoid or manage such situations if they should occur again. Just writing down the circumstances relieves some of your tension, and you can use the list later in discussions with your family and friends. The first blocks are filled in as an example.

SA Exercise 3

Analysis of Stress

Data	Cause of Stress	Reaction to Stress	How to Avoid/Manage Next Time
2/27	Couldn't get computer program to run.	Got mad — wanted to drop the course. Couldn't sleep.	Get started earlier. Get help. Check out program more thoroughly.

Time Management

Have you ever found that the work you have to do tends to take up all the time you have available? If you have, then you are a victim of Parkinson's Law. In order to get more use out of the time available, you need to learn how to manage your time well. Many students feel that they never have enough time, while others seem to carry heavy course loads, do well in their work, and have time for outside activities. Everyone has the same amount of time—it's what you do with your time that makes the difference.

In the Self-Awareness Inventory, a few of the questions related to self-discipline, the ability to control one's own behavior. College requires a great deal of self-discipline because it presents students with more choices than did high school. Instead of going to school in large blocks of time, perhaps from 8:00 A.M. to 3:00 P.M., the student goes to class for an hour, has a free hour, then has a two-hour lab, another free period, and one or two more hours of classes. Self-disciplined students learn to work independently and make intelligent decisions regarding the use of time. Other students will probably waste a great deal of time.

SA Exercise 4

If you want to manage your time more effectively, you will need to make some changes in your daily routine. Below is a list of typical ways that people waste time. Check those that apply to you and try to think of three other ways that you waste time. Add these to the list.

_____ Watching too much television

_____ Talking on the telephone for extended periods of time

_____ Entertaining drop-in visitors

_____ Hunting for something you misplaced

_____ Waiting for something or someone

_____ Having to do work over because it wasn't correct the first time

_____ Making frequent trips to a store when one trip would do

_____

_____

_____

Now that you have identified some of your personal time wasters, try to cut back on them so you have more time available for worthwhile activities. Some guidelines for helping you use your time effectively follow.

Establish your priorities. First, jot down how you spend your time now. Your list might include soccer, fraternity activities, part-time job, car repair work, television, school work, yearbook staff, and dating. Then select the three items on your list that should get top priority and rank them in order of importance. (If you are a full-time student, school work should be your top priority.) Your prioritized list might look like this: (1) school work, (2) part-time job, (3) yearbook staff. Now that you have decided what is most important to you, focus your attention on these activities and use any remaining time for the others.

Improve your reading and study habits. You have already taken a first step by enrolling in this course, where you can learn to use efficient study methods and improve your reading speed and comprehension. If you double your reading rate, you will be able to read some of your assignments in half the time.

Improve your concentration. Focus your attention on the task and keep irrelevant thoughts out of your mind. Have you ever read a page and, at the end of it, not known what you were reading? This happens when your eyes are on the page but your thoughts are somewhere else. Force yourself to keep your *mind* on the task—another exercise in self-discipline! You will save time by reading the page only once instead of having to start over several times.

Turn away interruptions. You can seldom avoid interruptions altogether, but you can reduce their effect on your concentration. If a friend calls you on the telephone, say you'll call back later. If someone invites you to go for a cup of coffee, say you're in the middle of something right now but would be glad to go later. If you stick with your task until you complete it, you will spend less time on it than if you make several starts and stops.

Block out distractions. Choose a place to work that is relatively quiet and where you are unlikely to be disturbed. This may seem impossible, but consider your choices. What about the library, an unused corner of a lounge, or the dorm room of a friend who is out? Avoid noisy places and places where you will want to join your friends for a hamburger or a video game.

Consider your learning style. Plan to do your most difficult work when your energy level is high. Schedule study periods according to the way you learn best. Remember how much sleep you require and what happens to you when you feel pressured.

Make use of short periods of time. Anticipate times of forced inactivity and have some work with you. For instance, if you have a dentist's appointment and you usually have to wait an hour, do some homework while you are waiting. Or, if you drive to school, play a tape of a lecture or of notes you have read into the recorder.

Make a weekly schedule and follow it. Use the form in SA Exercise 5 as a guide for one week's activities. First, fill in those blocks of time that are definitely fixed, such as times for classes or work. Then block out hours or partial hours for eating, sleeping, travel, extracurricular activities, or anything that you must do. Next mark time for studying. The rule of thumb says there should be two hours of studying for each hour of class time, but the amount actually varies in different courses. You will soon see how much time you have for other things you wish to do. If no time remains, you may be trying to do too much. Consider cutting back on your work hours, dropping a course, or giving up an extracurricular activity.

Make a schedule for the term. Use a date book in which you can record dates that assignments are due or on which certain responsibilities must be met. Be thorough. For example, if it is now January 8th and you have a term paper due on March 10th, write in a series of intermediate due dates for making an outline, completing the research, writing the rough draft, and so on.

Planning, scheduling, and making lists take time. By spending a little extra time at the beginning, however, you'll be able to make better use of the time that is available to you.

SA Exercise 5

Weekly Schedule

Time	Sunday	Monday	Tuesday	Wednesday	Thursday	Friday	Saturday
6:00–7:00							
7:00–8:00							
8:00–9:00							
9:00–10:00							
10:00–11:00							
11:00–12:00							
12:00–1:00							
1:00–2:00							
2:00–3:00							
3:00–4:00							
4:00–5:00							
5:00–6:00							
6:00–7:00							
7:00–8:00							
8:00–9:00							
9:00–10:00							
10:00–11:00							
11:00–12:00							

Chapter Note

1. Claudia E. Cornett, *What You Should Know About Teaching and Learning Styles* (Bloomington, Indiana: Phi Delta Kappa Educational Foundation, 1983).

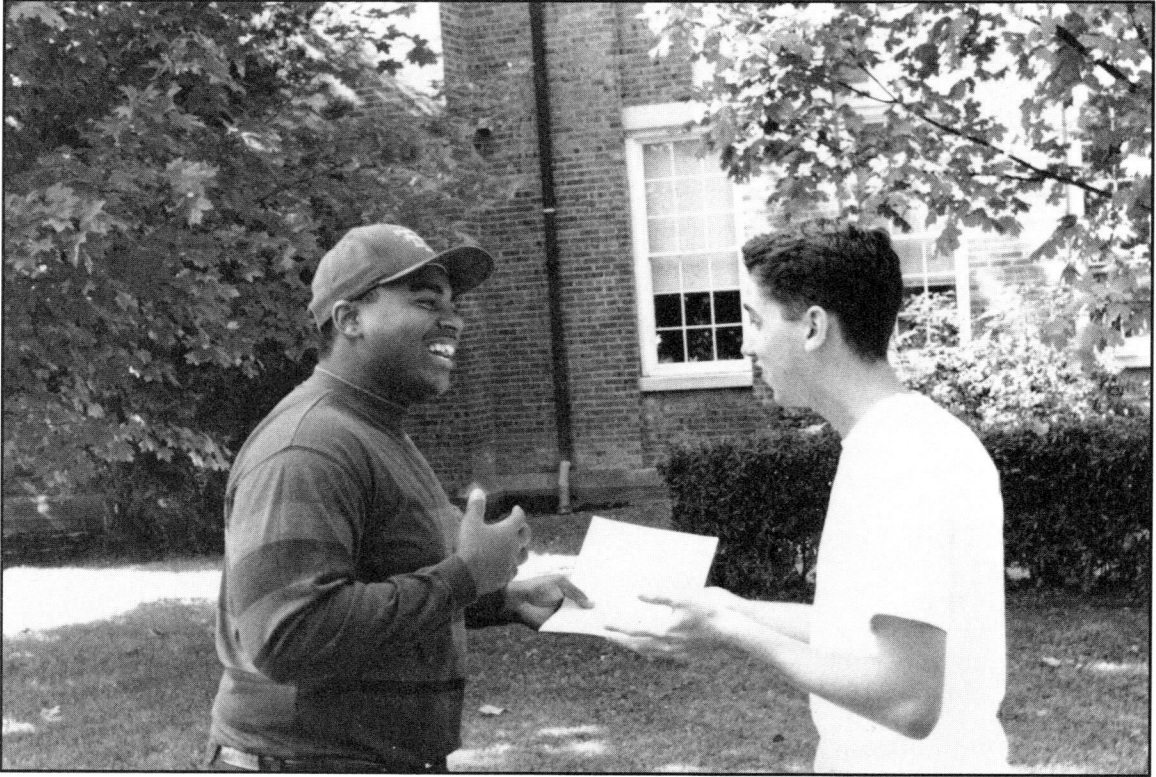

2 Study Skills and Spelling

Dale, a wide receiver on the football team, hurried over to join his friend Lonnie. "Is the coach going to have to find himself a new tailback?" he asked.

Lonnie grinned, shook his head, and held up his biology test, proudly displaying his grade of *B*.

"That's sure an improvement over the *D—* you made on the last test," Dale exclaimed, slapping Lonnie on the back. "How'd you do it?"

"I tried some of the stuff we read about in our reading class, and it paid off. I studied with Latonya and Andrea. We all read the study questions before we did our biology readings. We took notes on the points covered by the questions as we read. Then we got together and talked about the answers to the questions. I didn't do real well on some of the questions, but when I put what I thought with what Latonya and Andrea thought, I came out with better answers. I think they got some ideas from me too, but not that many. Anyway, while I was taking the test, I could remember some of the things we said to each other when we studied.

"We had also made up some silly sentences to help us remember lists. We laughed the whole time we did it, but one of the lists was on the test, and I got it all right. This stuff works! Now the coach can relax. I'm not going to be in trouble with my grades this semester. Biology is my hardest class."

Introduction

This chapter will help you improve two very important skills: study skills and spelling. Knowing how to study effectively and being able to apply spelling generalizations and strategies can improve the quality of your work. Read each of the following sections carefully and do the exercises to strengthen your study skills and spelling ability.

Study Skills

You may have trouble studying simply because you do not know how to study. You may make studying into a much more difficult task than it actually is. Many students find that, after they improve their study techniques, their study time becomes much more satisfying to them. Part of this chapter is designed to help you develop your study skills.

The Setting for Study

When you start to work on a reading-study assignment—or any assignment—you should look for the best study location available. A place with a quiet atmosphere will be best for study. The lighting should be adequate, and there should not be a glare on the work area's surface. You may not be able to find a perfect setting, but you can locate the best possible one available to you. If there is no reasonable place for you to study at home or in the dormitory, you could try studying in a library. Some advantages of doing so are the quiet atmosphere, the lack of distractions such as television and radio, and the easy access to reference materials.

Procedures for Study

Preparation

When you sit down to study, approach your task in a businesslike manner. Have all of your study materials—textbook, dictionary, class notes, paper, pencils—within reach so that you will not waste time searching for needed materials after your study period has started.

Methods

You will gain more from your reading-study activities if you use a good reading-study method, such as the SQ3R Method[1] or the SQRQCQ Method[2]. These techniques help you approach your assignments purposefully and methodically. SQ3R will help you retain more of what you read, whereas SQRQCQ will help you understand difficult mathematics statement problems.

The steps in the SQ3R Method are as follows:

SURVEY. Survey the material you are about to read by reading chapter titles, introductory paragraphs, major headings, and summary paragraphs in order to discover the main points that the author is presenting. Your survey should include an inspection of any visual aids included in the chapter also. This survey gives you a framework for organizing the details you will glean in closer reading of the material.

QUESTION. Make a question out of the first heading in the assignment. This step helps you to read purposefully, for you will be looking for an answer to the question that you have just formulated. Comprehension and retention are both better when reading is purposeful.

READ. Read to find the answer to the question that you have just formulated. You may wish to take notes as you read.

RECITE. After you finish reading the first section, try to answer your purpose question without referring to your book. This active question-answering process will help you remember the material longer.

NOTE: AT THIS POINT YOU SHOULD REPEAT THE QUESTION, READ, AND RECITE STEPS FOR EACH HEADING IN YOUR ASSIGNMENT.

REVIEW. At the end of the lesson, review the entire assignment briefly. You may go back over your notes or refer back to the chapter headings to refresh your memory and get an overview of the assigned materials, noting the relationships of the various points made in the lesson.

To practice using the SQ3R approach, follow this procedure with Chapter 10 in this textbook. The first step is to *survey* the chapter, so turn in this book to the first page of Chapter 10 and read the title. Then read the first sentence in the first *introductory* paragraph (found under the heading "Introduction") and skim through the rest of the paragraph. Do the same thing with the second introductory paragraph to see what the chapter will be about. Notice that the second major heading is "Concepts Related to Rate" and that three subheadings follow this heading. You will see that there is an exercise in this section and that the next major topic is "Physical Factors Related to Rapid Reading." The first subheading here is "Eye Movements," and two triangular-looking displays of words come next. You will want to look at these more closely later. A second subheading is "Vocalizations," followed by more exercises. "Increasing Your Rate" follows. You see a discussion of skimming next, followed by more exercises. The chapter ends with a discussion of and practice in scanning. You note that toward the end of the chapter the exercises get longer.

Now you have surveyed the chapter by looking through it and getting a general idea of the content. You are ready for the next step, *question*. You will need to turn the first heading into a question to set a purpose for reading the first part of this chapter. Go back to the beginning of the chapter where you see the heading "Concepts Related to Rate." In order to turn this heading into a question, all you have to do is add a few words so that the question says "What are some concepts related to rate?"

Look next at the three subheadings. You can turn the first one, "Flexibility," into a question by asking "What is flexibility?" For the next subheading, "Relation of Rate to Comprehension," you might ask "How is rate related to comprehension?" The final subheading in the section is "Role of Machines." Turn this one into a question by saying "What is the role of machines?"

Now you are ready to *read* the part of the chapter that goes with the first major heading and the three subheadings. Read it this time without doing the exercises. You may want to take some notes to help you remember important points. When you finish reading this section, you are ready to *recite*. See if you can answer the question "What are some concepts related to rate?" without looking back at your book or your notes. Do the same thing with the three questions taken from the subheadings. Then follow the same procedure with the next four sections of this chapter.

SS Exercise 1

Make questions out of the following headings and subheadings that appear in Chapter 10.

Heading or Subheading

Physical Factors Related to Rapid Reading _____

Eye Movements _____

Vocalizations _____

Increasing Your Rate _____

Reading Words in Groups _____

Procedures for Practicing Rapid Reading _____

Skimming _____

Purposes for Skimming _____

Techniques for Skimming _____

Scanning _____

Purposes for Scanning _____

When you have completed the first four steps of SQ3R for each part of the chapter, you are ready to *review*. Look back through the entire chapter to make sure you have in mind the major ideas that are discussed. Notice how the chapter begins by presenting some general background information on rate and then moves to specific techniques for rapid reading. Think of how this material can be useful to you.

Try to apply the SQ3R Method to any assigned reading you do this week. Don't feel discouraged if it takes you a little longer to study in this manner. You will find the study time you use now will lead to shorter review sessions for exams, because retention after using SQ3R is much greater than retention after a single reading of the material. One reason for this result is that the SQ3R method keeps you actively involved in your reading and requires you to continually react to what you have read. You will also find that as you practice using SQ3R, the time required to apply it will decrease as you become more familiar with the method.

The steps in the SQRQCQ Method for math are as follows:

SURVEY. This survey is a little different from the survey in the SQ3R Method. In it you read through the problem fairly rapidly to get a general idea of what it is about. You do not skip any material in this survey, but you do not take time to ponder over each separate statement.

QUESTION. You ask yourself: "What is being asked in this problem?"

READ. Next you read the problem through very carefully, paying attention to all facts presented and the relationships described.

QUESTION. Keep in mind the details you collected during the careful reading of the problem. Then decide what mathematical operations must be performed and, if more than one operation is involved, in what order the operations are to be performed. Ask yourself: "What operations must I perform? In what order should I perform them?"

COMPUTE. Now, carry out the computations that you decided on in the last "Question" step.

QUESTION. Finally, check the process that you carried out and decide if the answer you obtained seems to be correct. Estimate a reasonable answer. Ask yourself: "Is the answer I reached reasonable? Did I perform the computations accurately?"

Use this method with the next statement problems you are assigned to do in math class. Notice how applying these steps to the problems makes them seem more manageable because you have some direction in approaching them.

Wise Use of the Textbook

Your textbook has been designed to help you master the material presented. Most textbooks contain main headings and subheadings that help you find information you are looking for and also help you see the general organization of the material.

Many textbooks contain graphic aids that can help you to understand the concepts which are being explained in the textbook. These aids should be studied as carefully as the narrative material because they can enhance your comprehension of the textbook material. If you have difficulty reading graphic material in your textbook, refer to Chapter 8: Content Area Reading for help in learning how to interpret such material.

Your textbook contains other aids that you should be able to use effectively when you study. Not all textbooks contain all of the aids discussed below, but all textbooks will contain some of them.

Preface and/or Introduction

Many readers skip these important aids that appear in the front of the textbook. Skipping them is a mistake. The preface and introduction can give you an idea of the reason the textbook was written and the way in which the information is going to be presented in the body of the book. This background knowledge can help you approach the textbook in the best possible way. Did you read the preface to this textbook? If not, turn to the front of the book and do it now.

Table of Contents

The table of contents tells you what topics are covered in the book and the page number on which the coverage for each topic begins. In many cases chapter headings and subheadings are all listed so that you can easily find the information you are seeking. The table of contents eliminates the need for leafing through the entire book to locate a particular section that has the information you need.

As a check on your ability to use a table of contents, complete the following exercise.

SS Exercise 2

Write in each blank the page number to which you would turn to find information on the following main topics or subtopics in this book by referring to the Table of Contents.

1. Increasing your reading rate _____

2. Use of the dictionary _____

3. Use of context clues _____

4. Improving reading skills in the content areas _____

5. An effective study procedure _____

Index

An index is an alphabetical list of topics covered in a book. It is generally located in the back portion of the book and includes the numbers of the pages on which these topics are discussed. Most indexes have subheadings listed also. For example, an index of a book on methods of teaching reading might include the following topics and subtopics:

Basal readers, 54–70, 252–259
    description of, 54–58
    limitations of, 58–59
    vocabulary control, 56–57, 68
    workbooks, 60–67, 252

Some books will have more than one type of index. Nearly every textbook has a subject index. Author indexes are sometimes included to give you a chance to refer to the opinions, theories, and works of various people mentioned in the books. Check your textbooks to see what types of indexes, if any, that they contain. Remember that the index can be a useful tool in looking up specific facts when studying.

The brief exercise that follows will give you some practice in using an index.

SS Exercise 3

Refer to the preceding example of an index to discover the pages on which the following information should be located. Fill in the blanks with the numbers of the pages where the information should be found.

1. You have been asked to make a report on computer-assisted instruction. What pages would you check for information? _____

2. You want to know what the different types of context clues are. What pages should you read for this information? _____

3. You need to write a comprehensive report on basal readers. What pages should you use to obtain your information? _____

4. You have been asked for a written opinion of the workbooks accompanying basal readers. Where could you look for background information? _____

5. You believe that basal readers have some serious limitations, but you are not sure that authorities would agree with you. Which pages could shed some light upon this topic for you? _____

Glossaries

Many textbooks have glossaries of technical vocabulary that are intended to help students understand the specialized terms in the book. These glossaries are like little dictionaries, containing much of the information that you would find in a regular dictionary. The major difference between a glossary and a regular dictionary is that the glossary is concerned only with terms presented in the book in which it is contained. Many terms will not appear in a glossary. A glossary usually is located in the back of the book.

An extensive section on use of the dictionary is found in Chapter 3: Vocabulary: Part I. Refer to that section if you need help in using glossaries.

Bibliographies

A bibliography is a list of references on a particular subject or by a particular author. Most textbook writers include a bibliography of the books or articles from which they have obtained information either at the end of each chapter or at the end of the book. These bibliographies can be very helpful. You can turn to the books and articles listed to find more information on the subject or to clarify or explore ideas that you do not think the author explained clearly enough.

Use of the Library

Many assignments will require you to use the library. Term papers, in particular, generally call for library research. To use the library effectively and efficiently, you need to know the following things:

a. locations of different materials in the library (periodicals, reference materials, vertical file materials, audiovisual materials, photocopying equipment, card catalog or computer terminal used to obtain information about the books in the collection or to obtain access to databases subscribed to by the college, microfilm materials and readers, etc.);

b. how to use the card catalog, computer terminal, microfilm reader, and/or audiovisual equipment;

c. how to use the reference books (encyclopedias, dictionaries, atlases, etc.);

d. how to check books out;

e. policies for length of time you may keep a book; and

f. how to renew a book that you are not ready to return.

The librarian is a good source of this information. Don't hesitate to ask him or her for help in finding materials or using specialized reference materials or library equipment.

SS Exercise 4

Request an interview with your librarian, either individually or with one or more other students. Find out the answers to the following questions:

1. How are cards arranged in the card catalog?

2. What is the best reference source for information about a particular topic in periodicals?

3. What is a good source for biographical data about a famous person?

4. What kinds of materials are available on microfilm?

5. Who is available to help you use the microfilm readers?

6. What information is available through the library's computers and/or computer terminals?

7. Who is available to help you use the computer facilities?

8. What are the regulations related to use of videotapes, films, filmstrips, and other audiovisual materials?

9. Who is available to help you use audiovisual materials?

10. What are the library's hours? Do they change on weekends and during school breaks?

11. How long can you keep a book after checking it out? Can it be renewed if you are not finished with it by the due date?

12. What are the penalties for failing to return books or returning books late?

13. (Add your own question or questions.)

Organizational Skills

It is extremely helpful to organize the ideas that you encounter when reading. Four highly useful organizational skills are outlining, webbing, summarizing, and note-taking. Each of these is discussed below.

Outlining

An outline is a way to write down the ideas in a passage you have read (or a lecture you have heard) while showing the relationships between the major ideas presented and details that support the major ideas. (If you have difficulty recognizing the difference between main ideas and supporting details, turn to Chapter 5: Nature of Comprehension for help before proceeding with this section.)

Two widely used forms of outlines are the sentence outline and the topic outline. The sentence outline, as you might guess from its name, consists of complete statements. The topic outline makes use of key words and phrases. You should use the outline form that is most valuable to you as a study tool.

The importance of the ideas recorded in your outline is shown both by the numbers and letters used and by the indentation. Ideas of equal importance are designated by the same style of number or letter and the same amount of indentation. Do not indicate a division under any topic unless there are at least two points of nearly equal value that can be placed under the topic. (For example, never use an ''A.'' without a ''B.'' or a ''1.'' without a ''2.'') Unimportant or unrelated details should not be included in an outline.

The usual form for an outline is as follows:

Title
(The Main Thought of the Entire Selection)

I. First major idea
   A. Detail related to the first major idea
   B. Detail related to the first major idea
      1. Detail related to B
      2. Detail related to B
         a. Detail related to 2
         b. Detail related to 2
      3. Detail related to B
II. Second major idea

The following exercise will help you to develop your outlining skills.

SS Exercise 5

For outlining practice, fill in a topic outline for the following paragraph:

Many people enjoy owning pet birds. Parakeets are probably the most popular bird pets because they live contentedly in cages. Bird buyers are very careful not to choose as pets birds that become sick and discontented in captivity. People often enjoy teaching their pet parakeets to speak. Parrots and mynah birds are other birds that have the characteristics of contentedness in captivity and ability to learn to speak. Thus, they have also become quite popular as house pets. Canaries are highly rated as pets, too, even though they cannot be taught to talk. They are prized for their singing ability.

_____ (Title)

I. _____

    A. _____

    B. _____

II. _____

    A. _____

    B. _____

III. _____

    A. _____

    B. _____

IV. _____

    A. _____

    B. _____

Webbing

Some people are more comfortable organizing material with a web than they are with a standard outline. When using a web, you place the title or main idea of the entire selection in the center and then connect the major ideas related to this central idea to the title with spokes radiating from the center of the web. Similarly, details related to the major ideas can be connected by spokes radiating from the appropriate major ideas. A web would, therefore, have this form:

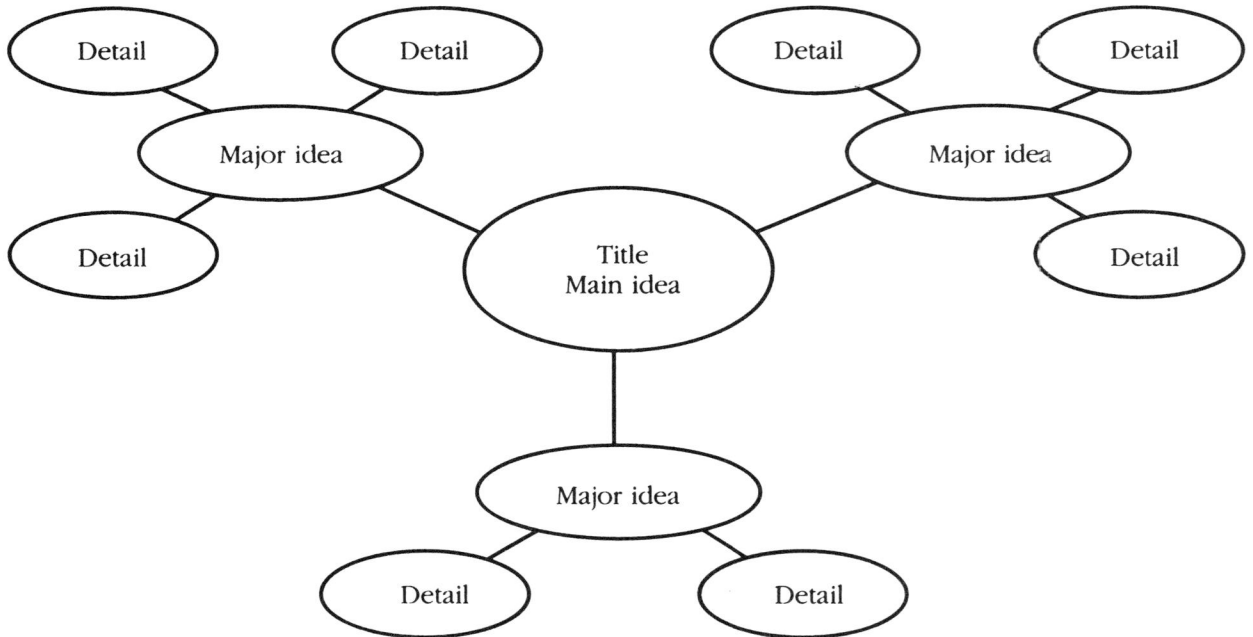

This web arrangement allows you to add ideas to the outline without having to rewrite the outline to allow space at the proper places, so going back to fill in details that you may have missed originally is a little easier when you use this procedure.

The following exercise will help you to see how webbing resembles outlining.

SS Exercise 6

For practice in webbing, make a web of the information in the paragraph presented in SS Exercise 5. Notice how you focus on the same major ideas and details as you did for that exercise; you simply record them in a different form.

Summarizing

Summarizing involves restating an author's material in a much more concise form. The author's main ideas should be included, but small details and all nonessential material, such as illustrative passages, should be omitted.

Writing a summary of material that you have just read will help you to remember the main points for longer than you would have remembered them after simply reading the selection. You can then use the summary to help you review for a test or for any other purpose.

If the selection is short, you can often simply use the topic sentences from each paragraph as your summary. In longer passages, you may need to look for the main ideas from each section and use them as the summary. In some lengthy selections, such as chapters from textbooks, the author may summarize the material in introductory or summarizing paragraphs.

Read the following article. Then select the best summary of that article from the choices presented below. Put a check beside the letter of the best summary.

A Wildlife Legacy[3]

The Mississippi Valley, as our forebears knew it, was magnificent. Here, pure water ran freely through braided channels. Wooded islands and marshy backwaters were interspersed for hundreds of miles—home to songbirds and waterfowl, furbearers and fish. Passenger pigeons swept endlessly across the skies. Limestone bluffs framed the wide valley and elk and bison grazed on prairie ridges.

With such abundant resources, no wonder the valley has been used by humans for centuries. It was an important focus of prehistoric Native American culture. Then by the late 1600's, European explorers began using the river as a travel route. Soon, white trappers and traders, soldiers and settlers were establishing a new culture; the river was used to transport furs and other goods. But during the 1800's, entire forests were logged and rafted down the river to sawmills. Steamboats carried an ever increasing cargo of passengers and machinery. Barges began hauling large quantities of grain and coal. As traffic increased, more attempts were made to control the river and make navigation easier.

By the early 1900's, visionary conservationists began expressing concern for the future of the river. Although locks and dams had not yet harnessed the river for navigation, a huge project was proposed in the early 1920's to clear and drain the bottomlands for farming. Will Dilg and his Izaak Walton League associates took their case for preserving the Mississippi Valley to Congress. As a result of their efforts, the Upper Mississippi River National Wildlife and Fish Refuge was established in 1924 to protect and manage the bottomland habitats for migratory birds and fish.

Today, the refuge helps sustain the most important corridor of fish and wildlife habitat remaining in the central United States. Actually, the importance of the refuge is even greater now due to habitat losses in surrounding areas. These losses have concentrated wildlife and related recreation along the floodplain of the Upper Mississippi, where both quantity and quality of natural resources still exist.

The river was free-flowing until a series of navigation locks and dams were constructed in the 1930's. The upper reaches of the pools that were formed behind each dam retain the early character of the river, with lushly forested islands separating many meandering side channels. The central portion of each pool supports extensive marshes and backwater lakes. The lower reaches, just above the dams, resemble large, deepwater reservoirs.

The vegetative diversity of the river's floodplain attracts fish and wildlife species that are varied and abundant. Marshes and lakes provide feeding and resting areas for migratory waterfowl. Diving ducks such as canvasbacks, scaup, and ring-necked ducks, along with tundra swans, are most numerous in open-water areas. Mallards and blue-winged teal make extensive use of shallow marshes. Wood ducks inhabit swampy backwaters in forested areas. . . . Many other migratory birds—such as herons, egrets, bitterns and rails—also use marshy habitats, and songbirds are abundant in woodlands and forest edges. Heron and egret nesting colonies (rookeries) are found in some mature forests. Big trees in isolated areas may also be used by nesting bald eagles. Large numbers of eagles concentrate along the river in winter to feed primarily on fish. The river supports an enormous variety of sport and commercial fish species. Over 100 kinds of fish occur on the refuge. Popular sport fish include walleye, sauger, catfish, northern pike, bass, sunfish and crappies. The natural resource departments of the states bordering the refuge maintain active fishery programs in response to this popular recreational activity.

_____ a. The Mississippi Valley was used by European explorers as a travel route and for transporting furs and other trade goods. Steamboats carried passengers and machinery, and barges hauled coal and grain. Navigation locks and dams were built along the river in the 1930's.

_____ b. The Mississippi Valley is a beautiful region and an important fish and wildlife habitat. For centuries people have used the Mississippi Valley for navigation and recreation. A wildlife refuge has been established to preserve the valley as a natural habitat. The many marshes and lakes attract migratory birds, and the river is host to many species of fish.

_____ c. Many fish and migratory birds live in the floodplain of the Mississippi Valley. There are diving ducks and wood ducks, and heron and egret rookeries are found in some forests. In the river, over 100 kinds of fish can be found, including walleye, catfish, northern pike, and bass. Fishing is a popular recreational activity.

SS Exercise 8

Read the following article. Then read the statements following the article. Place a check mark by the statements that probably would be included in a summary of the article.

Building a Quality Workforce[4]

By Ann McLaughlin

Quality goods and services must be the hallmark of the American economy if we are to continue to prosper in an increasingly competitive and sophisticated global marketplace. Price, of course, is an important factor. But we cannot compete on price alone with countries that pay their workers wages which make it impossible for them to purchase many of the consumer products they produce. Not only can't we compete on that basis, we shouldn't want to, or even try.

Japan's success in selling cars in America sometimes is cited as an example of market share built on price. The Japanese entered the American market by offering small, inexpensive, fuel-efficient cars at a time when gas prices were skyrocketing and American manufacturers were committed to large gas guzzlers. Whether this was serendipity or superior planning now is a moot point.

What is often overlooked is that while the Japanese may have gained a foothold on the basis of price, they solidified and expanded it by building cars that won a reputation for quality and dependability. Today, Japanese cars enjoy no price advantage over their

American counterparts but remain formidable competitors for market share.

Producing quality goods and services, of course, requires a quality workforce. And building a quality work force is perhaps the major challenge we face in seeking to maintain a competitive economy amid changing technology and changing markets.

Tomorrow's jobs will be more complex than anything we have known in the past. They will demand better reading, writing, and reasoning skills. Very few jobs will be created for those who can't read, follow directions, or handle basic math. Over half of the jobs created in the next 10 years will require education beyond high school.

We are fortunate in having a fairly accurate measure of what things will look like in the next 10 or 20 years. We not only know that jobs will be more complex, we have a pretty good idea who will be available to do those jobs. The number of new workers entering the labor force will decline substantially. And the profile of new entrants to the labor force will shift dramatically. About 80 percent of new workers will be women, blacks, Hispanics, and immigrants.

We must strengthen our efforts to bolster the quality of American workers—both those who are already in the labor force and those who soon will be. To do this, we must get business working with educators, and organized labor working with both of them. And we must ask ourselves what government can do—or quit doing—that will help raise quality and keep us competitive.

Business, labor, and government must work together to see that American workers are as prepared, as flexible, as protected, and as productive as possible.

To see that workers are prepared, we must develop new ways to relate literacy training to occupational skills. Young people must be taught the skills the job market demands.

To see that workers are as flexible as possible, we must reconcile the conflicting demands of work and family. Over the next 10 years women will account for two-thirds of new entrants to the workforce. Eighty percent of them are going to start families. Problems that once went by the name of "women's issues" have become basic economic issues.

Flexible hours, the use of sick leave to care for children, more part-time work, voluntary pregnancy leave for either parent, and high-quality day care are issues that must be addressed for economic and social reasons.

Modern technology and the rapidly expanding list of industrial chemicals have created complex new questions involving worker protection. But although the issues are changing, our commitment to worker health and safety must not. We must compete by improving quality and productivity, not by allowing basic employee protections to deteriorate.

By definition, quality workers are productive workers. And quality workers are most productive in a cooperative atmosphere. We no longer can afford adversarial labor-management relations.

Worker participation in various forms, such as integrated production teams, enhances worker morale and productivity, lowers costs, and improves quality.

America developed the world's most productive, prosperous, and dynamic economy by welcoming competitive challenges and meeting them with superior products. If we remember those lessons, and keep in mind that our human resources are our most precious asset, we can look to the future with confidence.

_____ a. Eighty percent of working women will be starting families in the next 10 years.

_____ b. The United States must compete in the workforce by improving quality and productivity.

_____ c. In the future business, labor, education, and government must work together to support American workers.

_____ d. High-quality day care is a significant labor issue.

_____ e. Japan can manufacture small, inexpensive, fuel-efficient cars.

_____ f. A quality workforce is needed to develop a competitive economy.

_____ g. Many new workers will be blacks, Hispanics, and immigrants.

_____ h. More than 50 percent of jobs over the next 10 years will need employees with advanced education.

SS Exercise 9

Read the following article. Then read the statements following the article. Place a check mark by the statements that probably would be included in a summary of the article.

Salt of the Dearth[5]

A recent issue of *Climbing Magazine* carried a suggestion concerning salt that might apply to skiers. Climbers for the past few years have been experimenting with combating the dehydrating effects of high altitude with increased salt intake. There's no set rule, just very gentle experimentation. *Climbing*'s article suggests as a rule of thumb that salt intake be increased for every 5,000 feet of climb.

A skier then going from a near sea level habitat, like the East Coast, to a 9,000-foot ski terrain, like the Rockies, might do well to salt his food a little more heavily a week or so in advance of—and also during—his ski vacation.

A pinch of salt helps your tissues hold a greater water supply. On the other hand, it is well known that you gain weight with more salt in your diet. The extra weight consists of water, a couple pounds of it, probably. This "water weight" disappears when your salt intake goes down again. Water weight is what you lose when you go on one of those miracle diets, which are not really miracles but merely salt deprivation.

From a ski vacation point of view, it's worth a little weight gain to feel less desiccated and more lively on the mountain runs. So salt away, but lightly.

_____ a. *Climbing Magazine* has been trying out some procedures to help skiers.

_____ b. Mountain climbers have been experimenting with increased salt intake to combat the dehydrating effects of high altitude.

_____ c. Extra salt is needed for every 5,000 feet of the climb.

_____ d. This procedure may be helpful to skiers also.

_____ e. A skier going from a near sea level habitat, like the East Coast, to a 9,000-foot ski terrain, like the Rockies, might do well to salt his food a little more heavily a week or so in advance of—and also during—his ski vacation.

_____ f. Salt helps your tissues hold more water.

_____ g. This causes you to gain "water weight," which disappears when your salt intake goes down.

_____ h. You lose water weight on "miracle" diets that are not really miracles at all because they are based on depriving the dieter of salt.

_____ i. It may be worth the added weight to feel better during your ski vacation.

Note-taking

Note-taking can serve as a memory aid in three ways. First, if you write down the main points in a selection as you read, you can use your notes to review the material later. This procedure will keep you from having to read the entire selection again because you cannot remember the main points. Second, the mere action of writing the main points will help to fix them in your mind, and you will probably remember them longer. Third, when you take notes in your own words, you are forced to think about the material that you are reading. As you will find out in a later section of this chapter, active involvement with the material you read can help you retain it.

The form you use in taking notes must be the one that is most helpful to you. Some students prefer to use an outline form or a web for note-taking. Others like to summarize what they have read in a series of brief paragraphs. You have had a chance to practice each of these techniques.

As a general rule, your notes should be as brief as possible while conveying the information you wish to retain. Do not copy the entire selection into your notebook. Notes should usually be in your own words, unless you are recording a quotation to be used in a research paper. Abbreviations are acceptable as long as you are sure you will remember their meanings when you are trying to interpret the notes.

When taking notes for a research paper, remember to record your sources carefully. It may be helpful to put each separate research note on a file card so that the notes can be easily rearranged when the paper is being written.

Listening

Listening is an important study skill for students at all levels. Much information is given in class through lecture. Other information emerges during class discussions. A poor listener will miss this information and will probably do poorly on tests because of this. In addition, many assignments are given orally in class. A poor listener's grades may suffer because of an incorrectly completed homework assignment.

Because your listening skills can mean the difference in doing well and doing poorly in your classes, you may need to follow these suggestions to improve your listening performance:

1. Sit as close to the front of the room as possible. It is easier to listen effectively if you do not have the distraction of other people between you and the teacher when he or she lectures.

2. Get ready to listen as soon as you enter your classroom. Open your notebook to the proper page, find your pencil or pen, write the date on the page, put your textbook in a convenient position, and then focus your attention on the teacher, even if class has not yet started. If you do these things, you will not miss important information while fumbling with your supplies.

3. Look at the teacher as he or she lectures, or look at the speaker during a discussion. Looking elsewhere may distract you from the topic being discussed and cause you to miss points that are made.

4. Just as you need purposes for reading in order to comprehend and retain the material well, you need purposes for listening to meet these same objectives. Before the speaker begins, think about *why* you are listening. Decide what you need to find out from the presentation, and listen for this information. You may wish to take notes as some of your reasons for listening are satisfied.

5. Think about what is being said in relation to things that you already know. If the information being provided does not agree with your prior perceptions, hold up your hand and ask the speaker a question to clear up your confusion.

Following these suggestions should help you to listen more effectively in class. Soon you may discover that these practices have helped you to earn better grades.

Retention

Just following study methods such as those discussed earlier will aid retention, but you can also help yourself remember the things you read in other ways. Ten additional ways to increase retention follow:

1. Read the material critically. Question the truthfulness of the statements. Distinguish between fact and opinion. Constantly evaluate the material by comparing information it contains to facts that you already know. This active involvement with the assignment will help you remember the details better.

2. If you have someone to study the material with you, spend some time discussing the major points. Talking about the ideas will help you remember them.

3. Try to apply procedures or ideas about which you have read. For example, carry out experiments described in the textbook if you can reasonably do so. Obviously, you cannot perform some experiments because they require material or equipment that is not available. Still, whenever you can apply ideas you have read, you are more likely to remember them.

4. Do your memorization at the end of your study session. The things you study last will be remembered better than those you study at the beginning of a lesson. New information may interfere with that which was studied earlier.

5. Always be sure you know *why* you are reading. If your teacher provides study questions, read them before you begin reading the assigned material. Hold these questions in mind as you read, searching for the answer to each one. If your teacher does not provide questions, check to see if there are

questions at the beginning or end of the chapter you are supposed to read. These questions can be used for your purpose questions. Or you can think about what questions you expect to be answered by the chapter, based upon the title and any other clues you have available (for example, the teacher's comments) and use these questions as purpose questions for your reading.

6. Take notes as you read. Just the physical act of writing an idea on paper may help set it more firmly in your mind.

7. Think about the reading topic before you begin reading. Jot down things that you already know about the topic. Also write down some things related to the topic about which you are not sure. Then read the material to verify your prior knowledge and clarify the points about which you were not sure. This is a way of providing yourself with a reading purpose without using questions.

8. Construct mnemonic, or memory, devices to help you recall lists. For example, if you wanted a way to remember the five parts of a textbook listed in this chapter (preface, table of contents, index, glossary, and bibliography), you might make up a silly sentence containing the first letter of each part and use this sentence to cue you when you are trying to recall the parts. Such a sentence might be: Paul took invisible grocery bags.

9. Always try to associate new material with what you already know. It is difficult to remember isolated bits of information, but fairly easy to remember something new when you relate it to your existing store of knowledge. For instance, if you are taking nature study and are already familiar with many wildflowers, you can remember new varieties by placing them mentally into the categories you already know.

10. Use appropriate metacognitive strategies for evaluating how well you understand and remember what you are reading. Take corrective measures, such as rereading and checking difficult vocabulary, when you think you may have trouble retaining important information.

Studying for Examinations

Some students have no idea how to study for examinations. They feel that they study a great deal and profit very little from their efforts. This section contains some hints on ways to study for exams.

The first thing that you should do when your teacher announces an exam is to find out what type it will be. You will use different techniques of studying for an objective test than for an essay test.

For essay tests you must be able to state main ideas and supporting details in your answers. Be as specific as you can. In this type of test the questions are likely to be quite broad in scope and chosen to cover the most important topics in the course. This approach allows the teacher to include only a few questions on the test. As you study, decide what major topics have been covered in class and in the textbook. Formulate some likely questions concerning these major topics and try to prepare some good answers for these questions. If you prepare answers for ten to fifteen important questions, the five or six questions that the teacher decides to ask are likely to be among those for which you have prepared.

There are several types of essay questions, so you should read each question carefully to see how you should answer it. If the question simply asks you to "discuss" an issue, you should organize your ideas and make a brief outline of what you want to say before you start writing the answer. Some essay questions require you to "compare and contrast." If this is the case, don't simply list or discuss issues on each side. Instead, carefully show how the issues are alike (compare) and then how they are different (contrast). "Cause and effect" essay questions also require you to relate one thing to another. Be sure your answer clearly differentiates between the cause and the effect, and then show how the cause contributed to the effect. Another type of essay question might require you to "trace the development" of something. You will need to begin with the origin and move through each of the steps sequentially. If you are asked to "evaluate, justify, criticize, analyze, or prove" something, you will have to consider your answer carefully. This kind of question means that you must think critically. Be sure your idea is valid before you start writing your answer.

Another type of essay question might ask you to "give reasons for" something. Be sure to clearly identify the reasons, perhaps by numbering them and underlining an introductory key phrase for each reason. If you make the reasons stand out clearly, your teacher will be able to see at a glance that you know the answer. You may need to discuss each reason briefly if the question indicates that some explanation is needed.

If the test is to be objective, you will have to be familiar with many details. The possibilities for questions are much greater than they are with essay tests. You should be aware of the types of questions that your teacher has asked in class and included on exams in the past. If the teacher asks for lots of definitions and dates, study the definitions and dates in your textbook and lecture notes carefully. For true–false and multiple-choice objective tests you should study the details so you will recognize them when you see them in print. For completion tests you must recall key terms and spell them correctly when you fill in the blanks.

When taking true–false tests, if the statement is partially false, consider the entire statement to be false. Read negatively-stated true–false questions very carefully to make sure you know how to answer. True–false questions that use absolute words, such as *all, never, only,* and *always,* are seldom true. With multiple-choice questions, choose the *best* answer if more than one answer could be correct. If you are sure that two of the answers are correct and an "all of the above" choice is given, the "all of the above" choice is correct.

Tests that require you to list items, especially sequentially, present special problems. Sometimes mnemonic devices can help you remember your lists. For example, if you need to remember the four types of articulation errors—substitution, omission, distortion, and addition—the key word "soda" may help you remember them. The "s" in soda can trigger the word "substitution" for you; the "o" can remind you of "omission"; and so on. The key sentence, "Days are soon over," can help you remember the same four items. The first letter of each word in the sentence is a clue to an item.

SS Exercise 10

Try constructing your own mnemonic device. Come up with a silly sentence to help you remember the layers of the atmosphere in order from lowest to highest. They are troposphere, stratosphere, mesosphere, ionosphere, and exosphere. Compare your sentence with the sentences of some of your classmates. Decide which one would help you remember best.

For any type of test, it is useful to learn definitions of terms. Definitions make ideal questions on objective tests, and they are helpful to know when answering essay questions. Correct usage of terms is impressive to teachers.

In addition to knowing what kind of test you will be taking, there are some other pointers that will help you prepare for your test.

1. Know *what* to study. Will the test include material from films, student reports, and handouts? How many chapters will be covered? How much of the test will come from the textbook and how much from class notes? If you are studying for a comprehensive exam, study your old tests.

2. Study and review regularly. Don't wait until the night before the test and cram. If you study every night, you will just need to review well before taking the test. You will also remember much better from regular, spaced studying than from cramming.

3. Listen well in class the day before a test. Often a teacher will tell you what to expect on the test, review some important points, or cover specific material that will be on the test.

4. If you need to study or review for several hours, take breaks periodically. For instance, after 45 or 50 minutes of studying, take a ten-minute break. Let your mind rest. Try telling yourself that when you learn a particular chapter, you will reward yourself in some way.

5. Remember your learning style. Underline key ideas, read aloud to yourself, jot down notes, or find another way to help yourself learn effectively. Study alone, with a friend, or in a study-review session with several others, depending on what works best for you.

6. Try to sleep well the night before the test. If you stay up too late studying, your mind will probably be cloudy and confused when you get your test. Avoid drinking liquids that contain caffeine, so that you won't have trouble falling asleep. After an intensive study session, find some way to relax before trying to sleep.

7. If the test is an early one, get up in time to feel fresh, eat something, and look over your notes one more time. A final review will help you remember what you have been studying.

Here are a dozen ideas that should help you do your best work *during* the test.

1. Be on time for the test, or a little early, to give yourself a chance to collect your thoughts before the test begins. Feel that you are as well prepared as you can be.

2. Be sure that you are ready. Sharpen your pencils, get out clean paper, or do whatever is necessary.

3. When you get your test, look through it first to see how long it is and what types of questions are on it.

4. Look to see how many points are given for each part. Then budget your time. You should either have your own watch or be able to see a clock. Be sure to allow enough time to complete the test—don't spend too much time on a section that is not worth many points.

5. Read and follow directions carefully. Is there more than one part to the question? Do you need to answer all of the questions, or do you have some choices? How do you indicate the correct answer— by underlining, circling, marking through, or something else?

6. Begin answering the questions. Go through the test and answer the easiest questions first. Then go back and try to fill in the rest of the answers. Sometimes you will think of an answer later, or another question on the test will help you recall the answer. Mark those questions you aren't sure of and come back to them.

7. Answer all the questions you are required to answer. If you aren't sure of an answer, use the best guess you have. It may be right!

8. When you finish, go back over the test. Check those questions you marked because you weren't certain, and make sure you answered everything. If you have enough time, proofread your essay questions for errors in spelling, punctuation, and grammar.

9. Be sure you are putting down the correct answer for that particular question. Many students miss points because they read the question carelessly and jump quickly to a conclusion. For example, don't write three *consequences* of the Civil War if the question asks for three *causes*.

10. Be careful about changing your answers. Often your first reaction is correct. Change an answer only if you feel sure your second idea is better than your first one.

11. When a teacher asks for your opinion, you will usually be safe if you repeat the opinion the teacher gave you in class. While some teachers really want *your* opinion, many teachers want you to give back their opinions on tests.

12. Remember that neatness, correct grammar, correct spelling, and good handwriting help. Teachers have many papers to grade, and they will look favorably on your paper if it is well written.

Reminder

Your technique for studying may greatly influence how much you gain from studying. The suggestions given in this chapter can help you to derive more benefit from your study. Refer to these suggestions any time that you feel your study method could use some improvement.

Spelling

Many intelligent people have difficulty learning how to spell words correctly. Yet, spelling is extremely important to you as you write English themes, send letters, or write term papers for classes. There are rules that will help you to become a better speller, but the English language is irregular and there are many exceptions to rules. Frequently used words that are spelled irregularly should be memorized.

There are two basic ways to become a better speller. One way is to become familiar with the rules that usually apply by learning them and making use of them when you are in doubt about the spelling of a particular word. The other way is to keep your own list of words that you misspell and refer to it frequently. In this way, you will avoid repeating your mistakes and will eventually master the problem of spelling. If you are in doubt about how to spell a word, look it up in the dictionary to make sure of the spelling. Then add it to your list.

Many words that are spelled differently are pronounced exactly alike or have small differences in their pronunciations. It is important to know which word is correct for the meaning conveyed within a particular context. Study the following pairs of words and their definitions.

1. accept: to receive without protest
   except: excluding

2. advice: opinion concerning action
   advise: to give advice

3. affect: to influence
   effect: result of a change

4. capital: city that is the seat of government
   capitol: building occupied by governmental representatives

5. cite: to quote a source
   site: a place

6. complement: to go along with, to complete
   compliment: to express praise

7. conscious: exhibiting awareness
   conscience: regard for fairness

8. council: an assembly
   counsel: advice that is given

9. elusive: tending to escape from grasp
   illusive: deceptive

10. loose: unfastened
    lose: to misplace

11. moral: ethical
    morale: a person's state of mind

12. personal: private
    personnel: a group of people, usually employees

13. precedent: an act used as an example
    president: chief or head officer

14. principal: adj., most important; n., head of a school
    principle: fundamental truth

15. proceed: to continue
    precede: to come before

16. stationary: in a fixed position
    stationery: writing paper

SS Exercise 11

In the following exercise, select the correct word to use for the meaning intended. Put the letter of the correct word in the blank space.

1. The score you make on this quiz will _____ your grade for the course. (a) affect (b) effect

2. He stopped in the store to buy some _____ . (a) stationary (b) stationery

3. The _____ object of the course is to increase reading proficiency. (a) principal (b) principle

4. We must _____ with the business at hand before starting anything new. (a) precede (b) proceed

5. The city council decided on the _____ for the new Chamber of Commerce building. (a) site (b) cite

6. Everyone came _____ the newest member. (a) accept (b) except

7. The true meaning of his statement was _____ , for I could not fully grasp what he was trying to say. (a) elusive (b) illusive

8. The girl would not listen to her father's _____ , for she felt he did not understand her situation. (a) advice (b) advise

9. Be careful not to _____ your contact lenses when you remove them. (a) loose (b) lose

10. The dome of the _____ building shone in the sunlight. (a) capital (b) capitol

11. Did you hear John _____ his wife on her appearance? (a) complement (b) compliment

12. Their _____ was low after losing five straight games. (a) moral (b) morale

13. The former judge offered his _____ , but it was refused. (a) council (b) counsel

14. The judge's decision was based upon a _____ established many years ago. (a) precedent (b) president

15. The office _____ were discouraged by the new policy concerning vacations. (a) personal (b) personnel

16. His _____ bothered him because he had taken unfair advantage of his friend. (a) conscience (b) conscious

Pronounce words carefully and your pronunciation may help you decide how the words should be spelled. Many words follow consistent spelling patterns, and careful pronunciation is the key to spelling these words correctly. Other words are not spelled phonetically, however, and some sounds may be spelled several different ways. For instance, the sound of a long *a* may be spelled *ay* (way), *eigh* (eight), *ai* (maid), or *ey* (they).

Be sure to listen carefully to the number of syllables in each word as you say it. Do not slur over any syllable or add any syllable that is not there. For each syllable that you hear there is one vowel sound or vowel blend, which may consist of a single vowel letter or a combination of vowel letters.

The following words are often misspelled because they are pronounced incorrectly. Study them and make sure you pronounce the syllables that are there. By learning to pronounce these words correctly, you will probably be able to spell them correctly.

Words in which letters or syllables are frequently omitted:

candidate	library	quantity
environment	literature	recognize
generally	occasionally	surprise
arctic	probably	usually
government	February	soldier
diamond	opera	finally
everybody	similar	particular

Words in which letters or syllables may be added:

athlete	entrance	lightning
disastrous	grievous	mischievous
drowned	height	remembrance
elm	hindrance	umbrella
twice	stole	once
across	nowhere	attack

Words in which letters are changed or transposed:

accumulate	hundred	irrelevant	prejudice
accurate	pronounce	perspiration	prefer
cavalry	pretty	larynx	prescription
children	introduce	particular	preserve

Many words are combinations of root words and prefixes (syllables that precede the root word) and/or suffixes (syllables that follow the root word). By learning some rules concerning the formation of these words, you can learn to spell them correctly. The following words show how prefixes and suffixes are added to root words.

Prefix	Root Word	Suffix	Whole Word
dis	place	ment	displacement
under	stand	ing	understanding
il	legal	ity	illegality

Sometimes when prefixes and suffixes are added, changes occur in the spelling of the words. The following rules and examples indicate when these changes are necessary.

1. Final y is changed to i, except before ing

Root Word		Suffix		Whole Word
lazy	+	-ness	=	laziness
bounty	+	-ful	=	bountiful
funny	+	-est	=	funniest
rely	+	-ance	=	reliance
fry	+	-ing	=	frying (no change before ing)

2. Usually drop the final e before a suffix beginning with a vowel, but not before a suffix beginning with a consonant.

Root Word	Suffix	Whole Word
approve	-al	approval
make	-ing	making
examine	-ation	examination
praise	-worthy	praiseworthy
change	-less	changeless
complete	-ly	completely

   Exception: Final e is not dropped before a suffix beginning with a if the e follows c or g
      Example: change—changeable

3. In words where the final syllable is accented, usually double the final consonant before adding a suffix if the word ends in a single vowel followed by a single consonant.

Root Word	Suffix	Whole Word
begin	-ing	beginning
run	-ing	running
stop	-ed	stopped
occur	-ed	occurred

4. Usually the final consonant is not doubled before adding the suffix in the following cases:
   a. If a word ends in a single consonant preceded by two vowels.
   b. If the word ends in two consonants.

Root Word	Suffix	Whole Word
trail	-ed	trailed
steer	-ing	steering
break	-ing	breaking
jump	-ed	jumped
turn	-ing	turning
truck	-ing	trucking

The plural of most words is formed by simply adding s to the root word. In some cases, however, this is not the procedure used. The following rules will help you decide how to spell the plural forms of words correctly.

1. For words ending in ch, sh, x, z, ss, or s, add es to form their plurals.

church	churches
brush	brushes
box	boxes
dress	dresses

2. For words ending in y preceded by a consonant, change y to i and add es to form their plurals.

city	cities
dairy	dairies
study	studies

3. For words ending in y preceded by a vowel, do not drop the y but add s to the word to form their plurals.

alloy	alloys
valley	valleys
tray	trays

4. For words ending in o preceded by a consonant, often add es to form their plurals.

potato	potatoes
tomato	tomatoes
hero	heroes

5. For Italian musical terms ending in o, add only s to form the plural.

solo	solos
soprano	sopranos

Many spelling errors occur as a result of confusion between ei and ie. Although there are some exceptions, the following rule is helpful. I comes before e except after c or when sounded like a. Study the following examples:

Normal order	After c	Sound like a
yield	receive	sleigh
relief	ceiling	vein
field	receipt	eight
friend	deceit	beige
believe	perceive	weigh

SS Exercise 12

1. Place the letter of the correctly spelled form of the word in the space preceding the choices.

_____ a. library   b. libary   c. liberry

_____ a. generly   b. generaly   c. generally

_____ a. mischievious   b. mischievous   c. mischeivous

_____ a. disasterous   b. disastrious   c. disastrous

_____ a. height   b. hieght   c. heighth

_____ a. perspiration   b. prespiration   c. perspration

_____ a. interduce   b. introduce   c. intraduce

2. Add <u>ing</u> to the following words. Make changes in the root words when necessary.

change   _____   plan   _____

select   _____   shop   _____

stoop   _____   cry   _____

3. Write the plural form of the following words.

play   _____   fox   _____

army   _____   dish   _____

sign   _____   tomato   _____

pass   _____   jay   _____

4. Fill in either <u>ei</u> or <u>ie</u> in each blank within the following words.

dec_____ve   gr_____f   pr_____st

r_____gn   b_____ge   rec_____pt

w_____ght   th_____f   p_____r

Some letters and combinations of letters cause special problems in spelling. Below are three pairs of word lists that include frequently misspelled words. Try to become aware of these trouble spots and notice which letters are used to spell the words correctly.

Study the following word lists.

ie	*ei*	*ent*	*ant*	*able*	*ible*
achieve	ceiling	adolescent	assistant	advisable	accessible
believe	deceive	apparent	attendant	applicable	audible
brief	foreign	correspondent	covenant	communicable	destructible
friend	height	dependent	defendant	durable	feasible
grieve	leisure	diligent	elegant	hospitable	flexible
handkerchief	neither	eminent	extravagant	irritable	irresistible
niece	perceive	imminent	ignorant	manageable	perceptible
pier	receive	innocent	irrelevant	predictable	permissible
priest	receipt	prevalent	observant	preferable	plausible
relief	reign	prominent	occupant	profitable	responsible
thief	seize	recipient	pleasant	reliable	sensible
yield	weird	reverent	restaurant	tolerable	susceptible

No two people are troubled by exactly the same words, but some words are more frequently misspelled than others. You will need to make your own personal list of problem words, but the following list contains words that are often misspelled by college students. Study these words carefully until you know them well, and you will avoid many spelling errors.

1. absence
2. accidentally
3. accommodate
4. accompaniment
5. advertisement
6. alleviate
7. all right
8. already
9. amateur
10. athlete
11. basically
12. bouquet
13. category
14. changeable
15. comparative
16. congratulations
17. continuous
18. cruelty
19. develop
20. disastrous
21. embarrass
22. emphasize
23. enough
24. envelope
25. erroneous
26. exaggerate
27. existence
28. extraordinary
29. familiar
30. fascinate
31. forest
32. frequent
33. hazardous
34. knowledge
35. laboratory
36. license
37. marriage
38. mathematics
39. necessary
40. ninety
41. occasional
42. occur
43. occurrence
44. organization
45. practice
46. preferable
47. privilege
48. probably
49. professor
50. pronunciation
51. psychology
52. quartz
53. quite
54. recognize
55. recommend
56. recipe
57. reliability
58. rhythm
59. schedule
60. separate
61. sergeant
62. similar
63. sophomore
64. statistics
65. strategy
66. succession
67. superfluous
68. surprise
69. symphony
70. technique
71. temperament
72. tension
73. theory
74. transferred
75. tremendous
76. ultimate
77. unnecessary
78. vacuum
79. validity
80. villain

SS Exercise 13

Spell the following words correctly by placing the right letters in the spaces.

1. *ie* or *ei*

   a. y____ld

   b. w____rd

   c. for____gn

   d. bel____ve

   e. n____ther

2. *ent* or *ant*

   a. dilig____

   b. observ____

   c. rever____

   d. depend____

   e. defend____

3. *able* or *ible*

   a. predict____

   b. irresist____

   c. access____

   d. applic____

   e. advis____

Place the letter of the misspelled word in the space in front of each line of words. If no word is misspelled, place the letter e in the space.

1. ____ a. probably   b. privelege   c. preferable   d. practice

2. ____ a. separate   b. schedule   c. sophmore   d. sergeant

3. ____ a. surprise   b. strategy   c. similar   d. symphony

4. ____ a. changable   b. bouquet   c. all right   d. already

5. ____ a. absence   b. accomodate   c. amateur   d. accidentally

6. ____ a. villain   b. theory   c. vacum   d. validity

7. ____ a. familiar   b. fascinate   c. forrest   d. frequent

8. ____ a. laboratory   b. license   c. knowledge   d. marriage

9. ____ a. envelope   b. existence   c. disastrous   d. develope

10. ____ a. recipe   b. reliability   c. rhythm   d. recommend

11. ____ a. occurence   b. organization   c. occasional   d. ninety

12. ____ a. psychology   b. pronunciation   c. professor   d. necessary

Chapter Notes

1. Francis P. Robinson, *Effective Study* (New York and London: Harper & Row, 1946), pp. 28–31.

2. Leo Fay, "Reading Study Skills: Math and Science," in *Reading and Inquiry,* ed. J. Allen Figurel (Newark, Del.: International Reading Association, 1965), pp. 93–94.

3. Excerpted from "A Wildlife Legacy," *Upper Mississippi River National Wildlife and Fish Refuge: Master Plan Summary,* U.S. Government Printing Office, 1988, pp. 1–4.

4. Ann McLaughlin, "Building a Quality Workforce," reprinted from *Business America,* May 9, 1988, p. 8.

5. "Salt of the Dearth," reprinted by permission from *Ski,* December, 1973, page 36.

3 Vocabulary: Part I

Mark looked at his class syllabus and frowned. He turned to Lee and said, ''This says, 'Plagiarism will not be tolerated. Evidence of plagiarism will result in a failing grade for the course.' What is 'plagiarism'? I sure don't want to fail the course, but I don't know what I'm not allowed to do.''

Lee shrugged and replied, ''If you haven't heard of it you probably aren't doing it, are you? Let's just get these reports for tomorrow out of the way so we can take in a movie tonight. I'm just going to copy a couple of paragraphs from this book and add an introduction and conclusion. It shouldn't take long.''

Michelle had overheard the entire conversation. She said, ''For something this important, we should find out exactly what that word means. A teacher mentioned something about it in a high school English class that I had. I think it's about doing your own work or something like that. Anyway that teacher thought it was a big deal too. Let's just look it up in the dictionary.''

Michelle looked the word up and said, ''Wow, Lee! I think copying that material into your report is plagiarism. It means taking passages from some source and using them as your own. You could have gotten into trouble for that.''

''Surely they know that we use reference books to get our ideas,'' Lee objected.

''Yes, but you're supposed to write it up in your own words or put their words in quotation marks. Either way you have to tell where you found the ideas. I remember that from that high school lecture now. I'm sure glad I looked this up. I might have copied some stuff for my report too,'' Michelle replied. ''I guess we had all better get busy now.''

''Hey, Michelle,'' Mark said as she started to walk away. ''Thanks. You kept us out of trouble. Why didn't I think of looking it up?''

Introduction

The size of your vocabulary is closely related to your ability to comprehend the things you read. There are many ways that you can improve your vocabulary. This chapter will help you become familiar with some vocabulary-building techniques. The next chapter will help you review special word types you should know.

What you refer to as your vocabulary is really a set of four overlapping and interrelated vocabularies. You have a listening vocabulary, composed of words that you understand when you hear them; a speaking vocabulary, composed of words that you can use correctly in speech; a reading vocabulary, composed of words that you understand when you see them in print; and a writing vocabulary, composed of words that you can use in your written communications accurately. Your listening vocabulary will probably be your biggest vocabulary, and your writing vocabulary will probably be your smallest vocabulary. When you add words to any one of your vocabularies, you increase the possibility of adding them to the other vocabularies. Therefore, work on your listening vocabulary may eventually result in increased speaking, reading, and writing vocabularies, for example. The work in this book on your reading vocabulary is likely to help you expand your listening, speaking, and writing vocabularies.

A person with a large vocabulary is often looked upon as an educated person, even though his or her formal education may be meager. A person who wishes to be successful in the study of a particular field or in work in a field must learn the vocabulary associated with that area. An instructor for a course or a supervisor on a job will evaluate your knowledge of an area of endeavor largely by the way you talk and/ or write about it. Use of exact terms will go a long way toward convincing others that you understand a subject.

Word Lists

One way that you can help to increase your vocabulary is through the study of word lists. These lists may have been prepared by others, or they may be self-constructed. Either type of list may serve a good purpose.

If you are embarking on the study of a particular field, such as biology, you ordinarily will have a textbook for that subject. Many textbooks in specialized subject areas have glossaries in the back which contain words that are essential to the understanding of the textbook material. Others may not have glossaries, but a glance through the index will disclose terms that are unfamiliar to you. The words from the textbook's glossary or index could form a meaningful word list for you to study. As you become familiar with the meanings of the words on your list, your reading in the textbook will become easier. In addition to studying the words that you originally listed, you may wish to list other unfamiliar words that you encounter in the reading of the textbook.

If you are interested in developing your vocabulary in many areas at the same time, you may want to form a word list without referring to an existing list. This word list would include every unfamiliar word that you encounter in your reading, regardless of the source. Words might come from newspapers, magazines, textbooks, novels, signs, or even television.

After you have the words that you wish to learn, you need to have a method for committing these words to memory and truly making them a part of your vocabulary. One good method is to list each word separately on a 3″ × 5″ index card. Look up the word in the dictionary and place a phonetic representation of the pronunciation in parentheses next to the word. For example, the phonetic representation for fraction is *frak'shun*. Sometimes it is helpful to list the part of speech, so that you will avoid using a noun in a sentence as though it were an adjective or verb. Next, list the dictionary definition that is appropriate for the context in which you found the word. Below the dictionary definition write the sentence in which you found the word. Enclose this sentence in quotation marks and indicate the source in parentheses beside the quotation. Then write an explanation of the meaning of the sentence without using the word with which you are working. On the back of the file card, use the word in an original sentence that shows your understanding of the word's meaning. Sometimes a sketch may be helpful to show your understanding of the word. For example, you might sketch a sailboat and draw an arrow to show the ''centerboard,'' ''rudder,'' or other part of the boat for which you have just learned the name. If you do not feel that you have time to record all of the above information on every word you wish to study, include those items that will be most useful to you. However, you should always include the dictionary definition that fits the context in which the word was found.

You should file your word cards alphabetically and review them frequently. A good procedure is to carry from five to ten of the word cards with you at all times. When you have to sit and wait in a dentist's or doctor's office, a barber or beauty shop, or any place at all, take out your cards and study them.

Try this method of vocabulary development for yourself. If you are enrolled in a reading improvement class, your instructor may wish to see your index cards and give you some suggestions for incorporating these words into your speaking and writing vocabularies.

IVo Exercise 1

The following words are ones that a high school graduate should recognize and understand when reading. Match each word with its definition to check your knowledge.

	Words		Definitions
_____	1. dissuade	1.	cure-all
_____	2. ostracize	2.	very cautious in spending money
_____	3. prognosis	3.	a forecast of future events
_____	4. spurious	4.	to turn from a purpose
_____	5. fallacious	5.	to move back and forth
_____	6. parsimonious	6.	misleading
_____	7. vindictive	7.	false, counterfeit
_____	8. fluctuate	8.	to banish from fellowship
_____	9. mutiny	9.	rebellion against authority
_____	10. panacea	10.	having tendencies toward obtaining revenge

If you did not do well on this exercise, you may wish to make some of the above words a part of your personal word study.

IVo Exercise 2

Take one new word that you have encountered in your reading this week. In the space below, write this word, a phonetic representation of the pronunciation, the part of speech, the dictionary definition that fits the context in which you found the word, a quotation of the context in which you located the word, an original sentence containing the word, and all the information that you can locate on the derivation of the word. This activity will give you a start on your personal word list.

Structural Analysis

Structural analysis is one approach to determining the pronunciations and meanings of unfamiliar words. Structural analysis involves the identification of prefixes, suffixes, root words, and components in compound words. It is best used in conjunction with context clues. (See next section.)

When you find an unfamiliar word in your reading, you may be able to decode it by analyzing the word's structure. First, check to see if the word is made up of two words that are within your present vocabulary. If it is, you will be able to pronounce the new word. You probably can come close to its meaning by combining the meanings of the two component words to formulate a definition that makes sense in the context where the word was found. If the word is not a compound word, you may still be able to decode it by finding that it is composed of a familiar prefix and root word, a familiar root word and suffix, or perhaps a familiar prefix, root word, and suffix.

To develop your power to decode unfamiliar words by using structural analysis, you must learn the meanings of many common prefixes, suffixes, and root words. The exercises following this section will help you achieve this goal.

Prefixes

A prefix is a word part that is placed before a root word to modify or change its meaning. The word "prefix" contains the prefix "pre-," which means "before," and the root word "fix," which means "to set or place." Therefore, the word "prefix" means "to set or place before." So, if you know the meaning of both the prefix and the root word, you should be able to understand the meaning of a new word.

Many common prefixes are useful in decoding unfamiliar words. The following ones are presented because of their usefulness and frequency of appearance in written materials.

Prefix	Meaning	Examples
1. a, ab	away, from, away from	abduct, avert
2. a, an	not, without	anhydrous, aphasia
3. a	on, in, at	asleep
4. ad	to, toward	administer
5. ambi	both	ambidextrous
6. ante	before	antebellum
7. anti	against	antitoxin
8. bi	two, twice	bicycle, bimonthly
9. circum	around	circumnavigate
10. com, con	together, with	combine, conspire
11. contra	against	contradict
12. de	from, away, down from	degrade
13. dis	apart from, reversal of	disconnect, dislike
14. ex	out of, beyond, formerly	exhale, exceed, ex-president
15. hyper	excessive, over	hypertension
16. hypo	under, less than ordinary	hypotension
17. in	in, into	income
18. in, il, ir	not	inactive, illegal, irregular
19. inter	among, between, together	interlace, intercollegiate, intermural
20. intra	within, inside	intracranial, intramural
21. mis	wrong	mislead

22.	mono	one	monorail
23.	multi	many, much	multicellular
24.	non	not	nonessential
25.	per	throughout	perennial
26.	poly	many	polygamy
27.	post	after	postdate, postscript
28.	pre	before	prejudge
29.	pro	in favor of, in place of, forward	proslavery, pronoun, proceed
30.	re	again, back	reinvest, retreat
31.	semi	half, partly	semicircle, semipermeable
32.	sub	under, below	subbasement
33.	super	over, above	supervisor
34.	trans	across, over, beyond	transcontinental, transgress
35.	tri	three	tricycle
36.	un	not	untrue
37.	uni	one	unicorn

Suffixes

A suffix is a word part that is placed after a root word to modify the meaning and/or change the part of speech. The following is a list of common suffixes you should learn.

Suffix	Meaning	Examples
1. able, ible	capable of being	manageable, edible
2. al	belonging to	theatrical
3. an	belonging to	American
4. ance, ancy, ence, ency	act of, state of being	assistance, emergence, compliancy, dependency

5. ant (noun), ent	a person who	occupant, superintendent
6. ant (adjective)	state of being	defiant
7. ar	belonging to, pertaining to	nuclear
8. dom	state or condition of being	freedom
9. ee	one who is	employee
10. en	made of, to make	wooden, whiten
11. ful	full of	joyful
12. fy	to make	amplify
13. hood	state of being	childhood
14. ic	of, pertaining to, resembling	angelic
15. ice	act, condition, quality	service, justice
16. ion, sion, tion	state or condition of being	tension, subjection
17. ism	state or condition of being, doctrine or practice of	barbarism, plagiarism
18. ist	a person who	humorist
19. ive	having the nature or quality of	active
20. ize, ise	to make, to make into	Americanize, compromise
21. less	without	childless
22. ment	state of being	imprisonment
23. ness	state of being	happiness
24. or	a person who	inventor
25. ous	full of	joyous
26. ship	state of being	friendship
27. tude	state of being	gratitude
28. ward	in the direction of	westward

Root Words

If you know the meanings of several root words, you will be able to figure out the meanings of countless other words because many different words can be built from the same root word. You will have to apply your knowledge of prefix and suffix meanings also, because these word parts will modify the meaning and/or change the part of speech of a word in which they appear. The following root words are common and are very useful to know.

Root word	Meaning	Examples
1. amor	love	amorous
2. anthrop	man	anthropology
3. aqua	water	aquarium
4. aster	star	astronomy
5. audio	hear	auditory
6. auto	self	autobiography
7. bio	life	biology
8. chroma	color	chromatic
9. chron	time	chronicle
10. cred	belief	incredible
11. cycl	circle, wheel	bicycle
12. derm	skin	dermatology
13. dict	speak	predict
14. dyna	power	dynasty
15. duct, duce	lead	conduct
16. ego	self	egotism
17. fact	make	manufacture
18. frater	brother	fraternity
19. geo	earth	geography

20. gram, graph	write	telegram, telegraph
21. helio	sun	heliotherapy
22. hetero	different	heterogeneous
23. homo	same	homogeneous
24. hydro	water	hydroelectric
25. jac, jec	throw	reject
26. junct	join	conjunction
27. loc	place	locate
28. loqu	speak	loquacious
29. manu	hand	manual
30. micro	small	microscope
31. mis, mit	send	mission, transmit
32. nom, nym	name	nominate, anonymous
33. pater	father	paternal
34. ped	foot	pedestrian
35. pel	drive	propel
36. photo	light	photograph
37. port	carry	transport
38. pseud	false	pseudonym
39. scrib, script	write	scribble, manuscript
40. scop	view	telescope
41. terra	earth	terrain
42. theo	god	theology
43. therm	heat	thermometer
44. tract	draw	contract

IVo Exercise 3

Define the following words, using the meanings of the word parts given in this section.

Example: trichromatic <u>having three colors</u>
(*tri—three, chroma—color, ic—of, pertaining to, resembling*)

1. abduct _____

2. anhydrous _____

3. bicycle _____

4. contradict _____

5. ex-president _____

6. hyperactive _____

7. hypodermic _____

8. inactive _____

9. illegal _____

10. irregular _____

11. interlace _____

12. misnomer _____

13. monorail _____

14. multicellular _____

15. nonessential _____

16. postscript _____

17. polychromatic _____

18. predict _____

19. propel _____

20. proslavery _____

21. pronoun _____

22. remake _____

23. semicircle _____

24. transmit _____

IVo Exercise 4

Define the following words, using the meanings of the word parts given in this section.

1. untrue _____

2. portable _____

3. incredible _____

4. freedom _____

5. employee _____

6. wooden _____

7. whiten _____

8. joyful _____

9. childhood _____

10. traction _____

11. Americanize _____

12. childless _____

13. happiness _____

14. inventor _____

15. joyous _____

16. westward _____

17. amorous _____

18. auditor _____

19. autobiography _____

20. autograph _____

21. dynamic _____

22. homonym _____

23. reject _____

24. pseudonym _____

25. manuscript _____

IVo Exercise 5

Choose the correct answer, and place the letter corresponding to that answer in the blank in front of the number of the item.

Example: _Posthumous_ fame refers to
        a. fame which is fleeting.
        b. fame occurring after one's death.
        c. fame occurring while one is alive.
(The answer is _b_. Knowing that _post_ means _after_ should provide a clue.)

_____ 1. If a person is <u>amoral</u>, he is
        a. extremely moral.
        b. lacking a sense of moral responsibility.
        c. concerned about the moral values of others.

_____ 2. An <u>antecedent</u> is something that
        a. goes before in time.
        b. goes after in time.
        c. occurs at the same time as.

_____ 3. The <u>antithesis</u> refers to
        a. the direct opposite.
        b. the most appropriate example.
        c. an early happening.

_____ 4. If you <u>bisect</u> an angle, you
        a. divide it into three parts.
        b. divide it into two equal parts.
        c. make it larger.

_____ 5. <u>Anthropology</u> is
        a. the scientific study of plants.
        b. the science of language.
        c. the science of man.

_____ 6. <u>Astronomy</u> is
        a. the scientific study of heavenly bodies.
        b. the scientific study of fossils.
        c. the scientific study of word meanings.

_____ 7. An <u>aquatic</u> sport is played
        a. in or on water.
        b. on a wooden surface.
        c. on the ground.

_____ 8. An <u>audience</u> is
   a. an assembly of hearers.
   b. something that is unpleasant.
   c. something that is unusual.

_____ 9. If something is <u>automatic</u>, it is
   a. having to do with cars or trucks.
   b. very powerful.
   c. self-acting or self-regulating.

_____ 10. <u>Biology</u> refers to
   a. the science of life.
   b. the scientific study of old manuscripts.
   c. the scientific study of stars.

_____ 11. The <u>circumference</u> of a circle is
   a. the middle or center.
   b. the line connecting the middle to the perimeter.
   c. the outer boundary or perimeter.

_____ 12. <u>Chronic</u> means
   a. acute.
   b. continuing for a long time.
   c. pertaining to color.

_____ 13. If two views are <u>contradictory</u>, they
   a. agree.
   b. don't agree.
   c. have no relationship to each other.

_____ 14. If something is <u>credible</u>, it is
   a. unbelievable.
   b. unreal.
   c. worthy of belief.

_____ 15. To <u>exhale</u> means to
   a. breathe out.
   b. breathe in.
   c. hold your breath.

_____ 16. A <u>dynamometer</u> is
   a. an instrument for measuring power.
   b. an instrument for measuring sound.
   c. an instrument for measuring time.

_____ 17. The <u>epidermis</u> is
    a. an illness.
    b. the outer layer of an animal's skin.
    c. an event.

_____ 18. <u>Egocentric</u> means
    a. self-centered.
    b. in the center of a circle.
    c. surrounded.

_____ 19. <u>Geology</u> means
    a. the science of man.
    b. the scientific study of life.
    c. the scientific study of the earth.

_____ 20. <u>Heterogeneous</u> groups are made up of
    a. people who are not alike.
    b. people who are alike.
    c. people who have dark hair.

_____ 21. <u>Multilateral</u> refers to something that
    a. has many sides.
    b. has only one side.
    c. has exactly two sides.

_____ 22. If someone says that your idea is <u>nonsense</u>, he means it
    a. is very sensible.
    b. makes no sense.
    c. is very important.

_____ 23. A <u>microscope</u> is used for
    a. viewing small objects.
    b. viewing large objects.
    c. viewing objects of all sizes.

_____ 24. <u>Polytheism</u> refers to
    a. belief in one god.
    b. belief in many gods.
    c. belief in humanity.

IVo Exercise 6

Choose the correct answer, and place the letter corresponding to that answer in the blank in front of the number of the item.

_____ 1. To <u>precede</u> means
    a. to go before.
    b. to come after.
    c. to occur at the same time.

_____ 2. To <u>resume</u> means
    a. to rest.
    b. to take for granted.
    c. to begin again.

_____ 3. <u>Semiautomatic</u> means
    a. partly automatic.
    b. completely automatic.
    c. not automatic.

_____ 4. <u>Subnormal</u> means
    a. the same as normal.
    b. less than normal.
    c. above normal.

_____ 5. A <u>superficial</u> examination is one
    a. that is very deep.
    b. that is done in secret.
    c. that only involves the surface.

_____ 6. If you have food in <u>superabundance</u>, you have
    a. very little.
    b. an adequate amount.
    c. much more than the amount you need.

_____ 7. If you are a <u>transgressor</u>, you are a person who has
    a. gone beyond the limits of the law.
    b. stayed within the limits of the law.
    c. studied the law.

_____ 8. A <u>tripod</u> is
    a. a camera stand that has four legs.
    b. a three-legged stand for a camera.
    c. an unstable camera stand.

_____ 9. An <u>unresponsive</u> person
    a. reacts favorably.
    b. does not react readily.
    c. reacts unfavorably.

_____ 10. A <u>unicorn</u> is
    a. a mythical animal with one horn.
    b. a mythical animal with two horns.
    c. a mythical two-legged animal.

_____ 11. <u>Hydrology</u> is the science concerned with
    a. water.
    b. earth.
    c. air.

_____ 12. A <u>conjunction</u> is a part of speech that
   a. takes the place of a noun.
   b. shows excitement.
   c. joins two words, phrases, clauses or sentences.

_____ 13. A <u>loquacious</u> person is
   a. silent.
   b. talkative.
   c. mean.

_____ 14. An <u>anonymous</u> note
   a. is short.
   b. has no name on it.
   c. is full of untrue things.

_____ 15. A <u>paternal</u> attitude is
   a. fatherly.
   b. brotherly.
   c. motherly.

_____ 16. A <u>pedestrian</u> is
   a. a person who rides.
   b. a person who walks.
   c. a person who swims.

_____ 17. A <u>photoelectric</u> cell has electrical properties that are modified by the action of
   a. light.
   b. water.
   c. air.

_____ 18. If the <u>terrain</u> is rugged,
   a. the ground will be hard to walk on.
   b. the weather will be bad.
   c. there is carpet on the floor.

_____ 19. <u>Theology</u> is
   a. the study of man.
   b. the study of animals.
   c. the study of God.

_____ 20. A <u>thermostat</u>
   a. is a numerical problem.
   b. regulates temperature.
   c. is the study of nature.

IVo Exercise 7

Suffixes may change the part of speech of a word. For example, "sand" is a noun, but "sandy" is an adjective. For each of the following items, choose the correct part of speech. Place the letter of that part of speech in the blank in front of the number of the item.

_____ 1. "Manage" is a verb, but "manageable" is
      a. an adjective.
      b. a noun.

_____ 2. "Assist" is a verb, but "assistance" is
      a. an adjective.
      b. a noun.

_____ 3. "Theater" is a noun, but "theatrical" is
      a. an adjective.
      b. a verb.

_____ 4. "Occupy" is a verb, but "occupant" is
      a. an adjective.
      b. a noun.

_____ 5. "Defy" is a verb, but "defiant" is
      a. an adjective.
      b. a noun.

_____ 6. "Nucleus" is a noun, but "nuclear" is
      a. an adjective.
      b. a verb.

_____ 7. "Employ" is a verb, but "employee" is
      a. an adjective.
      b. a noun.

_____ 8. "Joy" is a noun, but "joyful" is
      a. an adjective.
      b. a verb.

_____ 9. "Angel" is a noun, but "angelic" is
      a. an adjective.
      b. a verb.

_____ 10. "Serve" is a verb, but "service" is
      a. an adjective.
      b. a noun.

_____ 11. "Tense" is an adjective, but "tension" is
      a. a verb.
      b. a noun.

_____ 12. "Child" is a noun, but "childless" is
     a. an adjective.
     b. a verb.

_____ 13. "Happy" is an adjective, but "happiness" is
     a. a verb.
     b. a noun.

_____ 14. "Invent" is a verb, but "inventor" is
     a. an adjective.
     b. a noun.

_____ 15. "Joy" is a noun, but "joyous" is
     a. an adjective.
     b. a verb.

Context Clues

When you encounter unfamiliar words in your reading material, one excellent way of figuring them out is to use clues from the surrounding context. Often, reading the sentences directly before and after the sentence in which the strange word appears will make the meaning of the word obvious. Sometimes, clues to identification of the word will be found in the same sentence in which the word appears. The words and meanings identified by context clues may not be exact, but they will not be wild guesses: they will be educated guesses that are probably very close to the original ideas because of the thought which has been given to the surrounding material. Use of structural analysis along with context will be even more likely to produce a correct response. Use all the word recognition skills you have to help you with each unfamiliar word. If you cannot make an educated guess based on strong evidence, remember that you can go to the dictionary for the exact pronunciation and definition of the word.

The context provides you with many types of clues that you can learn to use successfully. Often an unfamiliar word is directly defined in the context. Sometimes an appositive will contain a synonym for the word. At other times the word may be contrasted with another word that has an opposite meaning. Words such as "but," "rather than," and "instead of" are among those words that signal contrasting ideas.

The following exercises will help you to develop your skill in using context clues.

IVo Exercise 8

Use the context in the following items to determine the meanings of the underlined words. Write explanations of the meanings of the underlined words on the lines following the items.

Example: Bill has a reputation for being *taciturn,* but he talked so much this evening that I'm beginning to believe that people have been mistaken about him. "Taciturn" must mean "untalkative." (The word "but" is a clue that it means something quite different from "talkative.")

1. Despite the fact that his friends tried to convince him to drink, Frank practiced complete abstinence. _____

_____

2. The doctor worked to alleviate, or relieve, the patient's pain. _____

_____

3. Taboos are common among these people. For example, the women are forbidden to show their faces in public. All of the people, except the religious leaders, are forbidden to walk on the grounds surrounding the temple, and even the religious leaders are forbidden to eat the flesh of birds. ____

_____

_____

4. The men were afraid that the natives would be hostile, but they found out, to their great relief, that these strange people were amicable. _____

_____

5. Dan was always making useful things out of useless ones and fixing broken things for his family. He always seemed to be engaged in constructive activities, rather than destructive ones. _____

_____

_____

6. Be careful not to associate closely with your classmates who have measles. You haven't had that disease, and it is contagious. _____

_____

7. I have never seen such a wonderful place to live! Look at this spacious living room! There's even room for them to eat breakfast in the kitchen, if they want to. I wish we had a commodious house like this. _____

_____

8. I can't sanction such actions. They go against everything I believe in. _____

_____

9. She is crazy if she thinks that medicine will rejuvenate her. She'd have a better chance of regaining her youth by searching for the mythical fountain. _____

_____

10. Don't go back to work too soon after this illness. If you exert yourself too much, you are likely to have a relapse. _____

_____

11. He hemorrhaged so badly that he died from the loss of blood. _____

_____

12. Thorough mastication of your food is important if it is to be digested properly. Most people don't realize how important it is to chew their food properly. _____

_____

13. There is no limit to God's power. He is omnipotent. _____

_____

14. You use many more words than are necessary in your writing. This redundancy makes your material less pleasant to read than it would be if the extra words were cut out. _____

_____

IVo Exercise 9

Use the context in each of the items to determine the best way to complete each incomplete sentence. Place the letter of the correct answer next to the number of the item.

_____ 1. It was extremely hard to get them all together, so I frantically tried to take care of all the important business before they began to disperse. Disperse means
   a. to scatter in different directions.
   b. to talk.
   c. to disagree.

_____ 2. I believed he was honest, but, when I caught him in a lie, I was disillusioned. A person who has been disillusioned
   a. has had an operation.
   b. has had his ideas shown to be wrong.
   c. has had a fit of anger.

_____ 3. Because this animal is only found in Africa, people consider it to be <u>endemic</u> to that country. Endemic means
   a. native.
   b. dangerous.
   c. useful.

_____ 4. Carl is a very successful businessman. You would do well to <u>emulate</u> him. Emulate means to
   a. laugh at.
   b. ignore.
   c. try to equal.

_____ 5. He already has a wife and three children that he is struggling to support. He doesn't need another <u>encumbrance</u>. An encumbrance is
   a. a burden.
   b. a job.
   c. a means of support.

_____ 6. He didn't use any single method, but tried to use the best of all the methods. His colleagues didn't agree with his <u>eclectic</u> approach. Eclectic refers to
   a. choosing from many sources.
   b. outstanding.
   c. one-sided.

_____ 7. You may say that she is a natural redhead, but I think that red color comes from the use of <u>henna</u>. Henna is
   a. a shampoo.
   b. a dye.
   c. a permanent.

_____ 8. You needn't be afraid that animal will eat you. It is <u>herbivorous</u>. Herbivorous means
   a. meat-eating.
   b. plant-eating.
   c. vicious.

_____ 9. He is continually <u>inebriated</u>. I don't believe I have ever seen him when he was sober. Inebriated means
   a. drunken.
   b. happy.
   c. sleepy.

_____ 10. This is an <u>infallible</u> sign that a hurricane is on the way. Only a simpleton would fail to prepare for the coming storm. Infallible means
   a. fallen.
   b. unreliable.
   c. certain.

_____ 11. The outlaw band traveled across the country looting and killing. Even after some of the gang members went to jail and paid their debt to society, their <u>infamy</u> kept them from taking useful places in society, for people knew of their past deeds and refused to believe that they had changed. Infamy means

    a. evil reputation.

    b. relatives.

    c. victims.

_____ 12. What you know about law could be written on the head of a pin. Your knowledge in that area is <u>infinitesimal</u>. Infinitesimal means

    a. accurate.

    b. large in quantity.

    c. extremely small in amount.

_____ 13. Why am I assigned every <u>onerous</u> task that comes up? It seems that other people get all the easy and pleasant tasks. Onerous means

    a. burdensome and distasteful.

    b. enjoyable and exciting.

    c. dangerous.

_____ 14. Please don't use so many direct quotations in your term papers. <u>Paraphrase</u> the author's ideas more often. Paraphrase means

    a. to copy the sources directly.

    b. to use only original ideas.

    c. to convey the same idea in different words.

_____ 15. This material is very <u>resilient</u>: it resumes its former shape regardless of how much stress we place on it. Resilient means

    a. elastic.

    b. difficult to store.

    c. slick.

IVo Exercise 10

In each of the following items is a word which is very close to the meaning of the underlined word and serves as a clue to that word's meaning. In each one find the word that is a clue and circle it.

1. This is an <u>insipid</u> meal. I will never become accustomed to such tasteless food.

2. Her <u>pallor</u> worried us. I don't think I have ever seen anyone quite as pale.

3. I can't stand to be merely a <u>spectator</u>, or observer; I like to participate.

4. She is too <u>inquisitive</u> for her own good. Her questions are making some people furious.

5. Young people today are so <u>apathetic</u>. They are even unconcerned about things that affect them directly.

6. I know it is not good to <u>procrastinate</u>, but I think I will postpone my housecleaning until tomorrow.

7. I hope she will <u>assent</u> to our plans. If she fails to agree to them, we may have to make some drastic changes.

8. Do you doubt my <u>veracity</u>? I have an excellent reputation for truthfulness.

9. When the teacher erased the board, she <u>obliterated</u> all the evidence of our mistakes.

10. Who had a <u>motive</u> for killing that nice man? I can't think of anyone who would have a reason to hurt him.

IVo Exercise 11

In each of the following items there are words which indicate that opposing ideas are being presented. Using your understanding of contrast clues, you can figure out approximate meanings for unfamiliar words. In each item *circle* the word or words which show that opposing ideas will be presented. Then *underline* the word or words that mean the *opposite* of the underlined word.

1. Rather than being a <u>probable</u> solution, his plan was very unlikely to succeed.

2. She thought that he was a <u>celebrity</u> she had met before, but he was an unknown who resembled the other man.

3. This deal was <u>legitimate</u>, not illegal.

4. I thought she would be <u>contrite</u> after her temper tantrum, but, instead, she seemed to be quite pleased with herself.

5. John thought that his son was seeking <u>approbation</u> for his actions, but the boy was really trying to upset his father by courting his disapproval.

6. Instead of being <u>permanent</u>, his appointment was only temporary.

7. Rather than being <u>brilliant</u>, he was a complete ignoramus.

8. He was a <u>cantankerous</u> old man, showing no evidence of good nature.

9. She intended to praise him, not <u>castigate</u> him, for going into the fire to save the young girl.

10. He behaved peacefully, not showing any <u>belligerence</u>.

Use of the Dictionary

The dictionary can help you determine the pronunciation and meaning of any unfamiliar word you encounter in your reading. In addition, you can find out the derivation and part of speech of the word and, in some instances, its synonyms, inflected forms, and idiomatic uses. Some dictionaries show the word in the context of a sentence.

You can check the dictionary to find the exact spelling of a word when you have a general idea of the spelling or when you know how the word begins. You can also check the dictionary to see whether or not a word should be capitalized.

To use the dictionary effectively to determine a word's pronunciation, you must be able to use a pronunciation key. The pronunciation key contains each symbol (diacritical mark) that the dictionary uses, along with examples of simple words for which the mark is needed. For example, a portion of a pronunciation key might look something like this:

Symbol	Reference Word	Symbol	Reference Word
ā	āce	ī	īce
ă	căt	ĭ	hĭt
ä	härm	ō	ōver
ə	sofə	ŏ	hŏt
ē	ēven	ū	tūbe
ĕ	sĕnd	ŭ	cŭp

If you find the symbol ä in an unfamiliar word you are trying to pronounce and you do not know how to pronounce the sound, pronounce "harm" and then place the vowel sound that you hear in "harm" into the new word.

In the dictionary respellings, both the symbols that are found in the pronunciation key and letters are used to help you figure out the pronunciation of the word. For example, the respelling "kwĭk" is the representation for the word "quick."

The accent marks (') given in the respelling of a word show you which syllables are stressed when the word is spoken. Multisyllabic words may have more than one accent mark. The syllable which should receive the most stress will have a thicker accent mark than syllables with slight stress. A syllable with relatively weak stress will not have an accent mark.

When you are using the dictionary to discover the meaning of a word, you must choose the meaning that fits the context in which the word was found. The dictionary lists several meanings for most words. You cannot simply choose the first meaning that is given, because the first meaning may not make any sense in the context where you found the word. Some of the meanings given may be specific to a certain subject matter area or a certain part of the world. For example, *Brit.* may be printed before a definition that is used primarily in England. The abbreviation *Geom.* may appear before a meaning used only in geometry textbooks. Meanings of a word are different when the word is used as different parts of speech. For example, a particular word is defined differently when used as a noun and when used as a verb. The abbreviation *n.* will appear before the definitions of the word when it is used as a noun. Other common abbreviations for parts of speech are *v.i.* for intransitive verb, *v.t.* for transitive verb, *adj.* for adjective, *adv.* for adverb, *pron.* for pronoun, *prep.* for preposition, and *interj.* for interjection. When searching for the meaning of a word, carefully choose the one that is most appropriate.

When looking up words in the dictionary, you probably realize that the alphabetical order of the entry words is helpful to you in finding the word you need. You may or may not be aware of another valuable aid to locating words in the dictionary—guide words. Guide words appear at the top of each dictionary page. The guide word on the left tells you the first entry on that page, and the one on the right tells you the last entry on the page. By determining whether or not the word you seek occurs alphabetically between the two guide words, you can decide if you need to look on that page for the word you need. For example, with the guide words "strut" (left) and "studio" (right) on a page, you can quickly decide that "stubborn" will appear on the page, but "stripe" will not.

IVo Exercise 12

Write the word represented by each phonetic respelling on the line beside the respelling. Refer to the pronunciation key in this section.

Example: fōn <u>phōne</u>

1. kăt _____
2. kāk _____
3. sĭ měnt' _____
4. ə wā' _____
5. jĕn' tlĭ _____

6. här mŏn' ĭk _____
7. lĭp' stĭk _____
8. mīn _____
9. nām' lē _____
10. ŏk' tān _____

11. rēch _____
12. rā' shō _____
13. shăd' ō _____
14. sĭks' tĭ _____
15. stăt' ĭk _____

IVo Exercise 13

Use your dictionary to look up the following words that you have encountered in earlier exercises. Write the phonetic respellings in the spaces beside the words.

1. alleviate _____
2. amicable _____
3. constructive _____
4. contagious _____
5. commodious _____

6. rejuvenate _____
7. relapse _____
8. mastication _____
9. omnipotent _____
10. redundancy _____

IVo Exercise 14

Use your dictionary to look up the following words that you have encountered in earlier exercises. Write the phonetic respellings in the spaces beside the words.

1. taciturn _____
2. disperse _____
3. endemic _____
4. emulate _____
5. encumbrance _____

6. eclectic _____
7. herbivorous _____
8. inebriated _____
9. infallible _____
10. infamy _____

IVo Exercise 15

You will find that many words are not pronounced the way their spelling seems to indicate that they will be pronounced. Generally, the reason for this situation is that the words have foreign origins. In the following exercise, fill in the blanks with the appropriate information from your dictionary.

Word	Language of Origin	Pronunciation
1. beau	_____	_____
2. boudoir	_____	_____
3. chamois	_____	_____
4. chef	_____	_____
5. corps	_____	_____
6. ennui	_____	_____
7. geisha	_____	_____
8. nee	_____	_____
9. vignette	_____	_____
10. verboten	_____	_____

IVo Exercise 16

In the dictionary you can find the comparative and superlative forms of many adjectives and adverbs. For example, if the entry word is "healthy," you will find "healthier" (comparative) and "healthiest" (superlative). Write the comparative and superlative forms of the following adjectives and adverbs on the appropriate lines following the entry words.

Entry	Comparative	Superlative
1. mad	_____	_____
2. lonely	_____	_____
3. long	_____	_____
4. many	_____	_____
5. much	_____	_____
6. bad	_____	_____
7. dry	_____	_____
8. fussy	_____	_____
9. timely	_____	_____
10. good	_____	_____

IVo Exercise 17

The dictionary will show you how to form the plurals of some nouns. For each noun listed below, write the plural on the adjoining line.

Noun	Plural
1. goose	_____
2. mouse	_____
3. calf	_____
4. tomato	_____
5. shoe	_____
6. shelf	_____
7. sheep	_____
8. lullaby	_____
9. index	_____
10. father-in-law	_____

IVo Exercise 18

The dictionary will tell you the principal parts of irregular verbs. For example, for the verb "see," the following principal parts would be given: "saw," past tense; "seen," past participle; "seeing," present participle. For the verbs listed below, fill in the principal parts on the appropriate lines.

Verb	Past Tense	Past Participle	Present Participle
1. fly	_____	_____	_____
2. go	_____	_____	_____
3. run	_____	_____	_____
4. swim	_____	_____	_____
5. drive	_____	_____	_____
6. drink	_____	_____	_____
7. fall	_____	_____	_____
8. do	_____	_____	_____
9. know	_____	_____	_____
10. sew	_____	_____	_____

IVo Exercise 19

Guide words help you find the words you seek more quickly than would be possible without their aid. Put a check mark by each of the following words that would be found on a page with the guide words "olive" and "once."

1. Olympian	_____	6. olfactory	_____
2. oil	_____	7. one	_____
3. ohm	_____	8. open	_____
4. omnipotent	_____	9. omit	_____
5. on	_____	10. omen	_____

IVo Exercise 20

In each of the following sentences the word "base" has a different meaning. Look up "base" in the dictionary. On the line following each sentence write the definition that applies to that sentence.

1. John had to slide into third base. _____

2. The base of the lamp was made of wood. _____

3. A base has the ability to turn litmus paper blue. _____

4. The computer does its calculations in base two. _____

5. Jean's brother is a corporal, and he lives on the military base. _____

IVo Exercise 21

Study the editorial cartoon on page 78 from *The Tennessean*; then answer the following questions.

1. What is the meaning of "light" that makes the cartoon funny? _____

2. What is the meaning that "light" usually has when people refer to "light reading"? _____

IVo Exercise 22

Use your dictionary to help you answer the following questions.

1. Could you use gentians to brighten up your home? _____

2. Could you play a tune on a metaphor? _____

3. Would you want a pentahedron for a pet? _____

4. Could you eat a pompano? _____

5. If you hit a man, would you want him to reciprocate? _____

6. If you had worked on your acceptance speech for weeks, would you be happy if someone said it stupefied him? _____

7. Would you use a tragopan on your car engine? _____

8. Would you like to have a hibiscus for breakfast? _____

9. Can you drink a drought? _____

10. Is an animalcule small? _____

Reprinted by permission from *The Tennessean*, July 24, 1983.

IVo Exercise 23

A reproduction of an actual dictionary page is presented in this section. Study it carefully, and answer the questions below.

1. Where is the pronunciation key for this dictionary page found? _____

2. What are the guide words on this dictionary page? _____

_____

3. What is the phonetic respelling of "brimstone" that is given in this dictionary? _____

_____

4. The sound that the "i" in "brimstone" represents can be discovered by pronouncing what word

   listed in the pronunciation key? _____

5. What is the language of origin of the word "brigadier"? _____

6. What are synonyms for "bright" when it means "shining or glowing with light"?

   _____ , _____ , _____ , _____

7. What is the past participle of "bridge"? _____

8. What is the present participle of "bridge"? _____

9. What part of speech is "brimful"? _____

10. What is the definition of the word "bridle" that fits the context for each sentence below?
    a. Saddle and bridle the horses for us.

    _____

    b. This bridle needs to be fixed before we go horseback riding again.

    _____

    c. You must learn to bridle your tongue, or you will get in trouble with the boss.

    _____

11. In the set of illustrations for the term "bridge," what type of bridge is shown in the number 2

    illustration? _____

12. What term, other than "bridge," is represented by an illustration, as well as a definition?

    _____

13. What is the part of speech of the word "brightly"? _____

14. What parts of speech are associated with the word "brine"? _____

_____

of a musical instrument — see VIOLIN illustration **c** : a raised transverse platform on a ship from which it is navigated **d** : GANTRY 2b **e** : the hand as a rest for a billiards or pool cue; *also* : a device used as a cue rest **3 a** : a musical passage linking two sections of a song or composition **b** : a partial denture anchored to adjacent teeth **c** : a connection (as an atom or bond) that joins two different parts of a molecule (as opposite sides of a ring) **4** : an electrical instrument or network for measuring or comparing resistances, inductances, capacitances, or impedances by comparing the ratio of two opposing voltages to a known ratio — **bridge·less** \-ləs\ *adj*

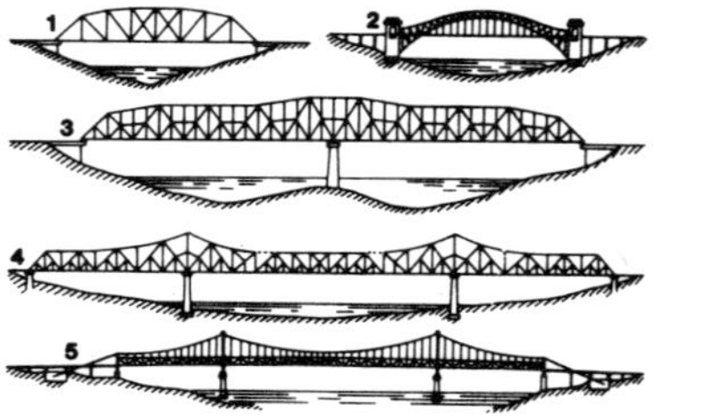

bridge 1a: *1* simple truss, *2* steel arch, *3* continuous truss, *4* cantilever, *5* suspension

[2]**bridge** *vt* **bridged; bridg·ing** (bef. 12c) **1** : to make a bridge over or across ⟨~ the gap⟩; *also* : to join by a bridge **2** : to provide with a bridge — **bridge·able** \-ə-bəl\ *adj*

[3]**bridge** *n* [alter. of earlier *biritch*, of unknown origin] (1843) : any of various card games for usu. four players in two partnerships that bid for the right to name a trump suit, score points for tricks made in excess of six, and play with the hand of declarer's partner exposed and played by declarer; *esp* : CONTRACT BRIDGE

bridge·board \ˈbrij-ˌbō(ə)rd, -ˌbȯ(ə)rd\ *n* (ca. 1864) : STRING 7a

bridge·head \-ˌhed\ *n* (1812) **1 a** : a fortification protecting the end of a bridge nearest an enemy **b** : an area around the end of a bridge **2** : an advanced position seized in hostile territory as a foothold for further advance

bridge·work \-ˌwərk\ *n* (1883) : dental bridges

[1]**bri·dle** \ˈbrīd-ᵊl\ *n* [ME *bridel*, fr. OE *bridel*; akin to MHG *brîdel* bridle, OE *bregdan* to move quickly — more at BRAID] (bef. 12c) **1 a** : the headgear with which a horse is governed and which carries a bit and reins **b** : a strip of metal joining two parts of a machine esp. for limiting or restraining motion **2** : something resembling a bridle in shape or function: as **a** : a length of secured cable with a second cable attached to the bight to which force is applied **b** : rigging on a kite for attaching line **c** : CURB, RESTRAINT ⟨set a ~ on his power⟩

[2]**bridle** *vb* **bri·dled; bri·dling** \ˈbrīd-liŋ, -ᵊl-iŋ\ *vt* (14c) **1** : to put a bridle on **2** : to restrain, check, or control with or as if with a bridle; *esp* : to get and keep under restraint ⟨you must learn to ~ your tongue⟩ ~ *vi* : to show hostility or resentment (as to an affront to one's pride or dignity) esp. by drawing back the head and chin ***syn*** see RESTRAIN

bridle path *n* (1811) : a trail suitable for horseback riding

Brie \ˈbrē\ *n* [F, fr. *Brie*, district in France] (ca. 1876) : a soft surface-ripened cheese with a whitish rind and a pale yellow interior

[1]**brief** \ˈbrēf\ *adj* [ME *bref, breve*, fr. MF *brief*, fr. L *brevis*; akin to OHG *murg* short, Gk *brachys*] (14c) **1** : short in duration, extent, or length **2 a** : CONCISE ⟨a ~ report⟩ **b** : CURT, ABRUPT ⟨a cold and ~ welcome⟩ — **brief·ness** *n*

syn BRIEF, SHORT mean lacking length. BRIEF applies primarily to duration and may imply condensation, conciseness, or occas. intensity; SHORT may imply sudden stoppage or incompleteness.

[2]**brief** *n* [ME *bref*, fr. MF, fr. ML *brevis*, fr. LL, summary, fr. L *brevis*, adj.] (14c) **1** : an official letter or mandate; *esp* : a papal letter less formal than a bull **2** : a brief written item or document: as **a** : a concise article **b** : SYNOPSIS, SUMMARY **c** : a concise statement of a client's case made out for the instruction of counsel in a trial at law **3** : an outline of an argument; *esp* : a formal outline esp. in law that sets forth the main contentions with supporting statements or evidence **4** *pl* : short snug pants or underpants — **in brief** : in a few words : BRIEFLY

[3]**brief** *vt* (1601) **1** : to make an abstract or abridgment of **2 a** : to give final precise instructions to **b** : to coach thoroughly in advance **c** : to give essential information to — **brief·er** *n*

brief·case \ˈbrēf-ˌkās\ *n* (1917) : a flat flexible case for carrying papers or books

brief·ing \ˈbrē-fiŋ\ *n* (1910) : an act or instance of giving precise instructions or essential information

brief·less \ˈbrē-fləs\ *adj* (1824) : having no legal clients

brief·ly \ˈbrē-flē\ *adv* (14c) **1 a** : in a brief way **b** : in brief **2** : for a short time

[1]**bri·er** \ˈbrī(-ə)r\ *n* [ME *brere*, fr. OE *brēr*] (bef. 12c) : a plant (as of the genera *Rosa, Rubus*, and *Smilax*) with a woody and thorny or prickly stem; *also* : a mass or twig of these — **bri·ery** \ˈbrī(-ə)r-ē\ *adj*

[2]**brier** *n* [F *bruyère* heath, fr. MF *bruiere*, fr. (assumed) VL *brucaria*, fr. LL *brucus* heather, of Celt origin; akin to OIr *froech* heather] (1868) : a heath (*Erica arborea*) of southern Europe with a root used for tobacco pipes

bri·er·root \ˈbrī(-ə)r-ˌrüt, -ˌrůt\ *n* (1869) : a root (as of the brier *Erica arborea*) used for tobacco pipes

[1]**brig** \ˈbrig\ *n* [short for *brigantine*] (1720) : a 2-masted square-rigged ship — compare HERMAPHRODITE BRIG

[2]**brig** *n* [prob. fr. [1]*brig*] (1852) **1** : a place (as on a ship) for temporary confinement of offenders in the U.S. Navy **2** : GUARDHOUSE, PRISON

[1]**bri·gade** \brig-ˈād\ *n* [F, fr. It *brigata*, fr. *brigare*] (1644) **1 a** : a large body of troops **b** : a tactical and administrative unit composed of a headquarters, one or more units of infantry or armor, and supporting units **2** : a group of people organized for special activity

[2]**brigade** *vt* **bri·gad·ed; bri·gad·ing** (1781) : to form or unite into a brigade

brig·a·dier \ˌbrig-ə-ˈdi(ə)r\ *n* [F, fr. *brigade*] (1678) **1** : BRIGADIER GENERAL **2** : an officer in the British army commanding a brigade and ranking immediately below a major general

brigadier general *n* (1690) : a commissioned officer in the army, air force, or marine corps who ranks above a colonel and whose insignia is one star

brig·and \ˈbrig-ənd\ *n* [ME *brigaunt*, fr. MF *brigand*, fr. OIt *brigante*, fr. *brigare* to fight, fr. *briga* strife, of Celt origin; akin to OIr *brig* strength] (14c) : one who lives by plunder usu. as a member of a band : BANDIT — **brig·and·age** \-ən-dij\ *n*

brig·an·dine \ˈbrig-ən-ˌdēn\ *n* [ME, fr. MF, fr. *brigand*] (15c) : medieval body armor of scales or plates

brig·an·tine \ˈbrig-ən-ˌtēn\ *n* [MF *brigantin*, fr. OIt *brigantino*, fr. *brigante*] (1525) **1** : a 2-masted square-rigged ship differing from a brig in not carrying a square mainsail **2** : HERMAPHRODITE BRIG

bright \ˈbrīt\ *adj* [ME, fr. OE *beorht*; akin to OHG *beraht* bright, Skt *bhrājate* it shines] (bef. 12c) **1 a** : radiating or reflecting light : SHINING, SPARKLING ⟨~ lights⟩ ⟨~ eyes⟩ **b** : SUNNY ⟨a ~ day⟩; *also* : radiant with happiness ⟨~ smiling faces⟩ ⟨~ moments⟩ **2** : ILLUSTRIOUS, GLORIOUS ⟨~*est* star of the opera⟩ **3** : BEAUTIFUL **4** : of high saturation or brilliance ⟨~ colors⟩ **5 a** : LIVELY, CHEERFUL ⟨be ~ and jovial among your guests —Shak.⟩ **b** : INTELLIGENT, CLEVER ⟨a ~ idea⟩ ⟨~ children⟩ **6** : AUSPICIOUS, PROMISING ⟨~ prospects for the future⟩ — **bright** *adv* — **bright·ly** *adv*

syn BRIGHT, BRILLIANT, RADIANT, LUMINOUS, LUSTROUS mean shining or glowing with light. BRIGHT implies emitting or reflecting a high degree of light; BRILLIANT implies intense often sparkling brightness; RADIANT stresses the emission or seeming emission of rays of light; LUMINOUS implies emission of steady, suffused, glowing light by reflection or in surrounding darkness; LUSTROUS stresses an even, rich light from a surface that reflects brightly without sparkling or glittering.

bright·en \ˈbrīt-ᵊn\ *vb* **bright·ened; bright·en·ing** \ˈbrīt-niŋ, -ᵊn-iŋ\ *vt* (1583) : to make bright or brighter ~ *vi* : to become bright or brighter — **bright·en·er** \-nər, -ᵊn-ər\ *n*

bright·ness *n* (bef. 12c) **1** : the quality or state of being bright; *also* : an instance of such a quality or state **2** : the one of the three psychological dimensions of color perception by which visual stimuli are ordered continuously from light to dark and which is correlated with light intensity — compare HUE 2c, SATURATION

Bright's disease \ˈbrīts-\ *n* [Richard *Bright* †1858 Eng. physician] (1831) : any of several kidney diseases marked by albumin in the urine

bright·work \ˈbrīt-ˌwərk\ *n* (1841) : polished or plated metalwork

brill \ˈbril\ *n, pl* **brill** [perh. fr. Corn *brȳthel* mackerel] (15c) : a European flatfish (*Bothus rhombus*) related to the turbot; *broadly* : TURBOT

bril·liance \ˈbril-yən(t)s\ *n* (1755) : the quality or state of being brilliant

bril·lian·cy \-yən-sē\ *n, pl* **-cies** (1747) **1** : BRILLIANCE **2** : an instance of brilliance

[1]**bril·liant** \ˈbril-yənt\ *adj* [F *brillant*, prp. of *briller* to shine, fr. It *brillare*, fr. *brillo* beryl, fr. L *beryllus* — more at BERYL] (1681) **1** : very bright : GLITTERING ⟨a ~ light⟩ **2 a** : STRIKING, DISTINCTIVE ⟨a ~ example⟩ **b** : distinguished by unusual mental keenness or alertness ***syn*** see BRIGHT — **bril·liant·ly** *adv*

[2]**brilliant** *n* (1690) : a gem (as a diamond) cut in a particular form with numerous facets so as to have special brilliance

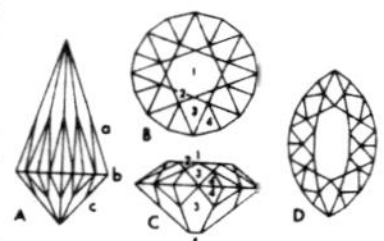

brilliant: *A* briolette; *B, C* American cut, top and side view; *D* marquise: *a* bezel, *b* girdle, *c* pavilion: *1* table, *2* star facet, *3* main facet, *4* corner facet, *5* culet

bril·lian·tine \ˈbril-yən-ˌtēn\ *n* (1884) **1** : a preparation for making hair glossy **2** : a light lustrous fabric that is similar to alpaca and is woven usu. with a cotton warp and mohair or worsted filling

[1]**brim** \ˈbrim\ *n* [ME *brimme*; akin to MHG *brem* edge] (13c) **1 a** (1) : an upper or outer margin : VERGE (2) *archaic* : the upper surface of a body of water **b** : the edge or rim of a hollow vessel, a natural depression, or a cavity **2** : the projecting rim of a hat — **brim·less** \-ləs\ *adj*

[2]**brim** *vb* **brimmed; brim·ming** *vt* (1611) : to fill to the brim ~ *vi* **1** : to be or become full often to overflowing **2** : to reach or overflow a brim

brim·ful \ˈbrim-ˈfůl\ *adj* (1530) : full to the brim : ready to overflow

-brimmed \ˈbrimd\ *adj comb form* : having a brim of a specified nature ⟨a wide-*brimmed* hat⟩

brim·mer \ˈbrim-ər\ *n* (1663) : a brimming cup or glass

brim·stone \ˈbrim-ˌstōn\ *n* [ME *brinston*, prob. fr. *birnen* to burn + *ston* stone — more at BURN] (14c) : SULFUR

brind·ed \ˈbrin-dəd\ *adj* [ME *brended*] *archaic* (15c) : BRINDLED

brin·dle \ˈbrin-dᵊl\ *n* [*brindle*, adj.] (1676) **1** : a brindled color **2** : a brindled animal

brin·dled \-dᵊld\ *or* **brindle** *adj* [alter. of *brinded*] (1679) : having obscure dark streaks or flecks on a gray or tawny ground

[1]**brine** \ˈbrīn\ *n* [ME, fr. OE *brȳne*; akin to MD *brīne* brine, L *fricare* to rub — more at FRICTION] (bef. 12c) **1 a** : water saturated or strongly impregnated with common salt **b** : a strong saline solution (as of calcium chloride) **2** : the water of a sea or salt lake

[2]**brine** *vt* **brined; brin·ing** (1552) : to treat (as by steeping) with brine — **brin·er** *n*

\ə\ abut \ᵊ\ kitten, F table \ər\ further \a\ ash \ā\ ace \ä\ cot, cart \au̇\ out \ch\ chin \e\ bet \ē\ easy \g\ go \i\ hit \ī\ ice \j\ job \ŋ\ sing \ō\ go \ȯ\ law \ȯi\ boy \th\ thin \t͟h\ the \ü\ loot \u̇\ foot \y\ yet \zh\ vision \à, k̲, ⁿ, œ, œ̄, ue, ue̅, ʸ\ *see* Guide to Pronunciation

4 Vocabulary: Part II

Meilu, a Chinese student, turned to her classmate Trina in despair. "I'll never understand my textbooks!" she exclaimed. "They just don't make any sense sometimes."

Trina looked at Meilu in surprise. "What things are bothering you?" she asked.

"My geography book says that Hong Kong was the doorway to China. Hong Kong is a city. I know that. What does it have to do with a door? And my education book talks about a tailor-made curriculum for social science. Social science doesn't have anything to do with sewing, does it?" Meilu complained.

Trina smiled. "Those are just figurative expressions," she replied.

"What does that mean?" Meilu asked.

"They are comparing Hong Kong to a doorway because that is the place where many people entered China, just as a doorway is the place that people enter a house. And the other book just means that the social science curriculum will be especially designed to fit the students, just as a tailor-made suit is especially cut to fit the wearer," Trina explained. "We have lots of figurative expressions in English. I guess that makes it difficult for people who haven't lived here all of their lives."

Introduction

Vocabulary development can be enhanced by attention to certain types of words and to special uses of words. Figurative language and idiomatic expressions use words in ways other than their literal meanings.

Special Types of Words

Some special types of words to be aware of when you are improving your vocabulary are *synonyms, antonyms, homonyms, homographs,* and *multiple-meaning words.* Proficiency with these word types will make your oral and written language more exact and will help you better understand the meanings and shades of meaning of words.

Synonyms

Synonyms are words that mean the same, or almost the same, thing, such as *pretty* and *beautiful.* The word "synonym" can be analyzed to discover the derivation of its meaning. "Syn" is a word part meaning "same," and "onym" is a word part meaning "name." It is important for you to realize the similarities in the meanings of synonyms and to distinguish different shades of meanings.

IIVo Exercise 1

For each of the sentences below, find in the Word List a word that is a synonym for the underlined word and place it on the line to the right of the sentence. You may use your dictionary, if necessary.

Word List
accustom
drunkenness
foreword
lawyer
reason
exhibit
surroundings

1. Perry was not interested in his current <u>environment</u>. _____

2. She read the <u>preface</u> of the book. _____

3. I would like to know the <u>motive</u> for his actions. _____

4. You will have to <u>habituate</u> yourself to this routine. _____

5. Her <u>inebriation</u> was evident to the police officer. _____

6. You should consider hiring an <u>attorney</u>. _____

7. I do not think he should <u>flaunt</u> his wealth. _____

IIVo Exercise 2

Answer each of the following questions on the line provided. If a word is unfamiliar, use your dictionary to discover its meaning.

1. Which is more desirable, to be called skinny or slender? _____

2. Would most people prefer to be called stingy or parsimonious? _____

3. Would you rather describe a gift you gave as cheap or inexpensive? _____

4. Would you rather be described as a novice or as a greenhorn? _____

5. What is the difference in declaring something and affirming it? _____

_____

Antonyms

Antonyms are words whose meanings are opposite, such as *hot* and *cold*. The word "antonym" can also be analyzed to discover the derivation of its meaning. The word part "anto" means "opposite," and the word part "onym" means "name." Recognizing such relationships among words can increase your comprehension.

IIVo Exercise 3

For each of the following sentences, choose and circle the antonym or antonyms for the underlined word. You may wish to use your dictionary.

1. The supply of food was <u>insufficient</u>. (inadequate, abundant, meager)

2. An intelligent decision is <u>crucial</u>. (unimportant, important, redundant)

3. Do not <u>lament</u> the change in command. (mourn, enjoy, relish)

4. To allow such conduct is <u>inconceivable</u>. (unimaginable, unthinkable, plausible)

5. He can <u>confirm</u> my findings. (ratify, support, refute)

6. This telephone is <u>antiquated</u>. (new, modern, obsolete)

Homonyms

Homonyms are words that sound the same, but have different meanings and spellings, such as *blue* and *blew*. In the word "homonym" the word part "hom" means "same," and the word part "onym" means "name." Knowledge of homonyms can help you write with more precision and accuracy, and it can also assist you in reading material orally.

IIVo Exercise 4

After each of the following words, write another word that is pronounced the same, but not spelled the same.

1. would   _____   6. dough   _____

2. heart   _____   7. pour   _____

3. hair   _____   8. foul   _____

4. pear   _____ or _____   9. feet   _____

5. great   _____   10. bore   _____

IIVo Exercise 5

For each of the definitions below, choose a word from those in IIVo Exercise 4, either one that was originally listed or one that you wrote in one of the spaces.

1. a place to build a fire _____

2. a rabbit _____

3. a fruit _____

4. a female deer _____

5. an internal organ of the body _____

6. an accomplishment _____

7. a male pig _____

8. to cut _____

Homographs and Multiple-meaning Words

Homographs are words that are spelled the same, but have different meanings and pronunciations. Examples are "contract," meaning "to decrease in volume," and "contract," meaning an "agreement." The first example is pronounced with the accent on the second syllable; the second example is pronounced with the accent on the first syllable. The word "homograph" contains the word part "homo," meaning "same," and the word part "graph," meaning "to write." In other words, the words are written the same way. Use of context is important in distinguishing among homographs. Words that are spelled and pronounced the same but have different meanings are frequently just called multiple-meaning words, but some people refer to them as homographs. Whatever label they are given, use of the context is important in determining their meanings.

IIVo Exercise 6

In each of the following sentences, the context is needed to determine the correct pronunciation of the underlined word. Place the letter of the correct pronunciation on the line next to the item number.

_____ 1. Yesterday I <u>read</u> a good book.
    a. rĕd
    b. rēd

_____ 2. William will <u>record</u> the scores for the contestants.
    a. rĕk′ ərd
    b. rĭ · kôrd′

_____ 3. Do you have a signed <u>contract</u>?
    a. kŏn′ trăkt
    b. kən · trăkt′

_____ 4. Molly will <u>wind</u> the clock.
    a. wīnd
    b. wĭnd

_____ 5. We trudged across the <u>desert</u> sands.
    a. dē · zərt′
    b. dĕz′ ərt

_____ 6. Tie her ribbon in a <u>bow</u>.
    a. bō
    b. bou

_____ 7. The farmer must <u>sow</u> the seeds.
    a. sō
    b. sou

_____ 8. Are you <u>content</u> with the assignment that you have?
      a. kŏn′ tĕnt
      b. kən · tĕnt′

_____ 9. Pay attention to the <u>minute</u> details.
      a. mĭn′ ət
      b. mī · nūt′

_____ 10. This is where you will <u>live</u>.
      a. lĭv
      b. līv

IIVo Exercise 7

Underline the correct meaning for each underlined word.

1. I was pleased to <u>land</u> such a large fish.
   a. a portion of the earth's surface
   b. catch

2. I have been known to <u>pore</u> over books on archeology.
   a. study
   b. a small opening in a membrane

3. He drew an <u>oblique</u> line.
   a. indirect
   b. slanting

4. They planned to <u>groom</u> her for the office of senator.
   a. curry
   b. prepare

5. His job was to <u>block</u> the linebacker.
   a. obstruct
   b. shape

6. How did you <u>anticipate</u> my wishes?
   a. foresee
   b. prevent by prior action

IIVo Exercise 8

Read the definitions for each word. Then read each sentence. Determine which meaning is intended for each underlined word. Place the letter of the definition which makes sense in the blank provided.

Example: run

    a. to move rapidly
    b. to compete
    c. to be in operation
    d. to extend in time
    e. to flow

1.   d   The film presentation will run two weeks.

2.   a   During recess the children run from one end of the playground to the other.

3.   b   The mayor refuses to run for a second term of office.

4.   e   When the snow on the mountain melts, the water will run into streams.

5.   c   The car will not run because it is out of gasoline.

I. flash

    a. to appear briefly
    b. to move rapidly
    c. to signal with light
    d. to sparkle
    e. equipment used to produce illumination

1. _____ Joe saw a beacon flash from the lighthouse, warning the sailors of the dangerous rocks.

2. _____ See the diamond flash in the bright sunlight.

3. _____ I saw a rabbit, startled by a dog, flash across my path.

4. _____ Tina saw the falling star flash in the sky and then disappear.

5. _____ He took the picture using his new flash attachment.

II. heavy

    a. having great weight
    b. filled with sadness
    c. violent, rough
    d. oppressive
    e. dense or thick

1. _____ Her heavy taxes were almost more than she could bear.

2. _____ The log was too heavy for the boy to move by himself.

3. _____ The cars crawled slowly through the heavy fog.

4. _____ His heart was heavy when he learned of the death of his friend.

5. _____ The small boat almost overturned in the heavy seas.

III. fall

    a. to drop down
    b. to collapse in ruins
    c. to be conquered
    d. a season of the year
    e. to occur or take place

1. _____ On the third day of the battle, it became apparent that the brave band of men would fall to the enemy.

2. _____ When the apples are ripe, they will fall to the ground.

3. _____ Leaves change color in the fall.

4. _____ Valentine's Day will fall on Thursday this year.

5. _____ The building should fall to the ground about three hours after the demolition crews begin working.

IV. break

    a. to come apart
    b. to force a way into
    c. to make known
    d. to pierce the surface of
    e. to tame or make obedient

1. _____ An unhatched bird can chip away at its shell until it breaks through.

2. _____ They were afraid that a thief would break into the house while the family was at church.

3. _____ Jane had to break news of the disaster to relatives of the victims.

4. _____ The trainer can break a wild horse in about a month.

5. _____ The fragile glass may break from the rapid temperature change.

V. set

    a. to adjust
    b. to put in a place
    c. to arrange
    d. to put in a mounting
    e. to affix a value

1. _____ She had her mother's sapphire set in a platinum band.

2. _____ He set his watch by the radio signal.

3. _____ The fine was set at fifty dollars.

4. _____ The elderly lady set the treasured picture on the mantle.

5. _____ Joe set the table to please his mother.

VI. sharp

    a. having a fine, keen edge
    b. shrewd; clever
    c. alert
    d. exactly
    e. abrupt, sudden

1. _____ The road made a sharp turn as we approached the mountain.

2. _____ The old trader was sharp and knew how to drive a hard bargain.

3. _____ Be there at five o'clock sharp.

4. _____ Only a sharp knife can cut that cord.

5. _____ Even though she was past eighty, her mind was still sharp.

VII. burn

    a. to consume as fuel
    b. to be destroyed by fire
    c. to feel strong emotion
    d. to cause a feeling of heat
    e. to undergo combustion

1. _____ The spaghetti sauce contained hot peppers that burned his mouth.

2. _____ The house burned to the ground when the fire department failed to arrive.

3. _____ She burned when she learned of the injustice to her brother.

4. _____ The old car burned too much gas.

5. _____ The charcoal was burning with an intense heat.

VIII. get
       a. to obtain, acquire
       b. to be sentenced
       c. to understand
       d. to catch or contract
       e. to arrive at

1. _____ She may get ten years for armed robbery.

2. _____ He will get the idea, after someone shows him what to do.

3. _____ She will get a new coat when her old one is worn out.

4. _____ The child could get chicken pox from the boy next door.

5. _____ He should get to the store just before closing time.

IX. give
       a. to make a gift or present of
       b. to pay
       c. to convey
       d. to grant
       e. to administer

1. _____ The Girl Scout will give first aid to the wounded dog.

2. _____ David wants to give his girl friend a box of candy for Valentine's Day.

3. _____ Please give my best wishes to the bride.

4. _____ He asked his father to give him permission to use the car tonight.

5. _____ It was necessary to give five dollars for the ticket.

X. play
       a. to participate in a game or sport
       b. to perform on a musical instrument
       c. to perform on the stage
       d. to release a steady stream
       e. to move quickly and lightly

1. _____ She will play the violin in the string quartet.

2. _____ We watched the sunlight play on the rippling water.

3. _____ A famous British actor will play the part of Hamlet.

4. _____ Sherry enjoyed watching the fountains play during the early evening hours.

5. _____ Jim can play basketball and baseball equally well.

Figurative Language and Idiomatic Expressions

Figurative language often involves comparing things that are unlike in most respects, but have some common trait which can be isolated to make the comparison illuminating for the listener or reader. Exaggerations are also often used to make points, although they are not meant literally. Some types of figurative language are explained below.

Similes

Similes are comparisons using the words "like" or "as." For example, the following sentence contains a simile: "Her cheeks were like roses." In this sentence, the girl's cheeks are being compared to some aspect of roses—in this case, the red color. No comparison of the thorns or other characteristics of roses is intended.

Metaphors

Metaphors are comparisons that do not use the words "like" or "as." For example, the following sentence contains a metaphor: "He was a pillar of strength." In the example, the man's strength is being compared with that of a pillar, which furnishes firm support.

Hyperboles

Hyperboles are extreme exaggerations. For example, the following sentence illustrates hyperbole: "I've told you that a million times." Although the speaker has not actually spoken the statement referred to a million times, the speaker means that the statement has been repeated very frequently.

Personification

Personification refers to giving an inanimate object or abstract idea the characteristics of a person. For example, the following sentence illustrates personification: "The ships danced on the waves." The ships cannot actually do dance steps, but the motion of the ships caused by the movement of the waves resembles the movements of dancers.

Euphemisms

Euphemisms are inoffensive expressions substituted for ones that are believed to be offensive. For example, the following sentence contains a euphemism: "Bill Smith passed away today." In this case the less offensive expression "passed away" is used in place of the more offensive term "died."

These are just a few of the more common figures of speech that appear in all types of printed material. You need to learn to interpret such figures of speech in order to read with understanding.

IIVo Exercise 9

The following are some well-known and often used similes. See if you can complete each simile by inserting the proper word in the blank. If you are not familiar with the expressions, use reasoning to try to determine which term would have the association that is being made attached to it. A list of words from which you should choose is provided.

Choose from this list.

1. cold as a	_____	1. fox
2. sly as a	_____	2. bug
3. mean as a	_____	3. frog
4. snug as a	_____ in a rug	4. snake
5. crazy as a	_____	5. loon
6. white as a	_____	6. tack
7. sharp as a	_____	7. goose
8. silly as a	_____	8. sheet

Idiomatic expressions have meanings that cannot be determined from combining the meanings of each of the words. The overall meaning of the expression must be determined by the reader. Some practice with such expressions will be helpful to you.

IIVo Exercise 10

Read the following items and choose the statement following each item that accurately explains the item's meaning. Place the letter of the correct response in the blank to the left of the item number.

_____ 1. John tried to hurry home to get in out of the biting wind.
    a. The wind was sinking its teeth into John.
    b. The wind was very cold and painful to John's skin.

_____ 2. As Jane left the house, she was swallowed up in the darkness.
    a. The darkness opened its mouth and swallowed Jane.
    b. The darkness kept Jane from being seen.

_____ 3. The car gulped gasoline so fast that I had trouble keeping the tank filled.
    a. The car burned a great deal of gasoline.
    b. The car drank gasoline thirstily.

_____ 4. My grandmother can spin a yarn better than anyone I know.
   a. My grandmother is good at taking yarn and spinning it.
   b. My grandmother can tell stories well.

_____ 5. At Christmas my husband gets excited and just throws his money away at the stores.
   a. My husband spends a lot of money at Christmas.
   b. My husband drops his money in the wastebaskets at the stores.

_____ 6. Sandra was heavy-hearted because she knew that she must move.
   a. Sandra's heart weighed a great deal.
   b. Sandra was sad about moving.

_____ 7. Sammy lost his temper on the playground.
   a. Sammy dropped his temper somewhere on the playground and couldn't find it.
   b. Sammy had an outburst of anger on the playground.

_____ 8. Let's put our heads together and see if we can solve this problem.
   a. Let's hold our heads together so they touch.
   b. Let's put together our ideas so that we will have a better chance to solve the problem.

_____ 9. Mike dug up the facts about the crooked politician.
   a. Mike used a shovel to dig up some facts that were buried in the ground.
   b. Mike did some research and located the facts.

_____ 10. Mother worked like a horse to get ready for the company.
   a. Mother went out into the field and pulled a plow.
   b. Mother worked very hard.

_____ 11. I have gained a ton over the holidays.
   a. I have put on some excess weight.
   b. I have gained 2,000 pounds.

_____ 12. The icy fingers of the wind caused me to shiver.
   a. The wind was so cold that it caused me to shiver.
   b. The wind put its cold fingers on me and caused me to shiver.

_____ 13. You mean old Joe finally kicked the bucket?
   a. Joe gave the bucket a blow with his foot.
   b. Joe died.

_____ 14. I hope you will take the boat off his hands.
   a. I hope you will buy the boat from him.
   b. I hope you will lift that heavy boat off of his hands before they are crushed.

_____ 15. After her opponent spoke, Denise took the floor.
   a. Denise ripped up the floorboards and left with them.
   b. Denise stood up to make a formal speech.

IIVo Exercise 11

Each of the following phrases has a special meaning. Place the letter of the word or phrase that means nearly the same as the special meaning of the first phrase in the blank beside the number of each phrase.

Example: <u>b</u> under the weather   a. carrying an umbrella
                                               b. not feeling well
                                               c. without education
                                               d. in the deep snow

If we say that a person is "under the weather," we mean that he or she is sick; therefore, the correct answer is "b. not feeling well."

_____ 1. in the dark

     a. without electricity
     b. during the night
     c. having poor vision
     d. uninformed

_____ 2. off the record

     a. on tape
     b. not official
     c. not turned on
     d. without music

_____ 3. of course

     a. naturally
     b. departing from the route
     c. never the same
     d. as a result

_____ 4. at wits' end

     a. making funny remarks
     b. end of the road
     c. completely at a loss
     d. as you please

_____ 5. in fine feather

     a. in very good humor
     b. light in weight
     c. a distinctive achievement
     d. as pigeons and doves

_____ 6. up to one's ears

     a. belonging to the group
     b. standing in deep water
     c. deeply involved
     d. unable to hear

_____ 7. over one's head

     a. more than six feet deep
     b. definitely superior to
     c. overly confident
     d. too difficult to understand

_____ 8. after one's own heart
    a. personally pleasing
    b. disappointing
    c. inclined to be sleepy
    d. highly emotional

_____ 9. near to one's heart
    a. concerning the anatomy
    b. within a short distance
    c. important to one
    d. a living relative

_____ 10. elbow grease
    a. lubricant for joints
    b. neglect of duty
    c. an abundant supply
    d. vigorous physical effort

_____ 11. off the track
    a. unable to trace
    b. away from the subject
    c. in complete control
    d. in great surprise

_____ 12. on the side
    a. the highest point
    b. in addition to the main subject
    c. increasingly difficult
    d. beside oneself

_____ 13. out of the picture
    a. no longer involved
    b. not in focus
    c. a window frame
    d. a painted window

_____ 14. picture window
    a. a large window
    b. a drawing of a window
    c. a window frame
    d. a painted window

_____ 15. under a cloud
    a. a silver lining
    b. a warning
    c. a sudden shower
    d. depressed or troubled

_____ 16. in the clouds
    a. foggy weather
    b. an unusual experience
    c. fanciful or impractical
    d. confidential

_____ 17. out on a limb

a. in a difficult position
b. falling suddenly
c. natural disaster
d. in great astonishment

_____ 18. in the red

a. politically inclined
b. strongly emotional
c. in a traffic jam
d. in debt

_____ 19. in the pink

a. delicately made
b. in good health
c. a rosy sunset
d. since the beginning

_____ 20. out of the blue

a. no longer depressed
b. startled
c. unexpected
d. questioning

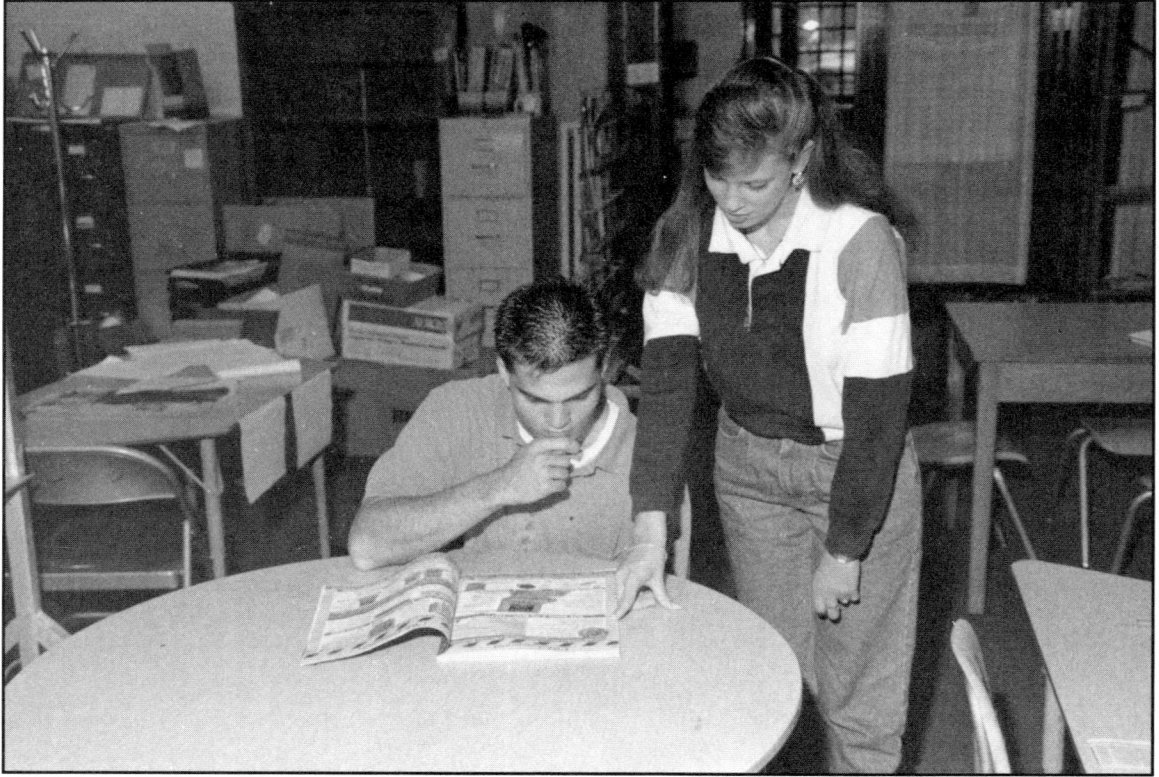

5 Nature of Comprehension

Clark was sitting at the table shaking his head when Sarah came into the classroom. ''Hey, why so glum? We don't have a test today, do we?''

Clark looked up and managed a smile. ''No. No test today. I'm just a little overwhelmed by these ads. I bought a computer so that I would be able to do a better job with my papers and such. Now it turns out that I need word processing software and maybe even a different printer to be able to do what I wanted to do. I thought when I bought all the pieces that were pictured in the catalog that I'd be okay. But it turns out that the only software that came with it just allows me to use the disk drive and, get this, *program* if I want to. It doesn't have the stuff that allows you to write papers. And when I told my English teacher about the computer, he said, ''You did get a letter quality printer, didn't you? All I know is that I have a nine-pin dot matrix printer. See, that's all the ad says about it. What did he mean by letter quality? Won't they all print letters?''

''You'll probably have to invest in another printer. Nine-pin means that each letter is formed by nine dots. That doesn't make a letter that looks like one a typewriter could make. Your teacher wants one that is as good as a typewriter letter,'' Sarah told him.

''I read the ad, but I didn't really understand what it meant. Nine-pin didn't sound inadequate because I had no idea what the pins did. Now I'm having the same trouble with these ads for word processing software. This one says 'WYSIWYG' on this line with no explanation. Is that good or bad? It also says 'Easy block moves' and 'auto-align.' I don't know what a block is and when I would need to move one, and I don't have a clue about the other term. There's some other confusing stuff here too. How will I ever decide?''

''I'll help you. My father has had computers for years. I've been using them myself for several years, and I know what all those terms mean. You just don't have enough experience with computers to allow you to read it with understanding,'' Sarah told him.

'' 'WYSIWYG' means 'what you see is what you get.' That means your printed page will look like what you see on the screen. You want that for sure. 'Easy block moves' means that you can move sentences and paragraphs around easily without having to rekey them—you know, like when your English teacher tells you that two or three of your sentences really belong in an earlier paragraph. You can just mark the beginning and the end of the sentences that you want to move, and then indicate with the cursor where you want them to go. The computer just moves them for you. And 'auto-align' means that your line lengths will be adjusted automatically when you insert something or delete something from your text and when you move sentences around. Those are both good features. Show me the rest of the ads, and I'll help you figure out their meanings. There's no substitute for experience in evaluating advertising claims.''

Introduction

Good reading depends largely on the quality of the reader's comprehension. Reading is more than word calling; it is the ability to understand or get meaning from printed symbols.

Comprehension is an active thinking process. It requires effort on the part of readers. They must draw on their experiences and previous knowledge and relate this prior knowledge and experience to what they read.

Clusters of related concepts that people bring to reading from their previous experiences are sometimes called schemata. (A single cluster is called a schema.) Readers at the college level have schemata related to many things that they will encounter in assigned reading materials. These schemata may be very rich and well developed, or they may be relatively incomplete. Rich, well-developed schemata that are related to reading assignments will help readers understand the material better. For example, if readers have traveled on small ocean-going vessels, the description of the difficulties of the *Mayflower* voyage is likely to be more readily understood, and if readers have traveled extensively in the Rocky Mountains, the difficulties facing pioneers who had only covered wagons and horses to use in the crossing will be more comprehensible to them than to readers unfamiliar with mountain travel. If readers have witnessed a tornado, the science book's explanation of this type of storm will be easier to comprehend than if they have never seen one. Readers who have had chicken pox will find a health book's description of this disease easier to understand than will readers who have not had this experience.

Readers must combine words, sentences, and paragraphs into meaningful ideas in order to comprehend. When the concepts and words are familiar, comprehension may come quickly and easily. When the concepts are new and strange and the words are technical, comprehension will come more slowly and will require much thought.

Comprehension can take place on many levels of difficulty. The easiest level is simply recalling what the writers have said in their own words. A higher level of comprehension involves interpreting the authors' ideas and expressing them in your own words. Other types of comprehension are applying knowledge to a particular situation and analyzing the material to see relationships. The most advanced level of comprehension is evaluation of the material or critical reading, which is discussed in Chapter 7: Critical Reading.

Units of Meaning

Meaning can be expressed through written words and their relationships to each other. In order to understand what you read, you should be aware of the connotations of words and the organizational patterns of larger units of meaning. You need to understand the meanings of units of varying lengths: words, phrases, sentences, paragraphs, and entire selections.

Words

Vocabulary and comprehension are closely related. If you have an extensive vocabulary, your comprehension is likely to be high. Chapters 3 and 4 dealt with understanding the meanings of words.

Phrases

A phrase is a combination of words that forms a meaningful unit. You probably have already developed a sense of phrasing, as phrases are the basic units of meaning that combine to form sentences. Reading in phrases should help both your comprehension and speed, as you will be thinking in terms of meaningful groups of words instead of single words.

Phrases can modify the meaning of a sentence. For example, a core sentence leaves much to the imagination. As phrases are added, you may need to change your mental image. Read the kernel sentence below and form a mental picture. Then read the sentences that follow and modify this image as new phrases are introduced.

The man was walking.
The wiry little man was walking.
The wiry little man was walking along a tightrope.
The wiry little man was walking along a tightrope with his arms outstretched.
The wiry little man was walking along a tightrope with his arms outstretched and an umbrella in one hand.
The wiry little man was walking along a tightrope high above the ground with his arms outstretched and an umbrella in one hand.

There are several easily recognizable types of phrases that form meaningful units. Examples of these are as follows:

Prepositional phrase—along a tightrope
Noun preceded by modifiers—the wiry little man
Verb with auxiliary forms—was walking

To derive the intended meaning from a phrase, you must think of the meaning of the entire group of words. The phrase as a unit often has a meaning that differs somewhat from the meanings of its separate words. Some phrases may be figures of speech or idioms. Examples of these phrases are found in Chapter 4.

Sentences

Words and phrases combine to form sentences. The full meaning of a sentence, however, is more than the combination of its individual words. Instead, each sentence is a complete thought relying for its meaning on punctuation, the arrangement of words in the sentence, and the meanings of its words and phrases.

Sentences in the English language have a fairly consistent structure. This consistency helps comprehension because the reader knows what to expect. The normal sequence for a sentence pattern is noun, verb, object. Modifiers as single words or phrases are interspersed to provide additional meaning. When reading quickly to grasp main ideas, it is important to be able to pick out the core, or kernel, of the sentence. This core contains the basic meaning of the sentence and consists of the noun and verb or the noun, verb, and object.

NC Exercise 1

In the following sentences, identify the kernel, or core, and underline the words that form this kernel.

Example: The French <u>explorers discovered</u> the heavily forested <u>area</u> in the early eighteenth century. ("Explorers discovered area" is a kernel containing the noun, verb, and object that form the core of the sentence.)

1. A huge plastic roof covers the new sports arena.
2. A grim-faced young man stepped out of the elevator.
3. People who do not own cars ride bicycles to work.
4. Pakistan has a shortage of teachers and schools.
5. The glorious sunset glowed in the sky.
6. The early settlers caught fish from the rivers.
7. Strong housing demands indicate prosperous conditions.
8. Unresolved grievances caused a long and bitter strike.
9. The workers ate a hearty lunch in the park during the noon hour.
10. After ten weeks of negotiations, a peace settlement was reached.
11. The spacecraft transmitted detailed pictures of the surface of Mars.
12. The Trans-Amazon Highway extends into areas rich with minerals and other resources.
13. More consumers than ever before are buying inexpensive electronic pocket calculators.
14. The winner of the Nobel Prize criticized the persecution of writers in the country he represented.
15. Relief for the nation's cities finally arrived in the form of a revenue-sharing plan.

16. Haunted by memories of his childhood, the writer returned to his home only to find everything had changed.

17. The new nation, struggling with limited resources, received much-needed help from the International Monetary Fund.

18. Through active participation in an outdoor program, the girls learned various skills that helped them build stronger bodies.

19. The child who had been lost for sixteen hours was found by a college student who had joined the search party.

20. Alone at last, the artist worked feverishly in order to complete the painting in time for the exhibition.

Paragraphs

A paragraph usually consists of a series of sentences that are related to each other and are centered around a single topic. It is a structured, organized unit of meaning. Writers end one paragraph and begin another when they are changing from one thought or phase of an idea to another.

Understanding the arrangement and the functions of paragraphs can help you develop comprehension, speed, and more efficient study skills. You will find that you can get the meaning from a paragraph more quickly when you understand how it is organized. Some types of paragraphs need to be read carefully while other types can be skimmed briefly. When you become skillful in analyzing paragraphs, you will be able to spot the main idea quickly and almost automatically organize the subordinate details around it.

It is common for a paragraph in an informational passage to have a main idea, which is usually contained in a single sentence. This sentence is called a topic sentence. The other sentences within the paragraph generally relate to the topic sentence and provide supporting material.

The topic sentence may be located anywhere in the paragraph. In most paragraphs, however, the topic sentence is the first sentence. In this case, it probably tells what the paragraph is about and points out what is to be discussed. Sometimes the topic sentence is the last sentence. When the first sentence is introductory or refers back to the preceding paragraph, the second sentence may be the topic sentence. Occasionally, there is no topic sentence, and the main idea is implied rather than directly stated. Then you must infer the main idea from the information presented.

Paragraphs may be developed in a number of ways. Five frequently used methods are explained briefly below.

1. Introduction: introduces the main idea, stimulates reader's interest, sets the mood.
2. Definition: defines or explains key words, ideas, or concepts.
3. Illustration: provides examples, anecdotes, illustrative stories; expands and clarifies.
4. Transition: provides a bridge from one topic to another; shows change of thought.
5. Summary/conclusion: summarizes major ideas and draws conclusions; emphasizes a final point.

As you become familiar with organizations and types of paragraphs, you may find that your reading is improving. If you are reading only for main ideas, you learn to spot topic sentences quickly and ignore details. You begin to look for introductory paragraphs, which help you anticipate the writer's ideas. You notice concluding and summarizing paragraphs, which bring out important points and reinforce major concepts. You realize that you need to read definition paragraphs intently, but that you can rapidly skim illustrative paragraphs. A thorough understanding of paragraphs should increase the quality of your comprehension and the efficiency of your reading.

NC Exercise 2

Read the following paragraphs and indicate by number the topic sentence in each, if there is one. Also, identify the type of paragraph by putting the letter of the type in the appropriate blank at the end of each paragraph.

Type
  a. *Introduction*
  b. *Definition*
  c. *Illustration*
  d. *Transition*
  e. *Summary/conclusion*

Example:

> There are two types of perceived frequencies. One is called *absolute pitch,* or the actual value as perceived in so many hertz or cycles per second. The other is the *relative pitch* or the frequency relationship between a certain note and a note played either with it or immediately before. Fortunately for music in general, very few people care about or can tell an absolute pitch, and it is only the *relative* relationship between notes on a frequency ratio basis that really matters. Thus, if *all* the notes produced change their absolute frequency slowly with time, very few listeners will notice. This also lets us move up and down a musical scale to get a different overall effect or to add variety or depth to a composition.[1]

The topic sentence in this paragraph is the first one because it introduces the subject discussed in the paragraph. The type of paragraph is definition because it defines and explains the terms "absolute pitch" and "relative pitch."

The answer is

Topic sentence	*Type*
1	b

I.   Man has always tried to capture sunbeams. Primitive man made fires in the sun's image to disperse the fearful dark of his cave, to bring benevolent warmth. Ancient men of all civilizations worshipped the sun as a god—central light of the heavens, nourisher of the earth. In ancient Egypt the Sun God Ra was dominant; his right eye—the Horus or "Sun-Eye," symbolizing the sun's disc—was the principal figure of mythical speculations. Early Greek religion concentrated on everyday life, rather than other worldliness, and sought for temporal blessings such as good crops, health, and peace. The word *Helios* meant both the visible sun and the Greek Sun God, clearly showing the Greek's direct deification of the sun.[2]

Topic sentence   *Type*

_____   _____

II.   In addition to these "normal" concomitants of skyrocketing growth, there is another problem that has troubled many thoughtful Virgin Islanders perhaps even more: the damage to the special character of the life and habits of the natives.[3]

Topic sentence   *Type*

_____   _____

III.   Music synthesizers generate three different kinds of electrical signals: audio signals, control signals, and trigger signals. The audio signals eventually emerge from the system as sounds. Control signals vary the audio signals to make them change loudness, pitch or quality. The performer can do these things manually, but it is easier and more convenient to let control voltages do the job. The trigger signals begin and end control sequences according to a preset program. Again, the performer could perform the trigger operations manually, but an electronic trigger circuit does the job better.[4]

Topic sentence   *Type*

_____   _____

IV.   In short, by all means read the consultant's literature, but don't be put off by its extravagant claims. We all have hopes for great achievement, management theorists as much as anyone else. And don't be swayed either by its evangelical qualities. After all, the author has to believe in his own method. Still, there is much to be learned from good consultants and much to be used, as long as *you* remain in control.[5]

Topic sentence   *Type*

_____   _____

V.   If you are looking for a place to get away from it all, consider the Lower Rio Grande Valley of Texas. This area and the cities just across the border offer a unique blend of Mexican and American cultures, with lots of agricultural interest thrown in.[6]

Topic sentence   *Type*

_____   _____

VI.   Have you ever spent a cozy December evening stringing popcorn and cranberries into a garland for your Christmas tree? Or gathered a few fragrant evergreen branches to spread on a mantel or holiday table? If you enjoy brightening your home with natural materials, consider using the beautiful bounty of seashore and forest—seashells and starfish, pine cones and nuts. With a little time and imagination, you can transform these mementos of a woodland walk or a stroll along the beach into a variety of colorful holiday decorations. Here are some suggestions to get you started.[7]

Topic sentence   *Type*

_____   _____

Entire Selections

An entire selection consists of a series of paragraphs organized into a cohesive unit of meaning. The paragraphs are not merely strung together in any sequence, but they proceed according to a logical plan. The writer invites the reader to come along as ideas are introduced, presented, explained, and brought to a conclusion.

When you are reading an article, a chapter, or a book, begin by surveying the material. Look for the writer's purpose and try to follow the line of thinking as ideas are developed. Mentally outline the main points and the supporting details as you read. Think of the selection as a single unit of meaning composed of many smaller units. When you have finished reading, identify the main point the writer has made.

NC Exercise 3

Articles, stories, and chapters usually have titles which indicate the main idea of the selection. In this exercise, select the best title for the article. The title you select should be the main idea of the article. Put the letter of the best title in the blank provided at the end of the article.

SNAG! It sounds like the result of a meeting of your sweater and the sharp edge of a countertop. However, snag is also a name for trees that have died, yet remain standing. Do not be fooled by the barren, decaying appearance of snags. For though they appear lifeless in contrast to their previous, verdant days, they in fact abound with life.

Host to a wide variety of wildlife, a snag plays a vital role in its environment. Imagine, for example, a beech tree. During life it created nutrients as its green leaves absorbed the radiant energy of the sun. Through the process of photosynthesis, sugars were made which nourished its leaves and roots and oxygen was also formed and released to enrich the atmosphere. Birds such as the robin, the scarlet tanager, and the red-eyed vireo nested among its branches, hidden safely in the crown of green leaves. Squirrels traveled over the beech's limbs, and woodpeckers scaled its trunk. The persistent shrill of the cicada which clung to the bark came often on warm summer afternoons. Twelve years, however, of heartrot disease killed this tree which had once so pulsed with life. Because the landowner realized the value of a snag, he left the tree standing on his woodlot. Today the beech provides a home, food, or a lookout for many varieties of wild creatures.

Much of the wildlife which now abides on that tree is only there because of the decay. The snag possesses a unique attribute valuable to each of them. Insects favor the dangling bark and softened wood of the snag. Various beetles and ants scramble beneath the bark, laying their eggs which soon hatch into larvae. Their action, along with decay such as bacteria and fungi, helps to loosen the bark's attachment to the tree. It is this dangling bark which attracts the brown creeper, a trunk scaler which will nest only under the peeling bark of a snag.

Another bird which finds the snag attractive is a red-tailed hawk, who hungrily scans its surroundings from its perch atop a jutting, leafless branch. This beech stands on a field's edge, so the hawk will make it a regular outlook post, keeping the rodent population below in check. Just below, a hole created by the pileated woodpecker has become home for the tiny screech owl, a secondary nester which nests in cavities excavated by other birds. It will take the hawk's place when the twilight hours approach. Downy and hairy woodpeckers pound their way up and down the tree trunk, probing for their meal of insects.

Not only birds and insects, but mammals too, make use of the "lifeless" beech. Once decay has sufficiently hollowed the inside, the snag becomes a den for a family of raccoons. Squirrels build their winter nest in another hole, and deer mice will raise many young in their nest at the beech's base.

It is largely because of these wildlife neighbors abiding on a snag that many people choose to keep a dead tree or two on their property; five snags per acre is best for wildlife use.

A tree's death only changes, not eliminates, the type of wildlife that uses it; its death in no way diminishes its value in the natural system.[8]

a. Life in Dead Trees

b. Snags: Homes for Insects

c. Decay of Lifeless Trees

d. Death of a Beech

NC Exercise 4

Select the best title for the article. It should represent the main idea of the article. Put the letter of the best title in the blank provided at the end of the article.

You can make a variety of Christmas ornaments with pine or spruce cones; . . . many are simple to prepare.

Create pine cone owls from pitch pine cones. Select two good-sized cones, hold them with the tops facing you and press the sides together. Then take them apart and dab Elmer's glue on the scales of both cones where they fit together. Press the cones together again and hold them till the glue dries. Fashion eyes of black and white felt and a beak of yellow felt, and glue them in place on the front of the top cone to make a face. Now let your imagination go to work. You can cut felt wings and attach them to the body of the owl to create an angel owl or add a bow tie for a Dapper Dan, an apron for a cook or a mortarboard for a scholar. Attach a gold thread to the top of your masterpiece and hang from your tree, or make several and line them up in a row on a window sill.

To make a pine cone skater, you need an acorn or hazelnut for a head, a red pipe cleaner for arms, a gay red crocheted cap, and a circle of felt-covered cardboard for a base. Begin by painting eyes and a mouth on the flat side of the acorn or hazelnut. Then glue the head onto the flat top of the cone. Twist a piece of red wool around the neck, crochet a bright cap to fit and wind the pipe cleaner between the scales of the cone with two ends protruding for arms. Then glue the merry figure onto the felt and cardboard base. Like pine cone owls, these figures can either be hung from the tree or set along a window sill.

Pine cones make beautiful miniature Christmas trees. Choose a large opened cone, spray it with clear shellac and attach its base to a Styrofoam block. On top balance a bright orange seed pod called a Chinese lantern; at the end of each scale nestle and glue a tiny shell, a cluster of three or four bayberries, a pumpkin seed or any other small appealing memento of the woods or shore.

You can also make attractive tree ornaments and mobiles with decorated pine cones. Glue sprigs of red berries from the woods or tiny straw flowers between the scales of the cone. For tree dangles, tie colorful ribbons to the top of the cone; for mobiles, tie heavy thread to the pine cones, and tie the thread, in turn, onto bent reeds or peeled sticks.

Spruce cones—longer than pine cones—make charming cone dolls. You need five large cones: two for the arms, two for legs and one for the torso. Wire the five cones together to form a figure. Cut a hole in the center of a red felt circle for the skirt and slip it over the torso cone. Make a poncho of red by cutting a long diamond of felt and slitting it in the middle. Use a Styrofoam ball for the doll's head. Glue sequins on the ball for eyes, add a strip of red wool for a nose, and fashion hair from plastic scouring pads. Attach the head to the top of the torso with a bent hairpin and complete the doll with a babushka made from a triangle of red felt.[9]

_____

a. Pine Cone Owls and Skaters

b. Decorations from Pine and Spruce Cones

c. Pine and Spruce Cones

d. Pine Cone Dolls

NC Exercise 5

Select the best title for this selection. It should represent the main idea of the selection. Put the letter of the best title in the blank provided at the end of the passage.

"The worst weather on the face of the earth," said one eyewitness Congressman of the snowstorm that nearly buried the inauguration of William Howard Taft in 1909.

Heavy snows began the day before and continued through the night, driven by a stinging, whistling wind. Branches and telegraph and telephone lines snapped under the weight of the wet, clinging snow, while the wind toppled trees and poles. Pedestrians were quickly driven indoors and carriages and streetcars were immobilized as a thick white mantle submerged the deserted streets of the Nation's Capital.

Six thousand shovelers struggled vainly through the night and forenoon to clear the area in front of the White House and Capitol, and the route between. As noon approached, the storm still howled on unabated. People stood huddled in doorways or peered out at an arctic landscape through snow-streaked windows. Postponing his decision until the last moment, Taft finally decided to take his oath of office in the Senate Chamber, rather than on the outdoor platform erected in front of the Capitol. Ironically, the snow stopped just a few minutes later and despite the icy, piercing wind, people began lining Pennsylvania Avenue for the inaugural parade.

Some 20,000 marchers sloshed past the snow-covered stands flanking the parade route. The wind howled through their ranks, playing particular havoc with the high-hatted representatives of various political clubs, while decorations and bunting whipped about in wind-torn shreds or sagged sadly under heavy burdens of snow. All in all, it was the worst Inauguration Day weather in the nation's history. Quipped President Taft to a reporter friend: "I always knew it would be a cold day when I got to be President." . . .[10]

_____

a. Inauguration Day Parade

b. Foul Weather for Taft's Inauguration

c. A Big Snowstorm

d. Shoveling Snow

Chapter Notes

1. Reprinted from the January, 1974 issue, *Popular Electronics,* Copyrighted 1974, by Ziff-Davis Publishing Company.

2. Excerpted from C. G. Scruggs, "Can We Catch More Sunbeams?" reprinted by permission from *The Progressive Farmer,* November, 1973, p. 41.

3. Excerpted from "A Children's Crusade in the Virgin Islands," reprinted by permission from *American Education,* July, 1972, p. 24.

4. Reprinted from the February, 1972 issue, *Popular Electronics,* Copyrighted 1974, by Ziff-Davis Publishing Company.

5. Excerpted from Rosabeth Moss Kanter and Barry A. Stein, "Much Ado About Management," *The Rotarian,* (November 1986): p. 17.

6. Excerpted from Tom Curl, "The Magic Valley," reprinted by permission from *The Progressive Farmer,* November, 1973, p. 70.

7. Excerpted from Phyllis Meras, "Over the Beach and Through the Woods—To Holiday Decorations from Nature," reprinted by permission from *Odyssey,* November–December 1973, p. 40.

8. Connie Adams, "SNAG: Dead Doesn't Mean Lifeless," reprinted by permission from *The Conservationist,* January–February, 1984, p. 35.

9. Excerpted from Phyllis Meras, "Over the Beach and Through the Woods—To Holiday Decorations from Nature," reprinted by permission from *Odyssey,* November–December, 1973, p. 41.

10. Excerpted from Patrick Hughes, "The Weather on Inauguration Day," *EDIS,* January 1981, pp. 3–4.

6 General Comprehension Skills

Gina and Tom, eating a quick lunch at the grill between classes, began discussing the frustrations of test-taking. "It's not that I don't know the material," Tom said, "but I have a really tough time trying to figure out what the teacher wants."

"What gets me are those essay questions with 'compare' and 'contrast.' I usually just put down all I know about the topic and hope it's okay."

"I know what you mean. 'Causes' and 'effects' are always problems for me. Who knows? Who cares?"

"The trouble is," added Gina, "that it doesn't seem to be enough to just write what you know. You have to figure out what angle the teacher is looking for from the way the question is worded."

After eating a big bite of his burger, Tom thought aloud, "I wonder if that reading course can give us any clues. When I glanced through the book, I saw a chapter that had cause and effect, compare and contrast—and other things they ask us. Maybe if we learn to *read* for those ideas, we'll be able to figure out how to answer those questions better."

Finishing her soda, Gina admitted, "You've got a point there. We've got a big sociology test Friday and Dr. Kell said it would be mostly essay. I think I'll look at that section in the book and see if I can use any of it for the test."

Introduction

Many skills are involved in comprehension. Those that are treated in this chapter are finding the main idea, locating details, arranging items in sequence, following directions, recognizing cause-and-effect and comparison-contrast relationships, observing clues to meaning, and drawing inferences. These skills do not operate in isolation, but are interrelated and must be used together for complete comprehension by the reader.

Finding the Main Idea

Identifying the main idea of a written selection is one of the most important comprehension skills. Sometimes the main idea is easily recognized, and other times it can only be inferred. Reading will be pointless for you unless you can pull the main ideas from the text to get the writer's message.

In any written passage there are relatively few main ideas. Each idea may be supported with introductory remarks, related details, and illustrations. You must strip away these excess words and sentences and focus on the main idea. As you progress through an article, you collect these main ideas and organize them into a meaningful pattern. When you are finished reading, you should be able to reduce the article to a few sentences that express the main ideas set forth by the writer.

Recognizing main ideas is important for reading rapidly. When you are seeking only main ideas or major concepts, you can extract each idea readily. You can then quickly proceed to the next idea without reading a lot of descriptive material. It may be that your purpose in reading is to study a passage thoroughly in order to learn facts and details for a test. Even so, it is best to begin reading for main ideas in order to grasp the meaning of the entire selection. After you have identified the main ideas, then look for the details that support each idea. In this way you won't simply memorize masses of unrelated facts, but you will know the main ideas with supporting facts for each.

To find the main ideas, observe the following procedures:

1. Read the title; it often provides the main idea of the entire selection. Pay special attention to what the title tells you. For instance, if the title is *Drama,* you can expect to find a few paragraph main ideas about drama. If the title of the selection is *The Development of Drama,* you should anticipate several paragraph main ideas, arranged in sequential order. If the title is *Kinds of Drama,* look for paragraph main ideas that identify several specific types or kinds of drama. These will probably be listed with descriptions following them. Be well aware of the topic and nature of the article before you begin reading so you can anticipate the main ideas that may be presented in the component paragraphs.

2. Preview or survey the article. Look for introductory remarks, which may lead into the main ideas of the paragraphs. Observe the headings and subheadings; they usually contain the main ideas. Look for a summary at the end, where the main ideas usually appear again.

3. As you read the article, look carefully at the first sentence of each paragraph. This may be the topic sentence, which expresses the main idea of the paragraph. The main idea, however, may appear elsewhere or not at all within the paragraph.

4. Look for key words that seem to occur fairly often. Words written in italics and other key words often point to the main idea. Look for nouns because they will indicate what the main idea is about. Then look for verbs that may tell what is happening to the nouns. Try to reduce sentences and paragraphs to key words that convey the essential meaning.

You can find main ideas in sentences, in paragraphs, and in entire selections. In the following exercises, select the main idea by reading a long sentence, thinking about the main idea or essential meaning, and reducing the sentence to a simpler form.

GC Exercise 1

Read the first sentence and think of its basic meaning. Then read the shorter sentences that follow. Place the letter of the short sentence that expresses the main idea of the first sentence in the blank space beside the first sentence.

Example:

_____ Although Delaware is the second smallest state in the United States, it has a large proportion of wealth because of its natural assets and its strategic location.

   a. Delaware is small.
   b. Delaware has much wealth.
   c. Delaware has assets.
   d. Delaware has a strategic location.

The correct answer is ''b.'' because Delaware's large proportion of wealth is the central idea of the sentence. The other facts are mentioned, but only in relation to the main topic. Read the following sentences carefully and place the letter of the correct answer next to the number of the item.

_____ 1. The Peru Current, located along the west coast of South America, is a cool ocean current believed to be caused by the winds which blow away the warm surface waters.
   a. The Peru Current is a cool ocean current.
   b. A cool current is located near South America.
   c. Winds blow away warm surface waters.
   d. The west coast of South America has warm surface waters.

_____ 2. In the early 1500s Copernicus showed that the sun was the center of the solar system, contrary to the beliefs of most ancient astronomers.
   a. The ancient astronomers thought Copernicus was contrary.
   b. Copernicus discovered the sun in the early 1500s.
   c. The sun was found to be the center of the solar system.
   d. Most ancient astronomers believed the sun was the center of the solar system.

_____ 3. Although it lays eggs, the platypus is a true mammal that lives along the streams of Australia and Tasmania.
    a. The platypus lives along the streams of Australia and Tasmania.
    b. The platypus lays eggs.
    c. Australia and Tasmania have streams.
    d. The platypus is a true mammal.

_____ 4. The oldest form of vertebrates, animals with backbones, resembled fish, but lacked jaws.
    a. Animals with backbones have no jaws.
    b. Early vertebrates were similar to fish with large jaws.
    c. Vertebrates are animals with backbones.
    d. Early vertebrates resembled fish.

_____ 5. An annual jumping frog jubilee, which draws entrants from all over the world, is held in Angels Camp, California.
    a. People from all over the world go to California.
    b. Angels Camp, California, has more jumping frogs than any other place in the world.
    c. A jumping frog jubilee is held annually in California.
    d. Frogs jump all over the world.

_____ 6. Commonly found in Asian countries, pagodas are towerlike buildings connected with the Buddhist religion.
    a. Pagodas are towerlike buildings.
    b. The Buddhist religion is commonly found in Asian countries.
    c. The Buddhists hold religious services in pagodas.
    d. People in Asian countries believe in Buddha.

_____ 7. The sundew plant feeds on insects by trapping them with its sticky leaves and absorbing them.
    a. Insects eat the sticky leaves of the sundew plant.
    b. The sundew plant traps and absorbs insects.
    c. The sticky leaves of the sundew plant attract insects.
    d. Sticky leaves trap the sun's rays.

_____ 8. With the help of recent discoveries, archeologists have determined that humans originated in Africa.
    a. Archeologists are African.
    b. Africans determined the origin of humans.
    c. Archeologists have found that humans originated in Africa.
    d. Archeologists have made recent discoveries.

_____ 9. The luxury liner _Queen Elizabeth_ caught fire in 1972 in the Hong Kong harbor.
    a. The _Queen Elizabeth_ was one of the world's finest luxury liners.
    b. The _Queen Elizabeth_ caught fire.
    c. There was a fire in 1972 in the Hong Kong harbor.
    d. Many fine ships are moored in the Hong Kong harbor.

_____ 10. Gypsies in bright-colored clothing once wandered through the United States in caravans.
   a. Gypsies once wandered through the United States.
   b. Gypsies wore bright-colored clothing.
   c. The bright-colored clothing worn by gypsies was moved in caravans.
   d. Caravans could once be seen on roads in the United States.

_____ 11. By taking measurements, scientists found that boys and girls grow most rapidly during the first two years of their lives.
   a. Scientists took measurements of boys and girls.
   b. Boys grow more rapidly than girls during the first two years of their lives.
   c. Children grow most quickly during their first two years of life.
   d. Measurements show that growth in children occurs during the first two years of their lives.

_____ 12. The streamlined greyhound, fastest of all dogs, hunts by sight rather than scent, since he can outrun the game he is chasing.
   a. The streamlined body of the greyhound enables him to run fast.
   b. The greyhound is the fastest of all dogs.
   c. The vision of the greyhound is better than his sense of smell.
   d. The greyhound hunts by sight.

_____ 13. Judging from suits of armor worn during the Middle Ages, human beings have increased in size over the past centuries.
   a. Human beings have increased in size.
   b. People wore armor during the Middle Ages.
   c. People who lived during the Middle Ages increased in size.
   d. The period of the Middle Ages occurred centuries ago.

_____ 14. Grain elevators are tall buildings that have machines for loading, unloading, cleaning, mixing, and storing grain.
   a. Tall buildings store grain.
   b. Machines load and unload grain.
   c. Elevators lift grain to the tops of tall buildings.
   d. Grain elevators are buildings where machines process grain.

_____ 15. In order to use a single pair of glasses for seeing near and distant objects, Benjamin Franklin invented bifocals consisting of two lenses of different focusing powers.
   a. Benjamin Franklin wore eyeglasses.
   b. Benjamin Franklin invented bifocals.
   c. Bifocals consist of two lenses of different focusing powers.
   d. Bifocals permit the wearer to see both near and distant objects.

GC Exercise 2

In each of the following paragraphs there is a main idea. Read the paragraph and look for the main idea. Then read the sentences that follow, and place the letter of the one which best expresses the main idea of the paragraph in the blank beside the paragraph number.

_____ I. Earthfill embankments shall be constructed to the neat lines and grades shown on the plans and established at the field location. Embankment materials shall be free of brush, roots, sod, large rocks, or other material not suitable for making compacted fills. The moisture content and methods of placing and compacting the material shall be of such that a firm, stable embankment results. Below the design water surface elevation, fill material shall be placed in horizontal lifts of such thickness that proper compaction and any prescribed densities are obtained.[1]

    a. Certain specifications must be followed in constructing earthfill embankments.
    b. Brush, roots, sod, and large rocks must be removed from embankment materials.
    c. Earthfill embankments must have proper compaction and prescribed densities.
    d. Firm, stable embankments result from low moisture content.

_____ II. And just as the athletes have improved, so too has their equipment. The ancient Greeks competed naked. Now skiers flash downhill in neoprene suits to reduce the aerodynamic drag. The early Romans took their cuts at feather-filled balls. Now computers determine that 432 is precisely the right number of dimples on a golf ball.[2]

    a. Skiers use neoprene suits to reduce aerodynamic drag.
    b. Early Romans and Greeks had unsophistocated approaches to athletic equipment.
    c. Both athletes and their equipment have improved.
    d. Computers decide how many dimples should be on golf balls.

_____ III. All of us have at one time or another gone to, or given, parties that seem to sparkle spontaneously from the time we entered or welcomed our very first guests. Why can't all parties be like these? Trying to uncover the secrets of the success of these parties is like trying to unthread the main theme of a happy melody from all of its little side notes and flourishes. We know it's there. We can even hum it from memory, but it's so hard to separate it, to make it stand out.[3]

    a. Parties with musical themes are best.
    b. It is difficult to determine what makes a party successful.
    c. Some parties are better than others.
    d. The best parties sparkle spontaneously from the first.

IV. Relatively few laws govern the operations of tobacco marketing. Some operations are controlled by custom, tradition, or precedent, of which some have been established by the courts and some have not. Other operations such as market opening dates, closing dates, and sales opportunities are controlled by an industrywide marketing committee composed of warehousemen, buyers, and growers. In some cases this committee is forced to make decisions in areas about which they have very limited information.[4]
   a. Tradition and custom determine how tobacco is marketed.
   b. A committee of warehousemen, buyers, and growers governs marketing operations.
   c. The courts establish traditions and customs.
   d. Tobacco marketing is loosely controlled.

V. From its advent two centuries ago on the frozen canals of Holland until the invention of the airplane, iceboating was man's fastest means of locomotion. Seventy-foot behemoths on the Hudson River raced crack passenger trains and won. Today's sophisticated racing boat will rocket over smooth, slick, early season ice at close to 100 miles per hour—four to five times the wind velocity. Many racing craft are one-man contraptions, but several current designs accommodate two people; some old-time craft carry as many as five. Thus the novice can savor the dynamic drama of iceboating as a passenger; runners thunder scant inches beneath you; the hull vibrates, becoming almost airborne; the sail snaps overhead with a loud report as the skipper changes direction. At its fastest point of sailing, one runner lifts off the ice and the whole boat heels in a thrilling maneuver.[5]
   a. Iceboating began in Holland two centuries ago.
   b. Iceboating is a fast, thrilling sport.
   c. Racing boats can carry from one to five people.
   d. Racing boats can travel at close to 100 miles per hour.

VI. The World's Fair in Knoxville, Tennessee, had something for everyone. Technically-oriented visitors were offered numerous exhibits on energy-development projects throughout the world. Those interested in different cultures were treated to artifacts, national treasures, and audiovisual presentations from many nations, as well as special troupes of musicians, dancers, and singers from abroad. People who preferred homegrown entertainment heard performances by local talent and well-known national celebrities. Finally, the lovers of carnival rides had an interesting supply in the Fun Fair area, including the tallest Ferris wheel in the world.
   a. The Knoxville World's Fair had the tallest Ferris wheel in the world.
   b. Many performers were at the Knoxville World's Fair.
   c. The Knoxville World's Fair had something for people with many different interests.
   d. There were energy-development exhibits at the Knoxville World's Fair.

VII. For football enthusiasts football fever is a year-round affliction. The summer is spent predicting the current strength of favorite teams, based on the previous year's recruiting and the returning players, and predicting potential wins for the upcoming season. The fall, of course, is spent in watching every move made on the gridiron by those favorites, celebrating when they win, making alibis when they lose, and replaying every game orally with anyone who will participate. The action leaks over into the winter, when bowl games dominate discussions. Spring brings spring practice and dawning hopes for next year.

    a. Football contests take place primarily in the fall.
    b. People who really follow football think about it all year.
    c. Summer is a time for predicting how teams will do in the upcoming season.
    d. Football is really played all year.

VIII. Prehistoric people began to use spoken language thousands of years ago. Primitive speech may have been simply an imitation of natural sounds, such as grunts and groans. Over a long period of time, humans refined their speech so that certain combinations of sounds represented specific thoughts or ideas. Language changed and grew as people discarded words they no longer needed, borrowed words from other languages, and invented words as labels for new ideas. Today there are about 3,000 languages throughout the world, not including dialects. Communication through language has made possible the development of religion, science, philosophy, and literature.

    a. Early people spoke in grunts and groans.
    b. Language remains much the same through the years.
    c. English is one of 3,000 languages used throughout the world.
    d. Language has developed over a period of thousands of years.

IX. The Maori people were the first to settle New Zealand. Of Polynesian origin, they migrated from Asia across the Pacific in a series of voyages that required great skill and courage. Their navigational feats are said to be rivaled only by those of the Vikings. They traveled in a southeasterly direction from one island chain to another in long native canoes. Early explorers arrived in New Zealand in the tenth century and some colonists came two centuries later, but the Great Migration took place in 1350, the year that marks the beginning of Maori history. These people brought with them their highly developed skills of wood carving, hand weaving, and the designing and constructing of elaborately carved houses and war canoes.

    a. The Maoris traveled with the Vikings to New Zealand.
    b. The Maoris migrated to New Zealand hundreds of years ago.
    c. The Maoris are skilled in wood carving, hand weaving, and building war canoes.
    d. The history of the Maori people began in the year 1350.

GC Exercise 3

Read the article that follows. Look for the main idea. From the following sentences, select the one that best expresses the main idea of the entire selection. Place the letter of the correct sentence in the blank beside the title of the article.

_____ Predation[6]

In the twilight of the fading day a silent form slides through the darkening sky as eyes search for the cause of the sound among the leaves. The owl half closes its wings and drops, feet closing on the leaves where a mouse had been a moment before. This time the mouse lived, using all the escape instincts built into it over the millions of years of evolution. The next time the owl might succeed. In the constant interplay between prey and predator a balance is reached. The predator must be successful only part of the time. Partial failure is the key to success. Enough mice, or other prey species, must survive to assure the continuation of that population. If the predator is too successful there would be the danger of destroying the food resource. On the other hand, in the case of owls and mice at least, the owl must be successful in hunting much of the time. If the mice were to live without some control of their numbers there would soon be so many that they would destroy their own food source, the plants. Starvation and disease would soon decimate them and the owls would either starve or have to leave.

In some instances the nutritional level of the predators is lowered enough so the number of young produced is reduced. This automatically takes some of the pressure off of the prey species allowing it to recover. So even in predation there is an interdependence.

Predation is not limited to wolves and tigers, but refers to any animal that kills another as a source for food. This is true whether they are one-celled protozoan hunters or complex creatures like whales and humans.

Among the local predators, the hawks and owls, with keen vision, unique flight patterns and sharp talons, attract considerable attention. Over the history of the human species these birds have been an integral part of our culture and folklore.

---

a. The owl is an important part of American culture and folklore.
b. There is a balance in the interaction between prey and predator.
c. Some mice survive their predators.
d. Without mice as a source of food, owls would soon starve.

Locating Details

Sometimes it is necessary to grasp details as well as main ideas. In science and mathematics the identification of fine points may be as important for comprehension as the recognition of the main ideas. When you read contracts or legal documents, it is important to examine the fine print before signing these papers. A small fact buried in a written agreement may cause a problem for the person entering the contract.

Reading for facts requires you to concentrate and give full attention to the task. With practice, you can improve your ability to concentrate. You must realize that all factual information is not equally important. As with main ideas, you may disregard some words and sentences that are used as introductory or illustrative material.

It is nearly impossible to remember everything you read, so you must be selective. Consider your purpose for reading, and determine what kind of information you are seeking. Do you need to know the procedure for making something? Are you planning to give an oral report? Are you locating facts for a research paper? Are you looking for answers to specific questions? Are you studying for a test? Will the test questions be objective, requiring knowledge of small details? Will there be essay questions, requiring knowledge of main ideas with supporting details?

When you know what facts you need, find ways of relating them to each other. It is difficult to learn many facts in isolation, but not nearly so hard to remember them when you perceive a relationship among them. Perhaps several facts are clustered around one central idea, and you can remember them in connection with the idea. It may be that another type of relationship exists, such as time sequence, cause and effect, contrast, or comparison.

One way to train your mind to pick up the important facts is to spot the main topic and answer the questions "who," "what," "where," "when," and "how" or "why" about this topic. A good newspaper story includes this information in the first sentence or two.

GC Exercise 4

Each of the following paragraphs is written as a newspaper story. Read each paragraph. Then answer the questions "who," "what," "where," "when," and "why" or "how" without rereading the story. When you have finished answering these questions, reread the paragraph to see if you have answered them correctly.

Example: As he was walking his dog early Tuesday morning, Sam Witherspoon discovered a leaking fire hydrant at the corner of Spring and Main Streets.

Who: _Sam Witherspoon_

What: _discovered a leaking fire hydrant_

Where: _at the corner of Spring and Main Streets_

When: _early Tuesday morning_

Why or How: _as he was walking his dog_

1. Statewide nominees will compete next month for engineering scholarships, which will be awarded on the basis of test scores. The competition will take place in Springfield.

   Who:

   What:

   Where:

   When:

   Why or How:

2. While fishing off the Florida Keys during his vacation, Herman Hayes caught a 257-pound swordfish by harpooning it from the bow of his sailboat.

   Who:

   What:

   Where:

   When:

   Why or How:

3. Over 100 school superintendents and principals attended a one-day seminar held on the campus of State University February 4. The educators met to discuss the implications of proposed school legislation.

   Who:

   What:

   Where:

   When:

   Why or How:

4. Mr. George MacKenzie will serve as librarian at the Senior Citizens Center for the forthcoming year. MacKenzie was selected because he had served for twenty years as a public school librarian.

   Who:

   What:

   Where:

   When:

   Why or How:

5. State Representative Lillian R. Hughes announced Wednesday that she will sponsor a bill during the next session of the legislature. It is designed to provide loans to small businesses throughout the state which are suffering from financial hardships.

   Who:

   What:

   Where:

   When:

   Why or How:

6. Before a crowd of 5,000 fans, State's Golden Rams romped over Tech's Flying Falcons 97–84 in Rye Memorial Gymnasium last night as a result of superb teamwork.

   Who:

   What:

   Where:

   When:

   Why or How:

7. Twelve choral groups from local high schools will participate in a singing festival to be held Friday night at 7:30 in the Community Center. Tickets are $2.00 and the proceeds will go toward a new regional park and recreation center.

Who:

What:

Where:

When:

Why or How:

8. Girl Scouts will canvass the city for the next two weeks to sell cookies during their annual cookie sale. Profits from the sale will be used by the Scouts for camping equipment.

Who:

What:

Where:

When:

Why or How:

9. Public school teachers throughout the state have been awarded a substantial salary increase for next year. This increase is based on the latest consumer cost of living index.

Who:

What:

Where:

When:

Why or How:

10. The internationally famous Austrian Choir Boys will present their traditional program of sacred music in the Hall for the Performing Arts on May 3 in a benefit performance for the YMCA.

Who:

What:

Where:

When:

Why or How:

GC Exercise 5

Many details can be found in the following article. As you read it, identify the facts concerning food that are presented. Then, answer the questions that follow the article without looking back at it. Place the letter of the correct answer in the blank beside the number of the question.

Food[7]

To Carry on Trips

The food taken on a snow survey trip should be dehydrated and high in protein and carbohydrates. If trips are 2 or more days long, canned or fresh food should not be carried. A minimum amount of equipment for reconstituting dried or processed food is usually a pot with a handle in which to melt snow. Examples of dehydrated food are beef, fruit, milk, coffee, chocolate, bouillon, and fruit juice. Chocolate bars are excellent emergency rations. All these foods are in grocery stores. Special survival food lists at sporting-goods stores contain all or part of these items.

In Shelter Cabins

For foot trips on which an overnight stay is planned, cabins are usually available. They are stocked with food before the snow season begins. Unless frostproof storage is available, emphasis should be on dehydrated rather than canned food. Freezing does not make canned food unfit for use as long as it stays frozen, but flavor does deteriorate. Thawed canned food should not be used, which makes it necessary to replace food in cabins each season.

The cache of food in these isolated cabins must be protected not only from rodents but also from freezing and theft. One method of food protection is to build a concrete pit, which has the bottom and sides lined with Celotex, beneath the floor of the cabin. This insulating board is nailed to pieces of plank, 1 inch by 4 inches, arranged to leave an airspace between the board and walls and floor. A heavy trap door in the floor with covered hinges and a padlock covers the pit. After the provisions in bags are lowered into the pit, a loose metal cover is placed in a recessed section at the top of the concrete walls and on top of this a layer of Celotex and bags of dry pine needles to fill the space right against the under side of the trap door. In stocking the cabin with food supplies something substantial should be left in the cabin within easy reach in the event of an emergency.

Another way to preserve food is in a locked box made of reinforced concrete placed in one corner of the cabin. This box should have inside length, width, and height dimensions of 40, 26, and 18 inches respectively.

_____ 1. What kind of food should be taken on a snow survey trip?
    a. dehydrated
    b. high in protein and carbohydrates
    c. both of the above

_____ 2. What kind of food should not be carried if trips are two or more days long?
    a. canned or fresh food
    b. dehydrated food
    c. chocolate bars

_____ 3. What equipment is needed to reconstitute dried or processed food?
    a. a blender
    b. a pot with a handle
    c. an egg beater

_____ 4. When an overnight stay is required on foot trips, what kind of accommodations are usually available?
    a. hotels
    b. cabins
    c. tents

_____ 5. When are the accommodations stocked with food?
    a. before the snow season begins
    b. just before each trip
    c. once a month

_____ 6. Why is canned food not recommended unless there is frostproof storage?
    a. It becomes unfit for use when it is frozen.
    b. Its flavor deteriorates when it is frozen.
    c. It takes up too much room.

_____ 7. What must the cache of food in these isolated cabins be protected from?
    a. rodents
    b. theft
    c. both of the above

_____ 8. What is one method of food protection?
    a. Build a concrete pit.
    b. Use a plastic bag.
    c. neither of the above

_____ 9. What is another way to protect food?
    a. Put it in a cardboard box.
    b. Put it in a locked box made of reinforced concrete.
    c. Put it on an open shelf.

Arranging Ideas in Sequence

One way of relating ideas is to recall them in sequence. Usually authors follow specific plans as they write and have reasons for presenting their material in a particular order. Their plans may involve logical sequences of ideas that build to reasonable conclusions. The plans may, however, involve recounting stories or recounting several events in situations where one event follows another in time sequence.

Learn to look for sequences as you read. In doing this, you will be identifying main ideas, finding supporting details, and discovering the author's plan. You may find that it is easier to remember information when you think of it in a logical order.

Sequences may be divided into three types. The first is chronological order, in which events are arranged in the order in which they occurred. Chronological sequence is important in studying history when the order of events must be remembered. The second type is process sequence, in which one procedure follows another, as in preparing a recipe or installing a program on a computer. Quite often the sequence in this case is crucial and must be followed precisely. The third category is logical sequence, in which one idea leads to another in the logical development of a concept or proposal. The author leads the reader, step by step, to accept the basic idea he or she is presenting.

GC Exercise 6

This exercise involves chronological sequence. Read the article in this exercise. After you have read the article, read the statement of the first event. Then read the list of three events that follows. Decide whether each of the events in the list occurred before or after the first event. If it occurred before, put "B" in the space. If it occurred after, put "A" in the space.

Entrance into World War II

A series of aggressive acts led to the involvement of the United States in World War II. In 1939 German troops invaded Poland, and only two days later Britain and France declared war on Germany. In its attempt to dominate the world, Germany next attacked Denmark and Norway. Allying itself with Germany, Italy declared war on Britain and France. In the summer of 1940, less than a year after entering the war, France surrendered to Germany. Pushing onward, Germany invaded Greece and Yugoslavia. The Axis powers then swept into Russia. On December 7, 1941, a memorable day for Americans, Japan attacked Pearl Harbor. The following day the United States declared war on Japan. Three days later Germany and Italy declared war on the United States, and the United States in turn declared war on Germany and Italy.

1. France surrendered to Germany.

    _____ Japan attacked Pearl Harbor.

    _____ Germany attacked Denmark and Norway.

    _____ Germany invaded Greece and Yugoslavia.

2. Japan attacked Pearl Harbor.

    _____ The United States declared war on Japan.

    _____ The United States declared war on Germany and Italy.

    _____ France declared war on Germany.

3. The Axis powers invaded Russia.

    _____ German troops invaded Poland.

    _____ Japan attacked Pearl Harbor.

    _____ Germany invaded Greece and Yugoslavia.

4. Italy declared war on Britain and France.

    _____ The United States declared war on Germany and Italy.

    _____ Britain and France declared war on Germany.

    _____ Germany and Italy declared war on the United States.

5. Germany attacked Denmark and Norway.

    _____ Germany invaded Greece and Yugoslavia.

    _____ Germany invaded Poland.

    _____ The Axis powers invaded Russia.

GC Exercise 7

Read the following passage and notice the order in which events occurred. Then read the statement of the first event and the list of three events which follows. If the event occurred before the first event, put "B" in the space. If it occurred after the first event, put "A" in the space.

The Westward Movement

A series of events, occurring during the late 1700s and the 1800s, enabled the settlers of North America to move westward across the continent. When Daniel Boone opened the Wilderness Road through the Cumberland Gap, pioneers began to build cabins and settle in Kentucky. Later, Clark's campaign won the Northwest Territory for the United States. The Northwest Ordinance, which was enacted three years later, provided for government and encouraged education in this area.

Other parts of the country also attracted settlers as more land became available. In the South, the Louisiana Purchase of 1803 opened a vast region beyond the Mississippi to settlers. Exploratory expeditions were sent westward to learn about this new land. Texas was opened to American settlers in the 1820s and was annexed by the United States in 1845. In the meantime, covered wagons had been arriving in the Oregon country, and Great Britain relinquished this land to the United States in 1846. As a result of the war with Mexico, which lasted from 1846 to 1848, California and the Southwest were also added to the United States. Settlers continued moving westward with the discovery of gold in California in 1848 and with the promise of free land provided by the Homestead Act in 1862.

---

1. Discovery of gold in California

   _____ Provision for free land by the Homestead Act

   _____ Northwest Ordinance

   _____ Annexation of Texas

2. War with Mexico

   _____ Opening of the region beyond the Mississippi

   _____ Acquisition of the Oregon country

   _____ Addition of California and the Southwest

3. Settlements in Kentucky

   _____ Opening of the Wilderness Road

   _____ Northwest Ordinance

   _____ Winning of the Northwest Territory

4. Acquisition of the Oregon country

_____ War with Mexico

_____ Annexation of Texas

_____ Discovery of gold in California

5. Winning of the Northwest Territory

_____ Addition of California and the Southwest

_____ Opening of the region beyond the Mississippi

_____ Settlements in Kentucky

GC Exercise 8

This exercise contains an example of process sequence. Read the article below and the statements that follow. Then arrange the statements in the correct order by placing a number in front of each statement to indicate its place in the sequence.

How to Change a Tire

When you have a flat tire while driving, you should drive the car as far off the road as possible before changing it. Engage your emergency brake and set the automatic transmission in park. If possible, place a block behind one of the wheels to prevent the car from rolling. Jack up the car, using the jack handle to remove the wheel cover or hubcap. Then use the wrench end of the jack handle to remove all the lug nuts. Be sure to place these in the wheel cover so that you can find them easily. The wheel can now be pulled off the axle. Pick up the spare tire and place the wheel onto the lug bolts. Replace and tighten the lug nuts. Put the wheel cover on and let the car down off the jack. Don't forget to remove the block of wood from behind the wheel before driving off.

_____ Remove the lug nuts.

_____ Place a block behind one of the wheels.

_____ Pull the wheel off the axle.

_____ Engage your emergency brake and set the automatic transmission in park.

_____ Put on the lug nuts and tighten them.

_____ Jack up the car.

_____ Remove the wheel cover with the jack handle.

_____ Place the lug nuts in the wheel cover.

_____ Remove the block of wood.

_____ Place the wheel onto the lug bolts.

133

GC Exercise 9

This exercise contains an example of process sequence. Read the article below and the statements that follow. Then arrange the statements in the correct order by placing a number in front of each statement to indicate its place in the sequence.

Plant A Bottle Garden[8]

Robert C. Baur

How can a garden get into a bottle? That's a question you can answer after planting one! Developed by Nathaniel Ward in 1829, bottle gardening is not as difficult as it seems.

While any clear glass bottle may be planted, ones with larger openings are suggested for beginners. Planting is done by poking, piecing and spreading with a wooden dowel. Other handy bottle gardening aids are a hook (a length of bent coat hanger wire) and a funnel (a tapered roll of stiff paper) through which soil and gravel can be poured. These tools should measure one handgrip longer than depth of planter—the larger the bottle, the longer the tools. Bottle should have a cork or other nonrusting closure.

Use dried decorator moss, aquarium gravel and crushed charcoal. For a growing medium, combine sifted garden soil, milled sphagnum moss and clean sand.

Most moisture loving foliage plants make good bottle garden subjects. Boxwood, small ferns and palms, and Strawberry Begonia (Saxifraga sarmentosa) are dependable plants and slip easily through narrow bottle necks. Brittle-stemmed, large-leaved plants should be avoided. Three small plants will fill a quart size bottle; tallest should not exceed five inches.

Start with a clean dry bottle. Moisten moss and squeeze nearly dry; cut into strips small enough to push inside. Piece strips together to form a lining about one-fourth the height of bottle. Press green side against glass; overlap edges carefully.

Pour in some gravel and charcoal for drainage and purifying. Tap dry soil through paper tube.

Make a hole for each plant's roots. Insert largest plant root-first in opening; push it inside with dowel pressed against lower stem. Tilt bottle to hold plant upright until you can anchor roots by spreading and packing soil over them. Add smaller plants and fill in gaps with bits of moss. Include a gravel patch for accent.

Tie a bit of cloth to wire to remove moss flecks and dirt streaks. Water lightly (about ½ teaspoon per plant). Replace cork.

Place container in a cool, bright location away from direct sunlight. Oxygen and moisture will recycle, so further watering is unnecessary. Moisture should continue to bead on glass. Water only if moss looks crisp and dry.

Uncorking will usually clear cloudy glass or dry out soggy interiors; to hasten the process, wipe off the glass. Use wire hooks occasionally to remove unwanted plants or to prune surplus growth and dead leaves.

Keep gift bottles long enough to know if they are functioning properly, then provide culture instructions to assure their proper care.

After planting one bottle, succeeding ones will be easier, and narrower openings will seem less challenging.

_____ Place the largest plant inside the bottle first by pushing it with a dowel.

_____ Piece strips of moss together to make a lining.

_____ Water lightly.

_____ Put some gravel and charcoal in the bottle for drainage and purifying.

_____ The container should be placed in a cool, bright location.

_____ Be sure the bottle is clean and dry before you begin.

_____ Remove dirt from the inside of the bottle with a bit of cloth tied to a piece of wire.

_____ The moss should be moistened and squeezed until it is nearly dry.

_____ Make a hole for the roots of each plant.

_____ Small plants should be added next.

_____ The cork should be replaced.

Recognizing Cause and Effect

Many paragraphs or reading selections contain cause-and-effect relationships. In this kind of relationship, something (the cause) appears to lead to or bring about something else (the effect). A cause is a reason for something; it explains why a condition exists. In order to complete the relationship, there is an effect or a consequence, which results from the cause. The effect tells what happens as a result of some stimulus or action.

Some cause-and-effect relationships seem simple and obvious, while others are misleading or difficult to recognize. The reader should not assume that there is always a cause-and-effect relationship just because there appears to be one. For instance, the cause-and-effect relationship seems fairly obvious in the following statement: "When it started to rain (cause), I got wet (effect)." In the next case, however, it is more difficult to determine if the relationship is actually a cause-and-effect situation: "The test was difficult (cause?) so I failed it (effect)." The difficulty of the test may have been part of the cause of failure, but failure could also have been due to insufficient studying, lack of concentration, or some other reason or combination of reasons.

The following words and phrases sometimes relate the cause to the effect: *so, because, therefore, as a result, if . . . then, in order that, where, when, due to, since,* and *so that.* While these words or phrases are not present in every case, they often signal a cause-and-effect relationship.

GC Exercise 10

Look at the following cause-and-effect sentences. In each one, underline the clause that is the cause once, and underline the clause that is the effect twice. Circle the word or words that serve as signals.

Example: I couldn't buy the book (because) I didn't have any money.

1. When the lightning struck the tree, it caught fire.
2. The toes of most woodpeckers are arranged so that they can cling to or climb up and down the sides of trees and branches.

3. My car wouldn't start this morning; therefore, I was late getting to class.

4. Yellow jackets live together and cooperate with each other, so they are called social wasps.

5. The chief cause of wind is the unequal pressure and temperature in different parts of the earth's atmosphere.

6. If uniform hard grains of quartz are used, then grindstones can grind quickly and withstand wear.

7. Where there is smoke, there is fire.

8. People who live in the wet lowlands of The Netherlands wear wooden shoes so that their feet will be drier and warmer.

9. As a result of spontaneous combustion of gases, a strange light called will-o'-the-wisp sometimes appears over marshy places.

10. Florida is a leading producer of watermelons, since the climate is mild and the soil is moist.

GC Exercise 11

The following article gives many causes and effects of drug addiction. One example of a cause and one example of an effect are shown on page 137. See how many more causes and effects of drug addiction you can find.

Drug Addiction

In recent decades, drug addiction has become a national problem, particularly among youth. Many young people are willing to risk serious health problems, breakdowns in relationships with loved ones, and possible death from overdose for the temporary "highs" induced by drugs.

With the breakup of many traditional family units, children lack the support, security, and guidance that a stable home environment can provide. Instead, many adolescents accept the standards of their peers, who pressure them to experiment with drugs in order to become part of a gang or particular social group. Others, not necessarily teenagers, become physically dependent on drugs as a result of taking them for medicinal purposes.

Young people frequently take drugs in order to get "kicks" or thrills, or to experience feelings of pleasure and elation. They believe that drugs will relieve their fears and anxieties and allow them to escape from reality.

Often the consequences are more than the drug users bargain for, however. Drugs reduce people's abilities to make judgments and to react quickly and accurately. Thus, people under the influence of drugs may be involved in automobile accidents. Sometimes drugs cause hallucinations, in which users have feelings of being persecuted by enemies. The users may then become dangerous to themselves and to others. Persons addicted to drugs often are unkempt in appearance and their grades frequently drop. Eventually, drug users may turn to crime in order to pay for the drugs they need to satisfy their cravings.

Causes	Effects
1. Desire for temporary ''highs''	1. Serious health problems
2.	2.
3.	3.
4.	4.
5.	5.
6.	6.
7.	7.
8.	8.
9.	9.
10.	10.
	11.
	12.
	13.
	14.
	15.
	16.
	17.

Recognizing Comparison and Contrast

You will find comparison-and-contrast relationships in some reading selections. Two or more things or ideas are shown as similar (comparison) in some ways and different (contrast) in others. Often the comparisons or likenesses are discussed together, and the contrasts or dissimilarities are then grouped together. Sometimes, however, they are mixed together and you have to look carefully to see how things are alike and how they are different.

Signal words can also be helpful in making you aware of comparisons and contrasts. For example, when two or more things are being compared, you may see words such as *like, as, with, also,* and *same.* When two or more things are being contrasted, the following words may appear: *but, however, although, yet, even though, instead, on the other hand, rather than,* and *while.*

When you are studying a passage that contains comparison-and-contrast relationships, you should organize the passage into its similarities and differences to help yourself think clearly about it. In the two examples below, the charts will help you classify the characteristics being compared and those being contrasted. You might want to make the same kind of chart for other class reading assignments where you find this kind of relationship. As you develop the habit of organizing your thoughts in this way, you will gradually learn to do it automatically as you read.

GC Exercise 12

Read the following selection. In the chart below, write comparisons, which show how the two things are alike, and contrasts, which show how the two things differ. An example is given.

I. Two frightening, legendary creatures are vampires and werewolves. A vampire is a corpse that rises from the grave during the night to suck blood from the neck of a sleeping person. The victim eventually dies and turns into a vampire. In order to stop the vampire from leaving the grave, someone must drive a stake through its heart. Werewolves, on the other hand, are men who are transformed into wolves at night. They eat human flesh and can be killed only by silver bullets.

Vampires and Werewolves

Comparisons	*Contrasts*
1. Active during the night	1. A vampire is destroyed by a stake driven through the heart, but a werewolf is destroyed by a silver bullet.
2.	2.
3.	3.

In the next selection, whales are being compared and contrasted with both fish and other mammals. Therefore, you will need to complete two charts.

II.   Although whales live in oceans and resemble fish in many ways, they are actually mammals. Both fish and whales have tail fins, but those of the whale are horizontal while those of the fish are vertical. Whales are warm-blooded in contrast to fish, which are cold-blooded. A whale's body is shaped like that of a fish, but it has two flippers that correspond to the two front limbs that most mammals possess. The typical hind limbs of the mammal are only two small bones embedded in the whale's hip muscles. Whales breathe with their lungs, as mammals do, instead of breathing through gills like fish. As with other mammals, whales give birth to live babies, and the young nurse from their mother's milk. On the other hand, most mammals are covered with hair, but whales have only a little hair on their heads. Unlike other mammals, whales have no sense of smell.

Whales

Comparisons with Fish

1.

2.

3.

Contrasts with Fish

1.

2.

3.

Comparisons with Other Mammals

1.

2.

3.

Contrasts with Other Mammals

1.

2.

3.

Following Directions

When reading directions, it is necessary to pay attention to both details and sequence. Every word and each step may be significant. This type of reading is slow and deliberate, requiring thoughtful attention. It is often necessary to reread directions in order to make sure you understand them.

There are many occasions when you must follow written directions, both in school and out. You need to know how to follow directions for completing registration forms, taking examinations, and doing homework assignments. It is necessary to follow directions when you are filling out tax forms and applications for jobs. You must be able to interpret directions to understand a diagram, a pattern, or a map.

The following guidelines may help you understand and follow directions.

1. Survey the directions in a general way to see what is to be done.
2. Look for a diagram, map, or other illustrative material that can help you form a mental image of the problem.
3. Forget any preconceived ideas you may have about how the process might be carried out, and read the directions with an open mind.
4. As you read, visualize what is to be done, step by step. Rehearse in your imagination the process from beginning to end.
5. Pay attention to key words, such as "first," "next," and "finally."
6. Get the process clearly in mind before starting. It may be necessary to reread parts of the directions.

GC Exercise 13

Read each of the following sentences and do what is suggested.

Example: Put an X on the third "t" and underline the next to the last word in this sentence. If you followed the directions, you put an X on the "t" in "third" and underlined the word "this."

1. Draw a circle around the smallest even number in the following series: 4, 9, 6, 3, 1.
2. If there are less than 15 words in this sentence, cross out the first word in the sentence.
3. If $7 + 5$ is more than $18 - 2$, place a check mark over the first word in the sentence.
4. Draw a line under the word in this sentence with the most syllables.
5. Add 7 to 4 and subtract 3. Multiply this answer by 2 and divide by 4. Write the answer on this line. _____
6. Draw a circle around the second letter of the word preceding the next to the last word in this sentence.
7. Put a check over the shortest word in this sentence and draw two lines under the middle word in this sentence.

8. If you are not able to read, draw a line under the last word in the sentence.

9. Cross out the third letter in the second word in this sentence, the fourth letter of the first word, and the first letter in the ninth word.

10. Cross out all the vowels in the following word: twelfth.

11. Put an X on the eighth word from the end if there is water in the ocean.

12. Unless you are more than ten decades old, circle the last word in this sentence.

13. Circle the next to the largest number and underline the sum of 2 + 5 in the following series: 12, 192, 291, 7, 9, 1009.

14. If there are 12 eggs in a dozen, write the thirteenth letter of the alphabet in the blank space. _____

15. If 15 is more than 13, write the word "false" in the blank space. _____

16. In the following group of words, circle the one that begins with the letter closest to the beginning of the alphabet; underline the word that follows the longest word; and cross out the word containing 4 consonants.

magazine   goat   eight   famous

Observing Clues to Meaning

Both punctuation and clue words or phrases assist the reader in comprehending the meaning of written material. Punctuation serves as a system of signals for clarifying meanings and providing patterns for words. The commas, periods, and question marks correspond to the pauses and intonations in speech that make speech comprehensible. If readers fail to observe punctuation marks, they can easily become confused and misled by what they read.

Writers also use certain words or figures to direct the reader's thought. These clues, placed in strategic places, cause the reader to pause and consider, prepare for a change of thought, or extend the same thought. Some clues, such as numerical listings and alphabetical listings, stand out clearly. Other clues are blended into the text and only a skillful reader can detect them readily. Learning to recognize and observe these clues can make comprehension easier.

Clue words appear in many places, such as at the beginning of the chapter when they introduce the ideas that will be discussed or at the end of the chapter when they pull together what has been said into a conclusion or summary. They may be used any place throughout the text to signal a change in thought, emphasize a point, or indicate that an illustration will follow.

Although sometimes clue words may have different meanings, they may be placed into categories that indicate their usual purposes. Seven types of clue words or phrases follow, with examples of each.

1. Reversal of thought: but, although, however, on the other hand, contrary to, whereas, yet, on the contrary, otherwise, nevertheless, until, not only.

2. Forward movement: and, likewise, in addition to, as well as, also, again, besides, moreover, furthermore, another

3. Additional explanations: for example, for instance, in other words, namely, like, as, such as, as well as, so that, in many respects

4. Relative importance or sequence: first, second, third; in the first place; 1, 2, 3; a, b, c

5. Subordinate relationships: because, since, for, although, as, in order that, even though, so that, when

6. Summary or emphasis: consequently, therefore, accordingly, in fact, in particular, indeed, in brief, to summarize

7. Conclusions: finally, as a result, in conclusion, therefore, consequently

GC Exercise 14

The following paragraphs contain clues to meaning. Write the clues in the spaces provided at the end of each article. Identify the clue by placing beside it the number that corresponds to that type of clue. Refer to the list at the end of the last section to find the number for each type of clue.

I.   The greatest and least-tapped natural resource of the Earth is the ocean. Not only is it important as a rich source of minerals and food, but its effect on the climate can govern the habitability of much of the land surfaces, and oceanographic features determine the safety with which men can travel on or near the surface of three-fourths of the globe.

Better information of many kinds is needed—for example, data on sea states, shoals, tidal waves, potassium, plankton, sardines, temperature, and turbidity.

Meteorological and other satellites, as well as *Gemini* and *Apollo* photography, have suggested many ways in which oceanography can benefit from space science and technology.[9]

Clue	*Type*
_____	_____
_____	_____
_____	_____
_____	_____
_____	_____

II.	Taking lessons, Shealy adds, does not reduce skier mishaps. In fact, skiers who took lessons had more accidents than skiers who did not, even when their ability levels were about the same. At the same time, as the skier progressed in skill the accident rate went down. This points up the key role of the ski school in the area's accident rate. If the ski school isn't doing a job, it contributes to the rate because skiers who take lessons but do not advance in skills have more accidents.[10]

Clue	Type
_____	_____
_____	_____
_____	_____
_____	_____
_____	_____

III.	Man's head is divided into two hemispheres, left and right. Until recently the theory was that these two sides of the brain were more or less interchangeable, like twin outboards. But the latest is that the two hemispheres do work in different ways.

Thé left is a verbally oriented hemisphere; it works out problems in linear or mathematical fashion, so that A leads to B leads to conclusion C—like that. The right hemisphere, on the other hand, tends to be more mystical; it processes information simultaneously, the gestalt technique.[11]

Clue	Type
_____	_____
_____	_____
_____	_____
_____	_____
_____	_____

IV.   College basketball has certainly been changed by the addition of the three-point goal. Whereas many teams still force the ball inside for high percentage shots, others are depending on long distance gunners. When these shooters are on target, the area under the basket opens up for some layups as defenses move out to guard against three-point shots. As a result, the team often begins to score inside because of its outside game.

Clue   *Type*

_____   _____

_____   _____

_____   _____

_____   _____

_____   _____

_____   _____

_____   _____

V.   Consumers naturally want food products that taste good, but they also look for other features. Because many people choose to spend their time doing things other than cooking, they look for ease of preparation. Others, faced with limited financial resources, must search for economical products as well as flavorful ones. As a result, food products available in supermarkets offer diverse features to entice different types of buyers.

Clue   *Type*

_____   _____

_____   _____

_____   _____

_____   _____

_____   _____

Drawing Inferences

Until now, this chapter has dealt chiefly with literal comprehension skills. These skills include following directions and recalling main ideas and facts that have been clearly stated by the writer. Interpretive comprehension skills call for a higher level of thinking. It is not enough to literally recall what the writer has stated, but the reader must also discover what the writer is implying.

Drawing inferences requires readers to make reasonable deductions based on the facts or evidence presented. Readers infer when they "read between the lines" in order to get additional insight into the author's meaning. Readers must be in tune with the writer's thinking and mood in order to pick up subtle and implied meanings. False inferences are sometimes drawn when readers overlook a point and get the wrong impression, or when they substitute personal convictions for those of the writer.

As you read the following section, think about what the writer is implying in addition to what he is stating.

Most people associate the word "synthetic" with "fake" and conjure up ideas of inferior versions of the genuine article. Perhaps it is only natural, then, that many people do not consider music synthesizers and their electronically produced sounds a legitimate part of real music. Electronic music has, admittedly, undergone rather gimmicky stages of development, but that is all over now. Today's sophisticated music synthesizers leave their gimmicky predecessors behind and take an important place in the evolution of legitimate music.[12]

Now read the statements that follow. If the statement can be inferred, write I beside the statement. If it should not be inferred, write N beside the statement.

1. _____ Electronic music is better than real music.

2. _____ Gimmicks have disappeared from electronic music.

3. _____ More people listen to electronic music than to real music.

4. _____ The quality of electronic music is improving.

5. _____ Music synthesizers produce electronic music.

The answers and the reasons for them are listed below.

1. N The writer explains that electronic music is now legitimate but does not imply that it is *better than* real music.
2. I The writer admits that electronic music has been gimmicky in the past, but he says that gimmicky stages are all over now. He is therefore implying that gimmicks have disappeared.
3. N The writer says nothing about listening to music.
4. I The writer says that music synthesizers are leaving their gimmicky predecessors behind and taking an important place in the evolution of legitimate music. He implies, therefore, that the quality of electronic music is improving.
5. I Although the writer does not clearly state this fact, he implies it when he says ". . . music synthesizers and their electronically produced sounds. . . ."

GC Exercise 15

Read each of the following selections. Then read the statements that follow. If the statement can be readily inferred from the selection, write I beside the statement. If it cannot be inferred or is simply a restatement of what the writer has already said, write N beside the statement.

I. Bullets and Transceivers[13]

According to the Department of Justice, two police officers—one in Miami and the other in Seattle—put transceiver radios in the same pocket in which they were also carrying loose pistol ammunition. In both cases, one round of ammunition exploded in the officer's pocket. The Law Enforcement Standards Laboratory found that, when loose ammunition makes contact with transceiver recharging studs, one of two things happens: If the cartridges are new and clean, providing firm electrical contact, they will simply discharge the radio battery. On the other hand, if the cartridges are dirty, making poor electrical contact, rapid generation of heat will occur. This detonates the bullet primer within a few seconds. The solution suggested was for police officers to carry and store cartridges separately from transceivers and batteries.

1. _____ The cartridges in the officers' pockets were dirty.

2. _____ It is dangerous to carry and store cartridges with transceivers and batteries.

3. _____ Police officers have lots of pockets in their uniforms.

4. _____ Police officers in Miami and Seattle use transceiver radios.

5. _____ The Law Enforcement Standards Laboratory produces large quantities of pistol ammunition.

II. Trip to the Top[14]

Matt Tobey, ski writer for the *New York Daily News,* was strolling along the sidewalk in Kitzbuhel one day not long ago, only to be accosted by Kitzbuhel hometown boy and triple Olympic medalist (1956) Toni Sailer, who knew Tobey on sight. Sailer insisted that Tobey come for a run down the Hahnenkamm, the biggest and meanest of Kitz's hills. Tobey protested he was in no way fit to ski with Sailer. But Sailer again insisted, and so Tobey found himself ascending with Sailer up the first stage, the second stage, the third stage and then off.

". . . I have never been up the third stage! What am I trying to prove?" Sailer left in a cloud of snow. Matt quickly skied back to the top of the third stage, rode all three stages to the bottom, buckled his skis back on and came skiing out onto the flat where Sailer was waiting.

"How was it?" said Toni.

"Fantastisch!" said Tobey.

1. _____ Ski writers are good skiers.

2. _____ Tobey gave the impression he had skied to the bottom of the hill.

3. _____ Toni Sailer was an expert skier.

4. _____ Tobey had never been on skis before.

5. _____ Tobey rode to the top of the ski lift because he thought he would be able to ski to the bottom.

III. Forestry[15]

The Forest Service of the U.S. Department of Agriculture keeps a continuing inventory of this country's vital timber resources, but some data are as much as 9 years old when reported because of the difficulties and cost of collecting information about woodlands. In many other countries, much less is known than in the United States about the current condition of forests.

Both foresters and naturalists need surveys of remote areas that are difficult to reach on the ground but can be monitored rapidly and repetitively from orbiting satellites. Such spacecraft can serve many countries virtually simultaneously.

Photographs from infrared sensors, whose colors represent variations in the reflectance of light rather than the colors the eye sees, can be used to detect insect damage and forest fires. Studies conducted by NASA have shown that such photographs can be obtained from orbital altitudes with equipment well within the reach of existing technology.

1. _____ Orbiting spacecraft can help to update the Forest Service's inventory.

2. _____ Infrared photography has special value for forest studies.

3. _____ Satellites can prevent forest fires and insect damage.

4. _____ Extensive technological developments must occur before photographs can be obtained that would be useful to the Forest Service.

5. _____ Other countries are generally better informed than the United States about forest conditions.

IV. A Children's Crusade in the Virgin Islands[16]

The Salt Pond Bay nature trail in the Virgin Islands National Park leads down to a small, curved, sandy beach in the southwest corner of St. John, smallest of the American Virgin Islands. It is a clean and sparkling place that looks out on the unbelievably blue Caribbean Sea. Less than ten miles westward but shut off from view by a promontory lies the sister island of St. Thomas, while 40 miles to the south the other sister, St. Croix, is usually lost in the distant haze. Probably this little beach at Salt Pond Bay has not changed much since Columbus, struck by the islands and their vast retinue of tiny islets, named them after St. Ursula and her 11,000 virgins.

Eastward across a narrow neck of land is another kind of beach—remote, rocky, and windward of the Atlantic, with the British-owned islands in the Virgin group dominating its ocean view. Here prevailing winds and currents have deposited among the rocks, as they have for thousands of years, the flotsam of the tropical sea: tree trunks and branches, coconuts, shells, fronds from banana plants, dead corals, and seeds from scores of trees, shrubs, and plants. But even in this remote place, more than 1,100 miles from the Florida tip of the American mainland, man's throw-aways are becoming mixed with those of nature. There are crates, bottles, and—more and more—an assortment of such objects as aluminum beer and soft-drink cans, and plastic containers that once held detergents, skin lotions, and cleansers casually dumped by passing ships and people on pleasure boats. Mixed in with this debris here and there are gobs of congealed tars—the offal of passing tankers.

1. _____ Columbus traveled to the Caribbean.

2. _____ People who take cruises are not very concerned about polluting the beaches.

3. _____ Before man came, nothing but clean sand was found on the beaches.

4. _____ St. Croix has a lot of pollution.

5. _____ The Virgin Islands are in an area of tropical vegetation.

V. Beware the Chilly Hypo[17]

Unlike the current popular usage, in which "hypo'd" means hopped-up or frantic, the Greek "hypo" is a prefix meaning "under." (Hypodermic equals "under the skin," get it?) So, when a doctor speaks of hypothermia, he doesn't mean super-hot—he is talking about freezing.

Ejnar Eriksson, an M.D. specialist in hypothermia with the Karolinska Institute in Stockholm, Sweden, gives this bit of advice for the skier caught out in a storm. "Get into a snow cave." The temperature outside may be at zero, says Eriksson, but that of the snow cave will never be lower than freezing, or 32 degrees Fahrenheit. Furthermore, a cave blocks out the wind, which cools off the body dangerously.

Eriksson has put people into temperature-controlled chambers held at 60 degrees and showed that sitting nearly naked at even this relatively mild temperature would cause loss of about half of a person's strength over a 24-hour period. In opting for a snow cave, therefore, your clothing has to be warm enough to prevent the slow drain of body heat. Another practical application: have an insulated parka with you on the lift, even if you don't use it. If the lift stops, you can be left hanging in cold circumstances.

Eriksson remarked that in the last stages before hypothermia becomes fatal the victim gets very sleepy, and sometimes suddenly feels deliriously hot. There have been many cases of people found in the snow, he says, with most of their clothes flung to the side.

"When found half-naked, believed to be dead," said Eriksson, "the police always suspect a sexual crime and nobody is allowed to come close to the body until a police doctor has arrived and they have taken photographs. I strongly suspect that in some cases the victims may still have been alive when found by police, but left there in the cold for hours, they may have died in the meantime.

"Resuscitation should continue for at least two hours after a body is found," said Eriksson. "It is extremely difficult to determine whether a patient suffering from accidental hypothermia is alive or dead."

1. _____ According to the reasoning in this article, hyposensitivity would mean less than normal sensitivity.

2. _____ A person's body temperature actually becomes higher during the final stages of hypothermia.

3. _____ People who get hypothermia often are people who have been mentally disturbed.

4. _____ Snow caves are often warmer than the air outside them.

5. _____ Exposure to low temperatures reduces a person's strength.

VI. Hearing Aids and HiFi[18]

There are over 20 million people in the U.S. that have some hearing problem. Most of these, about 15 million, could be helped with a hearing aid. Most such people have a hearing loss at the higher frequencies. Hence, those wonderful highs that a good hi-fi system produces are lost on such people. To them a modern stereo orchestral record may sound like the "tinny" phonographs of the 1920's. With a properly fitted hearing aid to restore the highs, the loss is compensated for to some extent. Here again is another case where electronics is helping the handicapped.

1. _____ Electronics can cure hearing problems.

2. _____ Everybody should wear a hearing aid to hear musical highs.

3. _____ Electronics can help the handicapped in more than one way.

4. _____ People who wear hearing aids can often appreciate hi-fi music more than when they did not wear them.

5. _____ Modern stereo records are better than phonographs of the 1920's.

Sometimes an author uses satire, a facetious style of writing, or an abundance of figurative language. This author doesn't expect the reader to take the article literally. Instead, the reader must find the intended meaning by looking beyond the surface meanings of the words.

The author of the following article gives investment advice, but he does so in a facetious or tongue-in-cheek style. He uses figurative language liberally. Read the article to see if you can infer the advice the author is giving in each rule. Then put a check beside the statement for each rule that best expresses the author's meaning.

Beware of the Dog—Or, Helpful Hints for the Amateur Speculator[19]

Richard Loller

When the stock market goes up, many otherwise sane and intelligent individuals get the itch to speculate. There is nothing intrinsically wrong with this. People speculate in the stock market constantly. The problem comes when people who have never before owned a stock try to get in on the action. More often than not, such a person will lose money.

Speculation is a high-risk undertaking. Its object is to beat the odds, to make a killing. Experienced speculators know just how hard that can be. The amateur, on the other hand, sometimes enters the market without a realistic picture of the dark side of the force. If you would like to try your hand at stock speculation with some chance of avoiding being whipsawed, sucked in, or taken to the cleaners, there are some elementary precautions you can take.

Rule #1: Never buy a stock your brother-in-law recommends. This is so obvious it almost seems as if it need not be stated. Yet, an amazing number of first-time speculators will trust their brother-in-law's savvy when it comes to stock selection, even though they'd never think of giving him the opportunity to help them pick a good movie or a nice restaurant.

Rule #2: Buy low, sell high. The stock market goes up and down in more or less regular cycles; so do individual stocks. But now is when you want to invest, not last year. You've got money that's burning a hole in your pocket *now*. What should you do? You should probably take a cold shower. But if you must plunge into the market, find a stock that hasn't already gone through the roof. When Brand X Inc. makes a series of spectacular new highs, the financial press lets everyone know about it. Buyers flock to get in on the ground floor. Bang! The bottom drops out, and there you are. Sorry. The ground floor was a long way back before the financial press ever heard of the stock. Don't chase stocks that are already high. Find a good one and buy it before it begins to skyrocket.

Rule #3: Don't get caught holding the bag. Let's fantasize a minute. Let's imagine that you've made a smart buy. You picked a stock with a lot of potential, and you bought it at a bargain price. Just as you hoped it would, it begins to climb. Now comes the hard part. When do you sell? This is the key question for a speculator. Unlike an *investor*, you aren't concerned with the long-term prospects of the stock. You want the maximum return for your money over the shortest period of time. But remember, what goes up must come down. Don't let greed trick you into holding on too long, trying to squeeze just a little more bang out of your buck. It could blow up in your face. When the balloon hits the fan, someone is going to be left holding a fast deflating bag. Don't let it be you. Sell when buyers are begging to buy, and pocket your profit. If you still haven't satisfied your speculative urge, then find another stock and start over.

Rule #4: Cut your losses. If you pick a loser, or the market goes rotten, it makes sense to salvage whatever you can. Maybe it's more noble to go down with the ship, but you'll make more money by admitting you goofed and jumping for the lifeboat.

Rule #5: Don't buy schlock stock. Stock is evidence of ownership of a share of a company. Companies sell stock with the object of bringing in large amounts of capital. In bull markets it is easier for companies to sell overpriced stock than it is in bear markets. Bull markets bring marginal companies out of the woodwork. Tiny enterprises run by Mom and Pop out of the back of their Winnebago may "go public" with an issue of 10,000,000 shares at 10 cents each. This is just the sort of stock your brother-in-law would love. Is the stock a bargain? Maybe so, maybe not. It is conceivable that Mom and Pop will work hard, make good decisions, and build their business into the next IBM. However, at this stage of the game you will almost certainly not be able to get enough information about the company to make any sort of judgment. Unless, of course, you live next door to Mom and Pop in the same trailer park. Little companies are like tadpoles hatching out in the spring. For every one that becomes a big frog, there are hundreds that fall victim to all the big fish out there waiting to gobble them up.

Rule #6: If you can't stand the heat, stay away from the hot stocks. You may have what it takes to become the shrewdest speculator since J. P. Morgan. You may be willing to spend countless hours digging up real bargains overlooked by the thundering herd. You may have the discipline to be satisfied with a realistic profit. But sooner or later, something is going to go really wrong. When it does, you may find that you weren't really cut out to be a speculator. If you toss and turn all night, lose your appetite, and have to fight down an overpowering temptation to kick the cat, then you might consider whether it's really worth the strain. If losing money is something you can't handle, then you might consider something other than stock speculation to occupy your time, something less nerve-racking—like defusing unexploded bombs.

Rule #7: Don't raid the cookie jar. It has been said that the worst thing that can happen to you on your first trade is for it to be successful. When your 100 shares at 2½ goes to 5⅜, bells ring and buzzers buzz. "Why didn't I buy 1,000 shares?" you groan. Visions of riches beyond your most avaricious dreams burn inside your feverish brain. Stop! Greed is a trap. This is the point where you start believing things like, "It's got nowhere to go but up," or "Sixty times earnings is dirt cheap for that stock." Decide *before* you begin to speculate how much you can afford to risk and stick to it. Never talk yourself into risking money you cannot afford to lose.

Rule #8: Be a winner. If you want to play the game, then learn to play it right. Study the market; do your homework; don't follow the herd. Do some original thinking. Make your selections; take your profits; cut your losses; and learn from your mistakes. You may not get rich, but you should do reasonably well. What's more, you may enjoy the process!

If, on the other hand, everything you pick goes bad—well, if you collect enough dogs you can at least start a kennel.

Rule #1   a. _____ Never trust your brother-in-law.

b. _____ Don't take the advice of someone who is not well informed about investments.

c. _____ Ask your brother-in-law's advice about movies and restaurants.

d. _____ Invest in your brother-in-law's business if you are a first-time speculator.

Rule #2   a. _____ Buy a good stock while its price is still low.

b. _____ Plunge into a cold shower to put out the fire that is burning a hole in your pocket.

c. _____ When the financial press identifies a stock that is reaching spectacular highs, you should buy it.

d. _____ As soon as you have some money, buy stock right away, regardless of its up-and-down cycle.

Rule #3   a. _____ As a speculator, you should hold onto a stock for its long-term potential.

b. _____ Don't sell until the stock has reached its highest point.

c. _____ If you deflate a balloon, it will come down.

d. _____ Don't wait too long to sell a stock that is going up on the market.

Rule #4   a. _____ Keep a stock until it makes money for you.

b. _____ If the market drops, hold on to your stock until it rises again.

c. _____ When a ship is sinking, get into a lifeboat.

d. _____ Sell a stock that has gone down in value or is not making any money.

Rule #5   a. _____ If you hear of a small, unknown company that is selling stock at a very low price, buy it while it is still a bargain.

b. _____ Be cautious about buying stock in small companies that are just starting operation.

c. _____ Buy stock during a bull market instead of a bear market.

d. _____ Buy stock in Winnebago, especially if you own a trailer.

Rule #6   a. _____ Defuse an unexploded bomb instead of kicking the cat.

b. _____ If you spend a great deal of time looking for bargains in the stock market, you will make a profit every time.

c. _____ Stop speculating in the stock market if you are becoming a nervous wreck from it.

d. _____ Continue to speculate in the stock market regardless of any effects on your nervous system.

Rule #7   a. _____ You should lose money on your first stock investment.

           b. _____ Don't risk money you can't afford to lose.

           c. _____ When you have good luck with a stock, put all of your money in the stock market.

           d. _____ If you are greedy, you will make more money.

Rule #8   a. _____ Before entering the stock market, learn how to invest wisely.

           b. _____ Buy stock in dog kennels.

           c. _____ When you play the stock market, do what others are doing.

           d. _____ You will get rich if you study the market.

GC Exercise 17

In this exercise you will have an opportunity to apply various comprehension skills. When you read the following article the first time, look for the main idea. After that, the questions will ask you to look for details, sequence, cause and effect, and inferences. Finally, you will need to summarize the article. You may want to look back through the chapter to refresh your mind on some of these skills.

Army Relief of Civilians, 1874–1875[20]

On a bright sunny day in July the S. C. Bassett family of Buffalo County, Nebraska, sat down to the mid-day meal. The sky seemed to darken and it was remarked that a squall might be approaching. Suddenly what sounded like hail first drop-dropped, rattled, then poured onto the roof and against the walls. On looking out, someone passed the cry of "Grasshoppers!" through the frame house.

In minutes the insects covered the earth to a depth of four to six inches. They moved through the grain fields, their feeding noises like a herd of cattle masticating. Corn stalks, even limbs, broke under their weight.

Quickly someone thought to throw bedclothing over the precious garden, but the hoppers ate not only through the blankets but into the subsurface onions and turnips. They chewed to ruin harnesses and munched off the grayness of weathered clapboards. Clubbed and stomped hoppers themselves were devoured by the horde. Creeks were stained with their excrement. Fish, turkeys, and hogs gorged on them to the extent that, when butchered, their own flesh tasted of the insect.

After a few hours of feeding in Buffalo County, the cloud re-formed and moved on. In that summer of '74 great areas of the upper plains were stripped of vegetation. Panicked neighbors offered a bounty of fifty cents a bushel for dead grasshoppers and many extreme remedies were proposed, including concussion bombs. But only heavy rains were an effective large scale natural control, drowning them.

It was soon reported that the isolated civilian farmers in the Military Departments of Dakota, Platte and Missouri faced winter without food and fuel reserves. Relief societies were formed. Committees traveled to the East with appeals, and churches and individuals responded. Controversy arose over the intensity of this new suffering inflicted upon the already beleaguered dry land immigrants. Tales circulated of both unfed children and misappropriated donations, misrepresentations of discomfort.

By February 1875 conditions were desperate enough that, in response to a Congressional resolution, the U.S. Army Subsistence Department arranged a Federal relief exercise. General Alfred Terry in the hard-pressed Department of Dakota detailed eighteen officers to canvass the counties and seek out "all cases of actual suffering, and to prevent imposture." Bacon, flour, greatcoats, hats, shoes and boots were distributed. From headquarters in Omaha, General George Crook directed a similar program for the Department of the Platte. In all, that winter the Army issued 1,957,000 rations to 63,500 adults and 43,900 children at a cost of about $150,000. And by 1881 the Army Signal Corps, in addition to its meteorological duties, manned locust control observation stations.

I. Main Idea
Put a check beside the statement that best conveys the main idea of the article.

_____ a. Grasshoppers travel in vast hordes.

_____ b. The U.S. Army provided relief from the grasshopper problem.

_____ c. Grasshoppers caused severe damage in the Midwest.

_____ d. There is no way to control an invasion by grasshoppers.

II. Details
Answer the following questions by looking carefully through the material.

1. What month and year did the grasshoppers come to Buffalo County, Nebraska? _____

2. How deeply did the grasshoppers cover the ground? _____

3. How did someone try to protect the garden? _____

4. How long did the insects feed in Buffalo County? _____

5. How much bounty did neighbors offer for a bushel of dead grasshoppers? _____

6. Where did relief committees travel for help? _____

7. What prompted the U.S. Army Subsistence Department to arrange federal relief? _____

8. Who assigned officers from the Department of Dakota to find cases of suffering? _____

_____

9. How many children received rations from the Army? _____

10. How much did the Army spend on rations? _____

III. Sequence

Arrange the following events in the sequence in which they occurred. Put numbers in the blanks beside the letters to indicate the correct order.

_____ The U.S. Army Subsistence Department arranged for a relief program.

_____ The Army Signal Corps staffed locust control observation stations.

_____ Grasshoppers arrived in Buffalo County, Nebraska.

_____ Neighbors offered a bounty for a bushel of dead grasshoppers.

_____ Grasshoppers destroyed grain fields in Buffalo County.

_____ The grasshoppers left Buffalo County and moved on.

IV. Cause and Effect

In the following cause-and-effect sentences, underline the clause that is the cause once, and underline the clause that is the effect twice. Circle the word or words that serve as signals or connectors.

1. The sky darkened when a horde of grasshoppers came.
2. Fish, turkeys, and hogs ate the grasshoppers so, when they were butchered, their own flesh tasted of grasshoppers.
3. Relief societies were formed because the farmers had no food.
4. Due to the insect problem, the Army Signal Corps set up locust control observation stations.
5. Conditions became desperate; therefore, the U.S. Army Subsistence Department provided federal relief.
6. As a result of the weight of the grasshoppers, corn stalks and limbs broke.
7. The grasshoppers drowned because of the heavy rains.

V. Inferences

Read the following statements and decide which of these contain inferences that you should be able to make and which contain inferences you should not make. In other words, some statements you can logically infer from the material in the article or your own knowledge, but other statements you cannot reasonably infer. On the lines below each statement, first write "yes" or "no" to indicate whether you can or cannot make the inferences. Then write your reason for making or not making the inference. An example is given.

Example: Grasshoppers are hungry creatures who eat almost anything.
yes   They ate anything they could find—vegetation, clapboards, blankets, harnesses, etc.

1. The people of the upper plains area had endured many hardships.

   _____ _____

   _____

2. The people had used all of their insect spray and it didn't work.

   _____ _____

   _____

3. Insect hordes continued to be a problem for years to come.

   _____ _____

   _____

4. The grasshopper problem spread all over the United States.

   _____ _____

   _____

5. People wanted to help the isolated farmers who had no food or fuel reserves.

   _____ _____

   _____

6. The U.S. Army Subsistence Department got rid of the grasshoppers.

   _____ _____

   _____

7. The grasshoppers worked fast.

   _____ _____

   _____

8. Grasshoppers can eat metal.

   _____ _____

   _____

9. People who had suffered from the grasshoppers needed food and clothing.

   _____ _____

   _____

VI. Summary

Write a summary of this article in three or four sentences. Be sure to include the major ideas.

Chapter Notes

1. Excerpted from "Irrigation Canal or Lateral Specifications," reprinted from *SCS,* October, 1977, pp. 320–23.

2. Excerpted from Gary Fennan, "Space-Age Sports," *The Rotarian*, September, 1988, p. 21.

3. Excerpted from Felicia Butsch, "A Twelfth Night Party to Remember," reprinted by permission from *The Progressive Farmer,* January, 1974, p. 99.

4. Excerpted from "Those Tobacco Marketing Woes," reprinted by permission from *The Progressive Farmer,* January, 1974, p. 45.

5. Excerpted from Natalie Levy, "Winter Sports for the Ski-None," reprinted by permission from *Odyssey,* November–December, 1973, p. 18.

6. Wayne Trimm, "Predation," reprinted by permission from *The Conservationist,* November–December, 1983, p. 18.

7. Reprinted from *Snow Survey and Water Supply Forecasting, SCS National Engineering Handbook,* Section 22, Soil Conservation Service, United States Department of Agriculture.

8. Reprinted through courtesy of *The Workbasket,* January, 1974, pp. 24–26.

9. Excerpted from "Science and Applications," reprinted by permission from *Space World,* March, 1971, p. 19.

10. Excerpted from "Binding Findings," reprinted by permission from *Ski,* December, 1973, p. 42.

11. Excerpted from "Try the Right Hemisphere," reprinted by permission from *Ski,* December, 1973, p. 36.

12. Reprinted from February, 1972 issue, *Popular Electronics,* Copyrighted 1974, by Ziff-Davis Publishing Company.

13. Reprinted from the January, 1974 issue, *Popular Electronics,* Copyrighted 1974, by Ziff-Davis Publishing Company.

14. "Trip to the Top," reprinted by permission from *Ski,* December, 1973, p. 41.

15. Excerpted from "Science and Applications," reprinted by permission from *Space World,* March, 1971, p. 18.

16. Excerpted from "A Children's Crusade in the Virgin Islands," reprinted by permission from *American Education,* July, 1972, p. 22.

17. "Beware the Chilly Hypo," reprinted by permission from *Ski,* December, 1973, p. 42.

18. Reprinted from the May, 1972 issue of *Popular Electronics,* Copyrighted 1974, by Ziff-Davis Publishing Company.

19. Richard Loller, "Beware of the Dog—Or, Helpful Hints for the Amateur Speculator," reprinted by permission from *Advantage,* October, 1983, pp. 20–21.

20. John Slonaker, "Army Relief of Civilians, 1874–1875," in Richard J. Sommers, ed., *U.S. Army Military History Research Collection, Vignettes of Military History,* vol. I, October, 1976, p. 12.

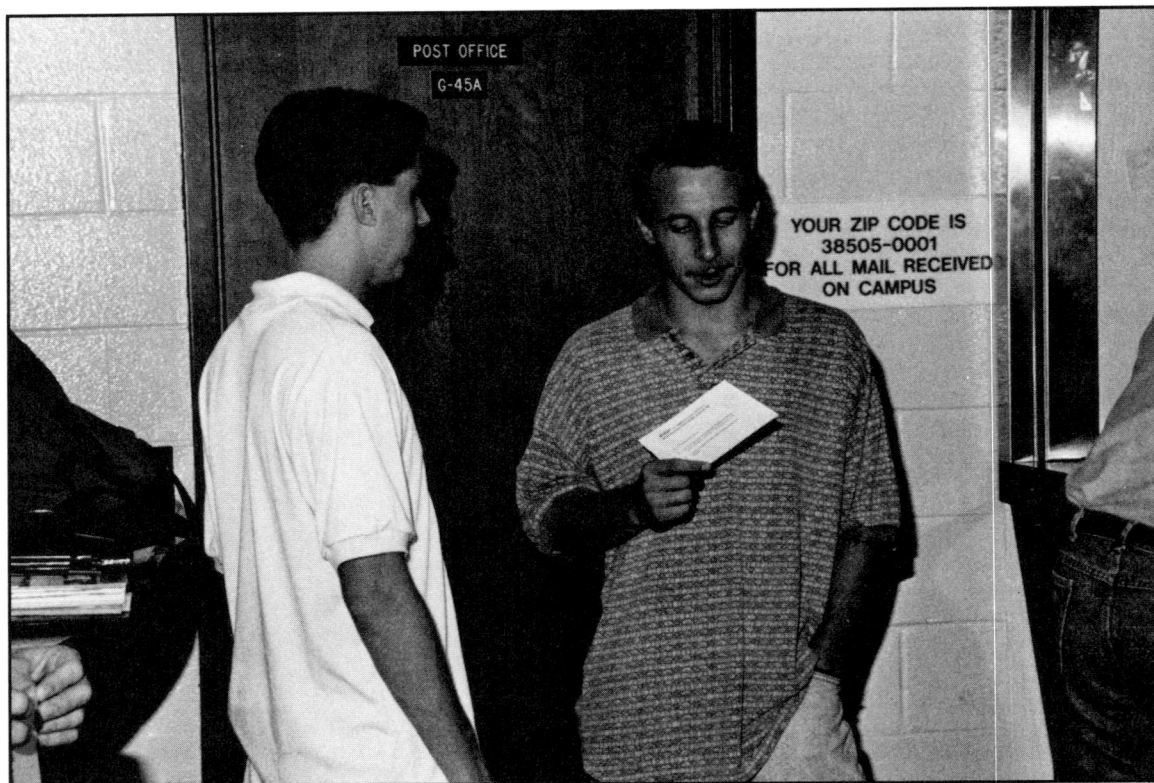

7 Critical Reading

Waiting in line at the post office, Ken and Tony recognized each other from class. "This is my first year to vote for president, but honestly, I don't know who's the best candidate," said Tony. "I get so confused when I hear the politicians on T.V. and read about them in the papers. How do I know what to believe?"

"I know what you mean," agreed Ken. "Promises, promises. I did get some good ideas about how to decide what you can believe and what's suspect, though. Things like how emotional words can sway your judgment and how to tell fact from opinion. Even the slogans politicians use can make you think a certain way—logical or not."

"Where did you find out about all of this?" asked Tony.

"It's in that course we're taking—the chapter on critical reading. Some of us were talking about how politicians and advertisers take advantage of us sometimes if we don't stop to think about what they're really saying—or not saying. It's easy to be fooled. Why, there's a whole bunch of propaganda types they use, and most of the time we aren't even aware of them."

"Wow. I'll have a look at that chapter myself. Maybe it will help me get my thinking straight about this election."

"Hey, Tony—pay attention. You're next in line. They want to know how many stamps you want."

Introduction

Critical reading, a high-level comprehension skill, is the process of questioning and evaluating printed material. It is closely associated with the reader's ability to think critically and to react intelligently to the writer's ideas.

The need for critical reading grows daily as the volume of reading material increases. Good citizens need to be able to read critically in order to weigh public issues and make intelligent choices among political candidates. Readers should be able to detect misleading advertising claims in order to recognize the best values and avoid spending their money foolishly. By applying critical reading techniques, readers will know how to make their own decisions instead of blindly accepting the persuasions of the writer as truth.

Critical reading can be developed and refined with practice. Readers can learn how to question what they read, distinguish between fact and opinion, detect faulty logic, and recognize propaganda. The techniques for reading critically presented in this chapter can help readers evaluate reading material and make judgments concerning its worth.

The Critical Reader

Good critical readers are able to go beyond the literal interpretation of what they read. They know how to question, analyze, and form judgments. They search for causes, consider the author's qualifications and purposes, and sort facts from opinions. Their minds are alert to unfounded assumptions, fallacious reasoning, and illogical conclusions. By thinking for themselves, they do not necessarily accept the biased viewpoints and propaganda of writers who are trying to influence them.

Unlike literal comprehension, critical reading requires readers to interact with the writer. Readers must understand the writer's message, question it, and react to it in terms of their own knowledge and experience. They are probing, comparing, and reflecting as they think along with the writer about the ideas that have been set forth. As a result of this interaction, readers have not only absorbed the writer's thoughts, but have also adapted them in light of their own background to fit their purposes.

Your first obligation as a critical reader is to understand the writer's message. Approach the reading with an open mind and a willingness to accept new ideas or another point of view. Even though you may have some doubts about the material before you begin reading it, give the writer an opportunity to present his or her position. Avoid letting your personal biases or prejudices interfere with clear thinking and objectivity.

As you begin reading and are becoming aware of the writer's thoughts, your mind should be analyzing and questioning the logic of what the author is saying. You should be skeptical toward unsupported assumptions and contrived relationships. You should be alert to faulty reasoning and illogical conclusions. Be aware of both the author's prejudices and your own as you make judgments about the material you are reading.

The more experiences and knowledge you have concerning a subject, the better qualified you are to read about it critically. When you are familiar with a topic, you can recognize misleading statements, make intelligent comparisons, and be aware of significant omissions. You find that the material either expands the concepts you already have or fails to harmonize with what you have experienced. You should have adequate knowledge to provide standards for reading critically, but it is impossible to know about everything.

When you are reading something outside of your experience, your critical reading ability is limited. For example, without some knowledge of the issues involved, it is difficult to know if a dam should be built in a certain location to provide power or if the area should be preserved in its natural state. You can, however, even without prior knowledge, read with an alert, inquiring mind in order to notice possible inconsistencies and biases.

Procedures for Evaluating Material

Asking yourself certain questions as you read helps you interpret the writer's ideas critically. No single list of questions applies in every situation, but certain types of questions are suitable for most kinds of printed matter. At first you may need to consciously ask these questions, but after you have formed the habit of questioning, you will probably find they occur to you automatically.

Begin by questioning the author's purpose. Many writers will try to persuade you to accept their beliefs. They might do this by telling you only one side of the story, making statements that are not based on facts, or using highly emotional words and phrases. Some writers are apt to be biased because of their sex, religion, political inclinations, or geographic background. For example, a Northerner might write the history of the Civil War from a different point of view than a Southerner. Sometimes the writers' purposes or biases may be obvious to you, and sometimes they may be subtle or hidden.

CR Exercise 1

Read the following article for the purpose of discovering the author's point of view. When you have finished reading the article, read the list of statements that follows. If you think the statement is probably true, write T beside it. If you think it is false, write F beside it.

Students Need to Grapple with "Significant Ethical Problems"[1]

"Delusions" spawned by the success of science

Universities have gone much too far in trying to produce value-free teaching and research. This happened primarily because scholars within universities were deluded by the thought that only completely objective, "scientific" inquiry was respectable and that values were not amenable to rigorous scholarship. There is, however, no totally objective science of political affairs or economics. Values always creep in.

For a long time, the success of science, along with the rewards and accolades society provided to scientists, caused people in other fields to delude themselves into thinking that they could achieve a completely scientific form of inquiry. Many scholars even distorted the reality they studied in order to make it susceptible to their "rigorous" methods of analysis. Now we are beginning to understand that while scientific methods have utility in softer fields such as the social sciences, they are not adequate to understanding all questions.

Another reason for the move away from dealing with values is that some people are more comfortable doing research in fields where they think that they may get reasonably certain answers. By contrast, in most important ethical issues, one can clarify the issue and satisfy one's feelings on the matter, but one cannot lay claim to achieving any sort of universally demonstrable, logical truth. Issues of value have no logical answer.

"A movement to introduce values"

Fortunately, there is now a movement to introduce values into the curriculum through courses in applied ethics that ask students to come to grips with significant ethical problems. Those courses do not try to indoctrinate students or tell them what they should think. They *do* try to help students become more sensitive to ethical issues and reason more carefully about those questions. They also acquaint students with the best writing that has accumulated on these matters over the centuries.

In this connection, I have been surprised and gratified to find that courses in moral reasoning are the most oversubscribed of any of the groups of courses we ask students to take as part of Harvard's new core curriculum. That suggests there is a genuine interest in these issues.

No one can be sure how much effect such courses will have on the quality of human behavior. But we do know that a number of people have gotten into ethical difficulty because they really didn't see a problem arising until it was too late. We also know that many people rationalize unethical behavior on the basis of reasoning that won't stand up under careful examination. If students are put in the habit of inquiring more rigorously into ethics, they will presumably find it easier to avoid these pitfalls.

Universities "have a greater reach"

There is a widely held belief among the public that institutions in the society, such as families and churches, are not as influential as they once were in transmitting values to individuals. If that is so, then universities should take even more seriously their responsibilities in these matters. We educate a much higher proportion of the citizenry than we used to and hence have a greater reach—and therefore a greater responsibility—to help fill gaps that exist as a result of the declining influence of other institutions.

But efforts by universities to teach students about ethical issues are likely to be limited in value and to produce cynicism if the institutions themselves are perceived to be ethically careless or insensitive. That doesn't mean we have to agree with the students or take institutional positions on public questions of the day, which I think would be wrong.

But we have to take seriously the ethical issues that confront the university and take the time to explain to students our attitudes on these questions. And when we disagree with the students, we should explain the grounds of disagreement with sufficient care so that any sensible person would recognize that moral questions have not been cavalierly tossed aside, ignored or subordinated to the selfish interests of the university.

1. _____ The writer believes that students who habitually think more deeply about ethics are less likely to rationalize unethical behavior than other students.

2. _____ The writer feels that universities should take institutional positions on current social issues.

3. _____ According to the writer, universities should strive to keep scholarly pursuits objective and scientific, completely unaffected by values or ethics.

4. _____ The writer believes that a completely scientific form of inquiry is possible.

5. _____ The writer feels that the university has an obligation to explain to students its stand on moral and social issues.

6. _____ The writer supports the idea of introducing values into the college curriculum.

7. _____ According to the writer, universities should accept a greater share of the responsibility for transmitting social values than they used to.

8. _____ The writer believes that logical answers can be found for issues of value through scientific methods of research.

CR Exercise 2

Read the following editorial to discover the editor's point of view. When you have finished reading the article, read the list of statements that follows. If you think the statement is probably true, write T beside it. If you think it is false, write F beside it.

Politics Leave Voters in the Cold[2]

C. Steven Doremus

Welcome to America, land of government of the people, by the people and for the political parties. It's a simple choice. The curtain closes on a voting booth, and the names of candidates representing two parties stare back at you. It's a choice that this nation is built on. While elections are still decided by majority rule, the decisions made by our elected officials are being influenced more and more often by party loyalties instead of public sentiment. Our votes are no longer cast for the individual whom we think will be most responsive to our needs and wishes. Instead, our votes now represent a nod of favor for the party that a candidate represents. Never mind the fact that most citizens do not have beliefs that fit squarely with one party or another. Money for re-election and power within the parties are directly linked to toeing the party line. In the simplest of terms, politics in America have become too political.

In today's world of media-based political campaigns, money is the key to victory. Money is used to buy air time for flashy television commercials that present candidates to the public as if they were automobiles or washing powder. Real issues are rarely discussed during campaign ads. Candidates would rather be shown kissing babies and shaking the hands of factory workers than taking stands on the concerns of constituents. The reasoning for such behavior is simple. At some point in the lawmaker's career, the well-being of his or her district may have to be sacrificed for the good of the party. Rest assured, the voters are expendable. The higher posts in political parties are not those that are elected by the public, but they are presented from the party to those who have made few if any waves for those pushing the party agenda. Candidates shy away from making promises that may have to be compromised later.

In the long run, the politicians are fighting for control of the nation's capital. The party with the most representatives can hold the opposition in a stalemate through the use of the Constitution's system of checks and balances between government branches. Majority rule is still the name of the game, but the majority is no longer directly affected by the decisions being made. When the voices of the voters are hundreds or thousands of miles away, the voice of the party takes on a greater role. Unfortunately, more often than not, the voice of the party is out to discredit the opposing party for its own benefit. Voters must find a way to show elected officials that it is their concerns, not those of the party, that they were chosen to fight for.

From the president on down, elected officials must be held accountable for actions taken on our behalf. We vote for representatives to represent us, just as the title implies. Too many taxpayers' dollars are being spent on playing politics instead of governing. We don't elect people to campaign for other party members, themselves or the party line. Voting for a Democrat or a Republican does not imply a blanket endorsement of every party issue. Even though the two-party system works well in elections, it is failing in our statehouses and legislatures. Too many important issues are being decided along party lines instead of according to voters' wishes. When a person takes an oath of office, he or she swears to defend the Constitution of this nation. Perhaps defense of one's party was left out of the Constitution for a reason. Party allegiances should be left in the voting booths, and the government of the people and by the people should return to working for the people, before we are all working for the benefit of the party.

1. _____ The writer thinks that politics play too big a part in the governing process.

2. _____ The writer believes that elected officials are often influenced more by voters' concerns than by party loyalty.

3. _____ According to the writer, a voter's beliefs are identical with the beliefs of the voter's political party.

4. _____ The writer thinks that voters are more likely to vote according to party affiliation than by a candidate's positions on issues.

5. _____ The writer contends that politicians are relying more on kissing babies and shaking hands to get votes than on making their positions clear on issues.

6. _____ The writer recommends abolishing the two-party system of government because it no longer works.

7. _____ The writer believes that the political party's interests should be more important than the concerns of individuals.

8. _____ The writer thinks that the amount of money spent during a political campaign strongly affects election results.

CR Exercise 3

Read the following editorial for the purpose of discovering the author's point of view. When you have finished reading the editorial, read the list of statements that follows. If you think the statement is probably true, write T beside it. If you think it is false, write F beside it.

Involvement: Key to College Success[3]

C. Steven Doremus

In the good old days, a college degree, even a bachelor's degree, carried a lot of weight in the job world. Now, with more and more high school graduates attending college, a degree alone is just not enough. Employers are looking for well rounded individuals who have experience ranging beyond sitting through hundreds of lectures. The key to success is as simple as getting involved, both in your school and your major. While the door to opportunity is still open in America, the chances of succeeding after college are increased if you go looking for that door instead of waiting for it to appear in front of you.

College freshmen often find out rather abruptly that time, specifically the proper management of it, is a source of constant worry. After the first term or two of classes, most students realize that they really do have time left over after classes. It is this realization that allows students to become involved in extracurricular activities. These activities can be involvement in student government, fraternities, sororities, professional organizations and clubs, but to get the most out of this precious time, students must find activities that will help them once they leave university life. For some majors, like education and journalism, these types of activities are built into their curricula. Education

majors go through the motions of teaching for the first time by student teaching, and journalism majors get their first taste of reporting and editing on student newspapers. For other majors, experience is harder to come by.

One way to get involved in your major is simply to get involved with your school. Most colleges participate in competitions with other schools in almost every field of endeavor. By sticking around after class, you can find out when these activities are taking place and how you can get involved in them. From these competitions, you can see what is involved in your selected field and make contacts that may help you when it is time to go job hunting. Another way of accomplishing the same thing is to make your part-time or summer job work for you. Try to find work that is at least related in some way to your major. While it may not be exactly what you plan to do, you can gain valuable insights that might place you ahead of the competition. Finally, get out on your own time and look at the kind of companies you want to work for. Most companies are only too happy to give tours and literature about their operations. Basically, you are placing your name in their minds before the other people you will be competing with, and you are building your knowledge of your major.

Like the old saying, every little bit does help in the competitive job market. While this list of tips is by no means complete, it serves to emphasize one point. Involvement and interest are essential to success before graduation, as well as after it. A direct connection between your activities and your major is not essential, but it is a good place to start. Social groups, for instance, may help you develop skills for meeting interviewers, and being on a speech or debate team might help you prepare for making corporate presentations. All kinds of possibilities exist, but you must make your time work for you because it can indeed be an investment in your own future. Every college graduate has a degree in one hand, but it's what you can carry in the other hand that might make the difference in who gets the job that you want.

1. _____ The writer believes that most employers consider academic achievement to be the only criterion for hiring new college graduates.

2. _____ The author feels that students who become involved in extracurricular activities are wasting their time, as far as employment is concerned.

3. _____ According to the writer, a student's involvement in campus organizations and activities can make the difference in whether or not the student is hired.

4. _____ The writer claims that one type of extracurricular activity is as good as another in terms of employment prospects.

5. _____ The writer feels that social groups have no value in preparing for a career.

6. _____ Time management usually gets easier after the first year, according to the writer.

7. _____ The author believes that some majors provide job-like experiences as part of their courses of study.

8. _____ The author implies that student involvement in campus activities is more important to employers than it used to be.

Sometimes you will read about something or someone from more than one point of view. During a political campaign you read about different candidates, with each one claiming to be the best. In different newspapers you read editorials about controversial subjects in which one newspaper supports the same issue that the other newspaper attacks. The sports editor in one town reports a ball game quite differently from the way the editor from the town of the opposing team does. Occasionally, history books may present different accounts of the same event, depending on the author's point of view.

CR Exercise 4

In the following exercise you will read two versions of an event that took place at Lexington Green on April 19, 1775. As you read, notice which country each reporter represents to understand the basic difference in the points of view.

What Happened? Or, Whose Version Do You Believe?[4]

John Shy

Military history is no better than the evidence it rests on. Trying to determine exactly what happened at Lexington Green on 19 April 1775 illustrates the point perfectly.

Captain John Parker, who commanded the militiamen engaged in the small but vitally important first battle of the American Revolution remembered it this way:

. . . on the nineteenth instant, in the morning, about one of the clock, being informed, that there were a number of the regular officers riding up and down the road, stopping and insulting people as they passed the road, and also informed that a number of the regular troops were on their march from Boston, in order to take the province stores at Concord, I ordered our militia to meet on the common in said Lexington, to consult what to do, and concluded not to be discovered, nor meddle, or make with said regular troops, if they should approach, unless they should insult or molest us; and upon their sudden approach, I immediately ordered our militia to disperse and not to fire. Immediately, said troops made their appearance, and rushing furiously on, fired upon and killed eight of our party, without receiving any provocation therefore from us.

But Ensign Jeremy Lister of His Majesty's 10th Regiment of Foot was also there, and he saw it—or at least told it—differently.

. . . the country people began to fire their alarm guns, light their beacons, to raise the country. However, to the best of my recollection about 4 o'clock in the morning, being the 19th of April, the five front companies was ordered to load, which we did. About a half an hour after, we found that precaution had been necessary, for we had to unload again, and then was the first blood drawn in this American Rebellion. It was at Lexington when we saw one of their companies drawn up in regular order. Major Pitcairn of the Marines, second in command, called to them to disperse, but their not seeming willing he desired us to mind our space, which we did, when they gave us a fire, then run off to get behind a wall. We had one man wounded of our company in the leg . . . also Major Pitcairn's horse was shot in the flank. We returned their salute, and before we proceeded on our march from Lexington I believe we killed or wounded either seven or eight men.

1. a. Captain Parker represents _____ .

   b. Ensign Lister represents _____ .

Put P for Parker or L for Lister beside each of the statements below to show the information reported by each of the men.

2. a. _____ The incident began at one o'clock in the morning.

   b. _____ The incident began at four o'clock in the morning.

3. a. _____ The country people began firing alarm guns and lighting beacons to raise the country.

   b. _____ The regular officers were stopping people and insulting them along the road.

4. a. _____ The American company was drawn up in regular formation.

   b. _____ The American militia met on the common to decide what to do.

5. a. _____ The American militia dispersed and did not fire.

   b. _____ The American company did not disperse and soldiers fired their guns.

6. a. _____ The regular troops received no provocation.

   b. _____ One man of His Majesty's 10th Regiment of Foot was wounded and a horse was shot.

7. a. _____ Seven or eight men were killed or wounded.

   b. _____ Eight men were killed.

To influence your thinking, the writer may appeal to your emotional or social needs. Advertisers frequently do this in order to persuade the noncritical reader to buy their products. Perhaps you can think of some commercials or advertisements that base their appeal on something other than the worth of the product. Some frequently used appeals are made to a person's desire for security, prestige, popularity, wealth, and pleasing appearance.

As you consider the author's reasons for writing, think about other aspects of the material as well. Often the policies of the publication determine the type of material that is published. You would not expect to find a notably conservative newspaper supporting a liberal candidate. Consider also the time the material was written. Times are changing and ideas that were valid twenty years ago may no longer hold true. Also, some authors are apt to be more competent than others in certain fields because of their experiences or educational background. For instance, a writer who has had children can probably write a more practical guide to child rearing than one who has never had children.

171

CR Exercise 5

This exercise will give you an opportunity to judge which person would likely be most competent to write about a certain subject.

Read the following statements and place the letter of the person who is probably best qualified to make the statement in the blank beside the statement.

1. _____ Laws must be passed to protect the quail from hunters.
    a. Game commissioner
    b. Lawyer
    c. Engineer

2. _____ The Supreme Court has the right to rule on the constitutionality of laws.
    a. College president
    b. Lawyer
    c. Personnel manager

3. _____ A highway lane should be at least eleven feet wide.
    a. Engineer
    b. State police
    c. Industrialist

4. _____ American colonists were at first loyal to Great Britain, but later rebelled against British rule.
    a. Historian
    b. School teacher
    c. Librarian

5. _____ The raven is a large bird that is a member of the crow family.
    a. Botanist
    b. Chemist
    c. Ornithologist

6. _____ The level of pitch is determined by the number of vibrations per second.
    a. Chemist
    b. Physicist
    c. Musician

7. _____ The people of Sweden can be seen sunning themselves in the cities during lunch hour.
    a. An American
    b. An African
    c. A Scandinavian

8. _____ The secret of enjoying a long life is to exercise regularly.
    a. A young mother of five children
    b. A recent college graduate
    c. An octogenarian

9. _____ The downhill race is one of the most exciting competitive skiing events.
    a. A sports commentator
    b. A newspaper editor
    c. A champion water skier

10. _____ The nation is in the midst of a crippling energy crisis.
    a. A representative of the steel industry
    b. A representative of the oil industry
    c. A representative of the electronics industry

As you question, suspend your judgment until you have thought through the material and can make a sound evaluation. You may be tempted to jump to conclusions, but it is far better to weigh all the evidence before making a decision. When you thoroughly understand the facts, you are ready to make your evaluation. If you read with an open mind and knowledge of the subject, you should be able to decide whether you support the writer's contentions or disagree with him or her.

In order to acquire the questioning habit, refer frequently to the list of questions that follows.

1. What are the policies of the publication in which this material appears?
2. Do I have sufficient background in this subject to make an intelligent evaluation?
3. How recently was the material written?
4. In what areas of the world was it written?
5. What do I already know about the writer?
6. Is he or she qualified to write on this subject?
7. What is the emotional tone of the material?
8. What is the author's stated reason for writing this material?
9. Does the writer have hidden motives?
10. To which of my needs is the writer appealing?
11. Is the writer's information complete?
12. Are the writer's facts correct?
13. Is the reasoning logical?
14. Are the conclusions justified?

CR Exercise 6

Thoughtfully read the following article from the November/December 1988 issue of *EPA Journal*, published by the U.S. Environmental Protection Agency. Consider the source of the article and your knowledge of the subject as you read. After you have read it, answer the questions that follow by placing the letter of the *best* answer in the blank beside the number of the statement.

Environmental Problems: The Situation[5]

What should be the nation's environmental priorities as we move toward the . . . 21st century? How should we go about the business of priority-setting? What criteria should determine our national priorities on the environment? . . .

Despite the controversies surrounding priority-setting, one point is indisputable: Whatever its outcome, the priority-setting process must be based on a firm understanding of the total universe of environmental problems now confronting the United States. . . .

Water

Water-pollution problems fall into three basic categories:

• *Protection of drinking water.* More Americans are receiving safer drinking water than ever before; the most severe public health effects from contaminated drinking water have been eliminated. However, there are still some less acute hazards associated with a number of specific contaminants, such as lead, radionuclides, microbiological contaminants, and disinfection byproducts. These hazards are particularly troublesome in small community systems, which have a low level of compliance with national drinking water standards.

One challenge facing the Agency is how to motivate the public to bear the costs of dealing with the growing number of contaminants EPA is now requiring public water systems to regulate. Another is to overcome the financial problems faced by these systems, especially the smaller ones.

In addition, EPA is concerned about protecting surface and ground-water sources of drinking water from further contamination. EPA and the states will need to continue working to improve wastewater treatment, as well as to deal with problems caused by toxic pollutants. The extent and significance of contamination by toxics has not yet been fully assessed, but the 1986 amendments to the Safe Drinking Water Act are requiring water systems to extend both their monitoring and treatment.

• *Protection of surface and ground water.* Protection of America's surface water has been the focus of concerted action for many years. Billions in federal funds have been spent to construct wastewater treatment plants, and industry has invested heavily in equipment to "pre-treat" its toxic effluents. Today the emphasis of surface-water programs is on consolidating the gains of the past, while transferring growing parts of their management to state and local officials. There is also a new effort to curb nonpoint pollution coming from agricultural and urban run-off.

Ground-water protection is a newer but ever-growing area of Agency concern. The major challenge today is to build capacity among state governments and Indian tribes for dealing with ground-water protection tasks, such as the safeguarding of wellhead areas. This is not always easy because of the scientific and regulatory complexity of the problems encountered.

• *Protection of critical and aquatic habitats.* Oceans, near-coastal waters, estuaries, and wetlands have been underprotected in the past. Their deterioration was highlighted . . . when swimmers fled beaches littered with medical waste and infected with fecal coliform.

More aggressive action is required—and required very soon—to save these aquatic habitats from further contamination, or even from destruction. The nation needs an integrated long-term waste management strategy, with ocean dumping no longer the "quick fix" alternative to other options.

Air

The past 18 years have brought improvements in U.S. air quality. For example, atmospheric levels of lead, ozone, carbon monoxide, airborne particulates, sulfur dioxide, and nitrogen oxides have all been reduced, in some cases sharply. However, the reduction of a problem does not mean its elimination, and the challenges ahead remain formidable.

The problem of ground-level ozone or "smog" has proven particularly difficult to control. For example, ozone standards are still not being met in over 60 major urban areas. Carbon monoxide standards are also being violated in many of these cities.

Another concern is sulfur dioxide—an important precursor of acid rain. In this case, individual vehicles are not the problem, but rather emissions from power plants that burn high-sulfur coal. New scrubber technologies are expected to play an important role in reducing the sulfur dioxide content of future emissions (as well as the nitrogen oxides that also cause acid rain). And there is wide discussion in Congress and elsewhere about how to deal with the acid rain problem.

There has been considerable progress in controlling large and intermediate particulates (dust, smoke, diesel exhaust, etc.), but smaller particles still require more rigorous controls. To deal with this problem, EPA has promulgated a new inhalable particulate standard that will require substantial enforcement efforts over the next few years.

The problem of air toxics also requires more attention. These are toxic chemicals released into the atmosphere by chemical factories and refineries. EPA is developing national standards for these substances; since 1984, the Agency has also developed and implemented a national air toxics program that is helping the states to monitor and control high-risk local problems.

A number of previously unrecognized problems have complicated the picture, such as radon and other indoor air pollutants, including asbestos, environmental tobacco smoke, formaldehyde, and airborne pesticide residues. More research is needed to identify and rank the exact health risks that result from exposure to individual indoor pollutants, or mixtures of multiple indoor pollutants. There is also a need for easy-to-operate, commercially available devices to monitor personal exposure to indoor air pollution, as well as better methods for diagnosing building-related illnesses, and correcting their structural causes.

Two other air-pollution problems have also risen to prominence . . . : global warming (the so-called "greenhouse effect") and stratospheric ozone depletion. The central challenge is to develop a better understanding of these problems, and how they relate to human health, agriculture, and natural ecosystems. There is also a keen need for new technologies and new chemicals that will not deplete the ozone layer, as well as ways of counteracting the build-up of gases linked to global warming.

Land

Air and water pollution are easier for most people to conceptualize than land pollution. But the fact remains that large portions of U.S. land are threatened by contact with toxic, radioactive, and other types of hazardous substances. Sometimes this contamination occurs through direct application, as with pesticides; it can also, however, occur as a result of improper disposal or storage of these substances, or their waste products.

Four major challenges face officials in government and industry who are now trying to protect our land:

• *Preventing future contamination from improper waste disposal.* Focusing on major generators, and storage, treatment, and disposal facilities, EPA is taking steps with the states to ensure the proper management of municipal and hazardous wastes. Many believe that municipal recycling and industrial waste reduction should become the centerpiece of a progressive national waste management strategy.

• *Cleaning up releases of hazardous substances.* One of EPA's most important responsibilities is to clean up the worst of the uncontrolled hazardous waste sites of the United States. Tremendous efforts will be required to develop the scientific and technical expertise needed for permanent clean-up remedies. The technical difficulty of cleaning up these sites can only be overcome by conducting research, developing technologies, and gaining further experience in the detoxification and destruction of wastes.

• *Tackling pollution from underground storage tanks.* EPA is helping the states to develop programs that will assist in managing underground storage tanks. Better tank design as well as leak detection devices are crucial to these efforts. The cleanup of areas already contaminated by leaking underground storage tanks is another major challenge that EPA and the states are now facing.

• *Emergency Planning and Community Right-To-Know.* The Emergency Planning and Community Right-To-Know Act of 1986 has redefined the way EPA, the states, and local government must deal with the presence of chemicals in individual communities. Better planning for chemical emergencies is already underway, and so is the gathering of information both to assist emergency planners and inform local citizens. Ongoing attention to these problems is certain to be a major EPA challenge in the years ahead. . . .

_____ 1. The main purpose of this article is to inform readers that
   a. the United States is facing critical environmental problems that demand solutions.
   b. environmental problems ranked in order of importance are (1) air, (2) water, and (3) land.
   c. there are no possible solutions for the nation's environmental problems.
   d. the EPA will pass laws controlling the use of the environment.

_____ 2. The questions raised at the beginning of the article
   a. are answered within each environmental category (water, air, land).
   b. are considered again at the conclusion of the article.
   c. can be easily resolved by environmentalists.
   d. are not answered within the article.

_____ 3. In regard to protection of aquatic habitats, the author believes
  a. ocean dumping continues as an acceptable solution for getting rid of waste.
  b. more aggressive action is needed soon to save these habitats.
  c. a short-term waste management strategy will suffice.
  d. the problem of protecting these habitats no longer exists.

_____ 4. Relative to air quality, the author states that
  a. research has identified precise health risks resulting from indoor pollutants.
  b. existing problems have been eliminated.
  c. new problems continue to arise.
  d. the problem of air toxics no longer requires attention.

_____ 5. According to the author, it is widely believed that
  a. combined government agencies will solve the nation's land pollution problems in the 21st century.
  b. municipal recycling and industrial waste reduction should be central to a national waste management program.
  c. billions of dollars are needed to establish new programs for reducing land pollution.
  d. most people can conceptualize land pollution easier than air or water pollution.

_____ 6. Throughout the article the author seems to be saying
  a. the future appears hopeless for solving environmental problems.
  b. nothing has been done in the past to protect the environment.
  c. some progress has been made, but difficult challenges lie ahead.
  d. by working alone, the EPA will be able to solve the nation's environmental problems.

The following questions are based on the critical questioning techniques in the section preceding this exercise. They should be answered in terms of your own background. Place the letter of the answer that comes closest to expressing your own thoughts in the blank beside the number of the question.

_____ 1. What do I know about the agency that publishes the journal in which this article appears?
  a. I am familiar with this agency. I know that it is reputable and I can assume the information is accurate.
  b. From my knowledge of this agency, I know it is sometimes biased. This article, therefore, may be slightly biased.
  c. I have never read anything from this agency, but I know of it from people whose judgment I trust.
  d. I know nothing about this agency.

_____ 2. Do I have sufficient background on this subject to make an intelligent evaluation?
  a. I am thoroughly familiar with the subject from reading of it in a variety of publications and hearing it discussed by competent people.
  b. I know something about the subject, but my knowledge is incomplete and my thinking may be biased.
  c. I have heard something about this subject, but not enough to form an opinion.
  d. I know nothing at all about the subject.

_____ 3. Was the material written recently enough so that the information provided is still valid?
   a. The information is recent enough to be considered valid.
   b. Most of the information is probably still valid, but new information may have become available recently.
   c. The information was probably written too long ago to be accepted without checking more recent sources.
   d. The information was written so long ago that it is completely out-of-date and totally useless.

_____ 4. The place of publication is Washington, D.C. Therefore, I can assume
   a. that the article accurately reflects the prevailing views on this subject since the subject is a concern of this country.
   b. that the article probably represents the thinking of American people.
   c. very little, because many different views are held on subjects within this country.
   d. nothing, because an article published in another country might present a more objective report.

_____ 5. What is the emotional tone of the material?
   a. The material is presented in a straightforward, objective manner.
   b. The material is basically factual, but some opinion statements and persuasive words can be found.
   c. Along with the factual material, emotional words and ideas are included that influence the reader's thinking.
   d. Although the material appears to be factual, it is actually written emotionally in order to stir up reader reaction.

_____ 6. What is the author's reason for writing this material?
   a. To provide the reader with important information.
   b. To discuss a topic that may be of concern to a limited number of people.
   c. To persuade the reader to think the same way he does.
   d. To present his own ideas for personal advantage.

_____ 7. Is the reasoning logical and are the conclusions justified?
   a. The situation is clearly stated, the reasoning makes sense, and the conclusions are well supported.
   b. Considering my limited background of knowledge, I think that both the reasoning and conclusions are probably correct.
   c. The reasoning appears to be based on incomplete information and the conclusions fail to consider the other side of the situation.
   d. Only one side of the case is presented and therefore the reasoning is biased and the conclusions are unjustified.

_____ 8. On the basis of the preceding eight questions, evaluate your ability to make a critical judgment of this article.
   a. I feel eminently qualified to evaluate this article critically.
   b. With only a few reservations, I am ready to make a judgment about this article.
   c. Since I have known little about the subject until now, I am unable to make a valid judgment without additional information.
   d. I am unable to make any evaluation of this article.

Forms of Critical Reading

Distinguishing Fact from Opinion

Discriminating between facts and opinions is one of your major tasks as a critical reader. Often they are woven together in a writer's account, and you may have difficulty determining which are the facts and which are the opinions. Although many readers assume that whatever appears in print is fact, printed material is often no more than someone's opinion.

There are several ways of distinguishing between verifiable statements of fact and someone's feelings or beliefs. You may verify or refute facts by checking the information in a reputable publication, getting confirmation from a respected individual, or observing for yourself. Your own experiences and knowledge can help you decide whether a statement is a fact or opinion. Certain words and phrases can also help you by indicating that the statement is likely to be an opinion. Some of these words and phrases are as follows: *I believe, he thinks, apparently, it seems as though, probably, may, should, it appears that, in the author's judgment, chances are, obviously, possibly, it is likely.*

CR Exercise 7

Keeping in mind that facts are verifiable, put F in front of each of the following statements that gives information as a fact. Put O in front of each statement that gives information as an opinion.

1. _____ Lightning often causes forest fires.

2. _____ School children should spend more time on sports.

3. _____ Spring is the best time of the year.

4. _____ There are more players on a baseball team than on a basketball team.

5. _____ I think basketball games are more fun to watch than baseball games.

6. _____ Billboards are placed along some highways.

7. _____ Highways would probably be more attractive without any billboards.

8. _____ The average annual temperature in Maine is lower than the average annual temperature in Florida.

9. _____ Florida is a pleasanter place to live than Maine.

10. _____ Thomas Jefferson wrote the Declaration of Independence.

11. _____ Columbus made a trip to America in 1492.

12. _____ Stover and Hartz are opposing each other in the race for city controller.

13. _____ Hartz will make a better city controller than Stover.

14. _____ The best vacation anyone can have is a week in the mountains.

15. _____ Lions can be found in Africa.

16. _____ Hurricanes, tornadoes, and floods have taken many lives.

17. _____ It is likely that weather control would be good for our country.

18. _____ Many people have dogs or cats as pets.

19. _____ Cats make better pets than dogs.

20. _____ Painting is the most creative of all hobbies.

21. _____ The public library in Moscow is one of the largest in the world.

22. _____ The Scandinavians are the hardest-working people in the world.

23. _____ Anne's new hair style is less attractive than her old one.

24. _____ General Eisenhower was the greatest man of World War II.

25. _____ The United States has 50 states.

Using Emotional Words

Some words are used to arouse emotions and stir feelings. Writers who want to make you think a certain way choose their words carefully to influence your thinking. You may suspect the authors are shading the facts to persuade you to their points of view when they use such words as *overwhelmingly*, *savagely*, *shocking*, *brutal*, *plunge*, and *destroy*.

CR Exercise 8

In each of the following sentences there is a blank space. Choose one of the three words following each sentence to complete the sentence. Place the letter of the word most likely to arouse the reader's emotions in the blank beside the number of the statement.

1. _____ The Club Room had been painted a _____ yellow.
   a. bright
   b. shining
   c. glaring

2. _____ The whole idea is _____ .
   a. foolish
   b. absurd
   c. grotesque

3. _____ I am _____ .
   a. terrified
   b. afraid
   c. frightened

4. _____ Bring me the note _____ .
   a. now
   b. instantly
   c. immediately

5. _____ Winters in Maine are _____ .
   a. cold
   b. freezing
   c. chilly

6. _____ The housewife _____ the walls until they were spotless.
   a. cleaned
   b. scrubbed
   c. washed

7. _____ He _____ into the icy water.
   a. leaped
   b. plunged
   c. jumped

8. _____ What is that _____ smell?
   a. awful
   b. horrible
   c. bad

9. _____ When she discovered that her priceless vase had been smashed, she was _____ .
   a. upset
   b. distraught
   c. dismayed

10. _____ The keynote speaker was _____ .
    a. dynamic
    b. strong
    c. powerful

CR Exercise 9

In the following statements the writer uses emotional words to persuade the reader to think positively or negatively about something. If the writer intends the reader's reaction to be positive, write P in the blank space. If the reaction is intended to be negative, write N. Underline the emotional words or phrases.

1. _____ Her beliefs are ridiculous and old-fashioned.

2. _____ Beagles are excellent house pets and make the best hunting dogs.

3. _____ This scheme to raise money is fraudulent.

4. _____ Gary Olsen is a skinny, emaciated fellow with dull hair.

5. _____ We wasted an hour listening to his silly chatter.

6. _____ She delighted us with her reflections on life during the 1950s.

7. _____ It is dreadful to have to get up early in the morning when you are still exhausted and need to sleep longer.

8. _____ The painting was filled with bright, glowing colors.

9. _____ The garish colors were a jumbled mess on the canvas.

10. _____ Like all good Americans, George Patel believes in justice for all.

CR Exercise 10

List the words and phrases from the following article that appeal to the reader's emotions. If they are intended to create positive feelings, write P. If they are used to create negative feelings, write N. Use your best judgment.

After 20 years of intense environmentalism in the United States, I'm struck by a common perception of little or no progress. . . . If anything, the sense of malaise and crisis has deepened over two decades. . . . The latest environmental outcry has apocalyptic overtones. The earth is warming, polar ice caps may melt, seas will rise and inundate coastal cities, and fertile plains could become barren deserts. With such alarm bells sounding, it is difficult to sort through the scientific evidence to see what is happening and why.[6]

_____ _____
_____ _____
_____ _____
_____ _____

CR Exercise 11

List the words and phrases from the following article that appeal to the reader's emotions. If they are intended to create positive feelings, write P. If they are used to create negative feelings, write N. Use your best judgment.

Flight is, for many passengers, a truly frightening experience. Having one's flesh hurtling along thousands of feet from the ground at hundreds of miles an hour makes the whole affair seem somewhat unnatural, if not downright suicidal. Volunteers to ride along would dwindle to a handful if it were not for one important ingredient: the implicit understanding that the pilot in command possesses both calm hands and a cool wit.

The ability to frighten passengers is certainly not a goal of the competent pilot; yet all too often, he accomplishes precisely that. It takes much less than an obviously hairy incident to open the floodgates of fear in a non-pilot. All that is required is just a little carelessness on the part of the captain.

Analogies that provide captains with godlike qualities are observations not to be taken lightly. From the passenger's seat, it appears that the pilot could cut everyone down like some terrible swift sword with a flip of a hand—an observation that is, in essence, reasonably accurate. The fact remains that "fear" is generated by the mind of the beholder, and a passenger's own opinion that disaster is imminent is enough to scare him half to death. The flight may be perfect from a safety standpoint, but the pilot must convince the passengers of that fact. Don't forget, however, that the non-pilot's ignorance can be an asset if you are in a bad situation and you're the only one who knows it. When a pilot puts unsuspecting passengers in an airplane, he has given himself an additional job. Besides the flying, he must watch over his riders and take reasonable steps to preserve their peace of mind.[7]

Words and phrases P or N

_____ _____
_____ _____
_____ _____

_____	_____
_____	_____
_____	_____
_____	_____
_____	_____
_____	_____
_____	_____
_____	_____
_____	_____
_____	_____
_____	_____
_____	

Impact of Slogans

Clever combinations of words, chosen for their emotional appeal, are used as slogans. These words may say little or actually be misleading, but their constant repetition makes an impression on people's minds. Without understanding their real meanings, people begin to support causes or buy products as a result of identifying their needs with these slogans.

Catchy phrases have been used by politicians and advertisers to persuade people to follow their wishes. Slogans have even been used to elect presidents. Hoover promised the voters "two chickens in every pot and a car in every garage." Supporters of Coolidge urged voters to "Keep cool with Coolidge," and Eisenhower probably won votes by using the slogan "I like Ike." History has been changed by such slogans as "Let them eat cake," "Taxation without representation is tyranny," and "Remember the Maine." "Uncle Sam Wants You!" may have persuaded some young men to join the armed services, while "Yankee go home" stirred feelings of resentment against American troops stationed overseas. Ecologists have used the slogan "Give a hoot—don't pollute." People buy products because they react to such slogans as "breakfast of champions" and "It's the real thing."

Think critically about slogans before you allow them to influence your behavior. What are they really saying? Are there facts to support the claims? What is the slogan trying to make you do? Before accepting a cause or product because of its slogan, investigate the subject intelligently and make your decision based on facts.

Awareness of Faulty Logic

Unwarranted assumptions often lead readers to accept false information. An assumption is a statement that is taken for granted or accepted as truth without proof or demonstration. Many statements are based on assumptions that are not necessarily true. If the assumption is not true, then the statement based on the assumption is probably also false. Therefore, before accepting the statement, examine the assumption to see if it is valid.

Assumptions may be used to introduce a statement or to justify a statement that has just been made. Sometimes they are easily recognized, and other times they are concealed within the statement. The following sentence contains an assumption followed by a statement based on that assumption. "Since we are a nation of sheep, a powerful leader can shape the minds of all people within the country." The assumption is that we are a nation of sheep and, therefore, will follow any powerful leader without thinking for ourselves. Since there is no real evidence to support this assumption, it cannot be considered as absolute truth. The clause that follows is based on the assumption. Because the assumption is unfounded, the statement that follows it has no justification and cannot be considered a fact.

CR Exercise 12

Read the following statements and identify the assumptions by underlining the part of the sentence that states the assumption.

1. Since all politicians are crooked, Joe decided not to enter the primary.

2. Latin is too difficult for most students to learn so it is no longer taught in the city schools.

3. I am not taking art because I can't do anything creative.

4. Donna Jenkins promised to build a new library when she is elected.

5. With a depression imminent, we won't buy a new car.

6. Since the stock will continue to increase in value, I bought 200 shares.

7. With morality at its lowest ebb, the church sponsored a crusade to retrieve sinners.

8. The coach's poor judgment was responsible for our defeat.

9. The concert on the mall was canceled because it is going to rain tonight.

10. Since girls are not well coordinated, they should not be permitted to play Little League baseball.

Some writers present only one side of an issue to promote their beliefs and conceal the opposing point of view. Uninformed readers may be persuaded by the writer's arguments. If they had known all the facts, however, they might have disagreed with the writer.

If you are unfamiliar with an issue, you may find it difficult to know if both sides have been presented fairly. Your best defense is to read more than one account of the subject and to select articles from publications that represent different views. Keep an open mind as you read, and look for possible opposing arguments.

CR Exercise 13

Read the following article. List the advantages and disadvantages of living in a big city as presented in this article.

Big-City Life

Living in the heart of the city is exciting! After dark the bright lights and the sounds of traffic in the street summon the city dweller to the night life found in the cafes and clubs. Cultural events with internationally known celebrities appeal to some, while professional sports teams attract others.

People who live in cities need not rely on cars for transportation, since taxis and public transportation are readily available. City dwellers have a larger selection of high-paying jobs than people who live in small towns. They also have access to leading universities staffed by world-renowned scholars. Special services are available through schools for exceptional children and medical specialists of all kinds.

The city offers many more attractions than the small town. There are museums, zoos, and amusement parks. Well-kept city parks provide opportunities to relax among flower beds, fountains, and tall trees. Shoppers can go from boutiques to discount stores to large department stores; the selection is abundant. Big-city living provides diversity and opportunities for everyone.

Advantages   *Disadvantages*

CR Exercise 14

Read the following article. List the advantages and disadvantages of living in a small town as presented in this article.

Small-Town Life

Life in a small town offers an escape from high-pressured, fast-paced city living. The air is clean and free from industrial pollutants. Nights are calm and peaceful with starlit skies overhead. As you walk down the streets of a small town, people greet you and call you by name. Neighbors gather at backyard cookouts and drop in for coffee.

In small towns people can drive to work quickly, without needing to cover the distances or cope with the traffic congestion of big cities. Downtown parking is rarely a problem. The entire community supports local sports events, theater productions, and cultural activities. Citizens become actively involved in the planning and operation of these events, instead of leaving them to professionals.

A small town is a good place to raise children. Because there is less crime than in the big cities, children are not often led astray. Scouting and organized sports keep them productively occupied, and woods and fields provide them with space to run and play. Small-town living is a wholesome, satisfying way of life.

Advantages   *Disadvantages*

If you listed only the information given in the articles, you found that each article presented only one side of the situation. No disadvantages were given in either case. If you read each article with an open mind, looking for opposing arguments, you could probably identify some of the disadvantages of each life style for yourself. When you are reading critically, suspect any article of being biased if the writer presents only one side of the situation.

In addition to using unfounded assumptions and presenting one-sided arguments, writers may employ faulty cause-and-effect reasoning. The reader should be careful to observe whether the effect is really based upon the cause, or whether the effect simply happened to occur after the cause. Sometimes it is difficult to be sure that the reason given actually produced the result. The following statement is faulty cause-and-effect reasoning. "Because a black cat crossed his path, the man lost his wallet." The black cat crossing his path had nothing to do with the man's losing his wallet.

CR Exercise 15

Read the following sentences to determine if the stated cause actually contributed to the effect. Write T if it probably did. Write F if there is no apparent relationship, if the relationship is uncertain, or if more information is needed for a decision.

1. _____ The rain caused the baseball game to be canceled.

2. _____ Because the couple dated on Friday the thirteenth, they broke up.

3. _____ He won the election because of his campaign promises.

4. _____ The house was destroyed by the fire.

5. _____ His girl friend's notes enabled him to pass the test.

6. _____ The blizzard caused the schools to be closed for five days.

7. _____ Because she dreamed of a wedding, the next day her boy friend proposed to her.

8. _____ Because he moved into the dormitory, his grade point average dropped.

9. _____ The candidate lost the election because a recent survey revealed a decline in her popularity.

10. _____ The large elm tree in front of the library died from the Dutch elm disease.

11. _____ As prices rise, unemployment increases.

12. _____ The arrival of a new president caused the company's profits to rise dramatically.

13. _____ Because she never graduated from college, she never amounted to anything.

14. _____ Foreign car sales increased as a result of the introduction of the Edsel.

15. _____ It won't work because it's never been done before.

16. _____ It must still be good since it has worked for twenty years.

17. _____ The test was unfair because I studied for it all night and didn't pass.

Detecting Propaganda Techniques

Propaganda is a way of spreading beliefs or opinions to further causes or damage them. It is used to persuade people to accept certain ideas and to act in certain ways. It may be used for either good or bad purposes. Frequently, propaganda misleads the public through half-truths, emotional words, and various other deceptive techniques. On the other hand, propaganda often provides useful information and is desirable. Most people agree that protecting their health and promoting worthwhile organizations are good purposes for propaganda.

Examples of persuasive techniques used by widely recognized organizations are given below. Each is a form of propaganda that is designed to appeal to the reader in a special way. Read the following paragraph on what Scouting does for a boy. How many positive words and phrases have been used to make you feel that the Scouts deserve your support?

Scouting develops a boy's initiative, self-reliance, leadership, good work habits, and all-round responsibility. It spurs his inner drive to excel. A boy also learns to care about other people, to respect them, and to want to help them. In total, Scouting prepares a boy to be a good citizen who asks "What can I give?" not "What can I get?"[8]

As you read the next paragraph, notice how the writer refers to doctors and surveys by the U.S. Public Health Service and the National Opinion Research Center. How does the writer use these specialists and organizations to persuade you to quit smoking?

Take It from the Doctors

They say cigarettes are lethal. And they ought to know. Your doctor will tell you that smoking can no longer be considered a gamble. Every cigarette smoker is injured in some way by this habit—though not to the same degree. And doctors aren't just talking. Many of them are taking actions: 100,000 doctors have already quit smoking cigarettes, an estimate based on surveys by the U.S. Public Health Service and the National Opinion Research Center.[9]

In the next paragraph, notice how the writer tries to persuade you to donate your blood by appealing to your desire to feel needed.

Every minute every day someone needs blood. It may be a friend or a relative. It may be someone you will never know. The need can be met only by persons like yourself, for this magic medicine can come only from people. There is no substitute.[10]

Although most people are aware of propaganda, they often fail to recognize it or realize how much it affects their thinking. Their gullibility prevents them from reading critically and asking questions about what the message really is. When they read "doctors recommend," they do not ask how many doctors were questioned, if the doctors recommend other brands as well, or if the doctors are a representative sample. If a product is "faster acting," they do not ask faster acting than what, how much faster acting, or whether it is more important to be faster acting than effective.

To avoid being persuaded against your wishes, you should be familiar with certain types of propaganda that are used frequently. Some writers quote portions of statements out of context, thus giving the opposite view from what was originally intended. For example, an advertisement for a play might contain the quotation "a brilliant, witty comedy" associated with a reviewer's name. Actually, the reviewer's entire statement may have been, "Instead of being a brilliant, witty comedy, the play was an utter disaster."

Seven specific types of undesirable propaganda techniques have been identified by the Institute for Propaganda Analysis. Familiarity with these techniques should help you distinguish between propaganda that provides information and propaganda that uses devious methods of persuasion. Descriptions and examples of the seven techniques follow.

1. Name calling. This method associates individuals or products with words that have negative connotations. Examples of words used in name calling are *slacker, unAmerican, scrawny, poor sport,* and *weak.* These words are used instead of facts to get the desired reaction from the reader.

Example: Senator Jones is a two-faced politician.

2. Glittering generality. Glittering generalities are vague phrases with positive connotations that convince the reader to accept or approve without examining the evidence. They may be slogans or generalizations that use such words as *American, Uncle Sam, freedom, truth, motherhood,* and *beauty.*

Example: Aaron Grissom believes in peace with honor.

3. Transfer. The transfer method of propaganda relates powerful symbols to people, products, or ideas. When the two are associated, the reader transfers his reactions to the new idea. Transfer symbols include the opinions of experts, the Flag, respected individuals, and prestigious organizations.

Example: Leading medical men claim Calso Capsules will cure the common cold.

4. Testimonial. This technique uses a prominent person, such as a movie star or athlete, to endorse a product or idea. If the reader admires the person, he or she may also wish to use the product, regardless of its true merits. Often the prominent person is being paid for his remarks, and what he says may not represent his true feelings.

Example: Superstar Diane Rogers says Cheewees are best for breakfast.

5. <u>Plain folks</u>. Politicians like to project a plain folks image in order to win the votes of the general public. By appearing as ordinary people, politicians imply that they are wholesome, good, and honest. Kissing babies, playing touch football, and riding tractors are examples of the plain folks approach.

Example: Bob Delgardie, candidate for mayor, was seen playing ball at the church picnic Saturday.

6. <u>Card stacking</u>. This method of propaganda tells only one side of a story in order to build a strong case for that point of view. Quotations are taken out of context; only part of the statistical data is presented; and half-truths are made to look like the complete truth. Only facts that support the concept are given, while none are given that damage it.

Example: This car is the latest thing in speed, power, and luxury.

7. <u>Bandwagon</u>. The bandwagon method gives the impression that everyone is buying a particular product or supporting a certain cause. Since many people want to be like everyone else, they may follow the crowd without thinking for themselves.

Example: All your friends are using Klenzo toothpaste. You try it too!

CR Exercise 16

Read the following sentences and decide which propaganda techniques they represent. Using the following code, place the appropriate letters in front of each sentence.

NC	Name calling
GG	Glittering generality
Tr	Transfer
Te	Testimonial
PF	Plain folks
CS	Card stacking
BW	Bandwagon

1. _____ Golden cigarettes last longer, taste better, use finer tobacco.

2. _____ Nine out of ten people use Gusto Shaving Cream.

3. _____ Cathy Butterfield, Olympic swimming champion, claims Formfit swimsuits are best.

4. _____ Buy new Blooze Soap in the giant, economy size.

5. _____ Twenty million Americans drink Golden Nectar tea. Why not you?

6. _____ Hi! I'm Hester Heatherstone. While I'm filming on location, I use Wonder-soft hand lotion to keep my hands smooth and soft.

7. _____ Surely you don't want to elect a slacker like Martin Schwartz!

8. _____ Senator Nakai rose to her position after having been a secretary.

9. _____ Ben Franklin Savings and Loan Association will help you save money!

10. _____ Leading physicians recommend taking Pilch Pills three times daily for increased vigor.

11. _____ An honest American, Richard Raves believes in freedom and love of all people.

12. _____ Our present student council president is a male chauvinist pig!

13. _____ Joan Bollinger, raised on a farm, wants to do what is best for the farmers.

14. _____ My opponent has shown himself to be narrow-minded and opinionated.

15. _____ Buy a Kwik-Kleen dishwasher—gets dishes cleaner, leaves no spots, has large capacity, and has more cleaning power.

16. _____ More people use Freshlips Mouthwash than any other.

17. _____ I'm Juan Garcia, pitcher for the Texas Stars. When I'm not pitching, I'm driving my new Speedster.

18. _____ John Carrington is clearly un-American in his views toward free speech.

19. _____ New Sheen dinnerware has attractive styling, a dishwasher resistant finish, and a sparkling shine.

20. _____ Senator Jones shook hands with the workers and kissed the babies.

21. _____ Beautiful girls use Frosty Hair Spray.

22. _____ The League of Voters supports Godfrey O'Hare for president.

23. _____ Everybody's dancing the Fling and Flop. Let us teach you how.

24. _____ Independent laboratory tests show Puresilk is best for your skin.

25. _____ Take the advice of Stan Stokely, track star: "Wear Whiz shoes!"

26. _____ Bill Tafoya is the laborer's friend.

27. _____ Buy the world's most advanced color television with instant push-button control. Beautifully made inside and out, this set offers every advantage.

28. _____ Vote for the referendum in order to give your children the kind of education they deserve in a free, independent society.

CR Exercise 17

Read the following possible advertisements. Make a check mark beside the ones that make use of obvious propaganda techniques.

_____ 1. The Mercury Messenger Service delivers your messages like a flash. Our messengers move on winged feet.

_____ 2. The Zippy Messenger Company offers 24-hour service. We guarantee that your message will be delivered within four hours, or your money will be refunded.

_____ 3. Mark Macho, all-professional football tackle, says, "You can always depend on Marv's Messengers to get there on time. I wouldn't trust anyone else."

_____ 4. Squeeky Sneakers are the shoes that everyone is buying. Don't be left out.

_____ 5. Runner Special tennis shoes have cushioned soles, sturdy arch supports, and tough canvas uppers. They are currently our most inexpensive track shoe. Come in and try some on.

_____ 6. Open a checking account with Bank of Midcity and receive 3% interest on your balance. You don't have to leave your money lying idle in our bank. And we are open 6 days a week for your convenience. Or simply use our bank-by-mail system. We wish to serve your needs.

_____ 7. Take it from a hometown boy like me, Dane Williams, this bank is a bank of the people. All of us appreciate you working folks who keep us going, because we are all working folks just like you. We'll take good care of your money.

CR Exercise 18

Study the explanatory material on propaganda. Then try to write an advertisement using one of the techniques described. Label your advertisement according to technique.

_____

_____

_____

_____

_____

Chapter Notes

1. Copyright, February 21, 1983, _U.S. News & World Report._

2. C. Steven Doremus, "Politics Leave Voters in the Cold."

3. C. Steven Doremus, "Involvement: Key to College Success."

4. John Shy, "What Happened? Or, Whose Version Do You Believe?" in Richard J. Sommers, ed., _U.S. Army Military History Research Collection, Vignettes of Military History,_ vol. I, October, 1976, p. 12.

5. Jack Lewis, "Environmental Problems: The Situation." _EPA Journal,_ vol. 14. November/December, 1988, pp. 27–29.

6. Excerpted from Bruce W. Karrh, "An Industry Official," _EPA Journal,_ November/December, 1988, p. 12.

7. Reprinted from the November, 1972 issue of _Flying Magazine,_ a publication of the Ziff-Davis Aviation Division.

8. "Questions Answered," reprinted by permission from Boy Scouts of America.

9. "Smoke Cigarettes? Why?" reprinted by permission from American Cancer Society, December, 1969.

10. "Life Preservers," reprinted by permission from Nashville Regional Red Cross Blood Center.

8 Content Area Reading

Jenny spotted Kim across the quad and waved excitedly. "Come here quick!" she called.

Kim hurried over to join her friend. "What's up?" she asked.

"There's a big sale going on in Thurston this afternoon. Fifty percent off all kinds of merchandise, including books. I know how much you love a book sale. A bunch of us are going to run over there now."

"How far away is Thurston?" Kim asked. "We have that big test at six o-clock, and it counts thirty percent of our grade for the course."

"Oh, it must not be far. See how close it looks on the map on this flier," Jenny said.

"Jenny, look here," Kim said, pointing to the corner of the map. "An inch equals 100 miles. Thurston is 3/4 of an inch from here. That's 75 miles. We'd never be able to get there and back in time for the test. Count me out."

"Really? How'd you think to check that? It looked so close."

"We've been talking about map reading in class. Dr. Kain mentioned that scale is an important thing that people often don't learn how to use. We practiced using the scale on a couple of maps in the textbook. I guess it is useful to know, isn't it?"

Introduction

Reading material in content area textbooks is very different from reading fiction. One difference is that in content area reading it is highly important to remember main ideas and details as you read. In reading fiction, on the other hand, retention of specific facts is relatively unimportant. Another difference is that facts are generally presented in rapid succession in content area materials, with understanding of later facts depending upon an adequate grasp of earlier ones. As a result, content area materials must be read carefully. Use of a study-reading procedure, such as SQ3R or SQRQCQ (explained in Chapter 2: Study Skills and Spelling), may be necessary for adequate understanding and retention of the material.

Specialized Vocabulary

Each content area presents you with specialized vocabulary. This vocabulary must be mastered before the content can be properly understood. The vocabulary problems in content area reading are of two types: familiar words used in unfamiliar ways and difficult specialized terms. You must be ready to cope with both types of vocabulary problems. A look at the specialized vocabulary problems of several fields follows.

Social Studies

The area of social studies includes such disciplines as history, government, economics, sociology, anthropology, and geography. All of these disciplines present special vocabulary problems.

Many words that you already have in your vocabulary may appear in social studies readings with new meanings. You must be able to determine these meanings by using both the context clues in the material and the dictionary.

In the following exercise, some of the terms may have unfamiliar meanings in social studies materials even though they have common meanings that are familiar to you. See if you can choose the correct meaning for each term. Then check your understanding of some specialized terms from various areas of social studies in the second exercise.

CA Exercise 1

In each of the following sentences, choose the correct meaning for the underlined term. Place the letter of the correct meaning in the blank beside the number of each item.

_____ 1. The workers at the plant were dissatisfied with their working conditions so they went on strike.
   a. act of quitting work
   b. act of hooking a fish
   c. act of knocking down all ten bowling pins with one ball

_____ 2. The settlers moved steadily across the <u>plain</u>.
  a. level land
  b. homely-looking land
  c. uncomplicated trail

_____ 3. The people were not satisfied with the tyranny of the king, and this dissatisfaction was the basis for a violent <u>revolution</u>.
  a. motion of spinning on an axis
  b. a gradual change over a period of time
  c. rebellion

_____ 4. It is against the law to discriminate against U.S. citizens because of their <u>race</u>.
  a. a contest
  b. a burst of speed
  c. a division of humankind having certain traits in common

_____ 5. The Appalachian <u>range</u> extends from Quebec to Alabama.
  a. a chain of mountain peaks
  b. to wander
  c. a stove for cooking

_____ 6. My uncle finally decided to <u>run</u> for mayor.
  a. to move rapidly
  b. to take part in an election
  c. to flow

_____ 7. The revolutionary felt that he could <u>rule</u> more effectively than the king.
  a. to govern
  b. to mark with straight lines
  c. to restrain

CA Exercise 2

In the list below, choose the correct meaning for each of the terms. Place the letter of the correct meaning in the blank beside the number of each item. Try to do the items without aid first. Then consult your dictionary to check your first reactions.

_____ 1. amendment
  a. a change
  b. a legal case
  c. a plan of action

_____ 2. century
  a. an amount of money
  b. the distance covered in most horse races
  c. one hundred years

_____ 3. culture
   a. a system of learned behavior patterns typical of a particular society
   b. a religious sect
   c. an unsuccessful invention

_____ 4. decade
   a. deterioration
   b. ten years
   c. a dispute

_____ 5. democracy
   a. disbanding of troops
   b. absence of laws
   c. government in which the people have the power

_____ 6. minority
   a. a group of people who work in the mines
   b. a group that has less than the controlling number of votes
   c. a group of people working in a political campaign

_____ 7. mores
   a. customs
   b. gruesome activities
   c. prevailing moods

_____ 8. prehistoric
   a. able to grasp
   b. a warning
   c. before the time of written history

_____ 9. primitive
   a. resembling people, things, or actions from the earliest ages
   b. a mammal
   c. first in importance

_____ 10. treaty
   a. free entertainment
   b. a formally signed agreement between two countries
   c. a narration of events

Natural Science

The natural sciences include such areas as biology, chemistry, earth science, and physics. As in social studies, the reading problems caused by specialized vocabulary can be enormous in the sciences. The following exercises will help you check your knowledge of science vocabulary.

CA Exercise 3

In each of the following sentences, choose the correct meaning for the underlined term. Place the letter of the correct meaning in the blank beside the number of each item.

_____ 1. The disease caused his muscle <u>tissue</u> to deteriorate.
   a. a group of cells in a plant or animal that has a special function
   b. paper squares
   c. a web

_____ 2. Many singers avoided that song because of the <u>pitch</u> of the last note.
   a. the highness or lowness of a sound
   b. a toss or throw
   c. the degree of slope

_____ 3. This process must be carried out in a partial <u>vacuum</u>.
   a. a device used to clean floors and carpets
   b. a gap
   c. a space which has had all or most of the air removed

_____ 4. The boy's mother made him gargle with a saline <u>solution</u>.
   a. the process of solving a problem
   b. a mixture in which the molecules of a dissolved substance are scattered among the molecules of the solvent
   c. the answer to a problem

_____ 5. An alkali is a very strong <u>base</u>.
   a. a starting point
   b. a chemical compound that turns litmus paper blue
   c. the number which is the foundation of a mathematical table

_____ 6. You may think it strange, but air is also classified as <u>matter</u>.
   a. something that is worthy of account
   b. a reason or cause
   c. something that has weight and occupies space

_____ 7. The <u>revolution</u> of the earth around the sun takes approximately 365 days.
   a. a complete change of circumstances
   b. a violent change in government brought about by the governed
   c. the movement of a body around a point in such a way that it returns to its initial position relative to the point

CA Exercise 4

In the list below, choose the correct meaning for each one of the terms. Place the letter of the correct meaning in the blank beside the number of each item. Try to do the items without aid first. Then consult your dictionary to check your first reactions.

_____ 1. Our nickel coin is made from an <u>alloy</u>.
    a. a substance made up of two or more metals united to form a compound
    b. a machine used to stamp out images in metal
    c. a person who designs and produces metal coins and medallions

_____ 2. The human ear can pick up sounds over a range of 130 <u>decibels</u>.
    a. a device that makes a ringing sound
    b. a unit used for measuring the loudness of sounds
    c. the distance at which a person is capable of hearing a very soft sound

_____ 3. After being lost on the desert, he was suffering from <u>dehydration</u>.
    a. badly burned skin
    b. loss of water
    c. lack of orientation

_____ 4. The dodo is now <u>extinct</u>.
    a. no longer living
    b. bad smelling
    c. unusual

_____ 5. <u>Friction</u> between the toy car and the floor caused the car to slow down.
    a. rollers
    b. carpet
    c. rubbing of one object against another

_____ 6. The <u>lava</u> poured out of the volcano.
    a. melted rock
    b. smoke
    c. poison gas

_____ 7. The <u>molecules</u> in water are more active than those in ice.
    a. bacteria
    b. dangerous microorganisms
    c. the smallest part of an element or compound that has the chemical properties of that element or compound

_____ 8. Many people are afraid of all <u>reptiles</u>.
   a. vertebrates that nourish their young with milk
   b. vertebrates that lay eggs and crawl on their bellies or on short legs
   c. gnawing mammals

_____ 9. Man belongs to the <u>species</u> "homo sapiens."
   a. a group of plants or animals that have common characteristics and breed exclusively in their group
   b. a group of animals that have superior intelligence
   c. a group of animals that live in a special area

_____ 10. Ethyl alcohol is a <u>volatile</u> liquid.
   a. fermented
   b. easily vaporized
   c. dangerous

Mathematics

Mathematics also presents vocabulary difficulties, even though many people do not think of vocabulary as being a problem in this field. Special symbols create a special vocabulary problem in mathematics. Even the reading of numerals themselves may cause difficulties. As is true in all of the content areas, multiple-meaning words often have special mathematical meanings that you may not know. The following exercises will help you to check your knowledge of mathematics vocabulary and symbols. Be sure to study the ones that you miss so that you will know them the next time you encounter them.

CA Exercise 5

Choose the correct meaning of each mathematical sentence. Place the letter of the correct meaning on the line before each question number.

_____ 1. $c(a + b) = ac + bc$
   a. The sum of a and b multiplied by c is equal to the sum of the products of a times c and b times c.
   b. The sum of c, a, and b is equal to the sum of ac and bc.
   c. When ca is added to b, the sum is equal to the sum of the products of ac and bc.

_____ 2. $a > b$
   a. a is less than b
   b. a is greater than b
   c. a and b are equal in value

_____ 3. $a < b$
    a. a is less than b
    b. a is greater than b
    c. a and b are equal in value

_____ 4. $a : b : : c : d$
    a. a plus b equals c plus d
    b. a times b equals c times d
    c. a has the same relationship to b as c has to d

_____ 5. $\sqrt{4} = 2$
    a. 4 divided by 2 equals 2
    b. the square root of 4 equals 2
    c. not given

_____ 6. Draw $AB \perp CD$
    a. Draw a square $ABCD$.
    b. Draw a rectangle $ABCD$.
    c. Draw the line segment AB perpendicular to the line segment CD.

CA Exercise 6

Match the metric units on the left to their equivalents on the right by placing the letter of the entry on the right beside the number of the correct metric unit.

	Metric Unit	Equivalent
_____	1. 1 centimeter	a. 0.62137 miles
_____	2. 1 meter	b. 10 centimeters
_____	3. 1 kilometer	c. 10 decigrams
_____	4. 1 decimeter	d. 264.18 gallons
_____	5. 1 liter	e. 0.3937 inches
_____	6. 1 gram	f. 100 square meters
_____	7. 1 kiloliter	g. 0.9081 dry quart
_____	8. 1 are	h. 3.29 feet

CA Exercise 7

Match the metric unit on the left with its abbreviation on the right by placing the letter of the abbreviation beside the number of the correct metric unit.

Metric Unit		*Abbreviation*	
_____	1. millimeter	a.	l
_____	2. centimeter	b.	cm
_____	3. meter	c.	kg
_____	4. kilometer	d.	mm
_____	5. are	e.	cl
_____	6. hectare	f.	ha
_____	7. liter	g.	m
_____	8. gram	h.	km
_____	9. kilogram	i.	g
_____	10. centiliter	j.	a

CA Exercise 8

In the list of numbers below, choose the correct meaning of each number. Place the letter of the correct meaning in the blank beside the number of each item.

_____ 1. 1001
    a. one hundred one
    b. one thousand one
    c. not given

_____ 2. 10,700
    a. ten thousand seven hundred
    b. one hundred seven thousand
    c. one thousand seven hundred

_____ 3. 1,000,000
    a. one thousand
    b. one hundred thousand
    c. one million

_____ 4. 100,000
     a. one thousand
     b. one hundred thousand
     c. one million

_____ 5. 70,500
     a. seventy thousand five hundred
     b. seven hundred five thousand
     c. seven thousand five hundred

_____ 6. 1,100,000
     a. eleven thousand
     b. one million one hundred thousand
     c. one thousand one hundred

_____ 7. 44,400
     a. four hundred forty-four
     b. four thousand four hundred
     c. forty-four thousand four hundred

_____ 8. 7,750
     a. seventy-seven thousand fifty
     b. seven hundred seventy-five
     c. seven thousand seven hundred fifty

CA Exercise 9

In each of the following sentences, choose the correct meaning for the underlined term. Place the letter of the correct meaning in the blank beside the number of each item.

_____ 1. Most of the arithmetic you will do is concerned with numbers in <u>base</u> ten.
     a. a starting point
     b. a chemical compound that turns the dye litmus blue
     c. the number that is the foundation of a number system in mathematics

_____ 2. In a division problem the <u>solution</u> is called the quotient.
     a. the process of solving a problem
     b. a mixture in which the molecules of a dissolved substance are scattered among the molecules of the solvent
     c. the answer to a problem

_____ 3. Four is the second <u>power</u> of two.
     a. the product obtained from multiplication of a number by itself
     b. degree of magnification
     c. electrical force or mechanical force

_____ 4. The two walls met at a ninety-degree <u>angle</u>.
   a. a figure that is formed when two straight lines meet at a single point
   b. a point of view
   c. a course that abruptly diverges from the original one

_____ 5. The fact remains: the earth is not a <u>sphere</u>.
   a. star
   b. a solid figure which has a curved surface with all points on the surface equally distant from the point within it that is called its center
   c. the environment in which a person exists

_____ 6. He did not notice the <u>exponent</u>, and, therefore, made a serious mistake.
   a. one who advocates
   b. a representative
   c. a symbol written above and to the right of a quantity that indicates the number of times the quantity is repeated as a factor

_____ 7. It is impossible to balance a <u>cone</u> on its apex.
   a. a solid figure with a circular base and sides that taper evenly to a point
   b. the fruit of some evergreen trees, composed of woody scales with a pair of naked seeds on each scale
   c. light-sensitive cells in the retina that react to color

CA Exercise 10

In each of the following sentences, choose the correct meaning for the underlined term. Place the letter of the correct meaning in the blank beside the number of each item.

_____ 1. He had fifteen tickets <u>minus</u> the two that he gave to his parents.
   a. in addition to
   b. less
   c. divided by

_____ 2. I want to know the length of the <u>perimeter</u> of the circle.
   a. the line that divides a figure into two equal parts
   b. the line from the center to the boundary line
   c. the outer boundary

_____ 3. She had fifty dollars <u>plus</u> the money from the sale of her guitar.
   a. including
   b. increased by
   c. less

_____ 4. The sign was shaped like a <u>trapezoid</u>.
   a. a plane figure that has four sides, two of which are parallel
   b. a device from which acrobats swing
   c. a line that intersects a system of lines

_____ 5. The teacher wants us to determine the length of the <u>radius</u> of this circle.
   a. the boundary line
   b. a line from the center of the circle to the curve
   c. a line that touches two points of the boundary of a circle

_____ 6. List the <u>axioms</u> used in the proof of each theorem.
   a. self-evident truths
   b. operations
   c. equations

_____ 7. The assignments included several <u>quadratic equations</u> to be solved.
   a. equations including two unknowns
   b. equations including unknowns raised to the second power, but to no higher power
   c. equations including unknowns raised to the fourth power

_____ 8. Referring to illustration 4, determine the length of the <u>hypotenuse</u>.
   a. the side of a triangle that is opposite a right angle
   b. any side of a triangle
   c. the height of a cone

_____ 9. Draw an <u>isosceles triangle</u>.
   a. a triangle containing a right angle
   b. a triangle with three unequal sides
   c. a triangle with two equal sides

_____ 10. <u>Square</u> the number five.
   a. multiply a number by itself
   b. multiply a number by two
   c. divide a number by itself

Health and Physical Education

Health materials present vocabulary difficulties, many of which are identical to some of those in the biological sciences. Some people may be surprised to discover, however, that physical education materials present some problems also. The following exercises will help you check your knowledge of health and physical education vocabulary.

CA Exercise 11

In each of the following sentences, choose the correct meaning for the underlined term. Place the letter of the correct meaning in the blank beside the number of each item.

_____ 1. The pupil is in the center of the <u>iris</u>.
   a. a rainbowlike play of colors
   b. the colored portion of the eye
   c. a flower

_____ 2. The pupil became larger as the available light decreased.
a. a scholar
b. the opening in the eye that allows light to enter
c. a boy or girl under the age of puberty

_____ 3. He has a ruptured disk.
a. semi-cartilaginous buffers between the vertebrae
b. a flat magnetic medium on which you can store computer programs and data
c. in flowers classified as composites, the central portion of the head

_____ 4. She had an attack of shingles.
a. pieces of wood used for covering roofs
b. signboards
c. an inflammatory skin disease that affects nerve endings

_____ 5. The pulp may die after decay penetrates to it.
a. living tissue in a tooth that contains blood vessels and nerves
b. a soft mass of vegetable matter
c. pulverized ore that has been mixed with water

_____ 6. We need a good guard to bring the ball down the court.
a. a person responsible for protecting property
b. a basketball player who is generally positioned away from the basket
c. a football player who is positioned next to the center in the line

_____ 7. He would be home free if he could get past the safety.
a. freedom from danger
b. a football player on defense who is deployed farthest behind the line, as the last line of defense
c. an act that results in the ball being declared dead behind the goal line of the offensive team

_____ 8. Jerry rolled a strike in the first frame.
a. score made when all bowling pins are knocked down on the first try for any turn
b. the result of swinging at a pitched ball and missing it
c. the result of having the fish take the bait

_____ 9. Try not to foul and give them the chance to make their free throws.
a. be offensive to the senses
b. cause illegal contact with an opposing player
c. be dishonest

_____ 10. The foul occurred when the ball was dead.
a. not alive
b. not in play
c. obsolete

CA Exercise 12

In the list below, choose the correct meaning for each of the terms. Place the letter of the correct meaning in the blank beside the number of each item. Try to do the items without aid first. Then consult your dictionary to check your first reactions.

_____ 1. cornea
    a. a hardened part of the epidermis of the skin
    b. a heart attack
    c. the transparent dome-shaped part of the coat of the eyeball that covers the pupil and iris

_____ 2. tumor
    a. an abnormal mass of tissue that develops from cells of pre-existing tissue
    b. a cancerous mass
    c. a damaged blood vessel

_____ 3. psychotherapy
    a. hypnotism
    b. treatment of mental disorders through mental and intellectual techniques, such as persuasion, psychoanalysis, and suggestion
    c. treatment given for imaginary illnesses (for example, sugar pills)

_____ 4. glaucoma
    a. a condition of the eye in which pressure builds up within the eye
    b. a state of unconsciousness
    c. a disease of the blood

_____ 5. antibiotics
    a. things that work against the body
    b. drugs that are effective against bacterial infections
    c. drugs that help lower blood pressure

_____ 6. tendon
    a. a band of fibrous connective tissue that joins a muscle with another part
    b. a tightly contracted muscle
    c. a delicate, easily injured part of the head

_____ 7. biceps
    a. the ball of the foot
    b. a part of the brain
    c. a large flexor muscle

_____ 8. sprain
    a. a minor break in a bone
    b. an injury in which blood vessels are ruptured
    c. an injury to a joint that involves torn ligaments

_____ 9. puck
   a. a flagrant foul
   b. a hard rubber disk used in ice hockey
   c. a knee protector

_____ 10. inning
   a. a division of a baseball game during which each side has a turn to bat
   b. a division of a football game into four equal parts
   c. a division of a basketball game into two equal parts

Personal Content Vocabulary Study

Not all vocabulary problems that you will encounter in your studies can be covered in this textbook. Therefore, you must develop a plan for dealing with difficult vocabulary that you find in your content textbooks. Here is one approach that you may wish to take:

1. Scan each content reading assignment for unfamiliar terms.

2. Make a list of the terms found.

3. Check to see if each term is defined in the context or has context clues that suggest its meaning. If so, try to state a meaning for the term, based on the context.

4. Check to see if the word contains one or more structure clues, such as a familiar prefix, suffix, or root word. Use your knowledge of the meaning of this word part or these word parts to help you determine the word's meaning. See if the meaning you construct fits the context that you studied earlier.

5. If context clues and structure clues point to the same likely meaning for the term, you have probably discovered the needed meaning and can proceed with the reading of the material without working further with this term. If the two types of clues do not agree or are not present at all, check to see if the term is listed in the book's glossary. If it is, choose the meaning that fits the context best from the meanings presented.

6. If the book has no glossary or the term is not listed in its glossary, look the term up in a dictionary. Choose the meaning that fits the context in which the term was found from among the meanings presented.

Following a procedure such as the one described here will help you to comprehend your textbook assignments better when you read them. It will also help you to do well on tests, for many test questions are based upon knowledge of vocabulary terms.

CA Exercise 13

For each class that you are currently taking, examine the most recent reading assignment for unfamiliar terminology. Follow the procedure described in this section to determine the meaning of each unfamiliar term identified. List the meaning that you determine from context, structural analysis, glossary, dictionary, or any combination of techniques for deciding upon word meaning. Together with one or more of your classmates, discuss the terms that you and they have located and defined. Help each other clarify meanings that may still be unclear. (Complete this assignment using your own paper to list terms and definitions. Your instructor may wish to collect your lists for analysis and discussion purposes, or you may simply share them with your peers.)

Reading Graphic Aids

Maps

In social studies courses and in some areas of science you will find it necessary to read maps. Some problems in mathematics courses may be based on maps also. When reading maps, you will need to be able to determine directions, locate natural and human-made features, understand map symbols, and interpret the scale of each map. To help you learn to use maps intelligently, a map of a nonexistent area will be analyzed.

When studying a map, first look for the title so that you will know what area is being represented. In the case of the first map in this section, the area represented is Sanders Island.

Most good maps will have a direction indicator. The direction indicator on the sample map is an arrow pointing toward the top of the map. If the point of that arrow is labeled "N," for north, east will be to the right; west will be to the left; and south will be at the bottom. Remember that the top of the map is not always north. North might be in the center of a map of the Arctic.

Parallels of latitude and meridians of longitude also can help you determine directions. Parallels of latitude are east–west lines that run parallel to the equator. Meridians of longitude are north–south lines that encircle the globe and meet at the poles.

To understand maps fully, you must be able to interpret the symbols included on them. An explanation of most symbols used on a map will be included in a section of the map referred to as the legend. Some map legends will not include such standard symbols as a dot, which represents a town, or a star, which represents a capital city. In the sample map, the legend contains only two symbols: dots to represent desert and inverted v's to represent mountains.

Since it is not practical to draw maps to the actual size of the area represented, the maps that you use have the areas reduced in size. The scale shows the relationship between a certain distance on the map and the corresponding distance on the earth. The scale on the map on page 211 is shown graphically and explained in words: "1 inch equals 40 miles." If two points on the map are one inch apart, therefore, you know that these two points are actually forty miles apart.

If you wish to describe the exact location of a point on the earth, you can do it by indicating the latitude and longitude. For instance, on the map on page 211, the city Tartac is located at 15 degrees north latitude and 27 degrees east longitude.

Now test your map reading skills with the following exercises.

CA Exercise 14

Study the map of Sanders Island pictured below, and answer the following questions about this map by placing the letter of the correct answer in the blank before the question number.

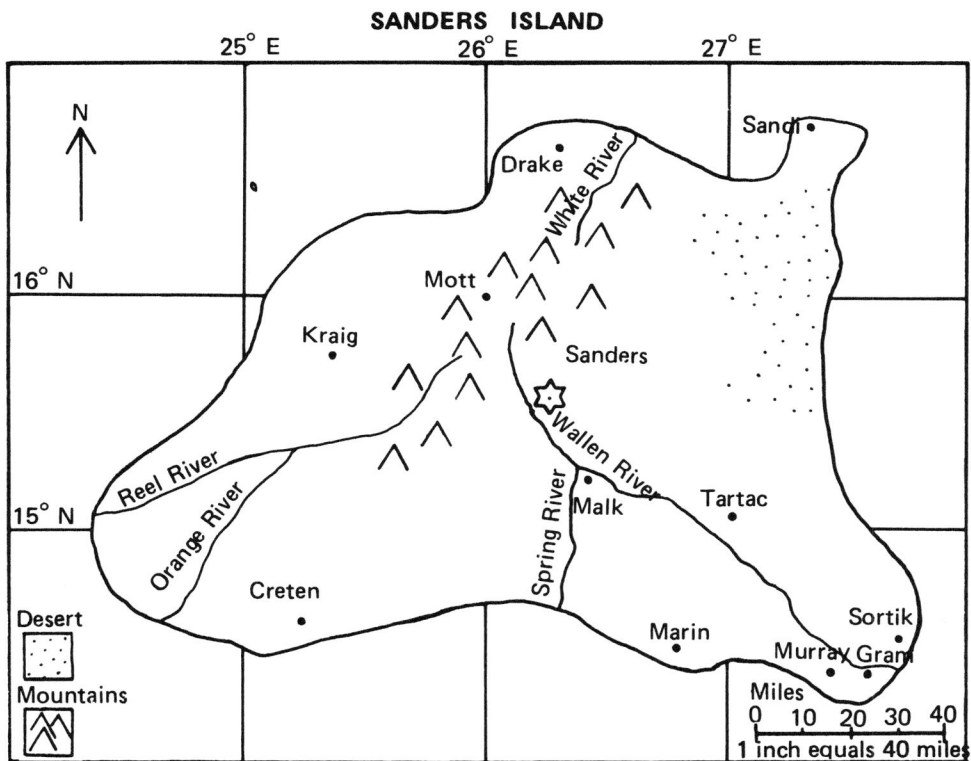

SANDERS ISLAND

_____ 1. Which of the following is farthest east?
   a. Creten
   b. Sortik
   c. Marin

_____ 2. Which of the following is farthest south?
   a. Tartac
   b. Drake
   c. Marin

_____ 3. Which city is located in the mountains?
   a. Mott
   b. Creten
   c. Gram

_____ 4. Which city is closest to the desert?
   a. Creten
   b. Gram
   c. Sandi

_____ 5. Which city is the capital city?
   a. Sanders
   b. Sandi
   c. Gram

_____ 6. Which city is closest to the Orange River?
   a. Creten
   b. Malk
   c. Drake

_____ 7. What is the distance from Marin to Gram?
   a. 20 miles
   b. 40 miles
   c. 60 miles

_____ 8. Which city is located at 16 degrees north latitude and 26 degrees east longitude?
   a. Drake
   b. Kraig
   c. Mott

_____ 9. What is the distance from Sanders to Malk?
   a. 20 miles
   b. 40 miles
   c. 60 miles

_____ 10. Which river flows past Gram?
   a. Spring River
   b. Orange River
   c. Wallen River

CA Exercise 15

Study the map below, and answer the questions about it by placing the letter of the correct answer in the blank before the question number.

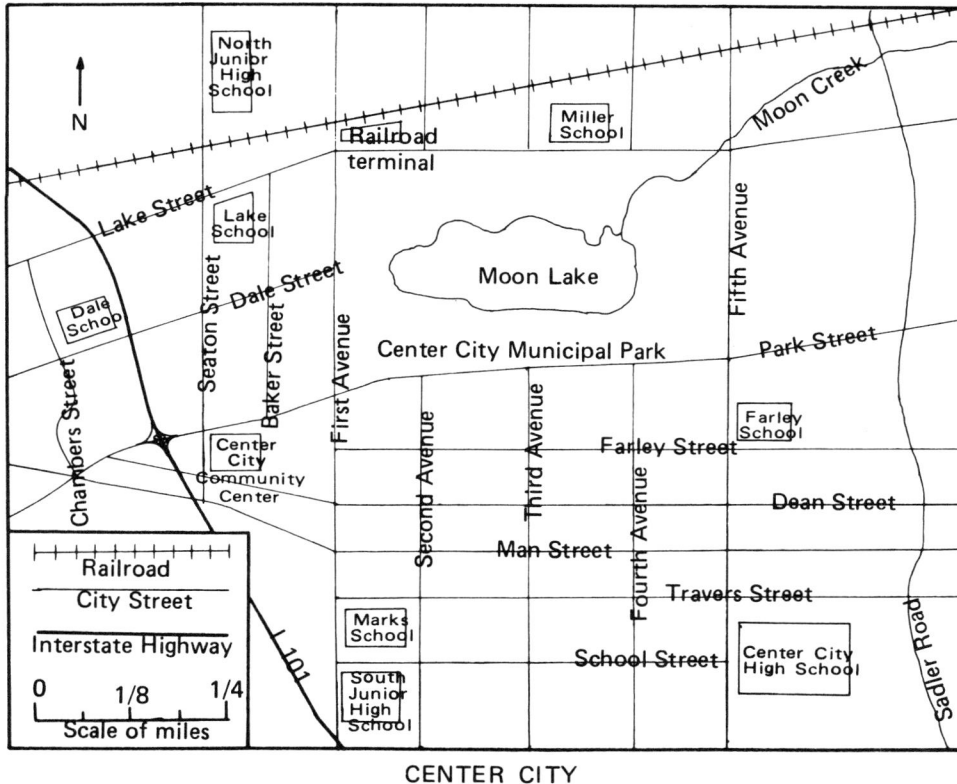

CENTER CITY

_____ 1. What area does this map represent?
   a. Park City
   b. Lake City
   c. Center City

_____ 2. Which school is farthest west?
   a. Dale School
   b. Center City High School
   c. Marks School

_____ 3. Which of the following schools is closest to a railroad track?
   a. North Junior High School
   b. Farley School
   c. South Junior High School

_____ 4. Which street has an interstate entrance and exit?
   a. Man Street
   b. Lake Street
   c. Park Street

_____ 5. Which of the following streets is not adjacent to the park?
   a. Lake Street
   b. Chambers Street
   c. Fifth Avenue

_____ 6. On which street are both North Junior High School and the Center City Community Center located?
   a. Seaton Street
   b. Dean Street
   c. Baker Street

_____ 7. Which of the following streets runs past the railroad terminal?
   a. Dale Street
   b. Lake Street
   c. Third Avenue

_____ 8. What is I 101?
   a. an interstate highway
   b. a railroad track
   c. a city street

_____ 9. How wide is Moon Lake at its widest point?
   a. ⅛ of a mile
   b. ½ of a mile
   c. 1 mile

_____ 10. If you are traveling on Dean Street, what is the distance between First Avenue and Third Avenue?
   a. ⅛ of a mile
   b. ¼ of a mile
   c. ½ of a mile

CA Exercise 16

Study the map below, and answer the questions about it by placing the letter of each correct answer in the blank before the question number.

FEDERAL RESERVE MAP OF THE UNITED STATES

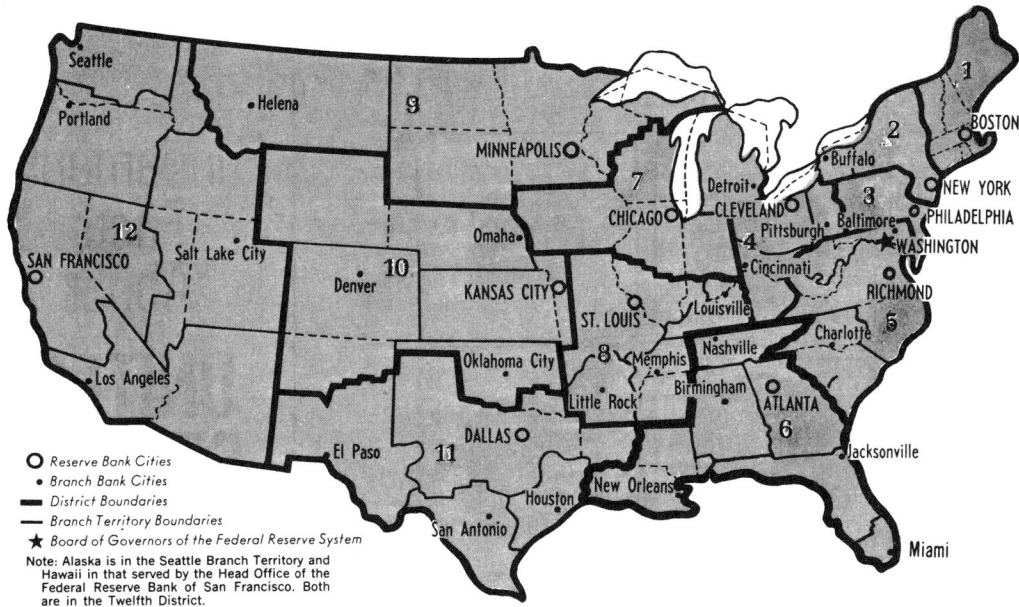

O Reserve Bank Cities
• Branch Bank Cities
▬ District Boundaries
— Branch Territory Boundaries
★ Board of Governors of the Federal Reserve System

Note: Alaska is in the Seattle Branch Territory and Hawaii in that served by the Head Office of the Federal Reserve Bank of San Francisco. Both are in the Twelfth District.

Source: *Fundamental Facts About UNITED STATES MONEY.* A Publication of the Federal Reserve Bank of Atlanta. Page 2.

_____ 1. What kind of information does this map contain?
  a. Locations of parts of the Federal Reserve System
  b. Zip code areas
  c. Time zones

_____ 2. Where is this map's legend?
  a. Across the top
  b. In the center
  c. In the lower left-hand corner

_____ 3. What is true of Denver?
  a. It is in District 12.
  b. It is a Reserve Bank City.
  c. It is a Branch Bank City.

_____ 4. What is true of Nashville?
   a. It is in District 6.
   b. It is in District 5.
   c. It is a Reserve Bank City.

_____ 5. What is true of Dallas?
   a. It is in District 8.
   b. It is a Reserve Bank City.
   c. It is a Branch Bank City.

_____ 6. How many Branch Territories are in District 12?
   a. 5
   b. 12
   c. 2

_____ 7. Where would you find the Board of Directors of the Federal Reserve System?
   a. Atlanta
   b. Dallas
   c. Washington, D.C.

Tables

Tables appear in some reading materials in all of the content areas. Reading tables may be difficult for you because so much information is contained in a relatively small space. Many facts or bits of information are presented in a concise list in a table. You must be able to extract from the list the information that you need.

In reading tables, as in reading maps, the title should be consulted first. The title will tell you what kinds of information the table contains. Headings of columns should also be noted. Using these headings as guides, you can then locate the specific information that you seek. As an example, examine the table below.

Band Concert Tickets Sold in the Years 1990–1993

Class	1990	1991	1992	1993
Freshman	50	61	44	49
Sophomore	57	53	75	38
Junior	52	66	51	89
Senior	191	201	193	190
Total School	350	381	363	366

If you want to find out how many tickets were sold by the junior class in 1991, first you look under the heading "class" until you find the entry "Junior." Then you locate the column labeled "1991." You look at the number in the column labeled "1991" that is directly across from the entry "Junior." In this case, you will find the number "66" at the intersection of the "1991" column and the "Junior" row. Therefore, you know that 66 tickets were sold by the junior class in 1991. Now try the following exercises to see if you really understand how to read tables.

CA Exercise 17

In the table used as an example on page 216, find the answers to the following questions. Place the letter of the correct answer in the blank beside the number of each question.

_____ 1. How many tickets were sold by the freshman class in 1993?
     a. 61
     b. 38
     c. 49
     d. 366

_____ 2. Which class sold the most tickets in 1992?
     a. Freshman
     b. Sophomore
     c. Junior
     d. Senior

_____ 3. Which class sold the fewest tickets in 1991?
     a. Freshman
     b. Sophomore
     c. Junior
     d. Senior

_____ 4. In which year were the total ticket sales the largest?
     a. 1990
     b. 1991
     c. 1992
     d. 1993

_____ 5. The tickets being sold were for what event?
     a. Bake Sale
     b. Junior-Senior Prom
     c. Band Concert
     d. Talent Show

CA Exercise 18

Study the table below. Then answer the questions following the table by placing the letter of the correct answer in the blank beside the number of each question.

Donations to Charities by Salaried Employees in Dollars

Charity	1990	1991	1992	1993
United Fund	1760	2000	2170	2155
March of Dimes	500	460	390	400
Easter Seals	125	100	120	105
Heart Fund	190	210	185	125
Boy's Town	50	0	0	25

_____ 1. What group made the donations shown in the table?
   a. Members of management
   b. Hourly workers
   c. Salaried employees
   d. Unemployed dependents

_____ 2. In what units are the donations listed?
   a. Cents
   b. Dollars
   c. Hundreds of dollars
   d. Thousands of dollars

_____ 3. What years are covered by the table?
   a. 1989–1991
   b. 1990–1993
   c. 1991–1994
   d. 1992–1994

_____ 4. Which of the following charities is not included in the table?
   a. United Fund
   b. UNICEF
   c. March of Dimes
   d. Heart Fund

_____ 5. How much money was given to the March of Dimes in 1990?
   a. $125
   b. $2170
   c. $500
   d. $460

_____ 6. How much money was given to the United Fund in 1991?
   a. $2000
   b. $2170
   c. $210
   d. $25

_____ 7. How much money was given to the Heart Fund in 1993?
   a. $185
   b. $105
   c. $125
   d. $120

_____ 8. In what year was the most money given to the March of Dimes?
   a. 1990
   b. 1991
   c. 1992
   d. 1993

_____ 9. What charity received no donations in 1992?
   a. March of Dimes
   b. Easter Seals
   c. Heart Fund
   d. Boy's Town

_____ 10. What charity received the largest donation every year?
   a. United Fund
   b. March of Dimes
   c. Easter Seals
   d. Heart Fund

CA Exercise 19

Study the table below. Then answer the questions following the table by placing the letter of the correct answer in the blank beside the number of each question.

TIME	MONDAY	TUESDAY	WEDNESDAY	THURSDAY	FRIDAY
	Classroom Training Schedule **Seasonal Police Officers** **Stone Harbor, N.J., Police**				
8:00 A.M. to 8:50 A.M.	Environmental Concerns	Patrol Operations	Motor Vehicle Stops—Criminal and Traffic	Handling the Juvenile Offender	Radio Communications Systems
	Table of Organization	Motor-Foot Traffic Marine			
9:00 A.M. to 9:50 A.M.	Policy—Rules & Regs	Investigative Division	The Drunk Driver	Crimes in Progress	Police Reports
		Investigations, Raids, Crime Prevention			
10:10 A.M. to 11:00 A.M.	Human Relations	The Use of Force	Summons Issuance Traffic & Borough	Evidence Locker Procedure	Police Equipment Familiarization
	Enforcement Attitudes				
11:10 A.M. to Noon	Basic Police Practices and Procedures	Prisoner Transportation and Processing	Testifying in Court	Crime Scene Responsibilities	Work—Schedule Recall Procedure Personal Appearance
	LUNCH	LUNCH	LUNCH	LUNCH	LUNCH
1:00 P.M. to 1:50 P.M.	N.J. Criminal Law	Prisoner Fingerprinting and Photographing	Responsibilities of Foot Patrol Duty	Controlled Dangerous Substance	City Orientation
2:00 P.M. to 2:50 P.M.	N.J. Criminal Law	N.J. Motor Vehicle Law	Emergency Medical Procedures	Arrest Search and Seizure	City Orientation
3:10 P.M. to 4:00 P.M.	N.J. Criminal Law	Accident Investigations	Police Ethics	Defensive Tactics	Final Examination
				Disarming Demonstration	

Source: Donohue, William B., "Summertime Cops," *FBI Law Enforcement Bulletin*, Vol. 51, No. 2 (February 1982): 7.

_____ 1. What information does this table contain?
   a. A court schedule for policemen
   b. A classroom training schedule for seasonal police officers
   c. A classroom lecture schedule for a professor of law

_____ 2. Where was the table developed?
   a. Stone Harbor, New Jersey
   b. New York City
   c. Stone Harbor, New York

_____ 3. What class is scheduled for Thursday from 10:10 A.M.–11:00 A.M.?
   a. Summons Issuance Traffic & Borough
   b. Prisoner Transportation and Processing
   c. Evidence Locker Procedure

_____ 4. During what time period would you find a disarming demonstration?
   a. 9:00 A.M.–9:50 A.M. Thursday
   b. 3:10 P.M.–4:00 P.M. Thursday
   c. 11:10 A.M.–12:00 noon Friday

_____ 5. During what time period would you find a lecture on New Jersey Criminal Law?
   a. 1:00 P.M.–1:50 P.M. Monday
   b. 3:10 P.M.–4:00 P.M. Monday
   c. Both of the above

_____ 6. When would you find a lecture on the Drunk Driver?
   a. 11:10 A.M.–12:00 noon Tuesday
   b. 9:00 A.M.–9:50 A.M. Wednesday
   c. 9:00 A.M.–9:50 A.M. Thursday

_____ 7. What is the lecture that immediately follows lunch on Monday?
   a. Controlled Dangerous Substance
   b. New Jersey Criminal Law
   c. Responsibilities of Foot Patrol Duty

Graphs

As you read in the content areas, you will often encounter graphs, which are designed to help you better understand the material that is being presented. These graphs may confuse you rather than help you if you have never learned how to read them. There are several different types of graphs that you must learn to read: picture graphs, bar graphs (vertical and horizontal), line graphs, and circle graphs.

When reading graphs, you should first read the title to find out what information the graph contains. Then you should check to see what is being compared. Some graphs have legends, which you must interpret. Finally, you should determine what conclusions can be drawn based on the information presented.

Picture graphs are relatively easy to read because the quantities presented on them are expressed in pictures. Fractions of pictures can cause confusion for some readers, however. A legend will show you what quantities are represented by the symbols. Sometimes the designated quantity has to be multiplied by a fraction, if only a fraction of a symbol is shown. Try the following exercise to discover whether or not you understand how to read picture graphs.

CA Exercise 20

Study the graph in this exercise. Answer the following questions by placing the letter for the correct answer to each question in the blank before the number of the question.

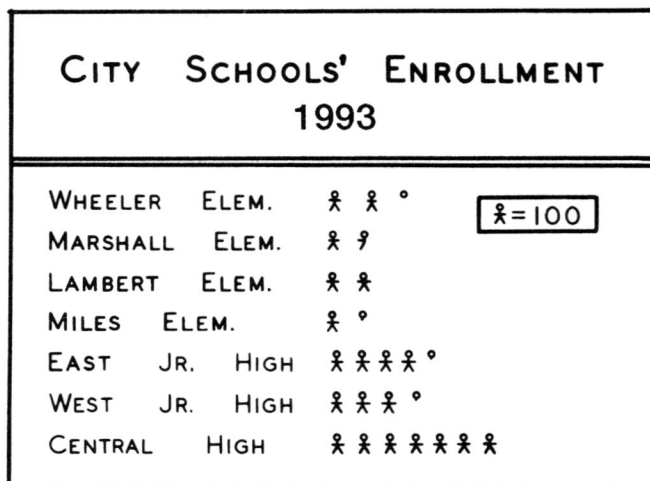

CITY SCHOOLS' ENROLLMENT
1993

WHEELER	ELEM.	♀ ♀ °	♀ = 100
MARSHALL	ELEM.	♀ ʔ	
LAMBERT	ELEM.	♀ ♀	
MILES	ELEM.	♀ °	
EAST	JR. HIGH	♀ ♀ ♀ °	
WEST	JR. HIGH	♀ ♀ ♀ °	
CENTRAL	HIGH	♀ ♀ ♀ ♀ ♀ ♀	

_____ 1. What is the subject of the graph?
    a. Number of Students Enrolled in City Schools in 1993
    b. Number of Students Enrolled in County Schools in 1993
    c. Number of Students Enrolled in City Schools in 1992
    d. Number of Students Enrolled in Elementary Schools in 1993

_____ 2. How many students does one symbol represent?
    a. one
    b. ten
    c. fifty
    d. one hundred

_____ 3. Which school had the greatest enrollment?
    a. Wheeler Elementary
    b. Lambert Elementary
    c. East Junior High
    d. Central High

_____ 4. Which school had about three hundred twenty-five students?
   a. Wheeler Elementary
   b. Marshall Elementary
   c. West Junior High
   d. Miles Elementary

_____ 5. How many students did Central High have?
   a. 200
   b. 300
   c. 700
   d. 1000

A bar graph compares quantities by using either vertical or horizontal bars, rather than using pictures. Try out your ability to read bar graphs by completing the following exercises.

CA Exercise 21

Study the bar graph in this exercise. Then answer the following questions by placing the letter of the correct answer in the blank before the number of each question.

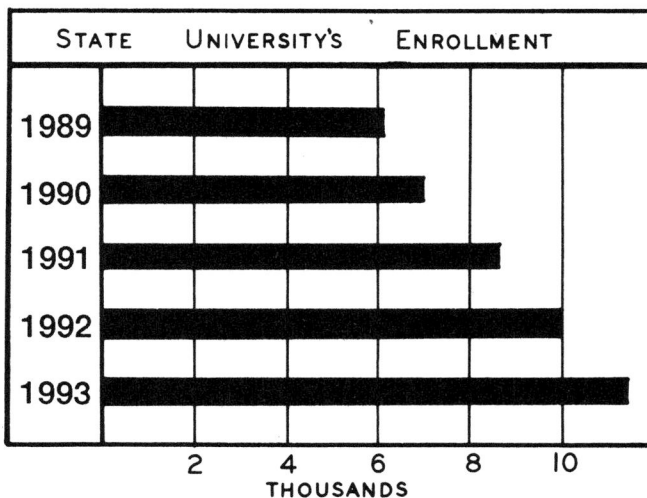

STATE UNIVERSITY'S ENROLLMENT

1989	
1990	
1991	
1992	
1993	

2   4   6   8   10
THOUSANDS

_____ 1. What was State University's enrollment in 1990?
   a. 700
   b. 7,000
   c. 700,000

223

_____ 2. In what year was State University's largest enrollment?
    a. 1989
    b. 1991
    c. 1993

_____ 3. In what year did State University's enrollment show the smallest increase from the previous year?
    a. 1990
    b. 1991
    c. 1992

_____ 4. In what year was State University's enrollment less than 7,000?
    a. 1989
    b. 1990
    c. 1991

_____ 5. In what year was State University's enrollment 10,000?
    a. 1991
    b. 1992
    c. 1993

_____ 6. Which of the following conclusions can be drawn from the above graph?
    a. State University's enrollment has steadily risen from 1989 to 1993.
    b. State University's enrollment has steadily decreased from 1989 to 1993.
    c. State University's enrollment has remained stable during the years 1989 to 1993.

CA Exercise 22

Study the bar graph in this exercise. Then answer the following questions by placing the letter of the correct answer in the blank before the number of each question.

_____ 1. In what game did the Wildcats score the most total points?
    a. 1
    b. 2
    c. 5
    d. 7

_____ 2. In what game did the Wildcats score the fewest total points?
    a. 1
    b. 2
    c. 5
    d. 7

224

TOTAL POINTS SCORED BY WILDCATS

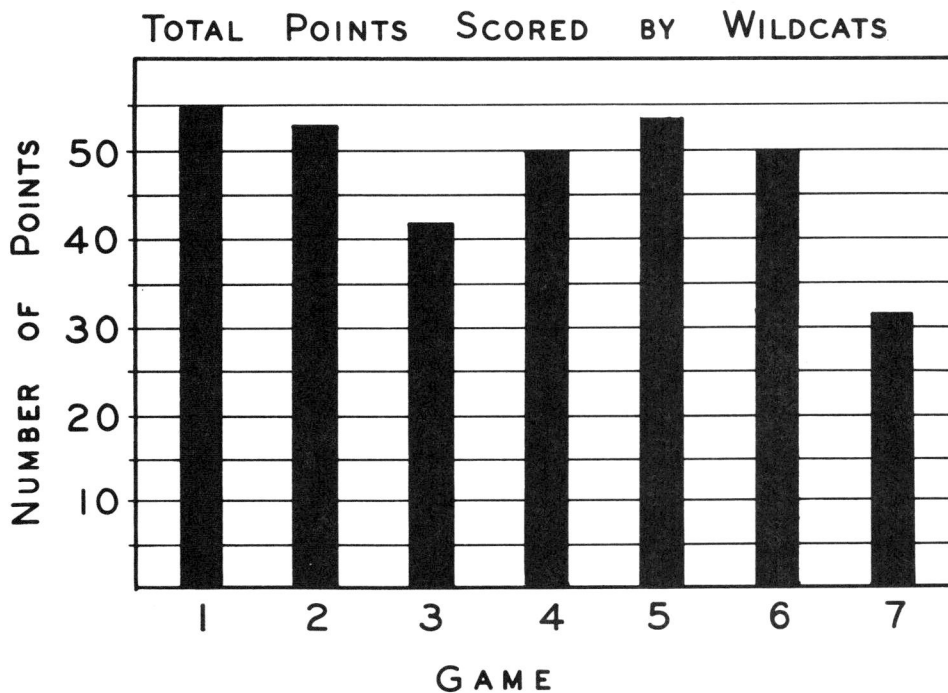

_____ 3. How many points did the Wildcats score in the first game?
  a. 55
  b. 53
  c. 42
  d. 50

_____ 4. In which of the following games did the Wildcats score 50 points?
  a. 1
  b. 2
  c. 3
  d. 4

_____ 5. In what game did the Wildcats score 32 points?
  a. 4
  b. 5
  c. 6
  d. 7

CA Exercise 23

Study the bar graph below. Then answer the following questions by placing the letter of the correct answer in the blank before the number of each question.

Value of Recreational Fisheries

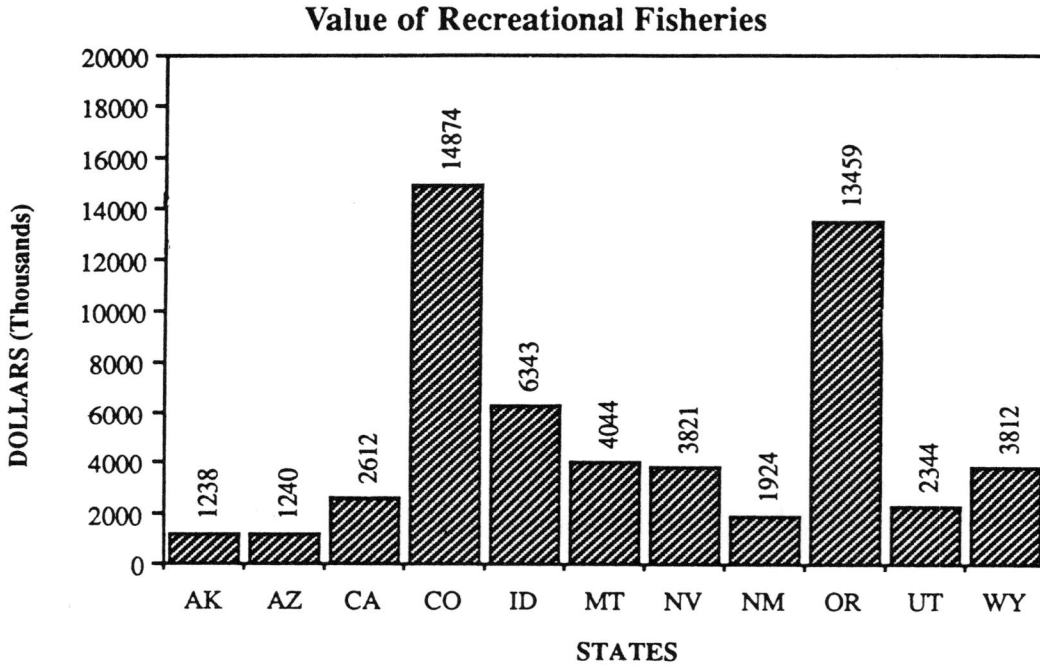

Source: *Status Report: Wildlife and Fisheries Program,* U.S. Department of the Interior, Bureau of Land Management, April 1988.

_____ 1. How much were the recreational fisheries in Wyoming worth?
   a. $4000
   b. $3,812,000
   c. $3812

_____ 2. Considering all of the states on the graph, which state's recreational fisheries were worth the least?
   a. Alaska
   b. Arizona
   c. New Mexico

_____ 3. Considering all of the states on the graph, which state's recreational fisheries were worth the most?
    a. Oregon
    b. Colorado
    c. Alaska

_____ 4. Which of these states had fisheries that were worth the most?
    a. Oregon
    b. Utah
    c. Wyoming

_____ 5. Which of the following states is not represented on this graph?
    a. Arkansas
    b. Alaska
    c. Arizona

Line graphs show changes in amounts over periods of time. The same types of information that are shown on bar graphs can be shown on line graphs. Test your understanding of line graphs by completing the following exercise.

CA Exercise 24

Study the line graph on Gene's Mathematics Scores on Weekly Tests (Winter Quarter). Then answer the questions about the graph by placing the letter of the correct answer in the blank before the number of each question.

_____ 1. Which week was Gene's mathematics score the highest?
    a. 1
    b. 3
    c. 5
    d. 7

_____ 2. Which week was Gene's mathematics score the lowest?
    a. 2
    b. 4
    c. 6
    d. 8

_____ 3. Which week did Gene's score drop the most when compared to the previous week?
    a. 1
    b. 3
    c. 5
    d. 7

_____ 4. What percent correct did Gene have the first week of the quarter?
    a. 40
    b. 45
    c. 50
    d. 55

GENE'S MATHEMATICS SCORES ON WEEKLY TESTS
(WINTER QUARTER)

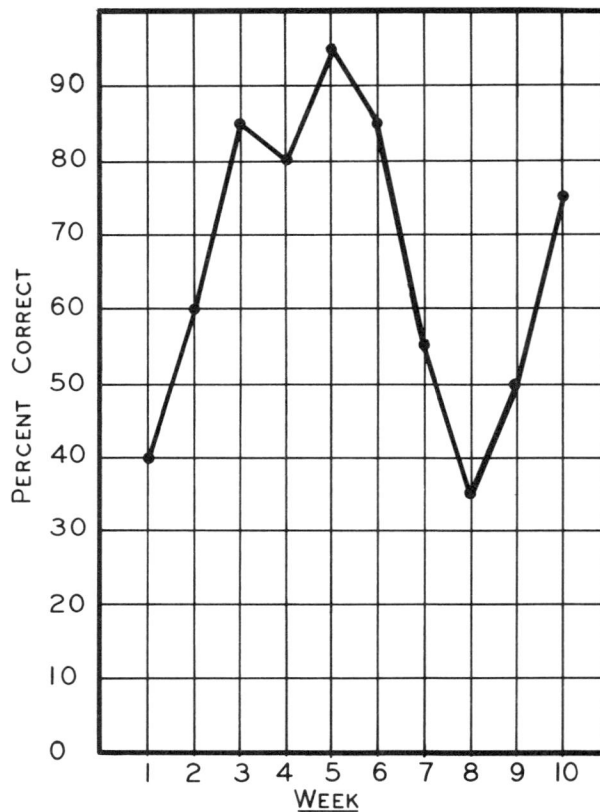

_____ 5. What percent correct did Gene have the fifth week of the quarter?
   a. 65
   b. 75
   c. 85
   d. 95

_____ 6. How many weeks was Gene's score less than 70 percent correct?
   a. 1
   b. 3
   c. 5
   d. 7

Circle graphs show the relationships of various individual parts to the whole. For example, a circle graph can show what percentage of each day you spend eating, sleeping, working, and relaxing, or it can show what percentage of your income you spend on food, clothing, shelter, recreation, and other goods and activities. Test your skill at reading circle graphs by completing the exercise below.

CA Exercise 25

Study the graph, below, on University Enrollment by College. Then answer the questions about the graph by placing the letter of the correct answer beside the number of each question.

UNIVERSITY ENROLLMENT BY COLLEGE

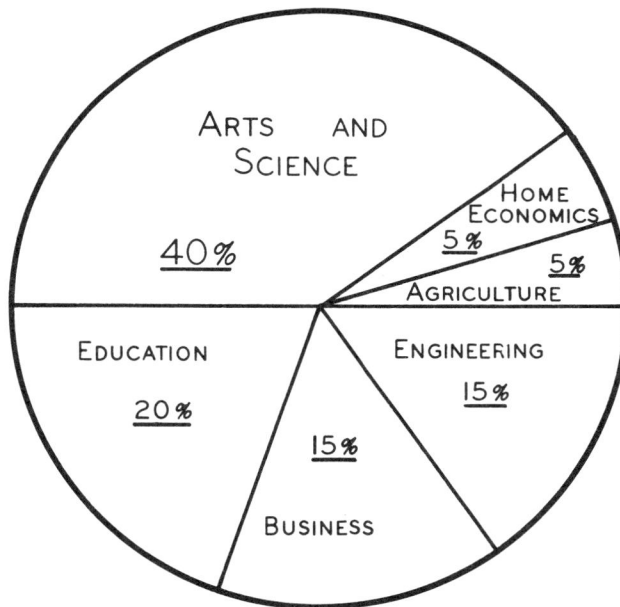

_____ 1. Which college of the university has the highest enrollment?
   a. Arts and Sciences
   b. Business
   c. Home Economics
   d. Agriculture

_____ 2. Which of the following colleges has the lowest enrollment?
   a. Arts and Sciences
   b. Education
   c. Engineering
   d. Agriculture

_____ 3. What percentage of the university's total student population is enrolled in the College of Home Economics?
   a. 40%
   b. 20%
   c. 15%
   d. 5%

_____ 4. What percentage of the university's total student population is enrolled in the College of Education?
   a. 40%
   b. 20%
   c. 15%
   d. 5%

_____ 5. What other college has the same percentage of the university's total enrollment as the College of Engineering?
   a. Arts and Sciences
   b. Business
   c. Education
   d. Agriculture

Charts and Diagrams

Charts and diagrams are found in many content area materials, particularly social studies, science, and health materials. When reading charts and diagrams, you will generally have to relate them to narrative material that they are designed to clarify. These graphic aids are somewhat abstract in nature because they attempt to simplify complex things in some way. For example, you may find three-dimensional objects represented in a two-dimensional format.

You should first check the titles of these aids to extract any information that they may contain. Then you should examine labels of various types. (Parts of diagrams often have verbal labels to further clarify the representations.)

Many charts have blocks of information connected by lines. The lines show which blocks are related. In organizational charts, for example, the lines connect supervisors with the people who are under their supervision. People near the tops of organizational charts have higher ranks than those below them on the charts.

In flow charts or diagrams, the direction of flow is shown by arrows. In other charts or diagrams, arrows may connect labels with the items being named.

The following activities contain examples of charts and diagrams from which information must be extracted.

CA Exercise 26

Study the chart below, and answer the questions about it by placing the letter of the correct answer in the blank before the question number.

Organizational Chart

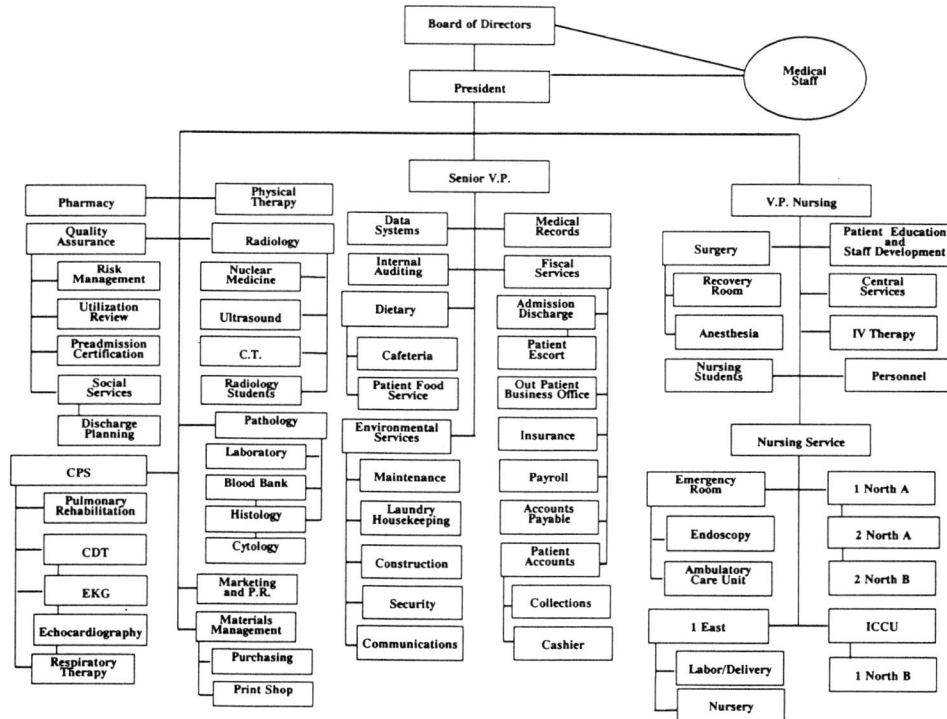

Source: Cumberland Medical Center, Crossville, Tennessee, 1992.

_____ 1. What type of information does this chart contain?
   a. Organizational structure of a bus company
   b. Organizational structure of a police force
   c. Organizational structure of a medical center

_____ 2. Who is the single most powerful individual in this organization?
   a. President
   b. Medical Staff
   c. Board of Directors

_____ 3. To what person does the Data Systems Department report?
   a. Vice President for Nursing
   b. Senior Vice President
   c. President

_____ 4. How many divisions does the Department of Radiology have?
   a. 13
   b. 4
   c. 10

_____ 5. Which Vice President is in charge of the Department of Environmental Services?
   a. None
   b. Vice President for Nursing
   c. Senior Vice President

_____ 6. What is a subdivision of the division of Social Services?
   a. Discharge Planning
   b. Preadmission Certification
   c. Quality Assurance

_____ 7. To whom does the President report?
   a. Nobody
   b. Medical Staff
   c. Board of Directors

The chart in CA Exercise 26 is one of a stationary situation. The chart presented in CA Exercise 27 shows movement of material from one place to another. The movement is represented by the direction of the arrows. This chart also has labels that represent places, people, and activities. Shades of black and gray on the chart also have meaning. This meaning is determined by referring to the key at the bottom of the chart.

CA Exercise 27

Study the chart on page 233, and answer the questions about it by placing the letter of each correct answer in the blank before the question number.

_____ 1. What type of information does this chart contain?
   a. It shows the movement of currency from place to place and some things that happen to it.
   b. It shows how money is spent.
   c. It shows how money is produced.

_____ 2. What does F.R.B. stand for in the chart?
   a. Financial Retrieval Bureau
   b. Federal Reserve Bank
   c. Federal Receiving Bureau

_____ 3. Where does the currency start out?
   a. With the public
   b. In a depository institution
   c. At the U.S. Treasury

Flow of Currency

From the U.S. Treasury...　　　*Through the Federal Reserve Bank...*　　　*To the Public and Back*

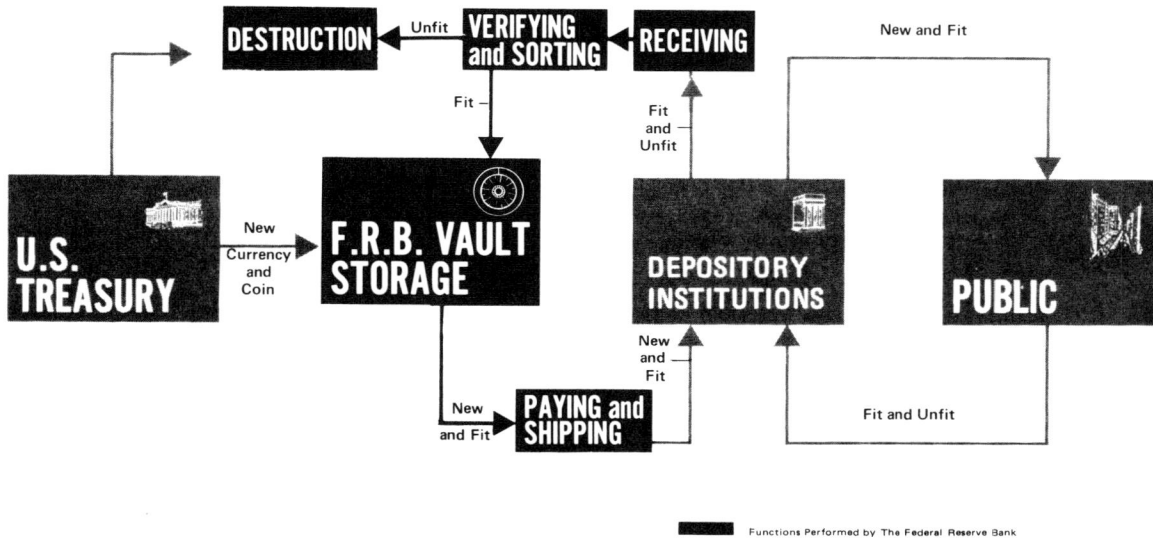

Source: *Fundamental Facts About UNITED STATES MONEY.* A Publication of the Federal Reserve Bank of Atlanta. Page 10.

_____ 4. What happens to unfit currency?
- a. It is given to the public.
- b. It is destroyed.
- c. It is returned to the U.S. Treasury.

_____ 5. What place is responsible for verifying and sorting fit and unfit money?
- a. U.S. Treasury
- b. Federal Reserve Bank
- c. Depository Institutions

_____ 6. What kind of money moves from the depository institutions to the public?
- a. New and fit only
- b. Fit and unfit
- c. Unfit only

_____ 7. Where would you take unfit currency to turn it in, according to this chart?
- a. U.S. Treasury
- b. F.R.B. Vault Storage
- c. Depository Institutions

233

The diagram in CA Exercise 28 helps you locate specific information on paper money. The labels are accompanied by arrows that point to the positions of the things being labeled.

CA Exercise 28

Study the diagram below, and answer the questions about it on the lines provided.

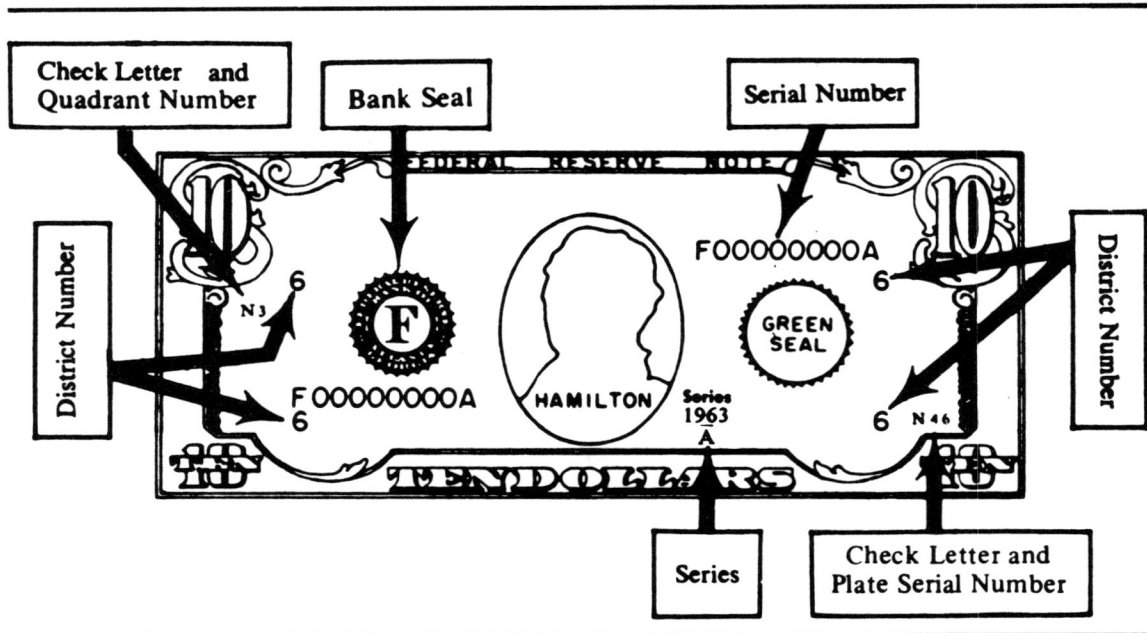

Source: *Fundamental Facts About UNITED STATES MONEY.* A Publication of the Federal Reserve Bank of Atlanta. Page 6.

1. Where is the Bank Seal located on this bill?

   _____

2. How many places does the district number appear on the exposed side of this bill?

   _____

3. What words are found written across the top of the bill?

   _____

4. How many places does the serial number appear on the exposed side of the bill?

   _____

5. What is the series for this bill?

   _____

6. What president is pictured on this bill?

   _____

7. What is this bill worth?

   _____

The diagram in CA Exercise 29 illustrates the sequence in a process. The arrows in the diagram show the movement from one step to the next. A diagram like this one helps you picture the steps described when you read a narrative that explains a process.

CA Exercise 29

Study the diagram below, and answer the questions about it on the lines provided.

MINTING NICKELS

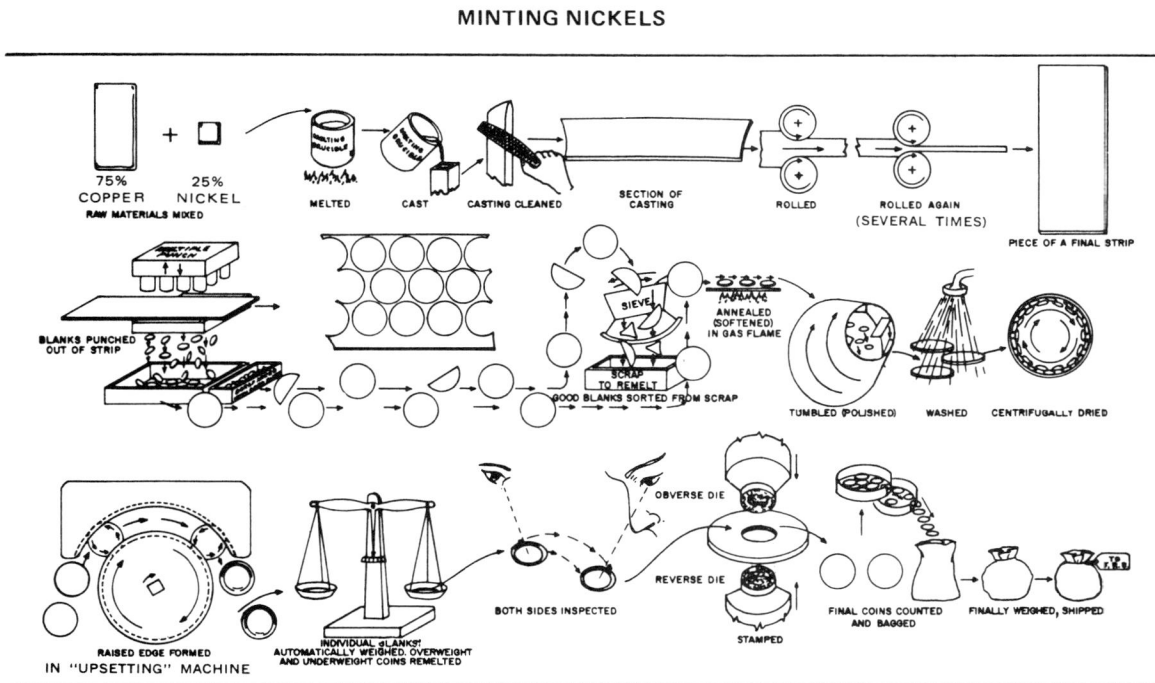

Source: *Fundamental Facts About UNITED STATES MONEY*. A Publication of the Federal Reserve Bank of Atlanta. Page 16.

1. What process is illustrated in this diagram?

_____

2. What are the raw materials that are combined in this process?

_____

3. What symbol tells you that you combine the raw materials?

_____

4. What symbol shows movement to the next step in the process?

_____

5. What process is used to combine the two raw materials?

_____

6. What piece of equipment is used to sort the good blanks from scrap?

_____

7. What happens immediately after the blanks are tumbled (polished)?

_____

8. What happens to overweight and underweight coins?

_____

9. What is the final step in the process?

_____

9 Application of Reading/Study Skills to Content Areas

Wanna threw up her hands in exasperation. "Why is it that I always do well in reading the short stories and novels in English class and have such a hard time with this sociology textbook?" she asked her friend Thad.

Thad looked down at the page she was studying. "I'd guess it has something to do with all of those new words you have to deal with in sociology. The short stories and novels probably use words that you already know."

"How do you know that there are a lot of new words in this? You haven't had time to read this page," Wanna said.

"In textbooks the new words are usually set off with bold print or italics to call attention to them. That page has lots of words in bold print. I'll bet you didn't know the meanings of all of them before you started reading it either," Thad replied.

Wanna nodded. "You're right about that. New words are about to drive me crazy. How are we ever supposed to understand all of this?" she asked.

"Well, I'll bet some of them have definitions right there in the text," he replied. "See that one? And some of them have some context clues, like comparisons and contrasts or examples. That one has a prefix that you probably know a meaning for, too. You just have to use all of the clues the author gives you. They put a lot of clues in those books to make them easier to understand. I was surprised when one of my instructors showed me all of the clues in one of our science textbooks. And most of the books have a glossary. You can use that as a last resort, even though it may slow your reading down a bit."

Wanna looked more closely at the page to which her book was opened. "Hey, you're right! I see two that have good clues and two that have definitions. I guess I just let the quantity of new terms get to me. Thanks for the tips."

Introduction

When you read a textbook selection, you need to understand what it is about. In order to do this, you should look at the title or heading and skim through the selection to get a general idea of the content. Try to find the main ideas of the paragraphs and see how they relate to the title. Then, as you read carefully, apply all of the comprehension strategies that you have learned in previous chapters to help you fully understand the content.

Social Studies

Look at the following selection from an introductory sociology textbook. Begin by reading the heading. What do you already know about the two main words? How are they alike or different? As you read the selection, see how these words are used in relation to sociology.

Positions and Roles[1]

1.   The pattern and predictability found in human groups is based on the existence of specific **positions** that their members occupy. A position in a human society is a ''bundle'' of activities that are important for the group's purposes or objectives. For example, in a university there are positions of student, teacher, dean, president, and so forth. In an industrial organization there are positions of lathe operator, foreman, accountant, shop steward, and so on. In a family there are positions of mother, father, wife, husband, daughter, and the like.

2.   Positions precede and are independent of the people who may occupy them. Each position in a social structure has a set of rights and obligations that the position's occupant will be expected to fulfill. Rights include material rewards, authority over others, and freedom to act in certain ways. Obligations involve the activities that must be carried out for the group to continue to exist. People in groups learn what is expected of them and what to expect of others when they assume certain positions.

3.   When positions are filled by people, the expectations are activated and applied to the position's occupant. Each position in a social structure is linked to some other position by its ''bundle'' of activities and by its rights and obligations. The positions of student and teacher are linked by reciprocal rights and obligations. The students' rights to clear, informative lectures and fair exams are the teachers' obligations. The teachers' rights to have students attend class and read assignments are the students' obligations.

4.   When we describe a social structure in terms of positions, what we have is a ''map'' of behavior but not the actual behavior of people in positions. Positions occupied by actual people are

transformed into roles. **Roles** are expectations about appropriate behavior for occupants of particular positions. Role expectations are held by both the role occupant and the people who interact with the role occupant. The actual behavior of people in positions is called **role behavior.**

5.   There are three main reasons why role behavior may be different from the map of behavior obtained from knowledge of the positions. First, when people occupy a position they bring to the position their own personality, values, and unique life experiences. Role occupants may choose to interpret the position in a way that is different from the usual. For example, a new chemical engineer working on fertilizers may feel that she has a professional responsibility to refuse to work on products that may be potentially harmful. She does this even though her position as an engineer does not give her the right to choose between projects; her role is to follow orders and leave it to others to determine a product's safety.

6.   The second reason is that role occupants may be exposed to multiple and conflicting expectations to which they must adapt. For example, a supervisor in a factory has role relationships with workers, managers, shop stewards, and other supervisors. In the process of reconciling conflicting or incompatible expectations his position as supervisor will be modified.

7.   The third reason is that people occupy many different positions and are therefore called upon to play different roles that sometimes involve contradictory demands. For example, a person may occupy the position of mother in the family and chief engineer at work. The expectations that her children and husband have of her as mother may call for more time at home in the evenings or weekends. However, the expectations that her colleagues have of her as engineer may call for working evenings and weekends. This is a situation of **role conflict.** Such conflict makes it difficult to fulfill either role in a satisfactory manner.

8.   Positions and roles, as elements of social structure, allow individuals to anticipate the behavior of others, to organize their own behavior and thus to provide pattern, regularity, and predictability to human behavior.

Now look over the selection quickly. What helpful clues are readily apparent? The first thing you may notice is that some words are in boldface (dark) print. These will be key words that you will need to learn in order to understand this selection. The second thing you may see is that paragraphs 5, 6, and 7 begin by stating reasons for something. When you read, you should pay special attention to these reasons. You may also notice that the words "for example" appear frequently. They signal that an example, probably to illustrate the main idea, follows.

Many words in this selection have specialized meanings as they relate to sociology. For nearly all of these words or terms, there are context clues that will enable you to figure out their meanings. As you read, look for the context clues that will help you understand the meanings of these words. (See Chapter 3 for more information on using context clues.)

Now read the selection again. You have a general idea of the content from the title, the key words in boldface print, and the clue words that announce there are three reasons. As you read, notice that most of the paragraphs begin with a main idea and continue with examples to support the main idea. This type of organization is often found in textbooks.

AP Exercise 1

I. Each of the following clauses gives a major idea from one of the paragraphs in "Positions and Roles." Put the number of the corresponding paragraph in the space in front of each clause.

   a. _____ Provides a summary.

   b. _____ Contrasts positions and roles.

   c. _____ Introduces three reasons for differing role behavior.

   d. _____ Compares rights and obligations (two answers).

   e. _____ Gives three different examples of positions.

II. You should have used several types of context clues to find the meanings of some of the difficult or specialized terms in this selection. These clues may have been *example, definition,* or *contrast clues.* Put the type of context clue beside each of the following words.

   a. Paragraph 1: position _____

   b. Paragraph 2: rights _____

   c. Paragraph 3: reciprocal _____

   d. Paragraph 4: "map" of behavior _____

   e. Paragraph 4: roles _____

   f. Paragraph 4: role behavior _____

   g. Paragraph 7: role conflict _____

III. A good way to read a selection is to mentally organize the important ideas. Until you get in the habit of doing this, you should write a brief outline of the major points to help you remember them. Try to organize this selection by completing the following outline.

I. _____
   A. Bundles of activities to meet group purposes or objectives
   B. Rights and obligations

II. _____
   A. Positions occupied by actual people
   B. Expectations about appropriate behavior for occupants of positions

III. _____
    A. Different interpretation due to experiences, values, and personality
    B. Adaptation to conflicting expectations
    C. Contradictory demands of different roles

AP Exercise 2

In social studies many familiar words and expressions take on new meanings. You can be easily confused unless you are familiar with how these words are used in your social studies textbooks. Many of the meanings used in social studies make sense if you understand the origins of the terms. In order to remember what these words or expressions mean, associate them with their origins or more familiar meanings whenever you see them. Read the story behind a pork-barrel bill in the following article.

Just What Is a Pork Barrel?[2]

The term pork barrel has its roots in the days when slaves fought over the special rations of salt pork that plantation owners sometimes dispensed from a barrel. Political observers later applied the term to the activities of lawmakers scrambling to get funding for public-works projects.

In a 1919 essay, *National Municipal Review* recalled that such plantation events often would bring "a rush upon the pork barrel" in which each participant "would strive to grab as much as possible for himself." It continued: "Members of Congress, in the stampede to get local appropriation items into the omnibus rivers-and-harbors bills, behaved so much like . . . slaves rushing the pork barrel that these bills were facetiously styled pork-barrel bills."

By the 1870s, lawmakers were making frequent reference to pork and pork-barrel bills, and the phrase became part of the American vocabulary.

Answer the following question to check your understanding of a pork-barrel bill by placing the letter of the correct choice in the blank.

_____ A pork-barrel bill is one that
    a. is written on a slip of paper and drawn from a pork barrel by a legislator.
    b. supports farmers who raise pigs and hogs.
    c. benefits a particular legislator's own constituents and personal interests.
    d. proposes legislation dealing with rivers and harbors.

In the remainder of this exercise, first read the origin or familiar meaning of each underlined term. Then find the meaning of the word or expression as it is used in a social studies context in the list that follows. Place the letter of the meaning you would expect to find in your social studies textbook in the appropriate space.

_____ 1. Iron is a strong metal and a curtain separates one area from another. The term <u>iron curtain</u> originated when it appeared in an article entitled "An Iron Curtain Across Europe" by Sir Vincent Troubridge in 1945. A few months later Winston Churchill accused Russia of drawing an iron curtain between Eastern and Western Europe.[3]

_____ 2. "Don't waste your powder on a dead duck" was a slang expression during the colonial days for anyone who was all "done in." Today the term <u>lame duck</u> is used instead of dead duck to indicate an impairment rather than a death.[4]

_____ 3. A <u>platform</u> is an elevated surface or flooring that serves as a foundation.

_____ 4. A <u>plank</u> is a large board that is sometimes used to build a platform.

_____ 5. An unknown horse that surprised everyone by winning a race was called a <u>dark horse</u> by the English people.

_____ 6. People often assemble in a <u>lobby</u> outside an auditorium or assembly room of the legislature.

_____ 7. A <u>revolution</u> is a turning around or spinning motion.

_____ 8. A <u>kangaroo court</u> tried gold diggers who resembled kangaroos by "jumping" the claim of another miner in an illegal manner.[5]

_____ 9. The odor from a <u>red herring</u> is so powerful that it interferes with the scent that a hunting dog is following.[6]

_____ 10. Philadelphia was an important city during colonial days and therefore attracted many shrewd lawyers. <u>Philadelphia lawyers</u> eventually resorted to making shady deals in order to win cases because of the strong competition.[7]

_____ 11. The signature of <u>John Hancock</u> on the Declaration of Independence was large and legible.

_____ 12. The lowest carving on an Alaskan totem pole must bear the weight of all the other carvings. Thus, the <u>low man on the totem pole</u> supports all of those who are above him.[8]

a. a group of people who join together in an effort to influence legislation

b. an irregular court which proceeds by leaps and bounds in an unauthorized, illegal way

c. an individual without status who does menial tasks for others

d. a public official who is finishing his term and has not been reelected

e. a political party's policies and principles which serve as a foundation for its program

f. a barrier of secrecy that prevents free communication

g. a means of diverting attention from the real issue, often used by politicians

h. a changeover from one form of government to another, often by force

i. someone who practices law in an unscrupulous manner

j. one of the principles that makes up the program of a political party

k. a little known contestant in a political race who wins unexpectedly

l. an individual's signature

Science

In order to read science textbooks with understanding, you must apply many of the reading skills that you have studied in this book. The next two exercises allow you to apply your reading skills to geology and biology textbook materials. You will be expected to use context clues and structure clues to word meaning, to use the dictionary to determine word meaning, to read diagrams, to determine sequence of events, to discover the directly stated details, and to apply other related skills.

AP Exercise 3

Read the following selection (Box 10.1) from a geology textbook and apply the reading skills you have become familiar with through this book to help you understand it.

First, look at the title of the selection to discover what it is about. Write the title here.

1. _____

The entire selection will center about this subject.

Next, locate unfamiliar terms in the selection. The first two you find may be "tilled" and "sheet erosion" in the very first sentence. Use the context to figure out the meanings for these words, if you can. There are fairly good context clues for both "tilled" and "sheet erosion." If you find "susceptible" to be an unfamiliar word, you will need to use your dictionary to locate a meaning for it, because there is not a good context clue. As you read through content material, you should list the unfamiliar terms you locate and try to define them with the help of the context or your dictionary. Some words that may be unfamiliar to you have been located in this passage and listed below. As you read the material, write a brief definition for each one as you encounter it. Be sure your definition fits the context. Notice that the italicized words in the selection have been included in this list. Words that are italicized are important to the understanding of the material. Always be sure that you understand their meanings. Notice that the diagrams help you understand the meanings of three important terms.

2. tilled _____

3. susceptible _____

4. sheet erosion _____

5. topsoil _____

6. contour plowing _____

7. furrows _____

8. contours _____

9. channelize _____

Box 10.1
Preventing Sheet Erosion on Farms

Tilled fields are particularly susceptible to sheet erosion because plowing and cultivating during the planting season remove the vegetation cover. Sheet erosion can remove as much as 60 tons of topsoil per acre in a single year. Farmers use several techniques to slow sheet erosion in their fields (figure 10.3).

In *contour plowing*, the furrows are plowed along contours (lines of equal elevation), rather than up and down the slopes. Furrows that run directly down a slope channelize sheet flow into small rivulets that increase the velocity of the water and thus wash down more soil. If the furrows run along contour lines, however, they are perpendicular to the direction of sheet flow. Each ridge and groove tends to retard the water, thereby reducing sheet erosion of topsoil.

In *strip planting*, two different crops are grown in alternating bands along contour lines. For example, a strip of hay might be planted downhill from a strip of corn. The dense growth and root systems of the hay slow any sheet flow moving downhill from the more widely spaced corn.

Terracing the land involves cutting or building flat surfaces, again parallel to the contours. The terraces may be so narrow as to hold only one row of plants, or wide enough for an entire field. The flat surfaces of the terraces slow the downhill flow of water and so decrease soil erosion.

Combinations of contour plowing, strip planting, terracing, and other techniques such as shallow and infrequent plowing can be very effective in slowing sheet erosion of topsoil. A recent development that looks very promising in further controlling sheet erosion is to mulch fields with organic matter to reduce raindrop impact and sheet flow. Mulching sometimes is done on untilled land into which seeds have been drilled. Such protection can essentially eliminate topsoil loss by sheet erosion.

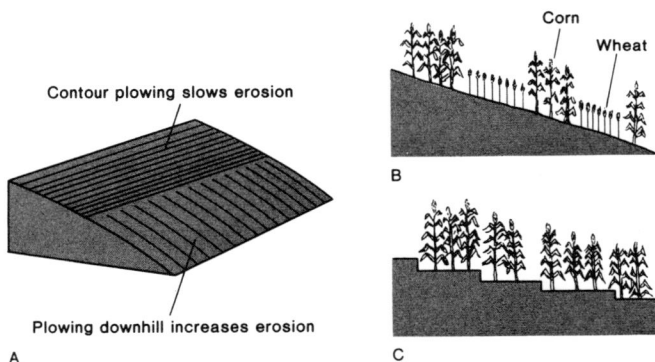

Figure 10.3 Methods of preventing sheet erosion. (*A*) Contour plowing. (*B*) Strip planting. (*C*) Terracing.

10. velocity _____

11. perpendicular _____

12. retard _____

13. strip planting _____

_____

14. terracing _____

_____

15. parallel _____

16. mulch _____

17. organic _____

Next look back at the selection. Did you notice that the meaning of "contours" was placed in parentheses directly after the word? Did you look at the diagrams in Figure 10.3, when the Figure was referred to in the text? Did you look again at each diagram in the Figure when that method of preventing erosion was discussed? Using the diagrams in this way can be very helpful to your understanding of the material.

Look at Diagram A in Figure 10.3. Does it help you picture the way erosion is slowed by contour

plowing, but increased by plowing downhill? _____ Can you see how the furrows that run downhill

would increase the flow of water in that direction? _____ If you answered "yes" to both of these questions, you have used the diagram effectively. Now look at Diagram B and answer the following questions.

18. What method of preventing sheet erosion is shown in this diagram? _____

19. What two crops have been alternated in this example? _____

_____

Now turn your attention to Diagram C and answer the following questions.

20. What method of preventing sheet erosion is shown in this diagram? _____

21. What type of surfaces do the terraces have? _____

Matter: Elements and Compounds[9]

Chemistry is the study of matter, and **matter** is defined as anything that takes up space and has mass. (*Note:* Sometimes, we substitute the term *weight* for *mass,* although the two are not equivalent. We can think of mass as the amount of matter an object contains. The weight of an object measures how strongly that mass is pulled by gravity. An astronaut's mass is the same as it would be on earth. However, as long as we are earthbound, the weight of an object is a measure of its quantity of matter, so for our purposes, we can use the terms interchangeably.)

Matter exists in many diverse forms, each with its own characteristics. Rocks, metals, wood, glass, and you and I are just a few examples of what seems an endless array of matter. The ancient Greek philosophers suggested that the great variety of matter arises from four basic ingredients, or elements. An **element** is a substance that cannot be broken down to other substances by ordinary chemical means. The Greeks imagined the elements of matter to be air, water, fire, and earth—supposedly pure substances that could not be decomposed to other forms of matter. All other substances were thought to be formed by blending various proportions of two or more of the elements. Even though the classical philosophers proposed the wrong elements, their basic idea was correct.

Today, chemists recognize 92 elements occurring in nature—for example, gold, copper, carbon, and oxygen. About a dozen more elements have been made in the laboratory. Each element has a symbol, usually the first letter or two of its name. A few of the symbols are derived from Latin or German names; for instance, the symbol for sodium is Na, from the Latin, *natrium.* Our modern elements fit the Greek definition: Elements cannot be decomposed to other substances by ordinary chemical means.

Two or more elements may be combined in a fixed ratio to produce a **compound.** Table salt, for example, is actually sodium chloride (NaCl), a compound composed of the elements sodium (Na) and chlorine (Cl). Pure sodium is a metal that explodes readily, and pure chlorine is a poisonous gas that was used as a weapon during World War I. Chemically combined, however, sodium and chlorine form an edible compound. This is a simple example of organized matter having emergent properties: A compound has characteristics beyond those of its combined elements.

From Neil A. Campbell, *Biology,* 2nd ed. © 1990 The Benjamin/Cummings Publishing Company, Inc., Redwood City, California, p. 22.

AP Exercise 4

Read the selection above from a biology textbook and apply the reading skills you have learned to help you understand it. First, look at the title of the selection to discover what it is about. Write the title here. 1. _____
The entire selection is about this subject.

Next, look at the first paragraph. Notice the word in boldface (dark) type. What is this word?

2. _____ The boldface type calls your attention to this word because it is important. Use

the context to find out what this word means. Write the word's meaning here. 3. _____

_____

What kind of context clue did you have to the meaning of this word? 4. _____

Sometimes extra information that gives you background or explains something related to the topic is offered in parentheses. What does the note in parentheses clarify for the reader of this paragraph? 5. _____

_____

What helped you to decide which terms in the parentheses were the most important? 6. _____

As you read, remember to be alert for unfamiliar words. Try to find clues for their meanings in the context, but if there are no clues, look them up in the dictionary. There are context clues in the first paragraph, not only for "matter" (as you have seen), but also for a number of other words. Some of the clues are more direct than others. Write the clues that you find for each of the following words:

7. mass _____

8. weight _____

9. quantity _____

10. interchangeably _____

You also may want to try structural analysis skills on unfamiliar terms before you resort to the dictionary. The term "interchangeably" has some structure clues, in addition to the context clues that are available. "Inter" means "between," "change" means "to switch," and "able" means "capable of." The "ly" tells you that this is an adverb. So "interchangeably" tells you that a reader or writer is capable of switching between the terms when he or she uses them. If "equivalent" is an unfamiliar word, you can use the knowledge that the "equi" means "equal" to help you understand its meaning. Now define the following two words, using your knowledge of structural analysis.

11. weightless _____

12. earthbound _____

Now look at the second paragraph. There is an example clue to the meaning of the word "diverse."

Study the context and then write a meaning for "diverse" here. 13. _____

What important word is signaled by the boldface type? 14. _____ What does it mean?

15. _____

_____

_____ What type of context clue is given for this word? 16. _____

Were the ancient Greek philosophers correct that the four basic elements are air, water, fire, and earth?

17. _____ What did the selection say that made you answer that way? 18. _____

Look at the third paragraph. How many elements do today's chemists recognize as occurring in nature?

19. _____ Does this number represent all of the elements in existence? 20. _____ What did the

selection say that told you that? 21. _____

What is the origin of the symbols for the elements? 22. _____

Look at the fourth paragraph. What is the topic of this paragraph? 23. _____

How did the author show you that this topic was important? 24. _____

What is the chemical symbol for table salt? 25. _____
Why was this symbol used? 26. _____

_____

_____

What does the word "edible" mean? 27. _____

Is pure sodium edible? 28. _____ Is pure chlorine edible? 29. _____ Is sodium chloride edible?

30. _____

Health and Physical Education

Health and physical education materials require the use of many different reading skills, just as materials in the other content areas do. This section contains an example of each of these types of reading materials.

Sequence is important in many health materials. First aid procedures depend upon understanding of sequence for their successful completion. Sequence involves putting important details in the correct order. Exercise 5 involves the need to recognize the correct sequence of actions. Exercise 6 involves many reading skills, including the reading of diagrams and tables.

AP Exercise 5

Read the steps in the two first aid procedures described in this exercise. They are designed to be used on a person who is choking. After you have read the two procedures, answer the questions that follow.

THE HEIMLICH MANEUVER[10]

with the victim standing or sitting

1. Stand behind the victim and wrap your arms around his waist.
2. Grasp your fist with the other hand and place the thumb side of your fist against the victim's abdomen, slightly above the navel and below the rib cage.
3. Press your fist into the victim's abdomen with a QUICK UPWARD THRUST. Repeat as often as necessary.
4. If the victim is sitting, stand behind the victim's chair and perform the maneuver in the same manner.
5. After food is dislodged, have the victim seen by a doctor.

THE HEIMLICH MANEUVER

when the victim has collapsed and cannot be lifted

1. Lie the victim on his back.
2. Face the victim and kneel astride his hips.
3. With one hand on top of the other, place the heel of your bottom hand on the abdomen slightly above the navel and below the rib cage.
4. Press into the victim's abdomen with a QUICK UPWARD THRUST. Repeat as often as necessary.
5. Should the victim vomit, quickly place him on his side and wipe out his mouth to prevent aspiration (drawing of vomit into the throat).
6. After the food is dislodged, have the victim seen by a doctor.

NOTE: If you start to choke when alone and help is not available, an attempt should be made to self-administer this maneuver.

What is the difference in use of the first procedure and the second procedure described in this material? 1. _____

_____

What is the key movement in the third step of the first procedure that is described? 2. _____

_____

How did the writer of this material indicate the importance of this movement? 3. _____

_____

Is a similar step included in the second procedure? 4. _____ Which step of the second procedure is it? (Give a number.) 5. _____

What is the first step of the second procedure? 6. _____

_____

What is aspiration? 7. _____

_____ How can it be avoided? 8. _____

_____

In both procedures, what is done after the food is dislodged? 9. _____

_____

AP Exercise 6

Read the following selection (pages 255–261) from an article related to physical education. Apply the reading skills you have become familiar with through this book to help you understand it.

First, look at the title of the selection to discover what it is about. Write the title here. 1. _____

A question that may occur to you after reading this title is "Who does 'yourself' refer to?" You may wonder why the person referred to is not included in the term "citizens." Check the footnote that tells the source of this article. It should provide a clue to the referent for "yourself." The title of the publication that the article appeared in should give you an idea of the referent. Write the title of the publication here. 2. _____

Now read the first paragraph of the article. A final bit of information in this paragraph should make you relatively sure who 'yourself' refers to. Write the referent here. 3. _____

In the first paragraph, what is said to be the most effective motivator? 4. _____

_____

Read the second paragraph to discover three other possible motivators. List them here:

5. _____

6. _____

7. _____

Read the third paragraph and answer the following question: What does "positive addiction" mean?

8. _____

_____ Why is running referred to in that way?

9. _____

_____

Read the fourth paragraph to find out what equipment is essential for running. Put the answer here.

10. _____

Read the fifth paragraph. What is a podiatrist? 11. _____

_____

Read the sixth paragraph to find out why a heavy shoe is best. Write the reason here. 12. _____

_____

In the seventh paragraph, what is meant by a "road test"? 13. _____

_____

Read the next three paragraphs. What can be done by runners to prevent injuries? 14. _____

_____

Read the descriptions of the warmup exercises. Study the diagrams that accompany them. Visualize each exercise described.

What does the arrow in the diagram of the quad flex exercise show you? 15. _____

_____

Which exercise do many people describe as a favorite because it can be very relaxing? 16. _____

_____

What may be a problem with this exercise? 17. _____

_____

How did the author attempt to ensure that you noticed this problem when you read the description?
18. _____
Are exercises like the hamstring stretches easier to do when you have the diagram to help you visualize the position, as well as the words? 19. _____ What limitations do the diagrams have in their helpfulness in the case of exercises? 20. _____

_____

Read the first paragraph after the descriptions of the exercises. What kind of life is a sedentary one? There is a context clue to the meaning of "sedentary." 21. _____

What is a congenital defect? 22. _____

Now read the next four paragraphs. What should you do before you start your running if you have been physically out of shape for several years? 23. _____

Read the next paragraph. Is it a good idea to run on the balls of the feet? 24. _____ What single word in the paragraph lets you know this? 25. _____ Use context clues and structural analysis to determine the meaning of "counterproductive." Write the meaning here.

26. _____

_____

Finish reading the article, and answer the following questions:

What types of fabrics should clothes for winter running be made of? 27. _____

_____

How can you keep your face from getting chapped in the winter? 28. _____

_____

What time of day should you do your running in the summer? 29. _____

_____

Examine the table in the article carefully. If a person is 20 years old, how fast should he or she be able to run a half mile? 30. _____ How fast should a 50-year-old person be able to run a mile? 31. _____ At what point in your running program do these times begin to apply? 32. _____

_____

Run—to Protect Citizens and Yourself[11]

Stephen D. Gladis

Running Safely

If fitness is vital to the police officer, and running is one of the best means to that end, there are four major areas which you should know about before you set one foot on the ground. Motivation, equipment, stretching and warmup exercises, and basic running techniques. Perhaps the most important of these is motivation. The journey of 1,000 miles must begin with the first step and for many it's the most difficult. Generally, "habituation process" is the most effective motivator. Man is a creature of habit and most of us are ruled by the clock. This phenomenon can be used to an advantage in running. Running at the same time of day will become part of your normal routine, and therefore you will tend to do it daily out of habit.

There are other motivators, too. Many people run with another person or with a group. You tend to run if you know someone else is waiting for you. Still others keep charts of their daily fitness as a contract with themselves. A glance at a calendar chart left empty for 2 or 3 days straight will motivate you to get out and run. In addition, the President's Council sponsors a Presidential Sports Award program, which provides patches, pins, and certificates for logging specific mile distances on an individual basis. . . .

Whether you use the calendar, the habit phenomenon, or the group approach, what does matter is that you motivate yourself to run. Running is a positive addiction. After a few months of daily running, you reach the point where you become dependent upon it. Your body begins to crave the exercise. Runners who get sidetracked with injury or illness actually go through withdrawal symptoms. This phenomenon has been reported by Dr. William Glasser in his book *Positive Addiction:* ". . . running creates the optimal condition for PA (positive addiction) because it is our most ancient and still most effective survival mechanism." Glasser has suggested that running is also a good cure for negative addictions, such as smoking, alcoholism, and drug abuse.[15]

Now that you are motivated to run, the next step is the right equipment. Above all else, running shoes are basic and essential. You can take or leave all of the beautiful warmup suits and emblazoned T-shirts, but a good pair of shoes are a must, not a luxury. The old adage, "you get what you pay for," is true regarding running shoes, and with more than 100 brands now being manufactured, there is a large variety to choose from.

There are some basics to follow when shopping for a good running shoe. First, make sure that there is adequate heel padding to absorb the tremendous shock of footstrike on hard surfaces. At least ¼ to ½ inch in the heel region is needed. Next, look at the shank of the shoe, the portion under the arch. Make sure that it is solid and rigid, so it can absorb the impact of the footstrike. Commercially made arch supports which are put into shoes are of little use. Normally, if you are in need of supports, they should be individually made for you by a competent podiatrist; however, a commercially manufactured heel counter is a must in a good shoe. The counter is a plastic or stiff fiber cup which holds the runner's heel snuggly in place and minimizes movement and knee injuries that can result from such movement. Nylon upper shoes are preferable to leather as leather tends to dry out, get hard, and lacks the flexibility of nylon.

Since shock absorption is more of a key factor in preventing injury, look for a heavy shoe. A 10 to 12 oz. shoe will minimize impact shock and the injuries sustained with it.[16]

Additional hints for purchasing running shoes are: Always try on the shoes with the same sock you will be wearing when you run. Put *both* shoes on and run around the shoe store for a "road test." Shoes feel differently when in motion. Don't be talked into a pair of shoes that don't feel right to begin with. . . .

Running requires little other equipment to get started. An old pair of shorts and a T-shirt will do the job. If the budget allows, nylon shorts ($3 to $4) and a nylon tank top ($4) are advisable. Nylon is durable, requires merely a rinse out and a quick drying time, is chafe proof, and needs no ironing. Socks are optional and after the feet get toughened are not really necessary. A sweatband is nice during the summer to keep the salt sting out of your eyes.

Knee pains, shin splints, and Achilles' tendonitis can plague the runner, particularly the new runner. The reason is simple—new runners know little or nothing about stretching exercises. Warmup or stretching exercises are probably the most neglected routine of many runners until they get injured. Muscles are stiff and need to be extended prior to and after vigorous exercises. If not, they tend to pull and sometimes tear.

Injuries of this nature take a long time to heal and are the reason that many quit running soon after they get started.

Many injuries can be prevented. The following basic stretching exercises suggested by the National Jogger's Association should be done regularly before and after each run to prevent injury: Hamstring stretcher, toe raises, wall stretch, the plow, quad and dorsi flex, and abdominal curls.

Quad and Dorsi Flex

The prime movers during a jog are the leg muscles at the rear of the leg. In order to maintain good balance, the muscles at the front of the leg must also be stretched and strengthened, particularly to help stabilize the knee, which may be traumatized during jogging. These exercises require a 3-to-5 pound weight, easily made from some rags (to act as a strap) and a couple of bricks or a can filled with sand or stones.

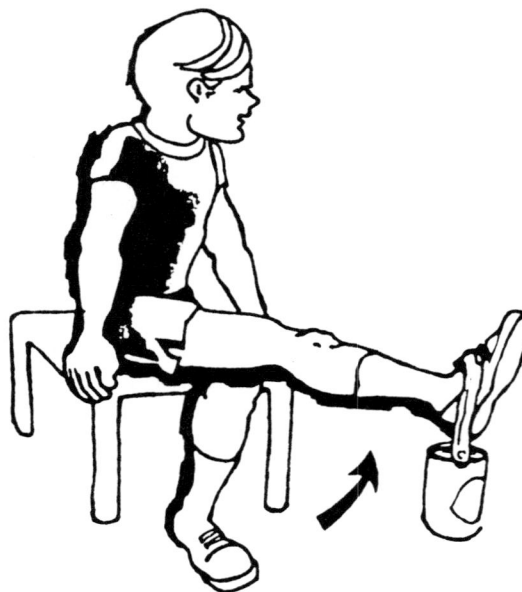

Illustrations courtesy of *Running & Fitness* (formerly The Jogger).

Quad Flex—Sit on a high table or bed with your leg out-stretched, weight over your foot. Straighten your leg into a tight contraction, flexing your quadriceps and the muscles on each side of the knee. Hold for 6 to 10 seconds and then relax, allowing your leg to bend no more than 15° at the knee, as this puts too much stress on the knee and can lead to injury. The knee may be bent to 90° to put the weight on and off. Repeat 10 times with each leg.

Dorsi Flex—This flex will strengthen the relatively underdeveloped shin muscles at the front of the lower leg, reducing shin pain and helping to develop a full range of motion in the foot. This will also help stretch out the foot. Sit on the same bed or table and allow your leg to hang. Flex your foot at the ankle, pulling your toes up toward your shin. Hold for 6 to 10 seconds, pulling your toes as close to your shin as possible without strain. Relax, stretching your foot as fully down as you're able. Repeat 10 times with each foot. A variation is to not hold the flex, but to assume the flex, return immediately to the relaxed position, stretching down, then flexing up again. Repeat with each foot 20 to 30 times. (Not pictured.)

The Plow

With practice many people describe this position as their favorite, as it can be very relaxing. It contributes not only to strength and flexibility, but also to balance and good upper-body carriage. This is especially good for loosening the lower back muscles tightened in our day-to-day activities and while jogging. *People with any history of back trouble should be especially cautious and gentle while trying to enter this posture. Do not strain.*

Using a thick rug or mat to protect you from the floor, lie flat on your back with your arms at your sides. Allow your body to relax. Breathe. If you so choose, close your eyes and relax for a minute. This may help tune you in to how tired or fresh you really are. With your palms against the floor, tense your abdominals and curl your knees up to your chest. Roll backwards until your weight is behind your head. Hold for 20 to 30 seconds, knees bent if necessary. Breathe.

Wall Stretch

Place your rear foot flat, *heel down,* toes straight ahead. Lean into the wall, stretching your posterior lower leg. Hold for 30 to 60 seconds. Repeat with other leg.

Repeat, this time bending each knee slightly and exaggerating the stretch even more fully. Hold 30 to 60 seconds. Repeat with other leg. Repeat both variations 2 to 5 times.

Hamstring Stretcher [Illustration on page 259]

This exercise stretches the posterior thigh muscles without stressing the lower back as can happen with more traditional toe touches.

Stand and cross one leg in front of the other. The toes of the front leg, but not the entire foot, should touch the floor parallel to the rear foot. Slowly bend forward from the waist and hips, keeping your rear leg straight, heel to floor. Relax your neck and arms and bend forward as far as comfortable. Hang, breathe regularly and deeply for 20 to 40 seconds. Stretch the other leg in the same manner. Repeat twice for each leg.

Abdominal Curl [Illustration on page 259]

The basic abdominal curl should be mastered before variations are tried. It particularly works the upper abdominals and takes the place of more traditional situps, which tend to strain the lower back. This exercise limits your motion to that part of the situp which uses your abdominals. Try not to jerk or bounce while doing it, as quality is just as important to good development as quantity. At first it may seem awkward.

Lie on your back with your head raised, knees bent, feet flat on the floor, arms folded across your chest. Curl yourself up only far enough so that your shoulder blades break

contact with the floor. (Note, your lower back should always remain fully supported by the floor in order to reduce any chances of strain.) Do not hold. Lower yourself back and relax. When you are curling up concentrate on your upper abdominals and allow them to do the work. Hold your head in a stable position and don't jerk. When you are uncurling it is not necessary to lower your head fully to the mat. Repeat 5 to 30 times. When you can complete 30 curls, try holding the flexed position for 6 to 10 seconds.

Strong stomach muscles provide the frontal support your back needs for pain-free posture and a smooth jogging style. The lack of this frontal support is often the cause of considerable back pain.

If you do everything as you should and you still get injured, by all means see a po-diatrist. Anyone who has been injured by running will tell you that most of the time the injury is foot-structure related. Each one of us has minor imbalances and flaws in our foot structure. In the everyday sedentary American life where automobiles and desk jobs abound, these imperfections never develop into a problem. But when you begin to add the stress of exercise to these congenital defects, injuries begin to occur. These injuries do not always confine themselves to the foot, but affect knees, hips, and shins as a result of foot imbalance and imperfection. Thus you need to see someone who knows about the biomechanical structure of feet—the podiatrist. . . .

A physical exam from your doctor is a most important step in starting. Ask him to pay special attention to your heart and lungs, and tell him you want to embark on a moderate jogging program. Take it easy the first few weeks. Many people make the serious mistake of trying to do too much too soon.

TIME STANDARDS						
Ages	¼ Mile	½ Mile	1 Mile	2 Miles	3 Miles	5 Miles
14–39	under 2:00	under 4:15	under 8:30	under 18:00	under 28:00	under 48:00
40–49	under 3:00	under 5:15	under 9:30	under 19:00	under 29:00	under 49:00
50–59	under 3:30	under 5:45	under 10:00	under 19:30	under 29:30	under 49:30
over 60	under 4:00	under 6:15	under 10:30	under 20:00	under 30:00	under 50:00

Note: Beginning runners should not attempt to measure their performances against these average times until they have achieved a level of conditioning that should include six months of running. The time standards are suggested by ''Runner's World.''

They try to run before their muscles are prepared and they try to run faster and farther than they should. If you have spent years getting out of shape, devote a few weeks to walking before you actually begin running.

People who have been completely inactive physically should begin with brisk daily walks. Do one block only on the first day and add about one block every other day for the first week. Then devote another week or two to brisk walking, progressing gradually to as much as 8 city blocks or about 2 to 2½ miles. (Pay no attention to the time required to cover this distance; it is the continuous effort that matters.) After the initial walking period, you can begin mixing in some jogging—a slow run, just faster than a walk.

Increase the distance and pace gradually. Be patient. As a rule of thumb, an overweight person who has been completely inactive should progress to a 1-mile nonstop jog within 6 months or less, including the initial walking period. An average person should work up to a steady 1-mile jog in 2 to 4 months. And the "regular exerciser" can work up to a mile jog in 2 weeks. In all cases, do not increase by more than one block or one lap (on a ¼-mile track) per day. (See Time Standards.)

The best place to start to talk about running technique is, of course, the foot. The basic footstrike of a long distance runner should be the heel. Many people erroneously run on the balls of the feet and several weeks later have Achilles' tendon problems. The stress is too great on the tendon if the ball of the foot hits first, so concentrate on heel first, or a flatfooted step. Your stride should be natural. Don't try to stretch it out. Let your legs go the way they want to. Run from the hips down—you don't need a lot of sway or bobbing up or down to help. Pick an object in the distance and concentrate on it while you run. If it moves quite a bit then you are bobbing too much. Your arms should be at least a 90° angle or even greater. Don't hold them too high—it's just a waste of energy that should be saved for the legs. Don't clench your fists tightly, just a loose fist will do. Good erect posture is essential and allows good airflow down the windpipe. Don't lean over or swing your arms across your chest as both are counterproductive. In running, the desired movement is forward, not upward or sideward. . . .

Generally, the extreme seasons, winter and summer, provide the greatest hazard to the runner. Here are some practical hints to reduce the discomfort and possible risks associated with winter and summer outdoor exercise.

Winter

1. Wear layers of clothing rather than one bulky piece.
2. Nylon stops wind effectively.
3. Wool insulates well even when wet from sweat. Cotton does *not.*
4. Mittens are more effective than gloves in the cold weather.
5. A thin coat of petroleum jelly or altitude cream keeps your face from getting chapped.
6. Run out against the wind and back with the wind to avoid freezing sweat.
7. Always wear a wool hat in winter—over 40 percent of heat loss is through the head.
8. On the coldest days (−0°) wear a wool scarf over your mouth to warm the air.

Summer

1. Wear lightweight shirt and shorts to permit evaporation and leave shirt untucked for ventilation.
2. Force ingestion of fluids.
3. Avoid running during the heat of the day (stick to early morning or evening).
4. *Never* wear a rubber suit to "lose weight"—that kind of weight loss can kill you.
5. Runners should keep track of their early morning weight to prevent chronic dehydration. (Sharp body weight differences of two to three pounds in any one day may indicate a problem.) . . .

FOOTNOTES

15. Dr. William Glasser, *Positive Addiction,* Harper & Row, New York, 1976.
16. Bob Anderson, (Ed.) *Runner's World Magazine,* (shoe issue), October 1977, pp. 33–89.

Chapter Notes

1. Reprinted by permission from pages 97–98 of *Sociology* by Robert Perrucci and Dean D. Knudsen; Copyright © 1983 by West Publishing Company. All rights reserved.
2. "Just What Is a Pork Barrel?" May 2, 1983, p. 20. Reprinted from "U.S. News & World Report, Inc." Copyright, 1983, U.S. News & World Report, Inc.
3. Ann and Dan Nevins, *From the Horse's Mouth* (Englewood Cliffs, N.J.: Prentice-Hall, 1977).
4. Ibid.
5. Ibid.
6. Ibid.
7. Ibid.
8. Ibid.
9. From Neil A. Campbell, *Biology,* 2nd ed. © 1990 The Benjamin/Cummings Publishing Company, Inc., Redwood City, California, p. 22.
10. "Choking: the Café Coronary." Reprinted by permission of Life Extension Institute.
11. Stephen D. Gladis, "Run—to Protect Citizens and Yourself," *FBI Law Enforcement Bulletin* (May 1978): 25–31.

10 Rate

Being from the same hometown, Maria and Susan often got together to share news from home as well as problems about courses they were taking. "I don't know what I'm going to do about American Lit," Maria confessed. "I'll never get through all of those pages I'm supposed to read. How does *anybody* ever find time to read so much?"

Susan asked, "Aren't you taking that reading-study skills course? I had it when I was a freshman and we learned how to read faster. That really helped me. I went from 185 words a minute to 420 words by the end of the semester. That means I can read more than twice as fast now as I used to read. You have to really concentrate, but you can do it if you want to badly enough."

"That sure would help. But I have my doubts. I'm always the last one finished when we have to read in class."

"There are some things you can do that will help—you don't have to read everything at the same speed, and you can learn to skim over things that aren't really that important."

"Well," admitted Maria, "I suppose it's worth a try. If I can't read faster, I'll never make it here. There's so much to read in college! It seems like I never finish."

"I'll give you some pointers," said Susan, "and you'll find out more about it as you get into the course. Now, tell me what's going on at home. Didn't you go home last weekend?"

"Oh, right—wait'll you hear what my mom told me. . . ."

Introduction

For many people reading improvement means the ability to read more rapidly. However, rapid reading as a skill cannot be fully developed until you have acquired an adequate vocabulary and sufficient comprehension skills to enable you to understand what you read.

As a college student, you may find you have barely enough time to complete your reading assignments and that there is little time left for reading the newspaper, an occasional novel, or a magazine. By learning to read faster, you would be able to cover your assignments in less time and have the remaining time for recreational reading. Learning to read rapidly does not come easily; it requires a great deal of effort to give up lazy habits and push relentlessly toward faster reading. However, if you apply the techniques for rapid reading presented in this chapter, it is reasonable for you to expect to double or even triple your present reading rates.

Concepts Related to Rate

Flexibility

It has been estimated that most adults read less than 250 words per minute. For most college students, this rate is simply too slow to enable them to finish reading all their assignments and review them for tests. On the other hand, proponents of some rapid reading programs claim that their students can ''read'' 2,000 to 5,000 words per minute. At this level the students are not actually reading, but they are skimming for main ideas.

Good readers learn to adjust their rates to their purposes for reading. They develop flexibility by changing speed according to the type of material. They know how to skim over a newspaper rapidly and how to read a poem slowly for pleasure. They can read detective stories quickly, but can also study textbooks with close attention.

It is just as bad to read everything very rapidly as it is to read everything slowly, because different situations require reading at different speeds. If you read your textbook too rapidly, you will not be able to absorb the information you must obtain. Most inflexible readers, however, read everything slowly and deliberately.

The goal of rapid reading, therefore, is not to read everything rapidly. Rather, the goal is to increase speed somewhat in all types of reading, and to develop a flexible reading rate that will enable you to read some material intently, read easier material more quickly, skim over some types of material at a quite rapid rate, and scan for specific bits of information.

Relation of Rate to Comprehension

Most people are afraid that by increasing their reading rate they will decrease their comprehension. They feel that they cannot understand as much if they cover the material more rapidly. However, just the opposite may be true. People who read slowly, word by word, often find it difficult to keep interested and their attention wanders. They lose track of the main ideas.

People who read rapidly must focus their attention on what they read. Instead of concerning themselves with each word equally, they are selecting key words and key ideas and putting these words and ideas together into meaningful patterns. Therefore, they may actually be getting more meaning from the text than those who laboriously read each word.

When you first begin doing exercises to increase your rate, you may find that your comprehension is dropping. This drop is not unusual and is likely to be temporary. Instead of decreasing your speed, try to maintain the same speed while increasing your concentration. Soon your comprehension should again be at a reasonable level. When doing rate building exercises, 70% or 80% is an acceptable level for comprehension.

One danger of reading too rapidly is that you may become so intent on reading the words quickly that you forget to think about the meaning. You must force your mind to move with your eyes. It does you no good to cover a page quickly with your eyes if your mind is not grasping ideas.

Ra Exercise 1

In the exercise that follows, read the first sentence to get the basic idea. Then read the five sentences that follow as fast as you can. In front of each sentence write "S" if the meaning is similar to the first sentence and write "D" if it is different.

Example: An antibiotic used to treat virus infections in chickens may be used in the treatment of human heart problems.

_____ a. Human heart problems may be treated with an antibiotic used to treat virus infections in chickens.

_____ b. An antibiotic used for chickens is of no value in treating humans.

_____ c. Antibiotics have been used to treat many patients.

_____ d. By using an antibiotic intended for chickens, doctors may be able to treat heart problems in humans.

_____ e. Chickens and humans have the same kinds of heart problems.

If you answered this example correctly, you would have placed an "S" beside "a." and "d." You would have written "D" before "b.," "c.," and "e."

Time yourself and try to finish in less than seven minutes.

1. Consumers do not have enough information to make intelligent buying decisions.

    _____ a. Many shoppers do not know the best products to buy.

    _____ b. People who shop often choose poor values because they do not know how to make better selections.

    _____ c. People should do their Christmas shopping early.

    _____ d. Teenagers are taking a larger share of the buying market than ever before.

    _____ e. Buyers need more facts before they can shop wisely.

2. Union leaders were undecided about postponing the coal strike scheduled to begin early next week.

    _____ a. Because of the shortage of fuel, greater amounts of coal are needed.

    _____ b. The coal strike, called for the beginning of the week, may be postponed.

    _____ c. The labor leaders were unsure about the projected postponement of the coal strike.

    _____ d. The coal strike, which is supposed to begin next week, may be postponed, according to labor leaders.

    _____ e. The strikers want better working conditions in the mines.

3. Nine terrorists who had occupied the French Embassy for three days released their four hostages today.

    _____ a. Four hostages were released by the terrorists who had held them captive.

    _____ b. The enemy troops captured nine men who became prisoners of war.

    _____ c. The hostages held in the French Embassy were turned loose today.

    _____ d. Terrorists let their hostages go today after keeping them prisoner for three days.

    _____ e. The prisoners had committed crimes against the State and were being sentenced to life imprisonment.

4. The Red Raiders finished fifth out of a field of six in the regional football standings.

    _____ a. The Red Raiders were second from the top in the region.

    _____ b. The Red Raiders basketball team won the regional championship last year.

    _____ c. The Red Raiders were next to the bottom in the region.

    _____ d. The new artificial turf will help the football team next year.

    _____ e. The Red Raiders tied for first place in the region.

5. The lawmakers voted to prohibit the importation of skunks into the state.

      ____ a. No more skunks can be brought into the state.

      ____ b. According to the lawmakers, all skunks must be removed from the state.

      ____ c. Skunks are a nuisance and belong only in state zoos.

      ____ d. The lawmakers decided to allow skunks to be exported from the state.

      ____ e. It is now illegal to bring skunks into the state from surrounding areas.

6. Legislation has been passed that permits persons convicted of capital crimes to enter a work release program.

      ____ a. A liberal rehabilitation bill now permits convicted criminals to participate in a work program.

      ____ b. Criminals will be allowed to enter the work release program.

      ____ c. Prisoners will be released from having to do any work.

      ____ d. A certain percentage of criminals will be set free in order to return to their homes.

      ____ e. All convicted criminals will be released from jail, according to recent legislation.

7. A small boy who had been kidnapped from his home was discovered safe a year later.

      ____ a. Kidnapping is a serious crime that carries a heavy penalty.

      ____ b. Small children must beware of kidnappers who might take them from their homes.

      ____ c. A young child was found safe a year after he had been kidnapped.

      ____ d. The parents of a young boy paid $5,000 ransom to the kidnappers.

      ____ e. The little boy was happy to be released from his kidnappers.

8. Aquaculture, or fish farming, offers a way of producing great quantities of fish to be used for food.

      ____ a. Fish can be found in unpolluted streams.

      ____ b. Fish scales and fish oil are used in manufacturing.

      ____ c. Aquaculture is a method of providing fish for food.

      ____ d. Great quantities of fish will be made available for food through aquaculture.

      ____ e. Fish farming will enable man to have more food by producing more fish.

9. A new vocational school is being built to serve the students of a three-county area.

   _____ a. Students will ride buses to the county seat.

   _____ b. Students from three counties will be able to attend the new vocational school.

   _____ c. Serving a three-county area, the new vocational school will provide training for many students.

   _____ d. Only students within walking distance will be able to attend the new vocational school.

   _____ e. A tri-county vocational school is being built.

10. Fire damaged twelve units of the motel during the night, but there were no reports of injuries.

   _____ a. There were no injuries when fire struck twelve units of the motel.

   _____ b. During the fire, twelve people were injured at the motel.

   _____ c. Fire damage to the motel was estimated at $12,000.

   _____ d. No one was injured during the fire at the motel.

   _____ e. It required twelve units of the fire department to extinguish the blaze at the motel.

11. Student government leaders from seventeen colleges and universities will meet to discuss issues in higher education.

   _____ a. Issues in higher education will be discussed by news commentators.

   _____ b. Student leaders are meeting for the purpose of discussing issues in higher education.

   _____ c. Seventeen colleges and universities will be represented at a meeting where issues in higher education will be discussed.

   _____ d. A discussion of student government in the school will be held by university professors.

   _____ e. To discuss issues in higher education, student leaders from seventeen colleges and universities will hold a meeting.

12. Reading is a thinking process.

   _____ a. Everyone should read great books.

   _____ b. It is necessary to think in order to read.

   _____ c. Recognizing words is reading.

   _____ d. Reading requires thought about the meanings of the words.

   _____ e. When a person reads, the person is thinking about what the words mean to her or him.

Role of Machines

Reading machines are often useful in helping you break through to a higher reading rate. By setting the speed on the machine at a higher rate than you normally read, your eyes are being forced to move more rapidly in order to keep up. You discover that your eyes are capable of moving faster and that you can read more quickly than you thought.

Reading machines have their limitations, however, and will do you little good unless you carry over this faster eye movement to reading that is not done with a machine. The machine has shown you that you can do it, but it is up to you to maintain this increased rate in the books and materials you are reading without the machine.

Physical Factors Related to Rapid Reading

Before you can become a rapid reader, you may need to break some bad habits developed during your childhood. Pointing with your finger, turning your head as you read, and whispering the words to yourself are habits that limit your reading speed. Making regressions, that is, letting your eyes go back to repeat what you have just read, also slows down your reading. Slouching in a chair or propping up in bed to read also tends to decrease your powers of concentration so that you cannot read as rapidly as you can when you are fully alert.

In order to read rapidly with comprehension, it is necessary to break these bad habits and substitute good habits for them. In this section are some ways of using your eyes and controlling vocalization in order to read more quickly.

Eye Movements

As you read, it may seem that your eyes are moving smoothly and continuously along the line of print. Actually, your eyes are moving in a series of rapid short jerks and pauses. Your eyes are only receiving visual impressions during the pauses or fixations. A poor reader will pause on each word, while a good reader will take in two or three words during each pause.

There are some ways of increasing your speed by controlling your eye movements. One way is to force your eyes to move rapidly across the line of print. Another way is to use your peripheral vision to increase your eye span. When you are focusing on a single word, your eyes can learn to pick up a word on either side of this word by using peripheral vision. Ra Exercise 2 and Ra Exercise 3 will help you develop this skill. Return to these exercises frequently to develop and maintain your ability to read a group of words in a single fixation.

Ra Exercise 2

Focus on the single word at the top of the list of words and phrases. Move your eyes down and read the next word. Continue moving your eyes downward, focusing on the word or words closest to the center line. Make a conscious effort not to move your eyes to one side or the other, but try to expand your eye span to take in the words on either side of the center line. Force your eyes to the outside edges without shifting their position. At first you may not be able to read anything but the middle word. After you practice awhile, you will be able to read short phrases and finally longer ones. When you can do this, you have increased your eye span so that you do not need to make a fixation for each word.

```
                        rate
                       vision
                     attention
                   concentration
                    for pleasure
                   more meaning
                  doing exercises
                increases eyespan
                  working on rate
               selecting key words
              covering the material
            powers of concentration
             develops reading skills
           limit your reading speed
        moving smoothly and continuously
```

Ra Exercise 3

Focus your eyes on the line that runs down the center of the pyramid. Without moving your eyes from the line, try to read the syllables on either side of the line. Keep stretching your span to the outside edges in order to increase the use of your peripheral vision.

```
              ad | pi
            mo .  | . ep
           eb . . | . . il
           si . . | . . uk
          fa . . . | . . . so
         ak . . . . | . . . . po
        id . . . . . | . . . . ba
      go . . . . . . | . . . . . re
     ti . . . . . . . | . . . . . . im
    ne . . . . . . . | . . . . . . et
```

Another way to increase your reading rate is to eliminate regressions. When you read a few words and then repeat the same words in order to make sure you got them right the first time, you are using twice as much time as necessary. Usually, your first perception is correct. If it is not right, the words that follow may redirect your thinking. Except in study reading, it is often worse to regress to check your first reading than it is to go on and risk being wrong. Regressions are often made from habit when there is no real need to verify what has just been read. When you make yourself keep going, you are also teaching yourself to pay attention to what you read the first time. Good readers rarely make regressions, except when they are doing study reading, and they read with a steady rhythm. They move their eyes with a minimum of fixations across the line of print, sweep their eyes back to the next line, and again move them rapidly across the line. It is important to develop a rhythmic pattern for reading and to avoid making regressions.

Vocalizations

Readers who vocalize are those who move their lips or say each word to themselves as they read. Some people are not aware that they are vocalizing, but they are actually reading word by word to themselves. If your silent reading rate does not exceed 250 words per minute, it is possible that you are vocalizing.

When you vocalize, you are limiting the rate of your reading. People rarely speak more than 150 words a minute. Although in reading you can pass this rate by slurring the words together, you still probably cannot get past 250 words per minute. Your mind is capable of absorbing much printed matter at a rate considerably higher than this. Adults should be able to read silently at three to four times their oral reading rate.

Vocalization is a barrier to rapid reading. It takes a great deal of effort to break this vocalization barrier to free yourself to read at far greater speeds.

If you are moving your lips as you read, you may be able to break this habit by putting your finger to your lips, holding your tongue between your teeth, or placing the knuckle of your forefinger between your teeth. At the same time force your eyes to move at a more rapid pace than you usually read. Machines can also be used to force your eyes to move so rapidly that you cannot say each word.

Another way you can overcome vocalization is by skipping over unimportant words and selecting only key words and phrases. All words in a reading selection do not have equal importance. Usually the nouns and verbs are most important, and the articles, pronouns, and prepositions are of least importance. Signpost words such as "not," "but," "however," and "only" are significant because they indicate a particular direction of thought. Also watch for words in italics, lists of main points, and summarizing statements.

Ra Exercise 4

In the following selection, key words and phrases have been italicized to separate them from less important words. Try reading only the italicized words in order to get the main ideas. At the end of the exercise place a check mark beside those sentences that express ideas from the article.

The *"Aids to Navigation,"* as they are now called, were *primitive affairs* back in the *old days for* the *sailing sloops on* the *Hudson River. Local people drove posts into* the *mud flats or hung lanterns on trees* or *poles near hazardous areas, or to mark* the *creeks.* Rocky *cliffs* were used to *sound* an *echo when* a *horn or bell* was *used nights, or in* a *fog.* However, *few traveled at night* unless necessary, *but "dropped* the *hook."*

The *U.S. Lighthouse Establishment* in *1789 hired "lamplighters"* to *service* and *place lanterns on* top of small wooden *structures.* Of course, *in winter,* the *river* was *closed* and *no lights* were *needed.*

The *first lighted tower* was *built* at *Stony Point* in *1826* of *stone from* the *old fort, famous in* the *Revolution.* The *keeper's dwelling* was *nearby.* This *round tower* is *now* a *tourist attraction in* a *State Park.* There were *nine "family stations" built later* with the *tower attached.* There were *other lighted towers* with a *keeper living nearby.* . . . [1]

1. ____ "Aids to Navigation" were primitive in the old days.

2. ____ Lanterns were hung from posts or trees in hazardous areas.

3. ____ Lighthouse keepers had to climb many steps to reach their lights.

4. ____ "Lamplighters" serviced and hung lanterns.

5. ____ A keeper's dwelling was built near to the first lighted tower.

6. ____ Lighthouses were built on rocks that jutted out into the water.

Ra Exercise 5

In the next article, insignificant words have been omitted from the text. Read to see if you can still identify the main ideas. Mark with a check those sentences at the end of the article that represent the ideas presented.

keepers   families   lived   years at   same
lighthouse,   wife or   son took over if
keeper died   rules   were   strict.   "Never let
light go out   ; use   lamp or   candle!"
(isn't   true today,   lights   unattended.)   "Ring
bell   in   fog."   old ones   wound up like   cuckoo
clock, with   heavy weight.   would run eight hours.
keeper   get up at night   start them   log
kept of date   hours rung, in case   ship ran aground   complained about
lack of   bell.   keeper had   alibi.   had to record   passing
of   ship,   assistance given   hours   ashore for mail   or
supplies.   twice a week,   family larder
kept well stocked in winter.   main chores   polish brass,
had to be spotless if   inspector   due.   included lamps

hand rails, door knobs,   oil cans   dust pans, wick boxes

          small items.   keeper had   lighthouse flag, white with

red border and   blue lighthouse   on   wide end.   flew

special occasions   uniform   seldom used   stored   for

burial.[2]

1. _____ Keepers and families lived at the same lighthouse for many years.

2. _____ The children of keepers went to school in boats.

3. _____ The keeper must keep the light burning and ring a bell in fog.

4. _____ The keeper had to polish brass.

5. _____ When the light went out, the ships would crash on the rocks.

6. _____ The keeper wore his uniform at all times when on duty.

Ra Exercise 6

Try eliminating the unimportant words in the following passage by marking a line through them. Mark out as many words as you can, but be sure you can still get the message.

The drinking water came from copper gutters off the roof, run through charcoal down into a cistern, and hand pumped as needed. River water was also hand pumped to pails for wash day. Some stations had a small pump in the kitchen sink, but the outlet pipe always froze in winter. In dry spells, the government tender could bring drinking water and pump it into the cistern. Usually, they had delivered coal oil to another station on the way up-river and used the same hose, so the water would taste and smell oily for some time.

The U.S. Coast Guard took over in 1938 and things changed. Now, ships of any size—with their modern compass, radio and radar— really don't need the lights or fog bells, and with their stronger hulls crash through the ice all winter. The Coast Guard icebreakers or tenders go back and forth to assist small ships, and even form a convoy to take several through heavy ice if needed. These seldom travel at night, but lay over until daybreak like a lighted parade at rest on the glistening ice. In summer, hundreds of cruisers, outboards, as well as the large ships from many foreign lands, travel day and night (especially the tugs and barges) with no thought of the lighthouses boarded up and keepers long gone.[3]

Increasing Your Rate

When you have been driving along slow city streets and you ride out into the country, you press the accelerator and force the car to move faster. At first, a speed of 40 seems fast compared to the slow city traffic. You press upward to 50 and feel that you are moving even faster. You surge toward 60, but settle back to cruise along at 55.

Your reading is like this. You may be on the slow city streets now, stopping and starting and moving along at an uneven rate. As you begin to increase your rate, you are like the driver leaving the city behind. You must push yourself to move faster, and the first increase you make seems fast compared to your former speed. Then you find you can force yourself to move even faster by exerting pressure. Eventually, you reach a speed where you have pushed yourself as far as you can. By dropping back slightly, you find that it is quite comfortable to be reading at a speed much faster than where you started.

Reading Words in Groups

When you have decided that you really want to read faster and are willing to work, following certain procedures will help you increase your speed. One of these is learning to read words in groups instead of one by one. As you increase your eye span, you find that your eyes can take in two, three, or even four words at a time. Reading words in groups will also tend to eliminate vocalization, for you are focusing on the group of words as a unit rather than each word by itself.

Your mind can absorb these words in groups more effectively than it can grasp single words, for ideas are often expressed in groups of words that are related to each other. It is more important to read every thought on the page than to read every word on the page. Reading in word groups will help both your speed and understanding.

Ra Exercise 7

In the following selection you will see how words can be grouped for meaning. Read it so that your eyes make a single fixation for each group of words and your mind absorbs each group as a thought unit.

If there is anyone   in the world   who should know   how to drive   on ice and snow,
it would have to be   the Swedes.   They have the weather,   for sure,   and they also
are affluent enough   to own   a lot of cars.
Every so often   the Saab automobile people   run seminars   on driving
on snow and ice.   The one   we got in on   was here   in the small logging town   of Torsby
in west-central Sweden.   There was ice racing   and a rally   but the real point
was safety   on the roads   in winter.
Safety itself   can be   a pretty dull subject   but if what you're doing
can lead you   into making good time   on bad roads   . . . safely . . .
it can become exciting.
A safety factor   that winter shares   with the rain and fog   of milder seasons
—and one often ignored   —is visibility.   If you can't see well   or be seen easily

you're in trouble.　The chap　who takes off　while peering　through a knothole-size
clear space　is no better　than a drunk　behind the wheel.　Either wait
until heat clears　all the windows　or scrape them　thoroughly.　And when it's murky,
drive with parking lights　or headlights.

There's no doubt　about it　that the best tires　for traction　in ice and snow
are studded snows.　And four　are better　than two.　But almost no one　goes for four
so settle　for two.　After that,　plain snow tires　and then radials.[4]

Ra Exercise 8

Identify the thought units in the following passage yourself. Place a slash (/) between thought units.

The cardinal rule of slick-road travel, whether slowly or at a hang-out speed, is never to do *anything* quickly. And moderate amounts of action usually are wisest. A quick turn often means loss of grip for the tires, a skid and sometimes the ditch or a tree. Too much of a twist on the wheel, too much brake or a stomp on the accelerator sometimes produce more spectacular results (such as a complete spin or a car that's facing backwards in traffic) but the results aren't anything to be proud of.

It's been said again and again—and it's still true: always turn toward the way you're skidding and not away. Sometimes turning into a skid can land you in the ditch, to be sure, but if you're in that bad a fix you'd have wound up there, anyway, except maybe at a different angle. Oftentimes it restores control.

One of the skills of winter driving that comes only with experience (and is harder to exercise with power steering) is the ability to feel the wheels, especially the fronts, becoming light and losing traction. Most mishaps on slick roads happen, not because of going fast or slowly, but because the driver fails to realize he's in trouble until too late.

Another obvious rule of good winter driving is planning ahead and driving ahead. Keep track of what's going on as far as possible ahead of you so that when you get there you're ready to turn, stop or whatever.[5]

Ra Exercise 9

Read each word and the phrases that follow. Put the letter of the phrase that means nearly the same thing as the word in the blank beside the number of the word. Do not read any more phrases than necessary in order to find the one that is similar in meaning. Try to read each phrase in a single fixation.

Example: _____ visible

a. dark as night
b. capable of being seen
c. obscured from sight
d. to stay with

You should have written the letter "b" in the blank space. "Visible" means nearly the same as "capable of being seen." Time yourself and try to finish this exercise within two minutes.

_____ 1. rapidly
    a. in a reasonable time
    b. day after tomorrow
    c. very quickly
    d. late at night

_____ 2. glimpse
    a. a brief look
    b. a steady gaze
    c. a glassy coating
    d. a mechanical device

_____ 3. echo
    a. a sudden noise
    b. refusal to speak
    c. system of communication
    d. repetition of a sound

_____ 4. far
    a. within reach
    b. at a considerable distance
    c. a place for animals
    d. side by side

_____ 5. empty
    a. half full of water
    b. brimming over
    c. containing nothing
    d. turned right side up

_____ 6. encourage
    a. to offer support
    b. to run away from
    c. to cause harm
    d. to distrust completely

_____ 7. hurricane
    a. a very fast movement
    b. an earthquake
    c. a walking stick
    d. a severe tropical storm

_____ 8. paralysis
    a. physical examination
    b. inability to move
    c. floating body of ice
    d. thick covering for a floor

_____ 9. neglect
    a. thoughtful attention
    b. willing cooperation
    c. failure to care for
    d. payment of taxes

_____ 10. hurt

    a. to feel physical pain
    b. to lend a helping hand
    c. to share a secret
    d. to hop on one foot

_____ 11. smash

    a. to burn with little smoke
    b. to put together
    c. to take apart gradually
    d. to break into pieces

_____ 12. sorrow

    a. a small bird
    b. a happy emotion
    c. mental suffering
    d. drowsy feeling

_____ 13. moment

    a. brief interval of time
    b. shifting position
    c. a large statue
    d. nearly a day

_____ 14. careful

    a. full of passengers
    b. proceeding with caution
    c. lack of thought
    d. wasteful spending

_____ 15. borrow

    a. a rabbit's hole
    b. to give away
    c. to place in the ground
    d. to obtain something on loan

_____ 16. perfect

    a. shattered to bits
    b. standing alone
    c. without flaw
    d. moderately good

_____ 17. start

    a. to set in motion
    b. to reach a conclusion
    c. to make a quick movement
    d. to produce a noise

_____ 18. late

    a. freedom from limitations
    b. after the expected time
    c. before the others
    d. toward the side

_____ 19. only

    a. many of a kind
    b. a wide selection
    c. part of a whole
    d. one of a kind

_____ 20. old
    a. having lived a long time
    b. standing in one place
    c. possessing youthful qualities
    d. in the early period of life

_____ 21. future
    a. movable articles in a room
    b. time yet to come
    c. having no useful result
    d. happening in the past

_____ 22. manager
    a. a box for feed
    b. one who controls or directs
    c. a skin disease
    d. under the domination of another

_____ 23. document
    a. to withhold salary
    b. to give medical treatment
    c. a pier or wharf
    d. a paper bearing evidence

_____ 24. reverse
    a. to hold in high regard
    b. to turn backward
    c. to study again
    d. to move forward rapidly

_____ 25. statistics
    a. an affair of state
    b. a sculptured form
    c. numerical data
    d. radio interference

Procedures for Practicing Rapid Reading

When you practice rapid reading, it is important to select easy, interesting material. Choose a familiar story, a book written for someone younger than you, or any light reading with no difficult words or concepts. The print should be large enough to avoid straining your eyes, and there should be enough space between the lines so your eyes can find the next line with ease. There should be several paragraphs to each page so that your eyes don't become lost in a page of solid words.

When you are working on speed, you must observe good study skills. Be sure that you are sitting up straight in a chair, that you have adequate light, and that you are relatively free of distractions. Establish a purpose for your reading, and then preview what is to be read. Give full attention to your reading task, and read the article as quickly as you can.

As is true for any other skill, rapid reading requires regular practice over a period of time. Working with a machine once a week for several weeks will not change your reading habits. Set aside a period of one hour daily when you are not tired and when you are willing to read under pressure. Continue these practice periods over months and years so that you will not slip back into lazy habits.

If you have been following the suggestion at the beginning of the book, you have been keeping a record of your reading progress. Record keeping is important to increasing speed, because it allows you to compete against yourself in trying to increase your reading efficiency. You should try to increase your speed and maintain or improve your comprehension each week. However, don't be discouraged if you seem to be standing still for a couple of weeks or even if you occasionally drop back. Plateaus in learning are natural, and they are usually followed by learning spurts during which you will again show progress. Dropping back may be explained by your own emotional and physical health or the difficulty and interest level of the material you are reading. If you follow the suggestions in this chapter and practice consistently, your reading rate will almost certainly increase.

Skimming

Skimming is the complex process of glancing over a page and selecting key words and ideas that provide needed information. It is one of the most difficult and advanced reading skills, but also one of the most useful. It requires an awareness of purpose, knowledge of organization, recognition of reading signposts, and efficient eye movements. Learning to skim takes practice, but knowing how to skim will save many hours of reading time.

Purposes for Skimming

It is important to know when to skim and when to read carefully. Skimming can be used for a variety of purposes, but it is not appropriate for studying for tests, reading critically, or appreciating fine literature. Skimming techniques can be applied to single pages, articles, or entire books. Some ways skimming can be used to save valuable time are listed below.

1. Surveying a reference book to see whether it is appropriate for a research project.
2. Choosing an appealing book for recreational reading.
3. Discovering the outstanding features of an entire book.
4. Locating specific information from a great deal of material that is irrelevant.
5. Grasping the important news in a newspaper.
6. Rapidly identifying the central thought of an article.
7. Increasing reading efficiency by a quick preliminary survey.
8. Locating the main idea or a sequence of ideas.
9. Assessing material that seems to contain nothing new, but may be too important to ignore.

Techniques for Skimming

Skimming techniques are a composite of all other good reading and study skills. To skim, you must avoid distractions and give full attention to your task. You must be familiar with the concepts and vocabulary so that comprehension will not pose a problem. Finally, you must be willing to skip over insignificant words and sometimes entire pages. You should let your eyes fly over the pages, picking out only what you need.

As you practice skimming, you will find that you are establishing patterns of eye movements. You may be reading across the first line or two of print to get the thought of each paragraph and then zigzagging across the page to pick out key words and ideas. You may find it helpful to use your finger to guide your eyes in moving rapidly in a zigzag pattern until this pattern becomes a habit. Force your finger to move quickly and your eyes to keep pace.

Ra Exercise 10

Practice skimming by reading the following paragraphs to find the sentence that does not belong. Write the number of that sentence in the space provided at the end of each paragraph. Work as fast as you can.

Clue: Look for a word or phrase that does not seem to fit with the rest of the paragraph.

Example:

[1]Nomads are people who wander about without having any settled home. [2]Usually they wander through a general region in a cycle determined by the seasons. [3]The Nootka Indians made the finest canoes in the world. [4]Although there are few true nomads today, there are some pastoral nomads who live in the deserts of Arabia, Central Asia, and North Africa. [5]They have a simple life and live in portable tents.

———

You should have written 3 in the blank space provided. The entire paragraph deals with nomads except for sentence 3 which mentions the Nootka Indians.

Time yourself. If you read all of these paragraphs in less than four minutes, you broke the vocalization barrier. If you read them in less than one minute, you were skimming!

1.　　[1]Mesquite is a thorny, low shrub that grows in dry climates. [2]Sometimes its roots may reach 60 feet into the ground in search of water. [3]The Sahara desert is the largest in the world. [4]The wood of the mesquite is used for fuel, to make fence posts, and to construct buildings. [5]The seeds or beans serve as food for cattle and the gum from the tree is used to make candies and Mexican dyes.

———

2.　　[1]Scheherazade was a legendary queen who married a Persian sultan. [2]The lute and the harp were two popular musical instruments during the Middle Ages. [3]The Sultan is said to have strangled each of his wives the morning after the wedding. [4]Since Scheherazade entertained the Sultan with stories each night, he allowed her to live. [5]These stories are found in the *Arabian Nights*.

———

3.   ¹With nuclear power, submarines can cruise underwater for almost indefinite periods of time. ²They may be the most important strategic force in the event of a nuclear war. ³Submarines were first used as weapons of war during World War I and played an even greater role in World War II. ⁴Most submarines are shaped like cigars. ⁵Cigarettes are hazardous to your health.

_____

4.   ¹Snowflakes are six-sided ice crystals that form when the water vapor in clouds freezes. ²No two snow crystals are exactly alike. ³ When lakes freeze, people can go ice skating. ⁴Snow crystals may be flat or they may form long needles. ⁵Sometimes snow crystals cling together to form flakes over an inch thick.

_____

5.   ¹Portland, Oregon, has a refurbished downtown area and a renowned rose garden. ²It hosts a major-league sports franchise and a variety of ethnic restaurants. ³In recent years Portland has acquired a theater with a planetarium-like dome. ⁴The Statue of Liberty stands in New York Harbor. ⁵With the addition of its theater, Portland has become a city of cultural significance.

_____

6.   ¹Montezuma was an Aztec ruler of Mexico who became emperor in 1440. ²He was a great military leader and increased the land holdings of the Empire. ³He built a huge dike to keep the waters from flooding his capital and constructed an aqueduct to bring in fresh water. ⁴As part of the public works program he started, many temples, water conduits, and hospitals were constructed. ⁵The great pyramids of Egypt were built as tombs for Egyptian rulers.

_____

7.   ¹Soybeans have been grown in China for about 5,000 years. ²The Chinese used them for food and medicine. ³Turnips are used for food. ⁴In the United States soybeans have been used for many years as a source of food, raw materials, and animal feed. ⁵They have more protein than beef and more calcium than milk.

_____

8.   ¹People who are deaf may communicate by a system of hand signs and gestures known as sign language. ²This form of communication has been used for thousands of years. ³Primitive people exchanged messages with sign language, and early monks who took vows of silence communicated in a similar manner. ⁴Morse code uses a system of dots and dashes and was invented by Samuel Morse. ⁵Sign language is also used for signals in sports.

_____

9.   ¹Mistletoe is an evergreen plant with thick clusters of green leaves. ²It lives as a parasite on the branches of trees. ³Meadow larks live in fields, meadows, and marshes. ⁴Long ago the Druids cut mistletoe from a sacred oak and gave it to the people for good luck charms. ⁵Today kissing under the mistletoe is a Christmas tradition.

_____

10.	¹Stonehenge, an ancient monument in England, is believed by some scholars to be a monument to the sun. ²Stars seem to twinkle in the sky because of the moving layers of the atmosphere. ³Many of the stones that make up this monument came from distances of 300 miles. ⁴Scientists have determined that Stonehenge is nearly 4,000 years old. ⁵Although many of the great stones fell or were carried away, the British government is now restoring this ancient monument.

_____

11.	¹One way to explore the strange world under the sea is by skin diving. ²Skin divers may use cameras encased in waterproof boxes to photograph their undersea exploits. ³Others carry rubber or mechanical guns to propel long spears. ⁴A swimmer must be able to use all the basic swimming strokes in order to earn a Red Cross Lifesaving badge. ⁵Sometimes the remains of ancient ships have been discovered by skin divers and treasures have been brought back for study.

_____

12.	¹Boa constrictors are found in the tropical parts of America. ²They kill animals for food by squeezing them with their long bodies. ³These snakes are not poisonous. ⁴Beavers live in lakes and streams. ⁵Boa constrictors can live for many months without food.

_____

13.	¹The Bridge of Sighs spans the canal between the Doge's Palace and the state prison in Venice, Italy. ²It was called the Bridge of Sighs because the prisoners walked across it years ago as they went from the prison to the palace for trial. ³Vienna, Austria, is a beautiful city. ⁴If the prisoners were found guilty, they were sent to their death. ⁵Many tourists visit the famous Bridge of Sighs today.

_____

14.	¹Mummies are embalmed bodies that have been preserved for thousands of years. ²Because the ancient Egyptians believed that the dead continued to live on in the next world, they felt that their bodies must be preserved forever. ³The embalmers were very skillful and could remove the brain through a nostril. ⁴Bodies were wrapped carefully in many layers of linen cloth and placed in coffins. ⁵Skeletons are used in the study of anatomy.

_____

15.	¹The largest known fish is the whale shark, which may be more than 50 feet long. ²These sharks have jaws wide enough to swallow a man. ³Fortunately, they are harmless and feed only on small sea plants and animals. ⁴Salmon swim upstream to spawn and sometimes leap more than 10 feet over swirling rapids. ⁵A baby whale shark was caught in Florida and weighed over 15 tons.

_____

16.	¹The Saint Lawrence Seaway permits large ocean-going ships to sail from the Atlantic Ocean to ports on the Great Lakes. ²Canoeing on lakes and rivers is a favorite pastime for many sports enthusiasts. ³The Seaway is the world's largest inland waterway for deep-sea navigation. ⁴It extends 182 miles from Montreal to the mouth of Lake Ontario. ⁵Grains from the Midwest and ores from Minnesota are shipped at low rates over the seaway.

_____

282

Ra Exercise 11

If you are reading columns, as in newspapers, your eyes may be going straight down the center of each column as you use your peripheral vision to pick up words on the edges of the columns. This exercise is written in columns. Focus your eyes on the center of the first column and move rapidly downwards. Do not move your eyes to either side, but let your peripheral vision work for you. Read to get the main ideas, and at the end of the article check those statements that represent the ideas expressed in or implied by the article.

Gold Nuggets in Your Attic[6]

Del Deterling

*Your "junque" may be an "antique" to someone else. Here's a way
to dispose of household items that is fast, easy, and profitable.*

"I hear a dollar. Who'll bid dollar-and-a-half? I have a dollar-and-a-half. Now two dollars. Two dollars. Who'll give two-and-a-half? Do I hear two-and-a-half? Two dollars. Two dollars. Sold to No. 23 for two dollars."

The sun was still high in the sky as the auctioneer's chant finally droned to a halt. My dad's lawn—covered from flowerbeds to curb with people, beds, chairs, boxes, pots, and assorted odds-and-ends only hours previously—suddenly was barren. Only the trampled grass, several bits of paper and string, and the few items remaining to be picked up by their new owners gave evidence that this had been the scene of a public auction.

In less than four hours, over 250 separate lots had been sold—ranging from a five-year-old washer that brought $105 to a bucket of kitchen items that sold for 50 cents.

In fact, everything sold.

Nearly every family finds itself in the position sometime of having to dispose of household goods. Maybe it's to get rid of stuff they don't want to move to town, or furniture and knickknacks that won't fit in with the decor of a new house, or to settle an estate.

Whatever the reason, disposing of household contents can be a chore. Trying to sell individual pieces can stretch out over weeks and months. Antique collectors, bargain hunters, and curiosity seekers come at odd, often inconvenient, hours. Somebody has to be there to deal with them.

Then there's the problem of putting a price tag on items when you have no idea what they are worth. And what do you do with those things that *nobody* wants?

For these reasons and others, a public auction is the best way to dispose of household goods. It's fast, convenient and fun.

"This way you get rid of everything in one day," says E. E. Orsak of Schulenburg, Tex., who handles more than two dozen household auctions a year. "People will buy things at auctions they ordinarily wouldn't touch.

You may get only 50 cents, but that's better than hauling it off to the junkyard.

"Besides, competitive bidding is the only real way of establishing the value of household items," Orsak adds. "Sure, you might get more for some things if you peddled them at the right places. But that takes time. Overall, you'll do better at an auction because everything sells."

A successful auction has to be planned.

• First, find an auctioneer. A professional usually will more than repay the cost of his services. He's fast and efficient, and he has the ability to coax that extra dollar out of a buyer.

Some auctioneers take a flat fee, but most work on commissions— up to 15% of gross sales, depending on what services they provide. It helps to get one with experience in auctioning household goods.

• Pick a time. Sunday afternoons are best, Orsak believes. "People will drive 100 miles or more on a Sunday to go to a country auction."

"Advertise to attract the attention of the type of buyers you want at your auction," Orsak advises. "If you have quite a few antiques, buy space in antique collectors' publications. Also use daily newspapers in nearby metropolitan areas, country weeklies, and local radio stations. Printed circulars may be justified if you have a large number of items to sell. List major items that will attract the attention of prospective buyers, such as antiques, bedroom suites, and freezers."

• Advertise. Cost is reasonable; attracting just a few extra bidders will pay the bill. And the more buyers on hand, the higher the bidding.

• Organize. Inventory all items for sale, and tag them with a number. On the day of the sale, display them for several hours ahead of time so buyers can see what is available. If possible, move all items to the auction area so they can be seen as they are sold.

• Save money by having family members keep sales records and collect the money. Designate someone to release items for loading after they have been paid for.

You'll be surprised at how many items have accumulated over the years. Some things that you may consider junk other people consider antiques. So as you prepare to clean out the attic, don't be surprised if you uncover a few "gold nuggets."

1. _____ Auctions are good ways to dispose of household goods.

2. _____ The best way to get rid of what you no longer need is to sell it to a junk dealer.

3. _____ Sunday afternoons are the best times for auctions.

4. _____ Competitive bidding is the only real way of establishing the value of household items.

5. _____ People usually enjoy auctions.

6. _____ It is not necessary to advertise when you hold an auction.

7. _____ A professional auctioneer is fast and efficient.

8. _____ Your junk may be a gold nugget for someone else.

Select interesting, easy reading material when you practice skimming. Try setting yourself a time limit of two minutes to skim through a chapter or an article and see how much you can find out in that amount of time. You may wish to ask a friend to time you so that you can give your complete attention to your reading.

Another way to force yourself to read faster is to use a commercial reading accelerator. This machine has a shutter which slides down over the page. The shutter forces your eyes to move quickly so that you can read the material before it is covered. If you don't have an accelerator, try using a 3″ × 5″ card. It is important to place the card above the lines you are reading and to move it down over the page faster than you normally read.

Scanning

Scanning is the process of moving your eyes rapidly over reading material in order to locate a specific piece of information. It isn't really reading, but it is selecting the one bit of information you need from written material. If you keep the image of what you are seeking clearly in mind, the answer should practically leap out at you.

Like skimming, scanning can save you much time if you learn to use it well. As you scan, your eyes flash down a column or dart quickly over a page, ignoring everything until they focus on the one word, phrase, or number you are trying to find.

Purposes for Scanning

You already may be using some scanning techniques when you look up a number in the telephone directory or find a word in the dictionary. You may not be applying your scanning ability to other areas where it can also be useful, however. Some ways you can use this technique are listed below.

1. Looking through your notes for some specific information you can't quite recall as you review just before a test.
2. Searching through the *Reader's Guide to Periodical Literature* for journal articles suitable for a research topic.
3. Looking for specific names, dates, titles, statistics, or topics in lists such as those found in indexes, dictionaries, telephone directories, or tables.
4. Locating specific answers to objective questions while you are doing a homework assignment.
5. Locating the infomation you want to find in schedules, such as television listings, course offerings, and travel schedules.
6. Finding a formula in an engineering or physics textbook.
7. Scanning the classified ads in the newspaper for a certain type of job or used car.
8. Looking at a calendar to find the day of the week on which a certain date falls.

Procedures for Scanning

When you scan, be sure you know *exactly* what you are looking for so you will recognize it when you see it. Is it a date, a number, a name, or a particular word? Will it probably be in quotation marks, in dark print, or in italics? Will there likely be a clue near it, such as "m.p.h.?" If so, watch for the identifying feature or clue that will help you recognize the answer.

You also need to understand the organization of the material so you know where to look. Is the material arranged numerically, alphabetically, chronologically, or in some other way?

You should now be ready to begin scanning the material. Move your eyes quickly; resist the temptation to read each word. Keep in mind what you are looking for and stop as soon as you think you have found it. Confirm your finding by checking the text immediately surrounding your answer. If you have found the right answer, you are finished. If not, continue scanning until you get the information you need.

Basically, there are three kinds of material you need to scan. For each kind, the procedure varies slightly. Some material is arranged in lists or columns, such as indexes and telephone directories. In this case, your eyes need only move rapidly downward. Some material is found in tables, charts, maps, or other types of graphic displays. In order to scan this type of material, you need to be familiar with the organization and then locate the logical position of the information you want. Other material is written in narrative form. For this type of material, you will need to move your eyes in a zigzag pattern, as in skimming, until you find a particular answer. The following exercises will give you practice in scanning each of these types of materials. (Additional exercises on scanning are in Chapter 12.)

Ra Exercise 12

Look at the list of telephone numbers on the next page.[7] Notice how it is organized. Practice scanning the columns to find the numbers for the following locations. As soon as you have found a number, write it in the space next to the name of the city. Try to fill in all of the blanks in one minute.

a. Denver, Colorado ⸻⸻⸻⸻⸻⸻⸻

b. Nashville, Tennessee ⸻⸻⸻⸻⸻⸻⸻

c. Philadelphia, Pennsylvania ⸻⸻⸻⸻⸻⸻

d. Wilmington, Delaware ⸻⸻⸻⸻⸻⸻

e. Washington, D.C. ⸻⸻⸻⸻⸻⸻⸻

f. Seattle, Washington ⸻⸻⸻⸻⸻⸻

g. Honolulu, Hawaii ⸻⸻⸻⸻⸻⸻⸻

Alabama
Birmingham 205-251-9454
Huntsville 205-534-5203
Mobile 205-433-6993
Montgomery 205-262-8304

Alaska
Anchorage 907-279-0653

Arizona
Phoenix 602-261-3560
Tucson 602-624-9042

Arkansas
Little Rock 501-372-3891

California
Bakersfield 805-861-4105
Carson 213-632-3555
El Monte 213-571-6902
Fresno 209-268-5395
Los Angeles 213-617-3177
Oakland 415-839-4245
Oxnard 805-485-7236
Riverside 714-351-6769
Sacramento 916-448-4367
San Diego 619-293-5020
San Francisco 415-863-4039
San Jose 408-293-5606
Santa Ana 714-836-2974
Santa Maria 805-928-7503
Santa Rosa 707-528-6233
Stockton 209-463-6005
Van Nuys 213-997-3293
Visalia 209-733-8194

Colorado
Denver 303-296-0462

Connecticut
Bridgeport 203-335-0070
Hartford 203-547-0015

Delaware
Wilmington 302-652-0272

District of Columbia
Call 202-628-2929

Florida
Ft. Lauderdale 305-523-3100
Jacksonville 904-353-9579
Miami 305-374-5144
Orlando 305-422-0592
Tallahassee 904-222-0807
Tampa 813-229-9255
West Palm
Beach 305-655-1996

Georgia
Albany 912-435-1415
Atlanta 404-221-6572
Augusta 404-722-9068
Columbus 404-327-0298
Macon 912-745-2890
Savannah 912-355-9632

Hawaii
Honolulu 808-546-7162

Idaho
Boise 208-383-0034

Illinois
Bloomington 309-828-6116
Champaign 217-398-1779
Chicago 312-886-9614
Peoria 309-637-9305
Quad Cities 319-326-1720
Rockford 815-987-4280
Springfield 217-789-0489

Indiana
Evansville 812-422-1026
Gary 219-884-4465
Indianapolis 317-634-1550

Iowa
Des Moines 515-284-6117
Quad Cities 319-326-1720
Waterloo 319-234-0817

Kansas
Wichita 316-264-3147

Kentucky
Erlanger 606-727-3338
Lexington 606-233-2889
Louisville 502-582-5599

Louisiana
New Orleans 504-529-2854

Maine
Portland 207-775-0465

Maryland
Baltimore 301-244-7306

Massachusetts
Boston 617-523-8602
Springfield 413-739-6624

Michigan
Ann Arbor 313-665-4544
Detroit 313-961-4282
Flint 313-238-4599
Grand Rapids 616-451-2034
Kalamazoo 616-343-0255
Lansing 517-372-2454
Mt. Clemens 313-463-9550
Pontiac 313-858-2336
Saginaw 517-753-9911

Minnesota
St. Paul 612-224-4288

Mississippi
Gulfport 601-863-3302
Jackson 601-960-4168

Missouri
Kansas City 816-421-3741
St. Louis 314-241-4700

Montana
Billings 406-656-1422
Helena 406-443-7034

Nebraska
Omaha 402-221-3324

Nevada
Las Vegas 702-385-1778

New Hampshire
Manchester 603-623-5778

New Jersey
Atlantic City 609-348-2636
Camden 609-966-3412
Newark 201-624-1223
Trenton 609-599-2150

New Mexico
Albuquerque 505-766-1102

New York
Albany 518-465-8318
Brooklyn 212-858-4461
Buffalo 716-856-9320
Manhattan 212-406-4080
Mineola 516-248-6790
Poughkeepsie 914-452-1877
Rochester 716-454-3330
Smithtown 516-979-0720
Syracuse 315-471-1630
White Plains 914-683-0134

North Carolina
Asheville 704-254-3044
Charlotte 704-371-6352
Durham 919-541-5283
Fayetteville 919-483-0735
Greensboro 919-378-1572
Raleigh 919-755-1498
Winston-
Salem 919-725-3013

North Dakota
Bismarck 701-258-8210
Fargo 701-232-9360
Grand Forks 701-746-0324

Ohio
Akron 216-253-1170
Cincinnati 513-421-8050
Cleveland 216-522-3037
Columbus 614-463-1898
Dayton 513-461-9755
Toledo 419-255-3743

Oklahoma
Oklahoma City 405-235-3434
Tulsa 918-599-0555

Oregon
Eugene 503-687-6737
Portland 503-294-5363
Salem 503-399-5784

Pennsylvania
Bethlehem 215-861-0325
Erie 814-459-7419
Harrisburg 717-236-1356
Philadelphia 215-592-8946
Pittsburgh 412-281-3120
Scranton 717-961-0325
Wilkes Barre 717 823 9552

Rhode Island
Providence 401-861-5220

South Carolina
Charleston 803-722-0369
Columbia 803-254-4749
Greenville 803-235-8093

South Dakota
Rapid City 605-348-3454
Sioux Falls 605-335-7081
Watertown 605-882-4979

Tennessee
Chattanooga 615-892-5577
Knoxville 615-521-7478
Memphis 901-525-2611
Nashville 615-242-1541

Texas
Austin 512-479-0391
Dallas 214-767-1792
Houston 713-850-8801
San Antonio 512-680-9591

Utah
Salt Lake City 801-355-9328

Vermont
Burlington 802-658-0007

Virginia
Bailey's
Crossroads 703-557-0034
Norfolk 804-441-3623
Richmond 804-771-2369
Roanoke 703-982-6062

Washington
Seattle 206-343-7221
Spokane 509-455-9213
Tacoma 206-383-4668

West Virginia
Charleston 304-343-3597
Huntington 304-523-0104

Wisconsin
Green Bay 414-433-3884
Madison 608-264-5349
Milwaukee 414-291-1783
Racine 414-886-1615

Wyoming
Cheyenne 307-634-1198

Ra Exercise 13

In order to scan for information in the Schedule of Classes on the next page,[8] you will need to look across the top of each column to see what kind of information is given and in which column it can be found. Then look down the first column to see how the subjects are arranged. You will need to know what the following abbreviations represent: M–Monday, T–Tuesday, W–Wednesday, R–Thursday, and F–Friday. Now scan the schedule for the six purposes related to the class schedule.

1. You need to take the nursing practicum, but you are concerned about the number of hours you need to be on campus. About how many hours do you need to attend class each week for NURS 371B-001?

   _____

2. You work full time during the day, but you would like to take a PE course one night a week to keep in shape. What course is available? _____

   What night does it meet? _____

3. If you take MUS 412–001, who will your instructor be? _____

4. What days and time does MUST 423–001 meet? _____

5. You have a job that keeps you off campus until almost 1:00 every day. If you want to take beginning tennis, what section will you need to take? _____

6. You commute forty miles to school and try to schedule all of your classes on Tuesdays and Thursdays. What section of PE 103 will you need to take? _____

SCHEDULE OF CLASSES[8]

CALL NO.	DISC.	CRS. NO.	SEC. NO.	TITLE OF COURSE	QTR HRS	SCHEDULE TIME	DAYS	BLDG. & ROOM		INSTRUCTOR
03645	MUS	−400	−001	SENIOR RECITAL	1	TBA	TBA	FA	264	LAMB, M
03651	MUS	−412	−001	CONTEMPORARY MUSIC	3	TBA	TBA	FA	374	BRAHMSTEDT, H
03655	MUS	−450	−001	PRIVATE CONDUCTING	1	TBA	TBA	FA	356	WRIGHT, R
03702	MUS	−450	−002	PRIVATE CONDUCTING	1	TBA	TBA	FA	107	WATTENBARGER, J
03713	MUS	−450	−003	PRIVATE CONDUCTING	2	TBA	TBA	FA	356	WRIGHT JR
03721	MUS	−450	−004	PRIVATE CONDUCTING	2	TBA	TBA	FA	107	WATTENBARGER, J
03723	MUS	−450	−005	PRIVATE CONDUCTING	2	TBA	TBA	FA	103	WATTENBARGER, J
02761	MUST	−423	−001	MUSIC IN THERAPY	5	1010A − 1200P	MW	FA	305	SUMMER, L
02765	MUST	−424	−001	MUSIC THERAPY PRACTICUM	3	TBA	TBA	FA	305	SUMMER, L
04987	MUST	−426	A −001	MUS THERAPY-EXCEPT CHIL	3	TBA	TBA	FA	305	SUMMER, L
02747	MUST	−451	−001	SPEC PROB IN MUS THERAP	1	TBA	TBA	FA	305	SUMMER, L
02753	MUST	−451	−002	SPEC PROB IN MUS THERAP	2	TBA		FA	305	SUMMER, L
02757	MUST	−451	−003	SPEC PROB IN MUS THERAP	3	TBA	TBA	FA	305	SUMMER, L
02767	NURS	−201	−001	INTRODUCTION TO NURSING	3	0110P − 0400P	W	NS	203	
02771	NURS	−313	−001	PHARMACOL ASPECT-NURS I	2	0110P − 0300P	T	NS	218	TATUM, D
02773	NURS	−315	−001	SURVEY OF PHARMA ASPECT	3	0510P − 0800P	T	NS	203	TATUM, D
02775	NURS	−323	−001	PROF NURS CONCEPTS III	3	0810A − 1100A	T	NS	218	RUSSELL, G
04889	NURS	−371	A −001	NURS PROCESS/PRACT III	5	0810A − 1100A	F	NS	218	CRAWFORD, L
						0110P − 0300P	F			
04891	NURS	−371	B −001	PRACTICUM	5	0710A − 0300P	WR	NS	110	KELLY, T
04909	NURS	−371	B −002	PRACTICUM	5	0710A − 0300P	WR	NS	112	DEPRIEST, S
04911	NURS	−371	B −003	PRACTICUM	5	0710A − 0300P	WR	NS	115	ADKISSON, C
04913	NURS	−371	B −004	PRACTICUM	5	0710A − 0300P	WR	NS	203	CRAWFORD
04915	NURS	−371	B −005	PRACTICUM	5	0710A − 0300p	WR	NS	119	RUSSELL, G
04917	NURS	−371	B −006	PRACTICUM	5	0710A − 0300P	WR	NS	218	WATKINS, L
02801	NURS	−422	−001	PROF ENTRY INTO PRACTIC	3	0110P − 0400P	W	NS	202	TAYLOR, P
02803	NURS	−433	−001	HEA ASSESSMNT IMPLEMNTA	3	0110P − 0400P	T	NS	110	TBA
02805	NURS	−433	−100	HEA ASSESSMNT IMPLEMNTA		0110P − 0400P	T	NS	110	TBA
02777	NURS	−437	A −001	NURS PROCES & PRACT VI	5	0810A − 1100A	T	NS	202	SADLER, M
						0110P − 0300P	T	NS	202	
02781	NURS	−473	B −001	NURS PROC & PRAC VI LAB	6	0810A − 1200P	W	NS	202	TAYLOR, P
						0810A − 0430P	RF	NS	202	
02735	NURS	−473	B −002	NURS PROC & PRAC VI LAB	6	0810A − 1200P	W	NS	218	MERHOFF, C
						0810A − 0430P	RF	NS	218	
02787	NURS	−473	B −003	NURS PROC & PRAC VI LAB	6	0810A − 1200P	W	NS	114	HANNA
						0810A − 0430P	RF	NS	114	
02795	NURS	−473	B −004	NURS PROC & PRAC VI LAB	6	0810A − 1200P	W	NS	215	SADLER, M
						0810A − 0430P	RF	NS	215	
02807	PE	−090	−100	CONDITIONING & AGILITY		0310P − 0400P	MTWRF	ES	114	RAGLAND, J
02817	PE	−100	C −001	MODIFIED SEASONAL SPORT	1	0610P − 0800P	R	HP	107	ROERNER, J
02827	PE	−101	A −001	BEGINNING TENNIS	1	0810A − 0900A	MW	HP	GYMC	WHITE, R
02835	PE	−101	A −002	BEGINNING TENNIS	1	0910A − 1000A	MW	HP	GYMC	WHITE, R
02841	PE	−101	A −003	BEGINNING TENNIS	1	1210P − 0100P	MW	HP	STAN	TBA
02847	PE	−101	A −004	BEGINNING TENNIS	1	1010A − 1100A	MW	HP	STAN	TBA
02853	PE	−101	A −005	BEGINNING TENNIS	1	1110A − 1200P	MW	HP	STAN	TBA
02857	PE	−101	A −006	BEGINNING TENNIS	1	0810A − 0900A	TR	HP	STAN	CAMPBELL, M
02863	PE	−101	A −007	BEGINNING TENNIS	1	0910A − 1000A	TR	HP	STAN	CAMPBELL, M
02871	PE	−101	A −008	BEGINNING TENNIS	1	1010A − 1100A	TR	HP	STAN	CAMPBELL, M
02877	PE	−101	A −009	BEGINNING TENNIS	1	1210P − 0100P	TR	HP	STAN	HOLLOWAY, M
02881	PE	−101	A −010	BEGINNING TENNIS	1	0110P − 0200P	TR	HP	STAN	HOLLOWAY, M
02887	PE	−102	−001	SWIMMING	1	0910A − 1000A	MW	HP	POOL	RIFL-NAIL, R
02895	PE	−102	−002	SWIMMING	1	1010A − 1100A	MW	HP	POOL	RIEL-NAIL, R
02899	PE	−103	−001	BOWLING	1	0810A − 0900A	MW	HP	STAN	ROERNER, J
				NOTE: OFF CAMPUS AND HAS FEE.						
02905	PE	−103	−002	BOWLING	1	0910A − 1000A	MW	HP	STAN	JEWELL, S
				NOTE: OFF CAMPUS AND HAS FEE.						
02913	PE	−103	−003	BOWLING	1	1010A − 1100A	MW	HP	STAN	JEWELL, S
				NOTE: OFF CAMPUS AND HAS FEE.						
02919	PE	−103	−004	BOWLING	1	0810A − 0900A	TR	HP	STAN	SALANSKY, G
				NOTE: OFF CAMPUS AND HAS FEE.						

Ra Exercise 14

1. In the article below, scan to find how many miles Holdfast had to run between Mobile and Nashville. Be sure to confirm your answer. Write the answer here. _____

Holdfast[9]

George C. Wallace

Captain Lukert hurried to stop a battle. Other men have raced to help start one.

Most people have read about the "message to Garcia" and how the brave Lieutenant Rowan took the message from President McKinley through miles of Cuban jungle to General Garcia. Some have also read about the feat of the Greek courier Phidippedes, who ran over 20 miles to Athens after the Battle of Marathon and, after uttering the words, "Rejoice, we conquer," fell dead. But few have read or heard about perhaps the greatest runner in history. He was Sleeping Bear of the Mohegan Tribe, better known as "Holdfast Gaines." This is his story.

The year was 1814, and General Andrew Jackson needed reinforcements to fight the British at New Orleans. His only source of men was the troops from Kentucky and Tennessee that General William Carroll could muster at Nashville. But Nashville was 600 miles away, and time was critical.

After studying his map, General Jackson told Holdfast that he could give him only ten days to deliver the message to Nashville, if the troops were to reach New Orleans before Christmas.

Holdfast started his epic run, November 7. There he was, a pure-blooded Mohegan Indian, running through the country of the Creeks, Cherokees, Choctaws, and Chickasaws, to bring down a bunch of badly mixed backwoodsmen so they could help a Scotch-Irishman save the French-Spanish city of New Orleans from the British Army. Through the days and some of the nights, his lean legs carried him along the Tombigbee River to Yowanni, Pontotoc, and Colbert's Ferry, and then along the Natchez Trace to Nashville.

General Carroll was having supper on the night of November 12, when Holdfast interrupted him to lay Jackson's message in his hands. When Carroll noted the date of the letter, he announced, in awe, that Holdfast had run the 600 miles from Mobile to Nashville in just six days.

Holdfast did not hear the excited talk throughout the night as plans were made to move down the rivers to Jackson's aid. He was asleep by the fireplace.

General Carroll and his 3,000 troops reached New Orleans in time to help Jackson defeat the British, thanks to the lost hero of the War of 1812, Holdfast Gaines, probably the greatest of all runners.

---

2. Now look back through the story to find the date that Holdfast started his famous run. Write the answer here. _____

Chapter Notes

1. Excerpted from Ruth Reynolds Glunt, "Never Let the Lights Go Out!" reprinted by permission from *The Conservationist,* December–January, 1972–73, pp. 24–25.

2. Ibid.

3. Ibid.

4. Reprinted from *Mechanix Illustrated Magazine, Copyright 1974 by* Fawcett Publications, Inc.

5. Ibid.

6. Del Deterling, "Gold Nuggets in Your Attic," reprinted by permission from *The Progressive Farmer,* December, 1973, p. 76.

7. "Tele-Tax," reprinted from the Department of the Treasury, Internal Revenue Service, Publication 1163 (Rev. 9-83).

8. *Schedule of Classes,* Spring Quarter, 1989, p. 47, reprinted by permission of Tennessee Technological University.

9. George C. Wallace, "Holdfast," in Richard J. Sommers, ed., *U.S. Army Military History Research Collection, Vignettes of Military History,* vol. I, October, 1976, p. 44.

11 Functional and Recreational Reading

Walking to their cars in the commuter parking lot, Rick and Jill were discussing all the forms they had to fill out as freshmen. "First of all," Jill complained, "there was registration. Not only did we have to figure out what courses to take, we had to complete those data sheets."

"That was only the beginning," said Rick. "There were the applications for a student loan, for work study, for housing. . . . It goes on and on."

"And it's not just at school. What about the loan for my car—insurance, too? And this year I'm going to have to do my own income tax."

"Lots of times the real problem for me is trying to figure out what the form means—what they want me to write in all those blank spaces."

"When I ask what something means," Jill added, "people just say, 'Follow the directions.' That's not always easy to do when you don't understand what the directions expect you to do."

"I wonder if there's some way to make it easier. . . ."

"I hope so—let me know if you find it. Here's my car—see you tomorrow."

Introduction

The last two chapters of this text deal with types of reading that are not primarily related to school work: functional, recreational, and professional reading. Chapter 11 offers examples of functional and recreational reading, two important applications for reading, and Chapter 12 presents material on professional reading.

Functional Reading

Many occasions require a person to use reading skills for practical purposes. Some examples of functional reading are following directions for completing insurance, application, and tax forms; reading labels to get information about products; reading directions for playing a new game, making something, or traveling to a destination; finding out how to place special types of telephone calls; and reading information necessary for carrying out tasks. In order to respond without error, the reader usually must read carefully, paying close attention to detail and sequence.

Completing Forms

The way you follow directions for filling out an employment application affects your chances for obtaining a job. Most employers prefer typed, or at least neat and legible, applications. An accurate, fully completed application takes time and careful reading, but the result tells a prospective employer that you are likely to be a good employee.

FR Exercise 1

Many application forms are several pages in length, too long for inclusion in this book, but the brief form that follows contains some of the questions that typically appear on applications. Read the form carefully. Then answer the questions about it to see if you paid close enough attention to detail to follow the directions without making errors.

1. How do you know if the job you are applying for requires a written test?
   a. Someone will tell you.
   b. It will be noted on the Federal Job Opportunity List.
   c. You will find out after your application is accepted.
2. What information is requested about your religious preference?
   a. none—it is a violation of privacy
   b. the name of your denomination
   c. when, and if, you observe a religious holiday

APPLICATION REQUEST FORM/TEST ADMISSION CARD [1]

U.S. OFFICE OF PERSONNEL MANAGEMENT
Memphis Area Office

PART A

This form is used for two purposes: (1) To request application forms or (2) to request scheduling for a written test. Positions requiring a written test are notated on the Federal Job Opportunity List. If the position does not require a test, the necessary application forms will be mailed to you.

POSITION REQUESTED: _____

GRADE OF POSITION APPLYING FOR: GS- _____ WG- _____

JOB LOCATION SHOWN ON FEDERAL JOB OPPORTUNITY LIST: _____

SEND THE NECESSARY FORMS TO APPLY FOR THE ABOVE JOB WHICH APPEARS ON YOUR CURRENT FEDERAL

JOB OPPORTUNITY LIST DATED: _____

PART B (APPLICANTS FOR WRITTEN TESTS MUST COMPLETE PARTS A, B, & C OF THIS CARD)

Do you claim Veterans Preference? ____YES, ____NO   If YES check either: ____5 pts. ____10 pts.

Dates of Active Military Service: FROM: _____ TO _____   Do you observe the Sabbath or religious holiday other than

Are You a United States citizen? ____YES ____NO   Sunday? _____

PRINT or type your COMPLETE name and address including zip code.

(First)	(Middle/Maiden)	(Last)

Number and Street, or RFD, or P.O. Box No.

City, State & Zip Code   Telephone

This card will be returned to you. Bring it with you when you report for written test.
IDENTIFICATION MAY BE REQUIRED FOR WRITTEN EXAMINATION.

MEAO-172-A

COMPLETE THE ABOVE INFORMATION FOR ALL REQUESTS
SUBMITTED ON THIS CARD

3. Which of the following purposes is *not* met by completing this form?
   a. to request application forms
   b. to request scheduling for a written test
   c. to request employment

4. If you need to take a written test, what do you do with this form?
   a. Mail it to the U.S. Office of Personnel Management.
   b. Bring it with you when you report for the test.
   c. Keep it until a job becomes available for you.

5. If a job does not require a written test, how do you get the application forms?
   a. Send this card and they will be mailed to you.
   b. Request them by making a telephone call.
   c. Pick them up in person at the Federal Job Opportunities Center.

6. If you are going to take a written test, what happens to this application form first?
   a. It is returned to you.
   b. It is destroyed.
   c. It becomes the property of the U.S. Office of Personnel Management.

Anyone who earns income in excess of a specified amount is required to complete an income tax form for the Internal Revenue Service (IRS). Although the reading level for the tax forms has been "simplified," the form still requires careful attention to detail.

When filing an income tax form, one of the first things to do is to decide which tax form best suits your needs. The IRS publishes a variety of forms, including those listed below.

Form 1040 EZ: income chiefly from wages or salaries for single taxpayers with no dependents and no itemized deductions

Form 1040 A: income from wages, interest, dividends; possibly including dependents, but no itemized deductions

Form 1040: income above a specified amount with itemized deductions and more complex financial transactions

In addition to these forms, there are numerous supplementary forms for special purposes, such as employee business expenses, interest and dividend income, profit or loss from business, and supplemental income.

You can get the form(s) you need free through the mail, from most libraries, or from a local IRS office. Before beginning to complete the form(s), gather together all related information, including records of income received from various sources and expenses that may be deductible. A W-2 form gives the amount earned from an employer, and it must be sent to the IRS with your tax form.

FR Exercise 2

Read the following case study and use the information to complete the income tax form[2] on page 298. Be sure to refer to both W-2 forms and the excerpt from the Tax Table on page 297.

Jean was enrolled in college full time and held two part-time jobs: one during the summer at home and the other near campus at nights and on weekends. She received $220 interest from a savings fund. Jean's parents do not claim her as a deduction.

After completing the tax form, answer the following questions:

Does Jean get a refund or does she owe the IRS? _____

What is the amount of refund or money owed? _____

Extracting Pertinent Information

Sometimes you may need to find information that relates to a particular situation. To do so, you must select what is pertinent from the other information. The two exercises that follow are examples of such situations.

1 Control number			This information is being furnished to the Internal Revenue Service. If you are required to file a tax return, a negligence penalty or other sanction may be imposed on you if this income is taxable and you fail to report it.
		OMB No. 1545-0008	

2 Employer's name, address, and ZIP code	6 Statutory employee ☐ Deceased ☐ Pension plan ☐ Legal rep. ☐ 942 emp. ☐ Subtotal ☐ Deferred compensation ☐ Void ☐

Q–Mart
1810 Russell Pike
Darryville, TX 82583

7 Allocated tips	8 Advance EIC payment

9 Federal income tax withheld 235.00	10 Wages, tips, other compensation 3900.00

3 Employer's identification number	4 Employer's state I.D. number	11 Social security tax withheld 280.00	12 Social security wages

5 Employee's social security number	13 Social security tips	14 Medicare wages and tips

19 Employee's name, address, and ZIP code	15 Medicare tax withheld	16 Nonqualified plans

Jean Jakes
1604 Maple Lane
Havertown, TX 82570

17 See Instrs. for Box 17	18 Other

20	21	22 Dependent care benefits	23 Benefits included in Box 10

24 State income tax	25 State wages, tips, etc.	26 Name of state	27 Local income tax	28 Local wages, tips, etc.	29 Name of locality

Copy C For EMPLOYEE'S RECORDS (See Notice on back.)   Department of the Treasury—Internal Revenue Service

Form **W-2 Wage and Tax Statement 1991**

---

1 Control number			This information is being furnished to the Internal Revenue Service. If you are required to file a tax return, a negligence penalty or other sanction may be imposed on you if this income is taxable and you fail to report it.
		OMB No. 1545-0008	

2 Employer's name, address, and ZIP code	6 Statutory employee ☐ Deceased ☐ Pension plan ☐ Legal rep. ☐ 942 emp. ☐ Subtotal ☐ Deferred compensation ☐ Void ☐

Burger de-Lite
1300 Main Street
Havertown, TX 82570

7 Allocated tips	8 Advance EIC payment

9 Federal income tax withheld 225.00	10 Wages, tips, other compensation 3760.00

3 Employer's identification number	4 Employer's state I.D. number	11 Social security tax withheld 270.00	12 Social security wages

5 Employee's social security number	13 Social security tips	14 Medicare wages and tips

19 Employee's name, address, and ZIP code	15 Medicare tax withheld	16 Nonqualified plans

Jean Jakes
1604 Maple Lane
Havertown, TX 82570

17 See Instrs. for Box 17	18 Other

20	21	22 Dependent care benefits	23 Benefits included in Box 10

24 State income tax	25 State wages, tips, etc.	26 Name of state	27 Local income tax	28 Local wages, tips, etc.	29 Name of locality

Copy C For EMPLOYEE'S RECORDS (See Notice on back.)   Department of the Treasury—Internal Revenue Service

Form **W-2 Wage and Tax Statement 1991**

If line 5 is at least—	But less than—	Your tax is—
1,400	1,425	212
1,425	1,450	216
1,450	1,475	219
1,475	1,500	223
1,500	1,525	227
1,525	1,550	231
1,550	1,575	234
1,575	1,600	238
1,600	1,625	242
1,625	1,650	246
1,650	1,675	249
1,675	1,700	253
1,700	1,725	257
1,725	1,750	261
1,750	1,775	264
1,775	1,800	268
1,800	1,825	272
1,825	1,850	276
1,850	1,875	279
1,875	1,900	283
1,900	1,925	287
1,925	1,950	291
1,950	1,975	294
1,975	2,000	298
2000		
2,000	2,025	302
2,025	2,050	306
2,050	2,075	309
2,075	2,100	313
2,100	2,125	317
2,125	2,150	321
2,150	2,175	324
2,175	2,200	328
2,200	2,225	332
2,225	2,250	336
2,250	2,275	339
2,275	2,300	343
2,300	2,325	347
2,325	2,350	351
2,350	2,375	354
2,375	2,400	358
2,400	2,425	362
2,425	2,450	366
2,450	2,475	369
2,475	2,500	373
2,500	2,525	377
2,525	2,550	381
2,550	2,575	384
2,575	2,600	388
2,600	2,625	392
2,625	2,650	396
2,650	2,675	399
2,675	2,700	403
2,700	2,725	407
2,725	2,750	411
2,750	2,775	414
2,775	2,800	418
2,800	2,825	422
2,825	2,850	426
2,850	2,875	429
2,875	2,900	433
2,900	2,925	437
2,925	2,950	441
2,950	2,975	444
2,975	3,000	448

Department of the Treasury—Internal Revenue Service

Form
1040EZ

Income Tax Return for
Single Filers With No Dependents (0)   **1991**

OMB No. 1545-0675

Name & address

Use the IRS label (see page 10). If you don't have one, please print.

LABEL HERE

Print your name (first, initial, last)

Home address (number and street). (If you have a P.O. box, see page 11.)   Apt. no.

City, town or post office, state, and ZIP code. (If you have a foreign address, see page 11.)

Please print your numbers like this:

9 8 7 6 5 4 3 2 1 0

Your social security number

Please see instructions on the back. Also, see the Form 1040EZ booklet.

Presidential Election Campaign (see page 11)
Do you want $1 to go to this fund?

Note: *Checking "Yes" will not change your tax or reduce your refund.* ▶

Yes No

Dollars   Cents

Report your income

1 Total wages, salaries, and tips. This should be shown in Box 10 of your W-2 form(s). (Attach your W-2 form(s).)   **1**

Attach Copy B of Form(s) W-2 here. Attach tax payment on top of Form(s) W-2.

2 Taxable interest income of $400 or less. If the total is more than $400, you cannot use Form 1040EZ.   **2**

3 Add line 1 and line 2. This is your **adjusted gross income.**   **3**

4 Can your parents (or someone else) claim you on their return?
☐ **Yes.** Do worksheet on back; enter amount from line E here.
☐ **No.** Enter 5,550.00. This is the total of your standard deduction and personal exemption.   **4**

Note: *You* **must** *check Yes or No.*

5 Subtract line 4 from line 3. If line 4 is larger than line 3, enter 0. This is your **taxable income.**   **5**

Figure your tax

6 Enter your Federal income tax withheld from Box 9 of your W-2 form(s).   **6**

7 **Tax.** Use the amount on **line 5** to find your tax in the tax table on pages 16-18 of the booklet. Enter the tax from the table on this line.   **7**

Refund or amount you owe

8 If line 6 is larger than line 7, subtract line 7 from line 6. This is your **refund.**   **8**

9 If line 7 is larger than line 6, subtract line 6 from line 7. This is the **amount you owe.** Attach your payment for full amount payable to the "Internal Revenue Service." Write your name, address, social security number, daytime phone number, and "1991 Form 1040EZ" on it.   **9**

Sign your return

Keep a copy of this form for your records.

I have read this return. Under penalties of perjury, I declare that to the best of my knowledge and belief, the return is true, correct, and complete.

Your signature

X

Date

Your occupation

For IRS Use Only---Please do not write in boxes below.

298

For Privacy Act and Paperwork Reduction Act Notice, see page 4 in the booklet.   Cat. No. 11329W   Form 1040EZ (1991)

FR Exercise 3

Read the following case study. Then read the excerpt from the OSHA standards manual[3] below and respond to the citations.

You are going to school part time and working full time as supervisor of a construction crew. A state inspector responsible for enforcing the Occupational Safety and Health Act (OSHA) visits you and takes special interest in the ladders you are using. He cites several infractions of the standards. Your safety manager decides to contest them, and he asks you to check the standards in the manual as part of the process.

Excerpt from OSHA Standards Manual

(iii) *Mason's ladder.* A mason's ladder is a special type of single ladder intended for use in heavy construction work.

(*a*) Mason's ladders longer than 40 feet shall not be supplied.

(*b*) The minimum dimensions of the side rails when made of Group 2 or Group 3 woods and rungs (Group 1 woods) of the mason's ladder shall be as follows:

| Length of ladder (feet) | Side rails | | Diameter | |
	Thickness (inches)	Depth (inches)	Rung (inches)	Tenon (inches)
Up to and including 22	$1\frac{5}{8}$	$3\frac{5}{8}$	$1\frac{3}{8}$	1
Over 22 up to and including 40	$1\frac{5}{8}$	$4\frac{1}{2}$	$1\frac{3}{8}$	1

(*c*) The width between the side rails at the bottom rung, inside to inside, shall be not less than 12 inches for all ladders up to and including 10 feet. Such minimum widths shall be increased by at least one-fourth inch for each additional 2 feet of length.

(*d*) Rungs shall be parallel and level and shall be spaced not less than 8 inches or more than 12 inches apart.

(5) *Trolley and side-rolling ladders—*(*i*) *Length.* Trolley ladders and side-rolling ladders longer than 20 feet should not be supplied.

(ii) *Dimensions.* The dimensions of the side rails shall not be less than the following for Group 2 or Group 3 woods:

Length of side rails (feet)	Thickness (inch)	Depth (inches)
Up to and including 10	$\frac{25}{32}$	3
Over 10 up to and including 20	$\frac{25}{32}$	$3\frac{3}{4}$

The minimum thicknesses of side rails provide for the cutting of a groove not over one-eighth inch in depth and shall be increased when grooves of greater depth are used. Flat steps shall have the following minimum dimensions for Group 2 or Group 3 woods:

Length of step (inches)	Thickness (inch)	Width (inches)
Up to and including 16	$\frac{25}{32}$	3
Over 16 up to and including 20	$\frac{25}{32}$	$3\frac{1}{4}$
Over 20 up to and including 24	$\frac{25}{32}$	$3\frac{1}{2}$
Over 24 up to and including 28	$\frac{25}{32}$	4

(iii) *Width.* The width between the side rails, inside to inside, shall be at least 12 inches.

(iv) *Step attachment.* Flat steps shall be inset in the side rails with one-eighth inch and secured with at least two 6-d nails at each end or the equivalent thereof. They shall be reinforced with angle braces or a $^3/_{16}$-inch steel rod.

(v) *Locking device.* Locking devices should be provided on all trolley ladders.

(vi) *Tracks.* (*a*) Tracks shall be wood, or metal (excluding cast iron), or a combination of these materials.

(*b*) Tracks for the top end of ladders shall be fastened securely and shall be so constructed that the wheels will not jump the track. Tracks shall be so designed as to provide for all probable loads to which they will be subjected.

(*c*) The supports shall be securely fastened by lag screws, machine, hook, or toggle bolts, or their equivalent.

(*d*) Track for side-rolling ladders shall be supported by metal or wood brackets securely screwed or bolted to shelving or other permanent structure at not over 3 feet.

(*d*) *Care and use of ladders*—(1) *Care.* To insure safety and serviceability the following precautions on the care of ladders shall be observed:

(i) Ladders shall be maintained in good condition at all times, the joint between the steps and side rails shall be tight, all hardware and fittings securely attached, and the moveable parts shall operate freely without binding or undue play.

(ii) Metal bearings of locks, wheels, pulleys, etc., shall be frequently lubricated.

(iii) Frayed or badly worn rope shall be replaced.

(iv) Safety feet and other auxiliary equipment shall be kept in good condition to insure proper performance.

(v) Ladders should be stored in such a manner as to provide ease of access or inspection, and to prevent danger of accident when withdrawing a ladder for use.

(vi) Wood ladders, when not in use, should be stored at a location where they will not be exposed to the elements, but where there is good ventilation. They shall not be stored near radiators, stoves, steam pipes, or other places subjected to excessive heat or dampness.

(vii) Ladders stored in a horizontal position should be supported at a sufficient number of points to avoid sagging and permanent set.

(viii) Ladders carried on vehicles should be adequately supported to avoid sagging and securely fastened in position to minimize chafing and the effects of road shocks.

(ix) Ladders should be kept coated with a suitable protective material. The painting of ladders is satisfactory providing the ladders are carefully inspected prior to painting by competent and experienced inspectors acting for, and responsible to, the purchaser, and providing the ladders are not for resale.

(x) Ladders shall be inspected frequently and those which have developed defects shall be withdrawn from service for repair or destruction and tagged or marked as "Dangerous, Do Not Use."

(xi) Rungs should be kept free of grease and oil.

For the following citations against your company, write "yes" if the company is in violation of the standards and write "no" if it is not in violation.

1. _____ You are using a mason's ladder 50 feet long.

2. _____ The spacing between adjacent rungs on the mason's ladder is 11½".

3. _____ On a trolley ladder, the inside width between side rails is 14".

4. _____ There is no locking device on your trolley ladder.

5. _____ The tracks for your trolley ladder are heavy-duty plastic.

6. _____ There is oil on the rungs of a ladder.

7. _____ Some of the rope you are using is badly frayed.

8. _____ The wooden ladders not in use are leaning against a steam pipe.

FR Exercise 4

The Veterans Administration (VA) notified you that your service-connected disability entitles you to special services. These services should enable you to overcome an employment handicap.

Read the vocational rehabilitation benefits[4] given below. Then write "true" or "false" in the blank beside each statement in response to the conditions given for receiving benefits.

Vocational Rehabilitation for Service-Disabled Veterans

Eligibility and Entitlement. You are entitled to a program of training and rehabilitation services if you have a compensable service-connected disability and the VA determines that you need these services to overcome an employment handicap. The basic period of eligibility is, generally, 12 years following the date you are notified of your entitlement to VA compensation for your disability. This period may be adjusted if you receive an upgraded discharge or are unable to train for a period as a result of medical conditions. The 12-year period may also be extended if you have a serious employment handicap and need additional time to complete your rehabilitation program.

Training and Other Rehabilitation Services. We provide evaluation and counseling to assist you in the development of a comprehensive rehabilitation plan designed to suit your particular needs. An initial evaluation will establish your eligibility and entitlement and determine whether you need extended evaluation, independent living services, educational or vocational training, or employment assistance.

If you have a serious disability, you may receive services under an extended evaluation program to determine and improve your training potential. Generally, an extended evaluation may not exceed 12 months, but extensions are possible.

If you enter a training program, up to 48 months or more may be authorized in colleges and universities, vocational schools, on-farm, on-job or apprenticeship programs, as well as special rehabilitation facilities. We pay the full cost of tuition, books, fees, supplies and equipment.

While in training, if you have unexpected financial problems, we may be able to provide you with a no-interest loan to help you through the period of difficulty. We can also arrange for tutoring services to assist you to complete your training program.

After you complete training, we will help you find a suitable job. This employment assistance may be provided for up to 18 months. You may be eligible for employment assistance as a total program or in addition to training. You may also qualify for job assistance if you took part in the VA or State rehabilitation program at some earlier time.

Subsistence Allowance. While you are taking part in training or in extended evaluation, you may receive a subsistence allowance in addition to disability compensation or military retired pay. This subsistence allowance may continue for 2 months following completion of training to provide financial support during the initial period of search for and adjustment to employment.

1. _____ You can get 4 years or more of education if you enter a training program.

2. _____ You pay for your own books, supplies, and equipment.

3. _____ After you complete the training, it will be up to you to find your own job.

4. _____ No-interest loans may be available in case of unexpected financial difficulties.

5. _____ If you receive disability compensation or military retired pay, no further allowance can be provided.

6. _____ The VA provides counseling services to help you plan your rehabilitation.

7. _____ The VA will pay for you to attend colleges and universities, but not for you to attend vocational school.

8. _____ Money is available for 12 months after you complete your training to help you during your job search.

Understanding the Newspaper

Daily newspapers are one of the best sources of information about what is going on in the nation and the world. Each day thousands of papers are published, but the average reader will probably only see one or two papers. Why are so many newspapers published, and how do people decide which ones to read?

Perhaps the most important reason for subscribing to a particular paper is the geographic area in which the paper is published. Readers want to know about things that are happening locally. Beyond this, however, are other considerations. Some newspapers are slanted toward liberal or conservative points of view; some openly support management or labor. Newspapers also differ in their approaches by either objectively reporting the news or by using sensationalism to attract readers. Newspapers may specialize by offering extensive coverage of world news or of business and finance. The reader must be aware of the type of coverage offered by each paper and decide what information is most important.

The format of a paper usually adheres to the following plan. The most prominent news stories are located on the first page with the most important items located above the fold of the paper. Often the lead story is located in the upper right hand corner. A brief index is found on the first page that helps readers locate specific parts of the paper. The classified advertising is usually found toward the end of the paper. Once readers have become familiar with a particular paper, they can usually find what they want quickly because editors try to be fairly consistent in the arrangement of the paper.

You may have heard certain terms used in journalism and not been sure of their exact meanings. Some common terms with definitions follow.

AP: Associated Press, a major news service

Banner or streamer: Main headline across the top of the front page

Byline: Reporter's name at the beginning of the story

Dateline: Place where the story happened—found at the beginning of the story; may also include the name of the news service

Editorial: Editor's opinion or commentary on an issue or story

Lead: First paragraph of a story

Masthead: Name of the newspaper at the top of the first page

Op-Ed page: Page facing the editorial page and featuring opinion columns

A newspaper must appeal to a wide range of reading interests and abilities because it is intended to reach a large number of people with varied backgrounds. The readability of the paper varies from a fairly low level of difficulty in some comics and society columns to a reasonably high level for some editorials and syndicated columns. There is something for everyone, but no one is expected to read an entire newspaper. Readers must decide for themselves what is important to them and read selectively. The following section deals with some of the major divisions of a daily newspaper and how to read them.

News Stories

News stories are intended to be factual, objective reports of what has been happening. Front page stories should be concise, timely, objective, interesting, accurate, readable, and balanced. The headline of the news story is actually its title, and the first paragraph of the story is a brief summary of the facts. Even though the first paragraph may consist of only a single sentence, it reveals the who, what, when, where, and sometimes how and why of the story. Details follow in order of decreasing significance. A news story may be considered an inverted pyramid, with the most important information compressed at the top and supporting details appearing in descending order. The words are simple, direct, and familiar whenever possible. News stories should contain no opinions, allusions, judgments, or theories. Readers who are pressed for time may learn all they need to know by reading the headlines and first paragraphs of news stories.

FR Exercise 5

Read the following news story. Notice how the main information is given in the first paragraph and supporting details are supplied in following paragraphs. The article could be cut off at almost any paragraph following the first without loss of essential information.

Light Plane Hits Rescue Truck, Two Men Killed[5]

Mark Mayhew
Banner State Correspondent

Ft. Campbell—Two aircraft attendants were killed here early today when a civilian aircraft slammed into the victims' crashtruck while making an emergency landing.

Authorities said the pilot, William F. Long, of Ohio, suffered only a fractured hip and cuts and bruises.

Military officials reported the Beech VE 18 aircraft, carrying a load of mail, had radioed the base for permission for an emergency landing and civilian attendants, Cleland Bedwell, Clarksville, and Herbert Rust, Hopkinsville, had driven to a ramp about 1,000 feet from the landing strip to await the plane's arrival.

The civilian aircraft, it was reported, which might have been running low on fuel, came into the landing strip from a southern direction and perpendicular to the landing strip, crashing into the parked truck occupied by Bedwell and Rust.

The unusual accident occurred at 3:15 A.M. and news of the crash was withheld pending notification of the victims' families.

The plane had departed Louisville and was en route to Paducah when Long radioed the Army airfield here for permission to land. Authorities reported he gave no reason for his request during the radio message.

Long was admitted to the post hospital. Bedwell and Rust were both dead on arrival at the hospital.

Reread the first paragraph and record the following information.

Who? _____

What? _____

Where? _____

When? _____

Why or How? _____

Editorials, Editorial Cartoons, and Syndicated Columns

Because of sources available and experience in analyzing news stories, an editor can offer insights into the news that may help readers see the issues in different perspectives. An editor holds a responsible position because an editorial can have a powerful impact on those who read the paper. On the editorial page the editor is free to comment on the international situation, to champion a cause, or to challenge a politician.

As you read an editorial, decide whether the editor's purpose is to interpret, persuade, criticize, or explore alternatives. Then consider the editor's position along with the positions of other writers and your own knowledge of the subject. You may decide to accept or reject the editor's view, but suspend your judgment until you have examined other sources.

FR Exercise 6

Read the following editorial and answer the questions that follow.

Frustration in the Classroom[6]

The Carnegie Foundation for the Advancement of Teaching recently surveyed 22,000 U.S. teachers to determine what they thought about their jobs, and the results should concern parents as well as educators. To the extent that certain factors are diminishing the teachers' effectiveness, society loses. That effectiveness is certainly diminished when a majority of teachers reported not only an overwhelming lack of support from parents but a feeling of "powerlessness in teaching."

The finding of a lack of parental support probably surprised few teachers, if any. While some parents believe that education is solely the responsibility of the teacher, those who think about it will realize that it must be a shared responsibility. Otherwise it will fail.

CFAT President Ernest Boyer said teachers "repeatedly made the point (in the survey) that in the push for better schools they cannot do the job alone, and yet there is a growing trend to expect schools to do what families, communities and churches have been unable to accomplish."

Can anyone doubt that? Consider that schools are not just expected to see that our youngsters are grounded in the basics during elementary school and prepared for college or the workplace in high school. We also expect them to watch for signs of child abuse (including sexual abuse), neglect, poor health, malnutrition and emotional problems. Schools are taking on major responsibilities for sex education, for programs aimed at curbing drug and alcohol abuse, and reducing the dropout rate. Have we left out anything?

We will concede that schools often assume these responsibilities by default, particularly in instances of abuse. And it's true that drug, sex and alcohol abuse programs are worthy subjects for schools in their responsibility to help shape productive members of society.

But Mary Hatwood Futrell, president of the National Education Association, is surely right in arguing that most parents don't know how important they are to their children's education. Parents, she said, "are a child's first—and potentially the most influential— teachers," and "even the best teachers cannot go it alone. Teachers need allies, and the allies they need most are parents."

With all their responsibilities, it's no wonder many teachers in the Carnegie survey reported a feeling of powerlessness. We suspect most teachers could cope with that if they weren't also inundated with trivial responsibilities. Among them: collecting money for school and PTA fund-raisers, processing reams of paperwork (a lot of it bureaucratically inspired), and passing out fliers from dance studios, baton instructors and sports organizations seeking to recruit student "customers."

Teachers also monitor students at recess and oversee the loading and unloading of buses. Those duties ought to be taken over by parent volunteers or paid aides—except there's no money for aides and in many households, both parents work. The upshot is diminished professionalism, which we suspect would fuel the CFAT's finding of powerlessness. Is that the case in Chattanooga and Hamilton County schools? Teachers?

1. What is the editor's main point? _____

_____

_____

2. Does the editor feel that the teachers in the survey made by the Carnegie Foundation were justified

in their responses? a. _____

Why do you believe that? b. _____

_____

_____

3. Does the editor believe that education is solely the responsibility of the teacher? a. _____

What makes you think he feels that way? b. _____

_____

_____

4. What two people does the editor quote to make points in this editorial?

    a. _____

What are the two organizations over which these people preside?

    b. _____

_____

Were the presidents of these two organizations good choices for people to quote? c. _____

Why do you believe that? d. _____

_____

5. In the fourth paragraph, the editor lists things other than educational factors for which teachers are expected to watch. What are they?

    a. _____

    b. _____

    c. _____

    d. _____

    e. _____

6. In the same paragraph, the editor suggests three other major responsibilities that schools (and therefore teachers) have taken on. What are they?

    a. _____

    b. _____

    c. _____

7. What did the editor mean by the statement that the schools often assume these responsibilities by default?

_____

_____

8. What is an ally? _____

9. Why do you believe teachers need parents as allies? _____

_____

10. In the seventh paragraph, the editor lists some trivial responsibilities with which teachers must contend. What are they?

    a. _____

    b. _____

    c. _____

11. In the last paragraph, the editor mentions duties of teachers that "ought to be taken over by parent volunteers or paid aides." Is he expressing fact or his opinion with the words quoted here?

    a. _____

How do you know? b. _____

What are the duties being discussed? c. _____

    d. _____

_____

12. Do you agree with the editor's case concerning the teacher's plight? Write a statement indicating why you agree or disagree.

_____

_____

_____

_____

FR Exercise 7

Look at the editorial cartoon on page 309 and then place a check in front of those statements that can be reasonably inferred from this editorial cartoon.

_____ 1. The cartoonist is alarmed about the filling of the world with toxic wastes.

_____ 2. The cartoonist thinks that the earth's shape will actually change to look like a toilet.

_____ 3. The cartoonist believes that the future of the earth is bright.

_____ 4. The cartoonist is suggesting that toxic wastes be flushed down toilets for disposal.

_____ 5. The cartoonist has a negative view of the world's future.

_____ 6. The cartoonist has used the shock value of the symbol of the toilet to draw the reader's attention to the point he wishes to make.

The Shape of the WORLD TO COME.

TOXIC WASTES

© 1989 M. Birdie Birdwell.

FR Exercise 8

Look back at the cartoon on page 78. List several ways the cartoonist shows the concept of "light summer reading." Then list the ways the cartoonist illustrates the unstated but assumed contrast of "heavy reading."

"Light reading"	*"Heavy reading"*
1. _____	1. _____
2. _____	2. _____
3. _____	3. _____
4. _____	4. _____

Syndicated columns are written by writers who have become well-known in certain fields. They provide the reader with in-depth views of the news and different points of view. The opinions expressed by syndicated columnists do not always agree with the positions held by the editorial staff of the paper. As with editorials, these columns should be read thoughtfully by those who are interested in exploring various aspects of the news. Readers learn to expect a certain style of writing or a certain point of view from a prominent columnist.

Features, Entertainment, and Advertising

The remainder of the paper serves many purposes. The reader finds articles on gardening, recipes, housekeeping hints, and child-rearing. The sports section is a small newspaper in itself with its own editorials, news stories, and special language. Financial pages help readers understand economic problems, interpret business news, and determine when to buy or sell stocks and bonds. Entertainment is provided through comic strips, crossword puzzles, book reviews, and serialized stories. Television listings and advertisements for theaters and restaurants offer sources of additional entertainment.

Newspaper advertising usually takes one of two forms: classified or display advertising. Classified ads serve you by providing organized lists of goods and services, which are indexed under major headings. They include such items as employment, real estate, rentals, merchandise for sale, and services available. Display ads provide information on sales being held by stores, new products on the market, and places to obtain specific items. While advertisements are often helpful, you must read them carefully in order to avoid being the victim of propaganda techniques.

General Procedures for Reading the Newspaper Efficiently

Twenty to thirty minutes is a reasonable amount of time to spend reading the newspaper. First, look at the headlines on the first page to see the important news of the day. From the headlines decide which articles interest you and read them. Some articles may be skimmed, while others should be read with special care.

The index on the first page tells you the special features of the paper and where they are located. You may select editorials, letters, and columns from the editorial pages in order to become familiar with different points of view. Reading the advertisements can help you decide where to shop and what to buy. You may also wish to read features of special interest, such as sports news or society columns.

Since different parts of the paper vary in reading difficulty and interest, they should not be read the same way. Stock market quotations should be read by first quickly scanning the columns for the stocks you want to know about and then carefully reading the day's quotations for those stocks. Editorials should be read thoughtfully and critically. Comic strips and light material can be read quickly and easily. The first paragraph of a news story should be read carefully and the rest can be skimmed.

Headlines help a reader see at a glance what the top news stories are. Banner headlines in large heavy type proclaim the main idea of the day's lead story. Secondary headlines summarize the main points of the story and prepare the reader for the details which follow. Most headlines are written in the present tense to give a sense of immediacy to the story. Small, unimportant words are omitted in order to economize on space. While headlines help the reader get the main idea of the story quickly, they can also be misleading. By cutting out words, the writer may give a false impression of what really happened. Headline writing can be a way of attracting attention and whetting the reader's curiosity by exaggerating the news. By using words in a certain way, a writer may slant a headline to reflect the paper's editorial opinions. Some headlines are confusing because words are used in unusual ways to fit the space, such as a word commonly used as a noun being used as a verb.

Newspapers don't always agree in their reporting, and some stories are later found to be false, so how do you know what to believe? One way to determine the accuracy of a news story is to question the source. If no source is given, you have reasons to doubt the integrity of the story. Be wary of such prefaces to statements as "It was alleged . . ." or "According to an undisclosed source. . . ." These statements may or may not be true.

Tips for Productive Reading of the Newpaper

1. Begin reading with a quick survey of the front page.

2. Have a purpose for reading each article. Turn the headline into a question and read to find the answer.

3. Use the newspaper as a source of new words for improving your vocabulary. Each day try to select some unfamliar words to learn.

4. Learn to read selectively. Do not waste time trying to read everything.

5. Develop flexibility in your reading rate. Skim whatever you can, but read commentaries slowly and critically.

6. Improve your reading rate by increasing your eye span. Focus on the middle of a column and read straight down with only one fixation per line.

7. Consider different points of view before forming opinions.

8. Watch for biased reporting, but keep an open mind.

Recreational Reading

Recreational reading is reading for enjoyment. Too few contemporary American adults read for recreational purposes. The tendency is to watch television, go to movies, or engage in some other activity that today's technology and mobility have made available. People who fail to read for pleasure, however, are forfeiting opportunities to enjoy new ideas, new people, and new places.

Reading can provide a lifelong source of entertainment, as well as information, for those who find pleasure in it. Books enable readers to vicariously experience everything that has ever been recorded: surf riding, jungle safaris, or skiing in the Alps. Books are companions during lonely evenings and time spent waiting. Books present readers with new ideas and help to expand their minds. Readers get clearer understandings of themselves by measuring their own attitudes and actions against those of the heroes and heroines from stories.

Some reasons for recreational reading follow. Perhaps you can think of others in terms of your own experiences.

1. To find escape, relaxation, and a change of pace from daily problems.
2. To keep informed about current events in order to know what is happening and to share views with others.
3. To increase knowledge of hobbies and special interests.
4. To stretch mental capabilities with new and complex ideas.
5. To gain pleasure from poetry and lyrical prose.

Ten Keys to Enjoying Recreational Reading

1. Become familiar with the library and what it offers, such as books, magazines, newspapers, films, compact disks, and audio- and videotapes.
2. Read book reviews and mentally note what you want to read.
3. Browse through the paperbacks wherever you go and occasionally buy one that appeals to you.
4. Subscribe to one or two newspapers and read them regularly.
5. Subscribe to magazines that provide you with information about your special interests.
6. Talk about what you read informally with others, or perhaps join a book club where books are reviewed and discussed.
7. Always have something to read with you while waiting in a doctor's office, eating alone, or waiting for someone you are to meet.
8. Set aside a special time each day for reading when you are unlikely to be interrupted.
9. Try new types of reading materials, such as biographies or short stories, so that you will be constantly enlarging your reading interests.
10. Have several types of reading materials accessible at one time so that you may select something that suits your mood.

Types of Recreational Reading

Many types of materials are available for recreational reading. Use of the newspaper both for obtaining information and as a means of entertainment has already been discussed. Readers may enjoy poetry, drama, mythology, science fiction, folklore, short stories, novels, or nonfiction. Often readers limit themselves to single types of reading that they find enjoyable but not challenging. As their reading tastes mature, they choose more diversified materials and select higher quality literature.

Magazines may either inform or entertain the reader. Specialized magazines include business, trade, and professional journals of interest to people in specific occupations. Weekly news magazines deal with current issues and must be read promptly if the information gained is to be up to date. Some magazines, such as *National Geographic,* may be kept and reread because they deal with topics of lasting value. "Pulp" magazines are so called because of the poor quality paper on which they are printed. These magazines often include sensationalism, emotionalism, and low-level journalism.

Nonfiction materials are often popular with readers who are interested in learning more about science, the arts, and the humanities. They prod readers into thinking about causes, relationships, and philosophical principles. They stretch readers' imaginations and thinking powers and offer them opportunities to lift their minds to the level of the writer's. Thought-provoking material gives readers ideas to consider during their free moments, and it ultimately makes them more worthy members of society.

A good novel can cause a reader to become deeply involved in the action. Some novels are light and entertaining. They permit the reader to skim through them rapidly and easily, catching the story line and bits of dialogue. Deeper novels require more concentration and thought; the reader must pause to consider, evaluate, and reflect. In some novels the plot holds the reader's interest and creates suspense and excitement as the climax is neared. Some novels are noted for their authenticity of setting and transport the reader to another time and place. Strong characterization—realism, consistency, growth—is often the mark of a powerful novel.

Light fiction, mystery stories, and best-sellers make entertaining reading, but you should also consider reading some classics in order to cultivate an appreciation for good quality literature. An abridged list of good books for recreational reading follows.

Good Books for Recreational Reading

Adams, Douglas. *The Hitchhiker's Guide to the Galaxy*

Adams, Douglas. *Life, the Universe, and Everything*

Adams, Richard. *Watership Down*

Anderson, Poul. *The Broken Sword*

Anderson, Poul. *Fantasy*

Andrews, V. C. Flowers in the Attic Series

Anger, Brad. *Ask for Love and They Give You Rice Pudding*

Anson, Jay. *The Amityville Horror*

Asimov, Isaac. Any of his works

Benchley, Nathaniel. *Only Earth and Sky Last Forever*

Benchley, Peter. *Jaws*

Bova, Bea. *Voyagers*

Bradbury, Ray. *Fahrenheit 451*

Bradbury, Ray. *The Illustrated Man*

Bradbury, Ray. *The Martian Chronicles*

Bradbury, Ray. *The Stories of Ray Bradbury*

Brancato, Robin. *Blinded by the Light*

Brancato, Robin. *Come Alive at 505*

Brooks, Terry. *The Elfstones of Shannara*

Brooks, Terry. *The Sword of Whannara*

Brown, Dee. *Bury My Heart at Wounded Knee: An Indian History of the American West*

Chrichton, Michael. *The Great Train Robbery*

Christie, Agatha. *And Then There Were None*

Christie, Agatha. *The Murder of Roger Ackroyd*

Christie, Agatha. *Murder on the Orient Express*

Clark, Mary Higgins. *Stillwatch*

Clark, Mary Higgins. *A Stranger Is Watching*

Clark, Mary Higgins. *Where Are the Children?*

Clarke, Arthur C. *Childhood's End*

Clarke, Arthur C. *2010: Odyssey Two*

Clavell, James. *Shogun*

Cook, Robin. *Brain*

Corlett, William. *The Dark Side of the Moon*

Donaldson, Stephen R. *The Chronicles of Thomas Covenant*

Doyle, Arthur C. *Sherlock Holmes: Selected Stories*

DeMaurier, Daphne. *Rebecca*

Duncan, Lois. Any of her works

Forsyth, Frederick. *The Day of the Jackal*

Gunther, John. *Death Be Not Proud*

Guy, Rosa. *The Disappearance*

Guy, Rosa. *The Friends*

Hemingway, Ernest. *Islands in the Stream*

Heinlein, Robert A. *The Number of the Beast*

Heinlein, Robert A. *Stranger in a Strange Land*

Herbert, Frank. Dune Series

Herriot, James. *All Creatures Great and Small*

Hesse, Herman. *Behind the Wheel*

Hinton, S. E. *The Outsiders*

Hinton, S. E. *Rumble Fish*

Holt, Victoria. Any of her works

Huxley, Aldous. *Brave New World*

Keller, Helen. *The Story of My Life*

Kemelman, Harry. *Friday the Rabbi Slept Late*

Kemelman, Harry. *Monday the Rabbi Took Off*

Kemelman, Harry. *Wednesday the Rabbi Got Wet*

Kerr, M. E. *Gentlehands*

Kesey, Ken. *One Flew Over the Cuckoo's Nest*

King, Stephen. *The Firestarter*

Knowles, John. *A Separate Peace*

Konvitz, Jeffrey. *The Sentinel*

Koontz, Dean. Any of his works

Kurtz, Katherine. *Deryni Checkmate*

L'Amour, Louis. Any of his works

Le Carré, John. *The Spy Who Came in from the Cold*

Lee, Harper. *To Kill a Mockingbird*

Lewis, C. S. Any of his works

Ludlum, Robert. *The Bourne Identity*

Ludlum, Robert. *The Matarese Circle*

MacLean, Alistair. *Breakheart Pass*

MacLean, Alistair. *Circus*

McCaffrey, Anne. Pern Series

McCullough, Colleen. *The Thornbirds*

Michener, James A. *Centennial*

Oppenheimer, Joan L. *Francesca, Baby*

Oppenheimer, Joan L. *The Lost Summer*

Orwell, George. *Animal Farm*

Orwell, George. *Nineteen Eighty-Four*

Peck, Richard. *Are You in the House Alone*

Peck, Richard. *Remembering the Good Times*

Potok, Chaim. *The Chosen*

Rand, Ayn. *Atlas Shrugged*

Rand, Ayn. *The Fountainhead*

Renault, Mary. *The King Must Die*

Salinger, J. D. *The Catcher in the Rye*

Scithers, George, ed. *Isaac Asimov's World of Science Fiction*

Scoppetone, Sandra. *The Late Great Me*

Scoppetone, Sandra. *Trying Hard to Hear You*

Silverberg, Robert, ed. *Science Fiction Hall of Fame: The Greatest Science Fiction of All Time*

Solzhenitsyn, Alexander. *One Day in the Life of Ivan Denisovich*

Steele, Danielle. Any of her works

Stewart, Mary. *The Crystal Cave*

Stewart, Mary. *The Hollow Hills*

Stewart, Mary. *The Last Enchantment*

Stewart, Mary. *The Merlin Trilogy*

Strasser, Todd. *Ferris Bueller's Day Off*

Swarthout, Glendon. *Bless the Beasts and Children*

Toffler, Alvin. *The Third Wave*

Tolkien, J. R. R. *The Hobbit,* or *There and Back Again*

Tolkien, J. R. R. *The Lord of the Rings*

Weiss, Margaret. Dragon Lance Series

White, T. H. *The Once and Future King*

White, T. H. *The Sword in the Stone*

Whitney, Phyllis. Any of her works

Zindel, Paul. *My Darling, My Hamburger*

Zindel, Paul. *Pigman*

Zindel, Paul. *To Take a Dare*

Chapter Notes

1. Application Request Form/Test Admission Card, U.S. Office of Personnel Management, Memphis Area Office.
2. Form 1040EZ, Department of the Treasury, Internal Revenue Service, Washington, D.C.
3. Excerpted from *Occupational Safety and Health Standards,* vol. 39, Part II, Washington, D.C.: Department of Labor, June 27, 1974, pp. 23515–23516.
4. Excerpted from "A Summary of Veterans Administration Benefits," Washington, D.C.: Department of Veterans Benefits, Veterans Administration, rev. September 1988, pp. 8–9.
5. Mark Mayhew, "Light Plane Hits Rescue Truck, Two Men Killed," reprinted by permission from *Nashville Banner,* January 13, 1976, p. 1.
6. Michael Loftin, Editorial page editor, *The Chattanooga Times*, February 1, 1989, p. A10.

12 Professional Reading

"Did you hear the good news?" Beth called over to Craig. "I'm getting to co-op this semester."

"That's terrific," responded Craig as he pounded Beth on the back. "That's what you were hoping for."

Beth winced, then said, "I know. It's really exciting. Not only will it be good experience, but it may lead to a job offer."

"When do you start?"

"In two weeks. There's only one little problem. I've got to read through so many technical reports—pages of data, sometimes with graphs and charts. I can really get bogged down trying to make sense of it all. Any ideas?"

"Seems like when we took that reading-study skills course together there was a section in the book about reading technical reports—how to skim and scan them to get the real meaning."

"I think you're right, Craig. I still have my book—maybe I'll check out that part of it and see if there's something I can use with my job. I really want to make a good impression."

"Good luck, Beth—I know you'll do a great job. See you tonight at the deli?"

"You bet—I'll be there."

Introduction

Successful people engaged in business or professional occupations spend a great deal of time reading various types of literature related to their work. They must read professional journals, business correspondence, and various types of reports. If they can learn to double their reading efficiency, they can consequently reduce time spent in reading by half. The time thus freed can be used for recreational reading or other activities.

Reading Technical Articles

When reading technical articles, previewing is a useful procedure. It provides the reader with a general framework for placing the details in an article, thereby enhancing retention of information. Previewing, like surveying in SQ3R, involves the following activities:

1. Reading the title and the author's name.
2. Reading the introductory material.
3. Reading all major headings and subheadings.
4. Noting italicized, bold-face, and other special-print words, phrases, and sentences.
5. Examining graphs, maps, diagrams, and tables.
6. Reading the summary paragraph or paragraphs.

After surveying an article in this way, you may find it unnecessary to do a detailed reading of the article either because the article does not cover the specific topic in which you have interest or because you already know the material presented.

If you are reading just to locate specific bits of information, you may wish to scan the pages for key words and actually read just the material related to the key words. If you only want to get the main idea of the material, you may wish to skim. You can run your eyes in a zigzag path down the page and cover pages quite rapidly. A discussion of skimming and scanning is found in Chapter 10.

PR Exercise 1

Study the table that follows to see what information it contains and how the information is arranged. Pay special attention to the title, the headings, and the way the information is organized. When you feel that you understand the table, read the questions that follow and scan the table to find the answers as quickly as you can. You may need to use a ruler or straight edge to follow the rows accurately. Try to complete the work in two minutes.

INDEXES OF INDUSTRIAL PRODUCTION [1]
(Seasonally Adjusted, 1985=100)

Quarterly	France	Germany	Italy	U.K.	Nether-lands	Europe Total*	Canada	Japan	Foreign Total*	U.S.
90:4	111.7	119.4	116.3	106.8	112.7	114.1	101.7	128.9	118.2	114.9
91:1	112.3	121.4	116.7	106.6	112.9	114.9	99.8	128.8	118.5	112.0
91:2	113.1	121.6	114.4	105.2	113.2	114.3	100.9	127.9	117.9	112.7
91:3	113.9	120.9	114.2	106.3	111.0	114.3	101.6	128.3	118.1	114.6
91:4	113.5	119.0	115.4	106.1	115.4	114.1	100.2	126.9	117.4	114.4
% Chg	-0.4%	-1.6%	1.1%	-0.2	4.0%	-0.2%	-1.3%	-1.1%	-0.6%	-0.2%
%Chgyy	1.6%	-0.3%	-0.8%	-0.7	2.4%	0.0%	-1.4%	-1.6%	-0.7%	-0.4%
Annual										
1987	102.9	102.6	107.6	105.8	101.2	104.4	104.1	103.2	103.9	105.9
1988	107.7	106.3	114.1	109.6	101.3	108.7	109.8	113.0	100.2	111.6
1989	111.3	111.4	117.6	110.0	106.5	112.1	109.6	119.9	114.6	114.5
1990	112.6	117.2	117.7	109.3	109.1	114.2	104.9	125.3	117.3	115.7
1991	113.2	120.7	115.2	106.1	113.1	114.4	100.6	128.0	118.0	113.4
% Chgyy	0.5%	3.0%	-2.1%	-2.9%	3.7%	0.2%	-4.0	2.2%	0.6%	-2.0%

Average weighted index.
%CHANGE=percentage change from previous period.
%CHANGE YY=percentage change from same period in previous year.

1. What was the index of industrial production for the United States in the first quarter of 1991? ____

2. What was the index for the Netherlands in the third quarter of 1991? _____

3. What was the monthly percentage change from the previous period for Italy? _____

4. Which nation had the highest quarterly index in the second quarter of 1991? _____

5. Was the index for the United States higher or lower than the Foreign Total index in the fourth quarter of 1991? _____

6. On a quarterly basis, what was the percentage change for the United Kingdom from the same period in the previous year? _____

7. Did Italy's index increase or decrease between 1987 and 1989? _____

8. On an annual basis, what was the percentage change for France from the same period in the previous year? _____

PR Exercise 2

1. Scan the article below to find what the letters ACP stand for. Write the answer here. _____

Integrated Crop Management[2]

The Integrated Crop Management (ICM) program helps farmers develop an overall crop management system that promotes the efficient use of agricultural inputs in an environmentally sound and profitable manner. It is administered by the Agricultural Stabilization and Conservation Service (ASCS) as part of the Agricultural Conservation Program (ACP).

The ICM practice is designed to encourage the adoption of farming methods that integrate many farming activities into a management system. It encourages producers to try different approaches of production by providing financial assistance to help defray the costs and overcome the risks of changing production methods. The long-term benefits of the ICM practice will be preservation and improvement in the natural fertility of the soil, prevention and abatement of agriculture-related pollution, increased farm efficiency, and conservation of the land.

Why ICM?

Each year, over 20 billion pounds of fertilizers and 1.1 billion pounds of pesticides are applied to U.S. land. Further, over 95 percent of rural Americans depend on wells as their sole source of drinking water. ICM practices are some of the most effective means of reducing run-off and seepage of nutrients and pesticides that affect water quality.
—by Jim Lucas, Assistant to the Director of Information, ASCS, USDA, Washington, DC

---

2. Return to the article and scan to find what percent of rural Americans depend on wells for drinking water. Write the answer here. _____

3. Return again to the article and scan to find out how many billion pounds of pesticides are used on U.S. land. Write the answer here. _____

PR Exercise 3

1. Scan the report on the next page to find out the meaning of the term "tsunamigrams." Write the answer here. _____

Tsunami Data Services[3]

One of the most complex, catastrophic and misunderstood natural disasters is the tsunami. These earthquake-generated waves have taken a tremendous toll of life and property. The Great Hoei Tokaido-Nankaido tsunami of 1707 claimed 30,000 lives and washed away 8,000 houses. More recently, a tsunami originating in the Gulf of Alaska on March 27, 1964 resulted in $11 million property damage in Crescent City, California and in Alaska.

EDIS' National Geophysical and Solar-Terrestrial Data Center (NGSDC) in Boulder, Colo., has compiled a set of data bases of direct interest to tsunami research and operations. The specific data holdings are as follows:

Seismological Data: Copies of seismograms from the World Wide Standard Seismograph Network of about 120 stations are available on 35 and 70 mm film and since 1978 on microfiche. Since 1972 this collection of about 5,000,000 seismograms has been augmented by about 150 additional stations worldwide for large magnitude (7.5 and larger) and special interest earthquakes. A program has begun to microfilm older seismograms worldwide for all large earthquakes for selected stations since 1900. Digital data from the very long period International Deployment Accelerometers (IDA) worldwide network of gravimeters are available since 1975 and from the digitally recording Seismic Research Observatory (SRO) and High Gain Long Period (HGLP) network since 1977. A digital Earthquake Data File has information on approximately 150,000 earthquakes, including whether or not a tsunami followed.

Hydrographic Data: The term "tsunamigrams" is used for tide records with evidence of tsunami activity. Nearly 1,800 tsunamigrams from U.S. tide stations are available on microfiche. Records in this collection date back to 1850. Future emphasis will be on the collection of records from international sources. Some data has been volunteered through the International Hydrographic Bureau and other data may come from the International Tsunami Information Center (ITIC). A few tsunamigrams have been digitized for review by selected researchers. Demand will determine future digitization of analog records.

Bathymetric Data: The data center has a collection of about 50,000,000 bathymetric observations of U.S. coastal areas collected since 1930 by the U.S. Coast and Geodetic Survey and the successor NOAA organization, the National Ocean Survey. These data are on magnetic tape and can be formatted to provide even space grids or profiles.

Photographic Data: A collection of 667 photographs of tsunami wave activity and effects has been compiled. A catalog describing the photographs is available from NGSDC.

The data center has printed catalogs on tsunamis in both Alaska and Hawaii. It operates a modest guest worker program and can provide space, access to computers, digitizers, plotters and data files to researchers who need to access large amounts of data. Data from the center are available at cost of copying or in exchange to scientists depositing data in the center.

2. Return to the article and scan to find out what the acronym HGLP represents. Write the answer here.

_____

_____

3. Return again to the article and scan to discover how many tsunamigrams from U.S. tide stations are available on microfiche. Write the answer here. _____

PR Exercise 4

Study the graph[4] below and answer the questions that follow.

_____ 1. About how long a period of time does this graph cover?
    a. 540 hours
    b. 6 years
    c. 18 months
    d. 14 weeks

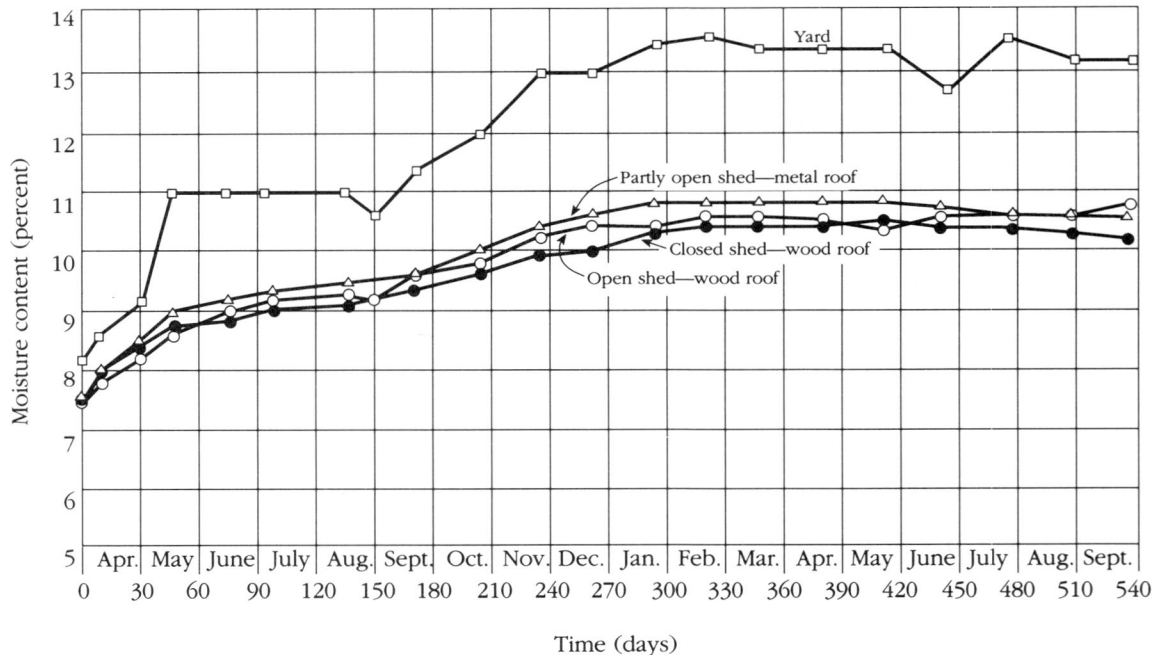

Figure 10.9. Change in average moisture content of kiln-dried southern pine 1- by 4-in flooring and 1- by 8-in boards during storage in solid piles within sheds and in a yard with a protective roof over each pile. (ML88 5557)

2. What does the line with open circles on it represent?
     a. yard
     b. partly open shed—metal roof
     c. open shed—wood roof
     d. closed shed—wood roof

3. In which type of storage is the percent of moisture content highest?
     a. open shed—wood roof
     b. closed shed—wood roof
     c. yard
     d. partly open shed—metal roof

4. At the end of the time given on the graph, what is the difference between the percent of moisture in a partly open shed with metal roof and a closed shed with wood roof?
     a. less than one percent
     b. slightly more than 1%
     c. between 10% and 11%
     d. a little over 13%

5. What change occurs in the percentage of moisture content in kiln-dried southern pine over a period of time?
     a. increases
     b. decreases
     c. remains the same
     d. goes down, then up

6. What is this graph mainly about?
     a. kiln drying procedures
     b. effects of storage procedures on kiln-dried southern pine
     c. types of sheds
     d. sizes of floor boards

PR Exercise 5

Study the map[5] on the next page and complete the following statements.

1. This map deals primarily with
     a. the Mexican railway system.
     b. mineral-producing areas of Mexico.
     c. Mexican cities.

2. A dotted line on this map represents a
     a. crude petroleum pipeline.
     b. river.
     c. natural gas pipeline.

_____ 3. Distance is measured by
   a. miles.
   b. kilometers.
   c. meters.

_____ 4. A railroad goes from Chihuahua to
   a. Torreon.
   b. Cananea.
   c. Durango.

_____ 5. According to this map, a city in Mexico is
   a. Veracruz.
   b. Belize.
   c. El Salvador.

_____ 6. Symbols such as Zn and Pb represent
   a. transportation routes.
   b. regions in Mexico.
   c. types of minerals.

_____ 7. There is a tanker terminal near
   a. Tijuana.
   b. Guadalajara.
   c. Tampico.

326

PR Exercise 6

Read the article below and complete the statements following it by placing the letter of the correct ending on the line beside each statement number.

Genuine or Counterfeit?[6]

Most industries focus their research programs on finding easier ways to manufacture their products, but security printers are constantly concerned with developing more difficult and more intricate methods. Genuine currency is distinctive because it is made through a detailed process with special paper and ink. The complicated and careful procedures not only make the currency durable, but also provide protection against counterfeiters.

The most persistent problem for counterfeiters, even with the latest technological knowledge, is the unique style of the artist transmitted in the engraving process to each note. United States currency notes are printed by the engraved intaglio steel plate method, and each feature of the design—portrait, lettering, scroll work, and the lacy geometric patterns—is done by an artist expert in his particular field. No photography enters into the creation of an engraved note, so that a camera can only picture a note and not make an actual duplication of it. A counterfeiter knows that a perfect counterfeit—one that would fool an expert—is practically impossible, so he must adopt a more modest objective. He tends to rely on his camera to produce work that will deceive an inattentive person.

Specially made paper is another important protection against counterfeiters. Its quality is far higher than paper generally available to the public and presents a difficult problem to would-be wrongdoers. Money paper has a particular feel, strength, a good appearance, and printability; it should have long life.

Can you spot a counterfeit? Perhaps the following suggestions, from the United States Secret Service, will show you how it is done.

1. STUDY genuine currency. Look closely at the workmanship of these features.

PORTRAIT

Genuine	Counterfeit
Stands out sharply from background. Eyes appear lifelike. Background is a fine screen of regular, un-broken lines.	May merge with background. Eyes, etc., may be dull or smudgy. Background may be dark, with some irregular and broken lines. Face may seem un-naturally white.

SEAL

Genuine	Counterfeit
Saw-tooth points around rim are even and sharp.	Saw-tooth points may be uneven, blunt, or broken.

SERIAL NUMBERS

Genuine

Figures are firmly and evenly printed, well spaced. On Federal Reserve Notes, prefix letter always agrees with District letter in seal.

Counterfeit

May be out of line, poorly spaced, printed too light or too dark. Prefix letter may not agree with District letter in seal.

SCROLL WORK

Genuine

Fine crisscrossing lines are sharp and unbroken.

Counterfeit

Lines may be blurred and are often broken.

2. PAPER used for genuine notes is very high quality. Small red and blue threads are in it, but may not be visible if the bill is badly worn or dirty. Counterfeit paper may feel different, or may be whiter than genuine paper. Threads may be imitated by fine red and blue lines made by a pen.

3. RUBBING a bill on a piece of paper is *not* a good test. Ink can be rubbed off genuine as well as counterfeit notes.

4. CONSULT an experienced money-handler if in doubt—a bank teller, for example.

5. IF YOU GET A COUNTERFEIT BILL . . .

   a. Write your name and the date on the back of it, so you can identify it later.
   b. Write down all the details about how you got it; WHO gave it to you? WHERE did you get it? WHEN did you get it?
   c. Contact the nearest U.S. Secret Service office, the local police, a commercial bank, or any Federal Reserve Bank.

Anyone convicted of passing a counterfeit may be fined as much as $5,000 or imprisoned for up to 15 years, or both.

_____ 1. The word "currency" means
   a. recent.
   b. money.
   c. movement of water.

_____ 2. The word "genuine" means
   a. real.
   b. valuable.
   c. one-of-a-kind.

_____ 3. Security printers constantly try to
    a. find easier ways to manufacture their products.
    b. develop more difficult and intricate methods.
    c. keep their procedures unchanged.

_____ 4. Genuine currency is made through a complicated process with special paper and ink, in order to
    a. make it attractive.
    b. challenge the printers.
    c. make it durable and provide protection against counterfeiters.

_____ 5. United States currency notes are printed by
    a. the engraved intaglio steel plate method.
    b. a photographic process.
    c. neither a nor b.

_____ 6. A counterfeiter generally
    a. expects to produce a perfect counterfeit bill.
    b. expects to be able to fool experts with his or her products.
    c. expects to be able to fool people who do not pay close attention to the money that they use.

_____ 7. Paper like that used for currency
    a. is readily available to the public.
    b. presents counterfeiters and potential counterfeiters with problems.
    c. is chosen to be ideal for photographic images.

_____ 8. If you find that the picture of a president on a bill has dull or smudgy eyes, you should suspect that
    a. the bill has gotten wet.
    b. the bill is a counterfeit.
    c. the bill is genuine.

_____ 9. If the saw-tooth points around the rim of the seal on a bill are blunt, you should suspect
    a. that you have a counterfeit bill.
    b. that you have a genuine bill.
    c. that there is no special significance to this feature.

_____ 10. If you rub a bill on a piece of paper and color comes off of it, you should suspect
    a. that you have a counterfeit bill.
    b. that you have a genuine bill.
    c. that there is no special significance to this occurrence.

_____ 11. If you think you may have a counterfeit bill, but are not sure,
    a. just go ahead and use it.
    b. throw it away to be on the safe side.
    c. check with a bank teller or other informed person.

_____ 12. The penalty for passing counterfeit money
    a. is relatively light.
    b. may be a fine or a prison term or both.
    c. is not specified in this material.

PR Exercise 7

The following article primarily relates to exports to the United Kingdom. The article has 5 parts, each part dealing with a slightly different topic. By skimming the article first, you should know which part contains the information you need to answer each question that follows the article.

"United Kingdom"[7]

- The U.S. and Foreign Commerical Service (US&FCS) in the American Embassy in London reports that U.S. manufacturers of smoke detectors have export opportunities in the United Kingdom. Most domestic fire detectors being sold there are battery-operated and are basically a "do it yourself" item. The market, according to Embassy sources, is "wide open" and the commercial staff has compiled names of U.K. firms that are anxious to talk to U.S. suppliers. Popular prices in the United Kingdom are running about $18.50 per unit. For details, contact the U.K. desk officer.

- American companies in the process industries that want to begin exporting to the United Kingdom and France have an excellent opportunity to get started exporting this October. The occasion is the MATCH-MAKER trade delegation that will visit London and Paris Oct. 24–28. Appropriate firms that want to find agents, distributors, licensees, or joint venture partners in these two markets will find the MATCHMAKER the most effective means to market penetration. . . .

- The American Embassy has produced an eight-page report on recent developments in the U.K. economy that summarizes financial market events, economic developments, and statistics in the public and private sectors. To obtain a copy, write to the U.K. desk officer.

- *An Assessment of British Technology* was recently completed by the U.S. and Foreign Commercial Service staff at the Embassy in London. The report, nearly 40 pages long, covers aerospace, advanced materials, computers, telecommunications, biotechnology, microtechnology, and government policy for science and technology. . . .

- The US&FCS in London has surveyed the British import market and identified specific sectors that have excellent potential for U.S. exporters. "Best sales" opportunities include computer hardware, franchising, telecommunications, advanced machine tools, automotive parts and accessories, hotel and catering equipment, industrial process controls, security and safety equipment, biotechnology, electronic components, Electronic Industry Production and Test Equipment (EIPT), and seafood. Each sector is treated in a four-page market summary. . . .

_____ 1. Who surveyed the British import market?
    a. US&FCS
    b. American Embassy
    c. MATCHMAKER
    d. Electronic Industry

_____ 2. Why are smoke detectors a good export opportunity?
    a. U.K. has many domestic fires.
    b. U.S. produces cheaper detectors.
    c. U.K. detectors are battery-operated and a "do it yourself item."
    d. U.K. lacks the raw materials to make detectors.

_____ 3. What is MATCHMAKER?
    a. a dating service
    b. a trade delegation
    c. a written report
    d. a type of smoke detector

_____ 4. Which is *not* mentioned as a "best sales" opportunity?
    a. electronic components
    b. hotel and catering equipment
    c. seafood
    d. textiles

PR Exercise 8

Read the article by Lee Bowman to find out how to be a good public speaker. Then answer the questions following it.

The Executive as Public Speaker[8]

Lee Bowman
"If your nose itches," says a speech specialist, "scratch it."

Whether or not the American business executive enjoys public speaking—and whether or not he is good at it—he is increasingly being called on to articulate the business viewpoint in the face of hostile charges ranging from excessive profiteering to polluting the environment. In effect, then, the executive is the voice of the company, conveying the corporate character through speeches, press conferences and appearances on the electronic media, and at every kind of public occasion from charity benefits to ribbon-cutting ceremonies.

Of course, some businessmen are lucky enough to be talented speakers. But a lot of them aren't—and they are the ones I'm thinking about. The problem is how to make an effective spokesman out of someone who literally is "unaccustomed to public speaking."

Step One is to take the mystery out of it. In my work with both businessmen and political candidates, I hammer home the first commandment of effective public speaking: Be yourself.

Think about it. An executive has already established his basic speech patterns and mannerisms, for better or worse. He has to work with what he's got. It's too late for elocution lessons. Anyhow, it isn't golden-tongued oratory we are after, but executives who can speak effectively.

I remember spending a delightful evening with the top man of one of the nation's largest corporations. He was marvelous company—urbane, lucid and witty. But the next day I heard him make a speech at a fund-raising dinner. Later I asked him, "What the hell happened to the guy I was having martinis with last night?" At the lectern he had become another person—cold, aloof and completely unconvincing. He wasn't himself.

The really effective speakers are the people who have learned that public speaking is little more than private conversation—amplified. Most important of all, they have learned to overcome the schizophrenic tendency of most inexperienced speakers to assume entirely different personalities when they step up to the lectern.

Unfortunately, "being yourself" isn't easy when you're confronted by a couple hundred skeptical faces or, worse, the cold-eyed lens of a camera. But it ought to be consoling to learn that practically everyone feels the familiar symptoms of stage fright—the wet palms, dry lips, parched throat and uncontrollable shaking of the limbs. They're not signs of incompetence; they're perfectly normal reactions to what is, after all, a high-stress situation. "Stage fright" is really a state of excitement generated by adrenalin-charged juices flowing through the body. Far from detracting from a performance, it can add to the speaker's effectiveness—provided he learns to channel it properly.

How can you use your inner tension to advantage? By letting your excitement, your emotions, come through. Show it, don't stifle it. If you don't seem to be interested in what you're talking about, what can you expect from your audience? And when you let your charged-up inner feelings come to the surface, you're going to come through as someone who means what he is saying; you're going to be a more effective speaker.

And while you're at it, get rid of your silly, senseless inhibitions. Too many inexperienced speakers seem to have the idea that their decorum should be stiff, proper and formal. Not so. If you feel like moving around, move. If your nose itches, scratch it. If you want to pull your ear lobe, pull it. They're all human mannerisms that any audience relates to. By doing what comes naturally, you relax yourself, you come through as a genuine human being, and you build rapport with your listeners.

Now let's run through a list of do's and don'ts. First—assuming that you're going to work from a fully prepared script—don't "write" your speech. What I mean is, put it down on paper but don't use a writing style; don't for God's sake, put it down the way you probably write business reports. In fact, if you're wondering how a long-time actor got into the business of consulting with public speakers, it is because speeches are—or should be—dialogue. So when you start writing your speech, *say* it, using the language that comes naturally to you, and then put those words down on paper.

Avoid the stilted words and phrases that plague many a businessman's speeches: "Thus we must conclude that," "I will now proceed to," and "Let me share with you my thoughts on this subject." When you're talking to your wife across the breakfast table, do you "share your thoughts" with her? Then why inflict that kind of pompous language on an audience you're trying to captivate?

Talking about language, don't hold back. If a little mild profanity expresses your feelings best, use it. If the latest government regulation is a helluva mess, say so. If you're damn glad the crisis is past, say it that way. You'll make your point more effectively.

Next, relax. Don't rush it. I've seen speakers plunge into their material, rattled by the suspicion that the mike isn't working properly. If you have any doubts, stop. Ask whether they can hear you in the last row. If your throat gets dry, stop again; take a sip of water. You'll put your audience—and yourself—at ease. You'll come through as a real pro.

Now it follows that what you're after is the complete attention of your listeners. But that attention should be riveted on your words, not some peculiarity of the way you are dressed. So dress conservatively. Don't wear a loud tie, or have a bunch of pens sticking out of your breast pocket. They are distracting. And on the subject of dress, I'll mention a couple of my pet peeves. The short-sleeved summer shirt may be comfortable, but too much bare arm is devastating to a speaker's image. What's even worse is the sight of an expanse of calf when you're sitting on the dais with your legs crossed. Always wear above-the-calf hose.

Having unburdened myself of a couple of don'ts, here are some do's. Do rehearse. Learn your speech and learn it well. There is nothing more annoying to an audience than the impression that the speaker is getting surprised every time he turns the page. Poor preparation is insulting to your listeners, so don't risk it.

And when I say "rehearse," I don't just mean read the speech to yourself. You should read it out loud, preferably in front of a critical and objective listener. And try to read it at a lectern, simulating actual speaking conditions as closely as possible.

The best tool I know for developing speech-making effectiveness is videotape. Run through your routine, then sit back and watch it. It can be strong medicine, but there is none better.

Once you have mastered the common sense rules, you'll do well on the podium—provided you observe one final rule: Keep it short. The best speaker in the world is going to outlive his welcome if he drones on too long. How long is too long? In my book twenty minutes is the upper limit for most occasions; and if you can cut it closer to fifteen, so much the better. You'll not only be able to get across a message that your listeners are likely to remember, you'll have their gratitude. And a grateful audience is the sure sign of an effective speaker.

_____ 1. If you wish to be an effective public speaker, you must
    a. change your personality to fit the topic.
    b. take elocution lessons.
    c. be yourself.
    d. none of the above.

_____ 2. Symptoms of "stage fright" are
    a. signs of incompetence.
    b. normal reactions to high-stress situations.
    c. sure to cause the speaker to fail completely.
    d. none of the above.

3. A good speaker
   a. eliminates all hand movements while speaking.
   b. moves around naturally.
   c. exaggerates body movements for effect.
   d. none of the above.

4. Speeches should be written
   a. in the language of formal business reports.
   b. in your conversational language.
   c. in very "proper" language.
   d. none of the above.

5. Speakers should dress
   a. conservatively.
   b. flamboyantly.
   c. casually.
   d. none of the above.

6. Speeches should be rehearsed
   a. by reading them silently.
   b. as little as possible.
   c. by reading them aloud.
   d. none of the above.

7. The best speakers
   a. keep their speeches short.
   b. give long speeches to give the audience "their money's worth."
   c. give long speeches to show how well-informed they are.
   d. none of the above.

PR Exercise 9

You will need to read the following article for three purposes. The first is to separate the information you are seeking from the extraneous material and identify only those points that are relevant to the assignment. Written material frequently contains more information than you need, and you should learn to extract only what is pertinent for your needs. The second purpose is to find the author's message or point of view so that you are aware of any bias or persuasive techniques. The third purpose is to evaluate the author's feelings in terms of your own knowledge and experience and then agree or disagree with the author. Now, read the article and observe the twelve points that organizations might consider in applying the concept of think time.

It's Thinking That Will Get Us There[9]

Much of the writing about the technology of the future has assigned to it the role of bringing to fruition our nation's dreams of prosperity. Our hopes seem to have been placed on the mechanical world of machines and computers. This is a grave mistake. The quality of our future will be determined by the quality of our minds.

The executive mind is always the major key to economic performance. But let's face it, far too few executives take the time to think, or encourage their colleagues to think.

There are many highly intelligent people who, because of their circumstances, are relatively poor "thinkers," and the result is a huge gap between what is and what can be. But the good news is: Thinking can be taught.

The Right Kind of Thought

Effective executives understand that there are many different kinds of thinking, including analytical thinking, creative thinking, short-range thinking and long-range thinking, to name a few. Each has its place and makes its contribution. However, unless the *right kind* of thinking process is applied to an issue, the end results will be distorted.

Unfortunately, most of our business education and experience teaches us *what* to think rather than *how* to think. As a result, much of our creative potential has been unexploited. We are conditioned to "solve problems" rather than to "seek opportunity." With a problem we look for a solution; with an opportunity we look for benefits.

In the past 50 years, startling advances in technology have added greatly to our standard of living, our productivity capacity and potential, and the prospects for a positive future. The challenge before us now is to add the power of the *mind* to the promise of technology.

From a functional standpoint, our mental capacities can be simplified as follows:
- Absorptive: the ability to observe and apply attention.
- Retentive: the ability to memorize and recall.
- Reasoning: the ability to analyze and judge.
- Creative: the ability to visualize, foresee and generate ideas.

Electronic brains and computers now have all of these capacities except the creative function, and it is highly unlikely that there will ever be a machine capable of creativity. That is what makes the creative executive such an irreplaceable resource. Creativity, however, is not the total answer. We must be able to identify and apply the appropriate mental process to the myriad of situations as they occur. If an immediate problem calls for a solution within a short period of time, a brainstorming session or a long-range planning session would be totally useless. Obviously, at a later date it might be very logical to look for creative ways to prevent the problem entirely, or plan on ways to minimize the possibility of a reoccurrence.

Start Them Thinking

Accountable think time is a process to encourage organizations and individuals to develop and apply more of their mental powers. To assure that your organization's best thinking is constantly being focused on opportunity and key issues is to put the odds of success overwhelmingly in your favor.

Opportunity is created where intelligent thought and purpose meet. Here is how some organizations have applied this concept:

1. Executives and employees participate in a thinking workshop. This workshop familiarizes them with the various approaches and effects of different styles of thinking.

2. Each year, as part of the budget preparation or the planning process, key individuals in the organization are allocated "accountable think time." In other words, they are *expected* to spend a predetermined amount of time thinking. A list of key issues is prepared to assure that thinking is directed toward issues and strategies that are consistent with the organization's mission, philosophy and goals. They know that they will have to report on the "output," but that it will be communicated after six months or a year, rather than after every session. This minimizes the pressure to produce valuable results.

3. Variations of this concept have been equally effective. One approach that has been consistently effective begins with the compiling of a list of issues "worth thinking about." Some organizations choose to identify "problem areas" that require major thinking; others focus on "opportunity" or "new market development." *The main thing is to identify key issue areas, positive or negative, that will produce significant benefits to the organization.*

4. After the list of key issues is generated, separate categories are set up for "current problem areas" and "opportunities." There should be a proper balance between the areas of concentration that focus on "problem solving" and those that are "entrepreneurial" in nature.

5. Each individual then selects from those items that are of particular interest to him or her. When people think about things that interest them, or utilize a special skill or talent that they have, the results are generally more positive, and the morale and motivation of the individual improves.

6. "Think time" is then scheduled for each person. It is OK to be flexible. However, there will probably be a tendency to let other "priorities" become more important than your think time. This is deadly and should be avoided. It's a matter of discipline and recognizing the ultimate payoff.

7. Think time should be at least two hours in length. A half-day is ideal. To get the mind really working requires a period of relaxation and concentration. In the executive's busy schedule, there is almost no time that is free of interruption. In addition, a preoccupation with problems and demands makes it difficult to focus on a specific problem or opportunity.

8. The conditions for thinking should be set by each individual. Some people think best in silence. Others prefer music. I like to think while jogging. The *quality* of thought is the important thing. Usually a relaxed, informal environment is best. No one is permitted to ask, "How are you coming along?" etc. Some people require longer incubation periods than others. The "thinkers," however, can ask questions or volunteer information as they wish.

9. At the end of the year, each individual is asked to present his or her best thinking on the subject that person chose to explore. The presentation is accompanied by a written report. Again, it is stressed that this is not a competitive exercise.

10. After the presentations have been made, those that seem to have continued potential are followed up and incorporated into the plan and budgeted for the coming year. Possibly a task force is initiated to explore the idea in detail and in depth.

11. A simple report format is used to make sure that the key points, strengths/weaknesses and costs/benefits, rather than the literary aspect, are the important characteristics. Clerical support should be provided so that the "mental" effort is the main focus of the process.

12. In order to maximize synergy, all members of the management team should be aware of the projects that each individual is working on. That way, they can refer books, articles, information and ideas to one another.

The above process can help the organization identify its best thinkers. It encourages innovation rather than the status quo.

Any organization without a conscious effort toward creating opportunity and renewal will stagnate.

The process described brings the organization's best thinking into focus on key issues, and it helps people grow. The more people's minds are exercised and stretched, the more the organization's potential is developed.

As an incidental benefit, through this process it is often discovered that many interpersonal problems are merely different perspectives on an issue, and can easily be resolved.

The "Corporate Visionary"

Recently, *The American Banker* carried an article by Michael Sullivan of First Union Bank of Charlotte, N.C., entitled, "The Corporate Visionary." The role of the corporate visionary, according to Sullivan, is to "force management away from an emphasis on current profits, short-range financial plans and economic forecasts, and to begin visualizing the organization of the future."

There needs to be a little more of the corporate visionary in all of us.□

I. In order to answer the question below, reread the twelve points and look for the major steps to follow in implementing a thinking workshop. While some of these points are actually steps in the procedure, others are merely explanatory. Reduce the list to the five or six essential steps and write each step clearly and concisely from management's point of view. The first step is given.

1. Decide which individuals should participate.

2.

3.

4.

5.

6.

II. Skim through the article again, this time looking for the author's views about thinking. Then choose the best answer for each of the following multiple-choice questions.

_____ 1. The author believes that the quality of our future depends on
    a. the mechanical world of machines and computers.
    b. the quality of our minds.
    c. our adherence to the status quo.
    d. executive-employee relationships.

_____ 2. According to the author, one of management's top priorities should be
    a. economic forecasts for the immediate future.
    b. current profits.
    c. visualizing the organization of the future.
    d. short-range financial plans.

_____ 3. Computers can now do all but which of the following:
   a. memorize and recall.
   b. analyze and judge.
   c. visualize, foresee, and generate ideas.
   d. observe and apply attention.

_____ 4. Thinking workshops should focus on
   a. effective report writing.
   b. short-range financial goals.
   c. problem solving.
   d. key issues.

_____ 5. Think time should occur
   a. in a two-hour or half-day block of time.
   b. at the end of the day in order to analyze what happened during the day.
   c. whenever the individual can find a few minutes to spare.
   d. during coffee breaks.

_____ 6. The author feels which of the following ideas is generally beneficial:
   a. all members of the management team know what projects others are doing.
   b. individuals compete for the best idea.
   c. executives allow other priorities to take precedence over think time.
   d. management sets the conditions for thinking for each individual.

_____ 7. The author believes that
   a. thinking encourages innovation rather than the status quo.
   b. the more thinking people do, the more the organization develops its potential.
   c. many interpersonal problems disappear when people realize they are simply different perspectives on an issue.
   d. all of the above.

III. React to the article by writing one paragraph explaining why you agree or disagree with the author.

Reading Business Correspondence

You can save time reading business correspondence by following a few simple steps. Automatically glance at the letterhead and categorize in your mind what type of information you expect to read. Look at the signature to see if you recognize the individual who has sent you the letter. By following these two steps, you are building a readiness for understanding the message of the letter.

Next skim over the body of the letter, picking out key words or phrases that indicate the nature of the business. The first paragraph may be a brief acknowledgment of a telephone call or communiqué, or it may consist of a courteous introductory remark. In this case, the intent of the letter will probably be expressed in the second paragraph. On the other hand, the writer may get right down to business and state the intent of the letter in the opening lines. Usually, the remainder of the letter deals with additional information about the main purpose or purposes of the letter. The concluding paragraph is seldom more than a closing remark or a line or two expressing anticipation of an answer.

Many business letters are somewhat formal and contain trite phrases that could easily be discarded. These phrases are included, however, to avoid the appearance of being rude or abrupt. As you read, you will save time by skipping over these pleasantries and picking out only the key words that get right to the heart of the business. The vocabulary and style of business letters are generally fairly simple to understand. Paragraphs in business letters are usually shorter than those found in literary works and may consist of only a sentence or two.

If the letter is a form letter, you will probably not want to give it the close attention you will give a personal letter. Although it is difficult to recognize a form letter every time, three features can reveal the style of a form letter. If the letter is addressed in a general way, such as ''Dear Customer,'' it is usually a form letter. If the letter is addressed to your name and address, it may still be a form letter if the type face of the heading does not match the type face of the body of the letter. A third way to recognize a form letter is to note the heading. If the letter has been sent from a large, well-known concern with which you are not knowingly doing business, such as *Reader's Digest,* the letter may be a form letter.

After you have read the letter, decide whether or not it requires an answer or any type of action. If it does require some sort of response, place it where you can take care of the business quickly to avoid having to reread the letter several times.

PR Exercise 10

Read the following letters as quickly as you can in order to answer these questions: (a) What is the purpose of the letter in a few words? (b) Is this a form letter? (c) Does the letter require an answer? (d) Does it require any action? If so, what?

1.   **Dodson Electric Company**

To all our customers:

XYZ has advised us that some of its black A, AB, and AC type portable cords may have been jacketed with material that could be conductive. While only under very unusual circumstances would there be any danger involved with this product, XYZ is recalling this material for further testing.

This relates only to black rubber jacketed cord purchased after October 1, 1992, and is identified by a reference to A, AB, or AC type on the jacket and a brown marker thread inside the jacket. The A and AB also have a single crown for further identification.

If you have any of the above material, please notify us. Our locations are listed for your convenience. Please consult your telephone directory for the number of the office nearest you.

Sincerely,

Edgar G. Pearson

a. What is the message of the letter in a few words? _____

_____

b. Is this a form letter? _____

c. Does the letter require an answer? _____

d. Does it require any action? If so, what? _____

2.   **Coswell Industries**

Dear Mrs. Harfield:

With reference to your phone call of yesterday, we have been able to secure a short film showing the Coswell trimmers. We are enclosing same herewith.

We are sorry to say that this is an extremely short film, but it is the only one that we have at the moment. We hope that this will give you a general idea of the operation of the Coswell trimmers.

We trust that this film will be of some value to you, and we thank you for your inquiry.

Sincerely,

John McFadden

a. What is the message of the letter in a few words? _____

_____

b. Is this a form letter? _____

c. Does the letter require an answer? _____

d. Does it require any action? If so, what? _____

3.

Division of Air Pollution Control
Department of Health

Dear Mrs. Harfield:

Thank you for your letter regarding the emission reducing program for the incinerator at your plant.

Inasmuch as the operation of this unit will be on such an indefinite schedule, we would not issue a permit for operation, but would have it on an emergency standby basis.

This would mean that you would maintain an operating log for this equipment and whenever it is necessary to operate it you would supply this office with the details. You should state the actual operating time, time started, time it was removed from service, reason for operation, and any other pertinent information.

Your cooperation in our program is appreciated, and if you have any questions feel free to call on us.

Sincerely,

George Hoskins

a. What is the message of the letter in a few words? _____

_____

b. Is this a form letter? _____

c. Does the letter require an answer? _____

d. Does it require any action? If so, what? _____

4.

Sales Department
Acme Wholesale Dealers

Attention: Purchasing Department Manager

Our records indicate that you are one of several customers from whom we have not received an order or quotation request recently.

Have our catalogs we've mailed been "borrowed" from your Purchasing Department and possibly misplaced? (A number of our commercial customers state that this frequently happens.) If so, please let us know and we will gladly forward additional copies for your purchasing facility.

Remember, our only reason for operating as a separate department is to serve you, our commercial customer, with quality merchandise at the right price. We've missed you and will appreciate the privilege of serving you again soon.

a. What is the message of the letter in a few words? _____

_____

b. Is this a form letter? _____

c. Does the letter require an answer? _____

d. Does it require any action? If so, what? _____

5. Berkley Brush

Dear Mr. Harris:

I have just received a special delivery letter from Mr. Jackson advising me that he has not as yet received the 10 untrimmed and uncleaned 18″ floor brushes that he needs for testing purposes on your machine.

This delay in getting the brushes is holding up delivery of your machine. Would you kindly have these shipped via air immediately so that your machine can be finally tested and shipped without further delay?

I would appreciate your advising Mr. Jackson directly that the brushes are being sent. Please send a copy of your letter to my office also.

Very truly yours,

Doris Fitzpatrick

a. What is the message of the letter in a few words? _____

_____

b. Is this a form letter? _____

c. Does the letter require an answer? _____

d. Does it require any action? If so, what? _____

6. Volunteer Machine Company

Dear Mr. Marshall:

This letter is in reference to your order #08–68–001–308 concerning repairs of one Auto Shaper Head for Model 40 Automatic Shaper. We were to advise you of the cost before proceeding with repairs.

The cost department advises me that the repairs would amount to approximately $607. If this estimate meets with your approval, kindly issue a letter of authority advising us to proceed with the repairs.

Sincerely,

Arthur Williams

a. What is the message of the letter in a few words? _____

_____

b. Is this a form letter? _____

c. Does the letter require an answer? _____

d. Does it require any action? If so, what? _____

Chapter Notes

1. "Indexes of Industrial Production." reprinted from *Business America,* June 1992, p. 18.

2. Jim Lucas. "Integrated Crop Management." In *Agriculture and the Environment. 1991 Yearbook of Agriculture.* Washington, D.C.: Government Printing Office, 1991, p. 182.

3. "Tsunami Data Services," reprinted from *EDIS,* January 1981, p. 23.

4. William T. Simpson, ed. *Dry Kiln Operator's Manual.* Washington, D.C.: Government Printing Office, U.S. Department of Agriculture, 1991, p. 227.

5. "Program Area and Accomplishments." In *Bureau of Mines Research 91.* Washington, D.C.: U.S. Department of the Interior, 1991, p. 95.

6. Excerpted from "Counterfeit?", a brochure distributed by the Federal Reserve Bank of Atlanta, Atlanta, Georgia. Illustrations of currency have been omitted because their reproduction is prohibited.

7. "United Kingdom," excerpted from *Business America*, April 11, 1988, p. 16.

8. Reprinted with the special permission of *Dun's Review,* January 1974. Copyright, 1974, Dun & Bradstreet Publications Corporation.

9. Harold R. McAlindon, "It's Thinking That Will Get Us There," reprinted by permission from *Advantage,* November 1983, pp. 89–92.

APPENDIX

Directions for Reading Rate Exercises

The following articles provide practice for improving your reading rate. Before you begin reading each article, scan it for a few seconds so you have some idea what to expect. Record your starting time in the blank provided at the beginning of each article. When you finish reading, record the completion time in the appropriate place. By subtracting the starting time from the completion time, you will have the elapsed time. Be sure to record this time in the proper place also.

Refer to the Reading Rate Table on page 408 in order to find the number of words you read per minute. This number should also be recorded in the blank at the beginning of the article. Then, turn to the rate chart on page 409 and mark the chart to indicate your reading rate. Next, answer the questions that follow the article by circling the letters of the correct answers. Then, have your instructor check your paper to see how many answers are correct. Record this information and the percentage of correct answers in the blanks at the beginning of the article. Also record the % correct on the comprehension chart found on page 409.

You may choose the articles in any order. They increase in difficulty from first to last article presented. Each week try to increase the number of words you can read per minute, but maintain a comprehension score of at least 70% to 80%. Your speed should increase each week as you practice your reading skills.

Reading Rate Selections

Rapid Reading I

1534 words

Starting time _____

Completion time _____

Elapsed time _____

Words per minute _____

Number correct _____

Percentage of comprehension _____

The New Flying Saucer Story*

It arrived in America on a golden autumn evening in a season of wonderfully mild weather, with almost no warning. The first voices that brought the news were from the Deep South.

We were fishing, said one, and all of a sudden there was a blinding light and some kind of glowing, pulsating blue object landed behind us. Then out came the men or the things or the creatures—he didn't know quite what to call them. Clearly, this man was trying his best to describe the experience. Just as clearly, whatever had happened to the two men was horrifyingly real to them for, as they spoke, the terror within them was easily discerned.

Thus began the new flying-saucer episode. The two fishermen were describing their experience on a riverbank in Pascagoula, Miss., and they were on national television. It was only the beginning. For five nights in a row, NBC's Nightly News carried some kind of UFO story. Predictably, the more the phenomenon was talked about, the bigger the story became . . . and the wilder. Those with fertile imaginations soon gave accounts of trips to Venus and talks with those from other planets.

By coincidence, the new UFO story began while the nation was wracked by extremely bad news—a shooting war in the Middle East and unbelievable political scandals in Washington. Perhaps UFOs were just a light diversion—something to take the mind off the awfulness of reality.

Except it would be difficult to convince a lot of people, especially the two fishermen in Mississippi.

It was not hard to view the return of flying saucers as something that in the end could be more menacing than Watergate or the guns of the Israelis and Arabs. Could it be that creatures from outer space, after previous scouting trips, were—are—finally coming to invade us?

Even the most recent history shows that almost nothing is impossible. Who could have imagined a man who was Vice-President at breakfast and a felon at cocktail time? Who could imagine a man walking on the moon? So flying saucers with humanoids coming to ravage and kill could be believed instantly. Orson Welles and his War of the Worlds on radio more than three decades ago proved that. Actors described the grotesque scenes as New Jersey was invaded and conquered. The people panicked.

*Reprinted from *Mechanix Illustrated Magazine,* Copyright 1974 by Fawcett Publications, Inc.

Then we found out that it was only a story. And years later the U.S. Air Force—no less—told us that most flying-saucer reports were either cases of misjudgment or outright hoaxes. Even the most advanced technology as we know it cannot produce a spaceship capable of an interstellar trip to the nearest heavenly body where advanced life could exist—a journey usually put at 26 *trillion* mi. So, therefore, it was highly unlikely that they could come here. And that was that—or was it?

"I was so scared that I couldn't believe it was happening. They were on us so quick we couldn't do anything. I doubt if we could have resisted them if we had tried to. I'm sure they are far more advanced than we are."

Those are the words of Charles E. Hickson, a 45-year-old shipyard worker, a man with a seamed, worried face and a balding head. He and a fellow shipyard hand, 19-year-old Calvin R. Parker Jr., had turned around to reach for bait when the spaceship, shaped roughly like an egg and exuding blue light, landed to begin the Pascagoula River Incident in Mississippi.

It was easily the most dramatic, intimate and *believable* UFO report ever made. Others had claimed to have been aboard spaceships and to have taken trips in them but invariably these people were alone (and invariably they were men, which could raise a question about the sexual preferences of our visitors from Out There). But here was a case in which *two* men were involved and, though one fainted, both could and did tell the same story.

"The creatures," reported Hickson, "were pale, ghostlike, about 5 ft. tall. They were sort of light flesh-colored, or more pale gray, with crablike claws for hands and rounded feet."

There were three of them, the two men agreed. They had two eyes, sharp ears and pointed noses with kind of a mouthlike gap beneath. And lots of folds in their skins. Most startling, they hovered about a foot above the ground, as if defying gravity, and there was no action in their legs as they moved. One made a buzzing sound and they picked up Hickson and Parker and carried them inside the spaceship—that's when Parker fainted. Some kind of mobile eye examined the two men, and they were taken out. The older man, Hickson, collapsed on the ground in terror and then—*buzzzzt!*—the spaceship was gone.

The men—left now in the quiet of the riverbank, exhausted, afraid and numbed—tried to think of what they should do. At first, it seemed obvious: say nothing because no one would believe them and they'd be laughed at. But then they knew almost immediately they couldn't do that. It wasn't a thing you could stand alone. They needed help and friendship. They called the newspaper. No answer. They called the sheriff. Help came, the story seeped out, the town was invaded by newsmen and TV cameras. Hickson and Parker became known around the world.

Surprisingly, there were few scoffers. One look at Hickson and Parker, wracked by inner turmoil and obviously suffering, could convince even skeptics that they were telling the truth. There was compassion instead of guffaws. The men finally were examined by doctors and researchers, including a period when hypnosis was used. Everybody agreed. The two Mississippians *were* telling the truth.

The Pascagoula River Incident, while immediate, electrifying and unique in a few aspects, fitted into a pattern known not only for years but for centuries. That's how long UFOs have been around. The flying-saucer story this time is not much different, despite its dramatic opening episode, from what we've seen before.

Strange objects flying silently through the skies were recorded as early as 100 B.C. By one reckoning, between then and 1800 A.D., some 500 UFO sightings were reported. The visitation rate from Out There speeded up considerably in the next century and three-quarters and earthlings thoughtfully produced more observers to report them. Between 1947 and 1967, it is estimated that no less than 5 million people in 70 countries saw UFOs. In all recorded history, the figure comes to a staggering 10 million observers.

But could they? All of them couldn't be wrong as to what they perceived, of course, but the fact is that man is no closer to knowing the answer to the crucial question than he was 20 centuries ago—has earth been visited by creatures from other worlds?

The Air Force used to be called upon to answer that question regularly. So the fly people expended a hideous amount of time, money and nerves on it. Well, it didn't work out. When asked about UFOs, the Air Force had to tell the truth—they didn't know.

It was about as bad an answer as you could give. Ha!, said the armchair experts, they know but they're just covering up. Afraid to admit they don't have a plane that can shoot one down.

The Air Force, tired of being kicked around, finally launched Project Blue Book, a big and expensive piece of research headed by a physicist, Maj. Hector Quintanilla, Jr. The object: a *definitive* answer to the old question. The answer (Sept. '67 MI) this time was even worse than the first. No, said the Blue Bookies, flying saucers do not exist because technology could not produce a spaceship that does all these things. Technology as we know it—no! Technology as they have developed it—yes!

The Air Force, at least, was ready for the flying saucer business this year. They've gotten smarter. They have nothing to do with UFOs now and know nothing about them. If you feel threatened by one, call the police. If you want someone to chase one in an airplane, better look into flying lessons.

As we said back there near the beginning, nothing really surprises us now and maybe this time we'll really find out. But history is against us. What we haven't found out in 2,000 years is likely to keep eluding us, by all odds.

UFOs tend to make people uneasy, to frighten them. History suggests our feelings should be otherwise. UFOs are somewhat like ghosts. We've had ghosts around since we've been here and never in that long history have they injured anyone. Frightened, yes. But never an actual injury. With the possible exception of two Brazilians who seemed to have suffered electromagnetic type burns from a UFO in 1957 and a horse that was killed in Colorado on the night of a spaceship visit, the little men from Out There—if they exist—have never exhibited harmful intentions toward us. So if you happen to run into a creature from another world, don't flee in alarm. Ask her in for a drink.

1. The space ship seen by the two fishermen was
    a. pale green with an eerie glow and shaped like a sphere.
    b. a glowing, pulsating blue object shaped like an egg.
    c. a silver mechanical monster with crablike claws.

2. Strange space objects have been recorded as early as
    a. 100 B.C.
    b. 500 B.C.
    c. 1800 A.D.

3. The writer feels that the fishermen's story was
   a. a hoax to fool the American people.
   b. just one more of many unfounded stories about UFO sightings.
   c. the most dramatic and believable UFO report ever made.

4. At this time, according to the article, the Air Force
   a. has nothing to do with UFOs.
   b. is conducting a massive research study concerning UFOs.
   c. tries to investigate all reports of UFO sightings.

5. The author feels that
   a. space people are likely to harm us.
   b. space people probably will not harm us.
   c. space people will capture us and take us back with them.

6. The creatures described by the fishermen
   a. were pale and ghostlike with crablike claws and rounded feet.
   b. were little green men with pointed heads.
   c. had bulging eyes and antennas on their heads.

7. At this time people on Earth
   a. know a great deal about UFOs.
   b. are learning much about UFOs.
   c. know practically nothing about UFOs.

8. The space creatures moved
   a. as they hovered about the ground without moving their legs.
   b. with rapid, jerky movements of their legs.
   c. in a swimming motion, using their arms to propel them.

9. The fishermen reacted to their experience
   a. with interest and curiosity.
   b. with fright and terror.
   c. with a sense of humor.

10. The main idea of this article is that
    a. flying saucers do not exist because technology cannot produce spaceships.
    b. men only imagine that they are visited by objects from outer space since we have no proof that these men exist.
    c. this most recent report of flying saucers, along with millions of other reports, indicates that objects from outer space may indeed be visiting the Earth.

Starting time _____

Completion time _____

Elapsed time _____

Words per minute _____

Number correct _____

Percentage of
comprehension _____

A Time for Walking*

Lew Dietz

A few years ago the first snowstorm came early to the region of my home in Maine. It was a wild, honking northeaster that paralyzed most of the state. Nothing moved for a good twenty-four hours. A power failure stopped the electric clocks. Time literally stood still.

I wasn't expected anyplace. Since everyone's car was plugged by ten-foot drifts, no one was expected anywhere. It was during this period of compelled immobility that I experienced a curious euphoria. The whole town and hundreds of other towns had supinely surrendered to nature. I was—perversely perhaps—pleased that modern man's pride in his conquest of his environment had been rudely dented. Pride goeth before a fall. In this case a fine winter snowfall.

The old-timers' tales of the long hard winters of the past notwithstanding, it is doubtful that Maine winters have changed for the better or worse in the course of the century. It is our attitude toward snow that has altered. Has modern man forgotten how to be properly grateful for a rousing snowstorm? Has snow become a total nuisance rather than a sometime joy and a boon to man? . . .

What, I asked myself, had become of that early American artifact, the snowshoe? Had snowshoes been relegated to the sad role of decorating the walls of ski lodges and providing wintry symbols for the covers of sporting catalogs? Why, it wasn't too far back—in my own lifetime in fact—that snowshoes were considered an absolute necessity everywhere in the chilly corners of the nation.

That was the year I dug my snowshoes out of the attic, where they had been gathering dust for a decade, and rediscovered the winter woods.

"Rediscovered," I say, because I once had been an habituate of the winter woods. Snowshoes had taken me rabbit hunting with my beagles—a whole series of rabbit hounds. Snowshoes had taken me on winter traplines. And one bitter winter more than a decade ago I had spent almost a solid week in the north woods chasing bobcats.

Looking back, I realize that in those winters on snowshoes I had learned more about nature and her laws than in all the other seasons rolled together. The northern winter is a quiet time, the season of nature's recuperation, but one need only to wander into the tucked-in wintry world to learn that life persists. Moreover, once the snow covers the earth, nature is an open book. Everything that lives and moves leaves its record on the snow.

*Reprinted from *Audubon*, the magazine of the National Audubon Society; copyright © 1972.

In New England, winter comes quietly like a stalking cat. Unlike the spring, which arrives with a sudden burst of life, or the autumn, which just as suddenly explodes into flame, the northern winter has a long slow fuse: it is a progressive silence that begins with the southern flights of birds and the final fading of the insect hum. The first snowfall covers the fallen leaves with a hushing blanket. And winter is here.

When rabbit hunting, I always preferred snow to bare ground. I could see the rabbit trails, check the crossings of both the dog and the rabbit. I got to know every trick the snowshoe hare uses to outwit the hound. I learned how a smart—or lazy—hound cuts some corners to counter the hare's stratagems. I became a part of the chase.

And, inevitably, I came to understand the snowshoe hare's place in the balance of nature. Clearly, the hare was not there for me and my hound, but to assure a food supply for the owls, the foxes, and the other predators that must survive in the harsh northern winter.

A snowshoe trek is most rewarding shortly after a fall of snow. There, just a few yards beyond the house, are the fresh stitcheries fashioned by a gray squirrel and a foraging field mouse. The mouse's trail vanishes into a grass clump and emerges again. On this pristine blanket—whiter than the whitest wash—you may see the end of the story. The mouse had made a dash for the base of a tree, where snow melts earliest and weed seeds are exposed. The lacy track ends abruptly where the marks of an owl's wings brush the snow.

Farther on, the dainty prints of a red fox punch black holes in the whiteness. The fox tracks run in line, not slightly staggered as a dog's. The tracks skirt the pasture and meet the fresh trail of a snowshoe hare. The fox had followed the hare's track for a few rods, then turned off. Possibly what the fox had in mind early that morning was one of the fat grouse that had been feeding in the scrub birch beyond the stone wall. At least he had headed up the slope, run the stone fence for

a few yards, then, leaping off, paused to consider the situation. Whatever the stratagem he had decided upon, it had worked. Soon I came upon a puddle of partridge feathers.

One January day I became involved in another of nature's small dramas. I came upon the paired slots of a bounding ermine— the winter weasel. I saw where the fierce little carnivore had come upon the chunky track of a hare. As I moved on the track, the grim story unfolded. Written was the instant in which the hare had become aware of the pursuing weasel. The bounding zigzagging tracks reflected the hare's panic.

To panic the hare was part of the weasel's plan. The weasel can't match the hare's speed on the snow. But what the weasel lacks in speed, it makes up for in dogged persistence. Darkness prevented me from reaching the end of this trail. I could only guess that somewhere beyond in that world of conifers and blue shadows, panic-induced exhaustion had closed the gap between quarry and hunted. Fear can cause a hare's heart to literally explode.

During those years on snowshoes the realization was borne in upon me that sudden death in the woods was too natural and commonplace to qualify as drama in nature's terms. The ultimate object of nature's stewardship is the welfare of the totality of things. It took me a while to escape from the trap of thinking of woods creatures in human terms and making sentimental judgments. . . .

Without the potential for symbolization, language, and culture, the behavior of lower animals cannot be construed as "cruel" from any but a human point of view. Yet, for instance, man seems to have a natural fear of the wildcats. Certainly the preservation of the bounty on bobcats in my own state can only be a reflection of that distaste, since there is abundant proof that bounties have never served a useful purpose.

Upon occasion bobcats do kill deer. One day years ago I came upon the fresh slots of a cat. It sometimes requires close examination to distinguish the cat track in the snow from that of the fox. I had learned from cat hunters that it is the slightly pigeon-toed tread of the cat that is the giveaway. I saw that day where the cat picked up a deer trail for a few hundred yards, then had abruptly swung off the trail. I guessed the cat's plan, and all too humanly I rushed to the rescue.

I arrived at least an hour too late. The bobcat had circled to waylay the young deer. Springing from the snow, the cat had leaped to the deer's back, and severing the nerve at the base of its neck with teeth and claws, had ridden the deer to the ground. The story was written there as clearly as if I'd witnessed it with my eyes. The cat had eaten a part of the haunch, then covered the carcass with snow to serve as a meal for another hungry day.

Later I came to respect the bobcat's rights as a hunter and to understand its place in the ecosystem. The northern winter, though a boon to some creatures, is a harsh test for others. The populations of some species, such as deer, must be pruned to a size that the winter range can support. By February the weak have long since perished. The late winter woods hold only the strong and the healthy.

Since many wild creatures are crepuscular and nocturnal feeders, there is no better time to observe life in the winter woods than at night under a moon. Years back, hunting in the north woods, I was snowbound by an early storm. Restive under confinement, I set out on snowshoes by the light of the full moon.

As I broke trail on the new snow, two deer crossed the woods road ahead of me. They paused to peer at me, more in curiosity than in fear. I sat down on a stump at the edge of a clearing where the remains of a lumber camp stood. As I rested, a great horned owl slid by, hunting on velvet wings. I heard no sound, though it passed so close I felt the breeze of its wings.

Suddenly, motion caught in the edge of my eyes. I spied a snowshoe hare cavorting crazily in the opening. As I watched in amazement another joined the first, and then another, soon a dozen or more hares were dancing, leaping, dashing about in the maddest of frolics. I had heard that sometimes woodland creatures become pixilated by the magic of moonlight in the snow. Now I could believe it. Whatever the magic was that made those hares joyous, reckless, or just plain lightheaded, it wasn't enough to deprive them totally of their protective senses. One careless motion of my hand and they vanished. In a glimmering there was nothing in the clearing but moonlight. . . .

Since the dawn of man, snowshoes have carried hunters across the surface of the snow. Surely they antedate the wheel, for snow shoes are as obvious a solution to a primitive problem as the caveman's club. Nor have snowshoes changed basically since the men of prehistory carried them across the land bridge that once connected Siberia with North America.

Trappers, game wardens, and timber cruisers, whose professions take them into the winter woods, have never hung up their snowshoes. The rediscovery of snowshoes as a means of pleasure is strictly a modern phenomenon. It was only this past year that I suddenly became aware that snowshoeing is enjoying a lively renaissance. . . . It appears that all at once thousands of winter-immobilized men, women, and children have discovered this simple and practical way of embracing and becoming involved with winter. . . .

Curiously, the increased sales of this most ancient of winter tools can be attributed in part to the explosive popularity of the newest mode of winter travel. Snowmobilers have learned by now that machines break down. When this happens, snowshoes can get you home.

Home, of course, means many things to many men. The special joy for the man who has learned to be at home in the winter woods is the quiet sense he gains of being a part of something larger than himself. Modern man lives in the confusion of a changing world. Never before has he had a greater need to know the ordered, changeless world that lies beyond his door.

1. When the wild snowstorm came to his home in Maine, the author felt
   a. panicky because of the resulting power failure.
   b. annoyed because cars could not get out on the roads.
   c. pleased and grateful for such a snowstorm.
2. The writer prefers snow to bare ground when hunting because
   a. he can travel on snowshoes.
   b. he can see the rabbit's tracks.
   c. it is quieter to walk in the snow.
3. Snowshoes
   a. have existed for centuries in basically the same form.
   b. are relatively new inventions found hanging on the walls of ski lodges.
   c. have never served any practical purpose.
4. Night is a good time to observe life in the winter woods because
   a. many wild creatures feed at night.
   b. there are no noises to disturb the animals.
   c. it is too dark for the animals to see you.
5. The tracks and patterns in the snow
   a. are a mystery to the writer.
   b. tell the writer the story of what has happened.
   c. are confusing because too many animals roam the woods.
6. To the writer, sudden death in the woods
   a. is a terrible thing.
   b. should be controlled by government regulations.
   c. is natural and commonplace.
7. One moonlit night the writer was amazed to observe
   a. a bobcat kill a deer.
   b. an ermine catch a hare.
   c. a dozen or more hares frolicking.
8. Snowshoe sales are increasing partly because
   a. snowmobilers have learned that their machines break down.
   b. they are needed as transportation because of the fuel shortage.
   c. the amount of snowfall is increasing.
9. By late winter
   a. nearly as many animals can be found as in early winter.
   b. only the strong and healthy animals have survived.
   c. nearly all the animals have perished.
10. The main idea of this article is that
    a. in the confusion of a changing world, man needs to experience the ordered, changeless world beyond his door.
    b. animals play, hunt, live, and die during the snowstorms in New England.
    c. showshoeing is becoming a popular new winter sport.

Starting time _____

Completion time _____

Elapsed time _____

Words per minute _____

Number correct _____

Percentage of
comprehension _____

Expedition to Everest*

Eric Perlman

WHAT COULD HAVE TEMPTED so prominent a group of United States doctors, scientists, lawyers, and businessmen to leave their familes and risk their lives against the most difficult and dangerous climbing route ever attempted on Tibet's towering Mt. Everest?

"Because it's there," is no answer. "Nothing ventured, nothing gained," comes closer. Even Sir Edmund Hillary, the first man to climb Mt. Everest . . . was drawn away from his philanthropic work in New Zealand and Nepal to join another assault on the world's highest mountain.

The U.S. Everest expedition left San Francisco, California, in September 1981, with great fanfare. We were an additional example of the growing cooperation between the U.S. and the People's Republic of China. When we arrived in the Tibetan capitol of Lhasa, the people greeted us with wide-eyed stares of disbelief. They had seen very few Westerners, and we presented quite a spectacle in our matching cowboy hats and gold-buttoned blazers. They crowded close to touch our white skin and feel our clothes.

Tibetans are a handsome people with a striking resemblance to the Navajo Indians of the U.S. southwest—strong faces with prominent cheekbones and flashing brown eyes. But Tibet is an occupied country. The Chinese invaded in 1959 and forced the Dalai Lama, the spiritual and temporal leader, to flee. Even after more than 20 years of occupation, whenever our Chinese guides wandered out of earshot, Tibetans sidled close and whispered, "Dalai Lama, Dalai Lama," a muffled cry of freedom that doubled as a request for pictures of him they hoped we might have brought with us.

I had brought no picture of the Dalai Lama, but through friends, I have been given a picture and a lock of hair of the second most revered leader of this religious people—the Gyalwa Karmapa—in hopes that I might place them on the summit of Mt. Everest. In the Jo-Khang Cathedral, the holiest temple of the Tibetan Buddhist faith, in a musty cubicle lit by yak-butter candles and adorned with multi-eyed demons and divinities on the walls, I unrolled my package. A pair of red-robed monks were sweeping the floor, but hurried over to see what I had brought. "Karmapa! Karmapa!" they whispered frantically and bowed at my feet to be touched by the picture and lock of hair. Within seconds pilgrims from throughout the cathedral crowded into the cubicle, whispering, "Karmapa," and

---

*Eric Perlman, "Expedition to Everest," reprinted by permission from *The Rotarian*, February 1983, pp. 33–35.

bowing to be blessed. Though their faith was not my own, their devotion impressed me. I touched each one on the head with the picture and packet of hair.

For four days, the Everest team rumbled through the Tibetan hinterlands in a caravan of five supply trucks loaded with climbing equipment. The roadway dust was so thick that we had to don surgical masks to protect the lungs, already burdened by the thin air at 4,270 metres (14,000 feet).

The end of the road was a muddy meadow at the foot of the high Himalayas. We unloaded the trucks. Soon, grizzled herdsmen in red felt boots drove their yaks into the meadow where the beasts would be loaded for the five-day trek to the base of Mt. Everest. The yaks looked like black water buffalo with stringy, matted hair and long horns. They did not look happy at the prospect of being put to work. Sir Edmund Hillary's handsome red duffle bag and bright blue backpack were strapped to the back of a recalcitrant yak. No sooner did the yak drivers release the animal and stand back to admire their work than the beast burst into a fury, bucking and leaping and throwing Sir Edmund's gear into the mud and dragging it through puddles of muck for almost 20 metres (65 feet). That was an ominous beginning to the organizational nightmare of hauling several tons of equipment on more than 100 yaks up and down rocky passes for five rainy days.

We located our base camp on a small, dry lake bed almost ten kilometres (six miles) from the foot of Everest. Our boxes of equipment made wind barriers around our tents. Most of the team wanted the yak drivers to leave as soon as possible to put an end to minor equipment theft and keep the yaks from further fouling the stream, our only source of water. Every evening, I played the guitar and sang old songs from home. Within minutes dozens of yak herders would cluster close to the door of my tent, peer in, and listen in rapt silence. Then they would laugh and sing their own songs to me. . . .

We found a route through the glacial rubble and established an advanced base camp at the foot of the mountain. Kurt Diemberger, an American Broadcasting Corporation television cameraman and climber of many Himalayan peaks, kissed the rock at the foot of the East Buttress and pronounced our intended route, "beautiful, but the hardest anyone has ever attempted on Everest." He should have known; he had already climbed the mountain once from the other, "easier," side.

For two weeks our route was shrouded in snow clouds. The summer monsoon storms stayed late. By September, the storms have usually passed, leaving a "window" of good weather that stays open one to two months, long enough to reach the summit of any mountain, then to get down and get away before the winter storm hits. But this year the window never opened. After a few days of good weather, blinding storms made the climbing tough.

In a heavy blizzard I hauled a load of extra ropes, pitons, ice screws, and snow flukes to a cache point 366 metres (1,200 feet) up the buttress. My climbing partner turned back at the base of the mountain; the weather was too miserable. Visibility was about six metres (twenty feet). My aluminum rope ascenders froze up in the wet snow and refused to grip on the icy ropes. It was time for me to head down.

Through storm and fear the climbing continued. Bright red and green fixed ropes-wound up rock cracks and ice runnels, over ridges and faces to the top of the towering East Buttress and its crown of ice that we began calling the "Helmet."

Day after day we hauled loads of food, hardware, and oxygen up to the higher camps, switched places with the lead team personnel and climbed until storms forced us down. When the weather cleared, we headed back up again.

Then the avalanche hit. It was 122 metres (400 feet) high, the biggest, most powerful avalanche any of us had ever seen in the Himalayas. It shuddered and roared, and totally destroyed the alternate route we had planned to take up the East Buttress. Blocks of snow and ice the size of apartment buildings crashed down the mountain side. Two team members had been climbing directly in its path only a few days before. Anyone in the way would surely have been killed. I saw it coming and snapped pictures as I backpedaled away from the shock waves. . . .

Gary Bocarde, a professional mountain guide and avalanche expert for the state of Alaska, rose with me before dawn at Camp 1, about 460 metres (1,500 feet) up the buttress. We melted snow for a breakfast of hot chocolate and cookies, then headed for the high camp on top of the Helmet at full speed. Climbing up the rock headwall, I scored 12 hits of rocks and ice on my hard hat. Large stones whizzed past our heads. We raced up ice gullies while spindrift avalanches swirled around our legs. It was snowing hard. We climbed well into the night, finally reaching the high camp after 14 exhausting hours on the ropes. . . .

Gary Bocarde and I went for a short exploratory hike on top of the Helmet. Gary felt the rest of the route was lethal. This season's onslaught of heavy snow, warm weather, more snow, then cold weather, had created the perfect avalanche death trap. He felt that the giant avalanche we had seen was just a foretaste of more to come, and from now on our climbing route would follow this dangerous avalanche path.

The heaviest storm we had seen so far raced in that morning. Gary and I decided to get off the mountain while we had the chance. Rather than argue its relative risks over the radio, we chose to let the rest of the team come up and see for themselves how bad the route was.

The storm finally cleared away, and the snow stabilized enough to allow a return to the top of the Helmet. One week after Bocarde and I went down, climbing leader Reichardt announced on the radio from Helmet Camp that the avalanche danger was severe and that too few team members were willing to risk continuing. He called for an evacuation. He also called for a return engagement. And, with better weather, a U.S. team will surely kick its way up the risky East Buttress route to the summit of Mt. Everest.

An explosion of shouts and curses burst from the trail toward home. All the yaks kicked their loads off into the dirt. They were reloaded. But the yak drivers were grumpy. So I pulled out the Gyalwa Karmapa's picture and lock of hair. The yak drivers were amazed. First they tried to swipe the packet out of my hands. When that did not work, they bowed to be touched on the head. Then they made gestures suggesting they wanted to eat the hair. Dutifully, I placed a single strand of the short black hair into the mouth of each yak driver. Since they believe that a person's spiritual power can be transferred by touch, word, or even a piece of clothing, they smiled happily, chewed, and swallowed the hair. They grinned and nodded in thanks for the gift. Then they turned to their yaks, and, with shouts and well-aimed rocks to the animals' rear ends, they herded the sullen beasts downward along the trail toward home.

Our team had not made it to the ultimate mountaintop. Yet we had tried mightily to fight the forces of nature, and were content with our performance. When we or our successors are ready for the next expedition, Mt. Everest will be there, waiting in all its terrible majesty.

1. The reason that a prominent group of people from the United States wanted to climb Mt. Everest is that they
   a. were getting paid to do it.
   b. liked the challenge.
   c. were part of a religious crusade.
2. The American expedition was met by the
   a. Navajo Indians.
   b. Dalai Lama.
   c. Tibetan people.
3. Many of the people from the area still revered
   a. the Dalai Lama.
   b. the leaders of the People's Republic of China.
   c. the mountain climbers from the United States.
4. Karmapa was a
   a. village near Mt. Everest.
   b. famous mountain climber.
   c. spiritual leader.
5. The supplies and equipment for the expedition were carried by
   a. water buffalo.
   b. yaks.
   c. camels.
6. The route taken by the expedition was
   a. the hardest anyone has ever attempted on Mt. Everest.
   b. the easiest side of the mountain.
   c. for beginning mountain climbers.
7. The weather was
   a. better than anticipated.
   b. about what the climbers expected it to be.
   c. a problem due to blinding storms.
8. The avalanche
   a. killed two team members.
   b. demolished the camp site.
   c. destroyed the alternate route.
9. The team
   a. made it to the mountain top.
   b. did not make it to the top this time but wants to return.
   c. lost many of its members and does not plan to return.
10. The main idea of this selection is that
    a. mountains are difficult but challenging to climb.
    b. the Chinese and American people can cooperate.
    c. conditions on mountains are hazardous and not worth the risk.

Rapid Reading IV

Starting time _____

Completion time _____

Elapsed time _____

Words per minute _____

Number correct_____

Percentage of
comprehension _____

Aboard the Orient Express*

Irene Rawlings

The Orient Express. The name conjures up mystery, intrigue, and romance. This is, after all, the very train that at one time or other carried Sarah Bernhardt, Scott and Zelda Fitzgerald, Mata Hari, Caruso, the Duke of Windsor and the beguiling Mrs. Simpson.

All right—not, strictly speaking, the *very* train. The fabled Orient Express, which set new standards of comfort and luxury from its first run in 1883, began its decline with the advent of air travel and gradually deteriorated until, consisting of one seedy sleeping car and three day-coaches, it made its last run in 1977.

Having traveled on the original Orient Express in the 1960's, I can positively attest to its shabbiness. We adventuresome students rode third-class. Traveling with us were several Yugoslav peasants and their livestock. I remember the faded women in their babushkas, the leathern men with their cardboard suitcases. The livestock was nothing major—mainly geese, ducks, and one small pig.

There being no dining car, we went pot luck with the Yugoslavs. In our backpacks we had Spam, cheese spread, and some wheat crackers; they had sausages, hard-boiled eggs, black bread spread with lard, and a sweet local wine. It took a strong stomach to eat the picnics we spread out—particularly since the food went more "off" as we traveled south and the weather got warmer.

We made our own sleeping arrangements. Two on the floor, head to toe. Two on each of the wooden seats and one in each luggage rack. The geese slept tied up in wicker baskets. But the pig—he was still pink and cute—had the run of the place.

The trip from Paris to Istanbul took four days. In the evenings we were entertained by gypsies who, proudly flashing their gold teeth, strolled through the cars playing czardas on their violins, singing Serbian love songs in an aching vibrato, and telling our fortunes. Shabby it may have been, but still romantic.

In 1977, five 1920s first-class passenger carriages from the Orient Express were sold at auction by Sotheby's in Monte Carlo. James Sherwood, head of the London-based Sea Container Corporation and a railroading enthusiast, was the successful bidder for two of these cars. One thing led to another and, eventually, Sherwood unearthed 35 more coaches. Some were purchased from railroad museums and from private collections. Others were found rusting on railroad sidings in various countries, particularly Spain and Portugal. Once these cars were acquired, the formidable and expensive task of restoring them began. It is rumored that more than $20 million went into putting the Venice-Simplon Orient Express back on the tracks.

The results are worth every penny. From the exquisitely worked marquetry panels (lovingly restored by Dunns, the same family-owned firm that made the originals) to the staff's uniforms (reconstructed by way of detailed sketches made from carefully studied old photographs), everything *feels* authentic. The Lalique-lit dining car, the mosaic-floored lavatories, the brass lamps with red silk shades, all contribute to the opulence expected by the upper-class traveler of the 1920s. The train has been described by Sherwood as "926 miles of unashamed luxury"—not what you would call a modest statement, but entirely true, it turns out.

Sherwood's restored Orient Express now travels from London to Venice and back three times a week, making it once again possible to experience the "Golden Age" of rail travel—elegant, but not speedy: London to Venice by air takes a little more than 2 hours, while the rail journey takes 24. But that is just about enough time for the leisurely traveler to relax and enjoy the surroundings.

A friend had advised me to travel from Venice to London; in the other direction, she said, the train was usually filled to capacity, meaning a crush at the bar and a wait in the dining car. On the Venice-to-London run, however, one can linger over coffee and brandy well into the Alps—as, indeed, one should.

The Orient Express I boarded late one Venetian afternoon bore no resemblance to the one I remembered from my student days. The cars were beautifully polished. They shone like patent leather. Raised brass lettering and elaborate brass escutcheons on the side of each car proclaimed its ancestry: Compagnie Internationale des Wagon-Lits et des Grands Express Européens. An aura of conspicuous glamour hung around the entire train. Even the stolid gondolier who delivered me to Santa Lucia station seemed impressed: He insisted on carrying my bags all the way to the train.

A liveried Wagon-Lits attendant, looking like a pencil-moustached matinee idol of the Twenties, showed me to my compartment. Would I prefer to have the train's amenities explained in English, French, or, perhaps, Italian? English would be fine. He described everything in the compartment, from the valet call to the ventilating system, while stowing the luggage in brass overhead racks.

After he left, I explored the compartment. A curved panel opened out to reveal the wash basin, complete with linen towels, crystal glasses, and Yves Saint Laurent soap. Another cupboard proved to be a tiny cedar closet; yet another held a cache of mineral water.

Having pulled all the brass levers and pushed all the porcelain buttons, I sank into the deep, tapestry-upholstered sofa to watch the Northern Italian countryside rush past: The Alps in the background, some farms, some small towns—but mostly vineyards. Nor was I doing the only watching: Residents of the region would lean from their balconies to point at the Orient Express as it passed; small children, dogs, and men on bicycles would stop for a better look.

The Wagon-Lits attendant returned with a bottle of the local wine—Soave—and a printed passenger list. I noticed three Counts, one Contessa, and a smattering of "Honorables"; no one I knew. I turned my attention to the Padua of Giotto's frescoes and the Verona of Romeo and Juliet, slipping past the windows as I sipped my straw-colored wine.

Once we stopped. I don't know why. But an entire bocce team stopped bowling on the village green to come over. They reached out to touch the shining paint. They outlined the raised brass letters with their fingers. They peered in through the brocade-curtained windows. Then, grinning and giving us the thumbs-up sign, they strolled unhurriedly back to resume their game.

As the train made its way into the snow-capped Alps, I made my way to the dining car. Darkness fell as I ate a delicious cold salmon in a delicate sauce. Afterward, I repaired to the bar-salon car for coffee, cognac, and jazz piano, fully intending to stay up until we passed through the Simplon Tunnel—but the cognac, together with the hypnotic murmur of wheels on rails, had its effect.

When I awoke, I was in France.

The French countryside came into focus after the second cup of coffee. Small clustered villages, some thatched roofs. And again vineyards, for this was the Côte d'Or, where French burgundy grapes are grown. Eventually, these pictures gave way to Paris, the Seine, Ile de la Cité, Notre Dame. Finally, Gare d'Austerlitz and a twenty-minute leg-stretch. I dutifully jogged the platform while my compartment was transformed back into a sitting room.

The train runs to the quayside at Boulogne, where we transferred to a Sealink ferry for the 90-minute Channel crossing. The ferry's verandah-saloon is reserved exclusively for Orient Express passengers, and, keeping us in the style to which we had now become accustomed, a steward served hot broth, coffee, and drinks while we stood on deck, taking in the sea air.

At Folkestone, polished wood and gleaming brass parlor cars originally built for the Pullman Car Company, Ltd., awaited us. A plaque on each gave its name and its pedigree: Audrey, from the now defunct Brighton Gelle; Phoenix, General de Gaulle's private car; Minerva, the favorite of the Queen Mother. These cars all ride on oversize white-walled wheels and have been meticulously restored down to the very pattern of the upholstery.

Afternoon tea—scones, Devonshire cream, watercress sandwiches, buttered toast wedges, strawberry jam, and sherry as well as tea—was served by a staff in brown and cream colored livery as the apple and cherry orchards of Kent rolled by. At 5:00—exactly 24 hours after we left Venice—we reached Victoria Station, and the conclusion that the journey had been entirely too short. I met no royalty, no heads of state, no spies, no rajahs, no monocled diplomats. True, the very words ''Orient Express'' still conjure up mystery, intrigue, and romance, but I encountered none of the first two. Just plenty of romance.♥

1. The Orient Express is
   a. a train.
   b. a bus.
   c. a luxury van.

2. Compared with the Orient Express of today, the Orient Express in the 1960's was
   a. much more elegant.
   b. about the same.
   c. much shabbier.

3. The Orient Express now travels from
   a. Paris to Istanbul.
   b. London to Venice.
   c. Istanbul to Hong Kong.

4. James Sherwood
   a. traveled with geese and a pig.
   b. restored the Orient Express.
   c. accompanied the author.

5. Passenger carriages were found
   a. at Sotheby's auction in Monte Carlo.
   b. in railroad museums and private collections.
   c. both of the above.

6. On her recent trip, the author met
   a. three Counts and one Contessa.
   b. Yugoslavs and gypsies.
   c. no one of importance.

7. In addition to traveling on the Orient Express, the author
   a. took a Sealink ferry across the Channel.
   b. flew by airplane part of the way.
   c. rode in a private car through the Simplon Tunnel.

8. Today the service on the Orient Express is
   a. excellent.
   b. adequate.
   c. inadequate.

9. The trip today takes
   a. 2 hours.
   b. 24 hours.
   c. 4 days.

10. The main idea of this article is that travel today on the Orient Express is
    a. quick and efficient.
    b. luxurious and romantic.
    c. full of mystery and intrigue.

Starting time _____   Number correct _____

Completion time _____   Percentage of
                                          comprehension _____
Elapsed time _____

Words per minute _____

W. H. Jackson: His Camera Helped
Start a National Park*

Boyd Norton

If it hadn't been for the merest element of chance—a lover's quarrel—America might have been deprived of one of its great pioneer photographers and, possibly, its first national park.

William Henry Jackson was an incredible man. Born in the age of daguerreotypes, he lived to see the development of Kodachrome. He was, at various times, a painter, Civil War soldier, a bullwhacker on a western wagon train, and a horse wrangler. But his most famous exploits were with a camera, and he is best remembered as the man whose photographs helped convince Congress to establish Yellowstone National Park 100 years ago.

Jackson was born in 1843 in Keeseville, N.Y., and at an early age showed great artistic talent. By the time he was 18, he was earning a respectable salary as a photographer's artist in Rutland, Vt., a job entailing the retouching and coloring of portraits. The job afforded him the opportunity to learn the skills of photography: the manipulation of the cumbersome cameras, the coating and developing of the large wetplates. But his career was interrupted by the Civil War, and he left Rutland to serve a two-year stint as a volunteer in the Army of the Potomac. His stay with the Union Army was uneventful except for an involvement in a less bloody part of the battle of Gettysburg. In later years, his sketches and paintings of army life in the Civil War period would come to be highly prized by collectors.

Returning to Vermont, he soon became engaged to be married and accepted a well-paying job in Burlington with another photographer. It was here that a quarrel with his fiancee caused him, on sheer impulse, to forsake his career and his wife-to-be and head west.

From 1866 to 1867, he traveled across the western frontier, first as a driver on a wagon train as far as Salt Lake City. He went on to California, then decided to head east again, this time signing on as a horse wrangler herding some 200 horses to be sold in Omaha. When he arrived in Omaha in 1867, his life took another fateful turn. To earn money for his continued journey east, he obtained a job as a photographer's artist once again. Within a short time, he found himself in a position to buy out his employer with a

---

*Boyd Norton, "W. H. Jackson: His Camera Helped Start a National Park," reprinted by permission from *Popular Photography,* August 1972, pp. 67–68, 102–103.

small down payment and, with his brother who came west to join him, the "Jackson Brothers, Photographers" was established.

Jackson's love of the outdoors led him to pursue contracts with the western railroads to photograph the scenery along their routes and these pictures soon gained him a modest fame and reputation—so much so, in fact, that in July of 1870, Dr. Ferdinand V. Hayden, head of the United States Geological Survey, was leading a series of yearly expeditions to map and survey portions of the Rocky Mountains West, and he asked Jackson to serve as official photographer. He eagerly accepted and, in later years, wrote, ". . . if any work that I have done should have value beyond my own lifetime, I believe it will be the happy labors of the decade 1869–1878."

In the summer of 1871, at the age of 28, Jackson left with the Hayden expedition to explore that mythical region known as the Yellowstone. Even in 1871, most of the West had been explored and few places remained unknown. Except for one. That region in the northwest corner of Wyoming, headwaters of the Yellowstone River, was still something of a *terra incognita,* at least as far as much of the public was concerned. In actual fact, the Yellowstone country had been explored as early as 1807, and the fur trappers of the 1820s to 1840s knew the area well. But when men such as the legendary Jim Bridger brought back tales of smoking hills and boiling springs, no one believed them. Thus Hayden and Jackson were to prove or disprove the legends of Yellowstone.

Jackson's equipment for this, as for so many of his other wilderness expeditions, consisted of three basic cameras: an 8 × 10, his "miniature" 6½ × 8½, and a stereo. (There was a lucrative market in those days supplying the many owners of stereopticons with scenics.) His portable darkroom was a specially made tent that he used for both coating and developing his plates. The plates were glass, several hundred sheets of various sizes for the different cameras. Together with the necessary chemicals, his gear weighed over 300 pounds, and for most of the trip it was carried by pack mules.

Few today can appreciate the labors of obtaining a photograph then. In Yellowstone, when he found a scene he liked, it meant unloading all the gear from the mules, setting up one or more cameras on tripods, and focusing and composing on the groundglass. Then, when the dark tent was erected, he disappeared in its confines to begin sensitizing a plate. Actually, the tent was not completely dark, being lined with a yellow muslin to allow a dim yellow-orange light to filter through—a "safelight," in a sense. The emulsions of Jackson's time were orthochromatic, sensitive primarily to the blue end of the spectrum. . . .

Subsequent development, fixing, and drying were carried out in a manner not much different from today. Storing and transporting the delicate glass plates was often a problem, however. But Jackson managed it, and only on one occasion a few summers later did an ornery mule cause the breakage of exposed plates.

There were other problems as well. Besides being an artist, photographers such as Jackson had to be well versed in the art and science of chemistry and sensitometry, and only after long experience did a photographer acquire the necessary "feel" for his working medium. There were many variables to cope with, such as available water supply. Sometimes the chemicals were mixed with water dipped from an icy mountain stream. At other times, as in Yellowstone, the hot, mineral laden waters of pools and springs were sometimes used. And then there was exposure. The plates were relatively insensitive, compared with today's films, corresponding very roughly to an equivalent film speed of ASA 0.01! But, of course, there were no ASA indexes, nor were there any light meters. A long working familiarity with his emulsions enabled a photographer to estimate the proper exposure—often as long as four or five minutes in bright sunshine if he chose to stop his lens down for maximum depth of field and definition.

The process was laborious, made doubly so by the terrain. Jackson photographed from mountain top to canyon bottom, packing all the bulky gear along, and he loved every exciting minute of it. At times there were logistic problems, as when he desired to photograph the magnificent 200-foot-high Tower Falls from the bottom of the steep gorge. There was no room for his dark tent down there, barely room to set up a camera. His only solution was to set the dark tent on the rim and, after preparing a plate, he would wrap the holder in moist blotting paper to keep it from drying out, and then slip and slide down the steep walls of the gorge to his camera. Placing the plate in the camera, he would make his exposure and then, working as quickly as possible, extract the holder, wrap it once more in blotting paper, and scramble several hundred feet back up the canyon walls to develop the plate before it dried. The procedure was repeated several times to insure a good negative and Jackson later wrote of the experience in his autobiography, *Time Exposure:* "The end of the day found us exhausted but very proud."

He had good reason to be proud, for these and his other photographs were among the very first to be made in this strange and wonderful place. In his wanderings with Hayden that summer, Jackson photographed many of the now well-known features of Yellowstone: the delicate steaming terraces of Mammoth Hot Springs, the awe-inspiring gorge and lower falls of the Yellowstone River, the immense and lovely Yellowstone Lake, and countless geysers and mud pots and springs. Jackson's photographs were remarkable and proved that, indeed, this was a land of enchantment and wonder. His work also proved to be very timely.

The previous summer, members of the Washburn expedition had been so impressed with the beauty of Yellowstone that, out of their enthusiasm for this place, a strange and wonderful concept emerged: a national park to preserve and protect this place for all people. Then, as now, there were callous exploiters who were only too eager to make a quick profit from such places, and Congress had to be convinced that this radical idea should be adopted.

When Jackson returned from Yellowstone he was summoned to Washington and there, for several months, prepared prints of this marvelous region. Jackson's friend, the famed artist Thomas Moran, had also been on the expedition of the previous summer and both the paintings of Moran and Jackson's amazing photographs helped convince an indifferent Congress that this place should be preserved. In March of 1872, the bill was passed establishing Yellowstone as the nation's—and the world's—first national park.

One might assume that this was the peak of an already amazing career, and yet Jackson continued his work with the Geological Survey for several more summers. It might almost be said that where he pointed his cameras, national parks seemed to follow. Yellowstone, Yosemite, Grand Teton, Mesa Verde (he was one of the first discoverers of the ancient cliff dwellings), Chaco Canyon, Rocky Mountain National Park, all came into sharp focus on his groundglass, and all were ultimately made a part of the National Park Service of the United States.

Later, his cameras literally spanned the globe. A three-year junket around the world took him to the Orient, Asia, Australia, and Europe. He traveled across 3,000 miles of frozen Siberia in a horse-drawn sleigh, and he photographed steaming tropics. But in later years, he confessed that his most exciting days were roaming the wild West.

Jackson never lost his excitement over photography. At the age of 96, on another trip west, he experimented with a miraculous new film called Kodachrome. In his enthusiasm he remarked that if he had it all to do over again, ''I should wish to do everything in color.'' This amazing man continued to photograph and to paint right up to his death at the age of 99.

Today, photography plays a vital role in conservation. The magnificent and lavish books produced by the Sierra Club and Friends of the Earth have become renowned for publishing excellence and superlative photography, and it becomes difficult to imagine the prodigious effort of a man who, in his photographic career, produced some 40,000 plates under the most trying circumstances. Yet Jackson played a key role in alerting this nation to the beauty of unspoiled lands and helped share a national conscience toward conservation.

1. The reason the author believes a lover's quarrel may have contributed to the establishment of America's first national park is that
   a. Jackson's fiancee refused to travel west with him.
   b. Jackson's quarrel with his fiancee caused him to forsake his career and head west.
   c. Jackson volunteered to serve in the Army of the Potomac as a result of his quarrel.

2. A significant event occurred in Jackson's life when he
   a. became a driver on a wagon train to Salt Lake City.
   b. bought a photography business in Omaha.
   c. became a horse wrangler and herded about 200 horses to be sold in Omaha.

3. Jackson gained modest fame and reputation when he
   a. began photographing scenery along the western railroads.
   b. began retouching and coloring portraits.
   c. sketched and painted army life during the Revolutionary War.

4. Some of Jackson's happiest and most productive years were spent from 1869 to 1878 when he
   a. served in the Union Army and became involved in the battle of Gettysburg.
   b. had a well-paying job in Burlington, Vermont, and was engaged to be married.
   c. served as official photographer for an expedition to the Rocky Mountains West.

5. Taking pictures during the time when Jackson was photographing Yellowstone was
   a. very similar to taking photographs today.
   b. much simpler than taking pictures today because there was no color film available.
   c. much more difficult than making photographs today, partly because of the cumbersome equipment.

6. One of the main problems Jackson faced in his photography at Yellowstone was
   a. coping with the rugged terrain.
   b. finding people who were willing to look at his pictures.
   c. getting the pack mules to carry his equipment.

7. During the photographic process, Jackson sometimes had to mix chemicals with
    a. water from icy mountain streams.
    b. minerals found in creek beds.
    c. rainwater kept in blotting paper.

8. Jackson's photographs were instrumental in establishing Yellowstone as a national park because they
    a. showed the cool blue and green colors of the region.
    b. convinced the public of the need for a conservation program.
    c. helped convince Congress that this area should be preserved.

9. After photographing Yellowstone, Jackson
    a. retired while still a young man in order to travel through the West.
    b. continued to photograph other areas, many of which later became national parks.
    c. invented Kodachrome film.

10. The main idea of this selection is that
    a. Jackson's remarkable photographs played an important part in establishing the first national park
    b. Jackson traveled across the western frontier because of his love for the outdoors.
    c. Yellowstone is one of America's most beautiful and unusual national parks.

Rapid Reading VI

1625 words

Man Under Machine*

Richard Trubo

The next time you begin to yearn for "the good old days," maybe you'd better count your blessings. Just compare today's automobile driving with grandfather's around the turn of the century. The early motor vehicles caused so many problems that some disgusted auto owners traded their cars in for something more dependable—like a horse!

The automobile was not considered a first-class mode of transportation, even as it continued to grow in popularity. In the early 1900s there were 21 million horses in America, but only 4000 automobiles. And the four-legged animals always received first priority.

In Washington, D.C., car traffic was restricted to a six-mile-per-hour speed limit. Higher speeds were outlawed because the lawmakers thought cars might frighten the horses on the road. Even Theodore Roosevelt, the first American president to drive an automobile, had to observe the restrictive speed laws.

The early cars had many opponents. Woodrow Wilson, while president of Princeton University in 1906, called the motorcar "a picture of the arrogance of wealth."

Farmers pressured legislators to discourage driving because car noise alarmed their horses and chickens.

Pennsylvania's Anti-Automobile Association demanded that all motorists driving on country roads at night send up aerial flares every mile, then wait ten minutes for the roads to clear.

Chugging along at the top legal speed of four miles an hour, motorists in Urbana, Ohio, were required under city ordinance to sound their car bells or horns any time they came within 50 feet of an intersection. Other towns forced drivers to stop their cars completely any time they came near a horse pulling a wagon, surrey or sled. Under New York state law, a motorist who encountered a resting horse and rider could be required to pull off the road and turn off the car motor until the horse and rider decided to mosey on.

Mitchell, South Dakota, banned cars completely for a time, and early speed restrictions reached the depth of absurdity in a New England town where this sign was posted: THE SPEED LIMIT THIS YEAR IS SECRET. VIOLATORS WILL BE FINED $10.

*Richard Trubo, "Man Under Machine," reprinted by permission from *Odyssey,* November–December 1973, pp. 32–34.

Out-of-state motorists were unwelcome in many places. Maryland refused to allow nonresidents to travel on its roads unless they paid a fee. In Missouri, each *county* charged drivers to travel through. It cost $30 to drive across the state from east to west, $50 from north to south.

Where the laws against cars did not seem stiff enough, disgruntled farmers often took action of their own. Tales were told of farmers who buried rakes in dirt roads, upturned teeth barely protruding through the dust. Other weapons used against the auto included empty bottles, frequently implanted early on Sunday to deter weekend drivers. One farmer buried the blade of a crosscut saw in a popular road; every car that ran over it immediately punctured all four of its tires.

Many newspapers opposed the advent of the motorized vehicle. When a large group of automobiles passed through Manchester, New Hampshire, in 1905, the *Manchester Union* termed the visit an "unmitigated nuisance," and "an outrage that ought to be stopped once and for all. . . ." Continued the paper: "If these people think of coming here another year, we hope the law against speeding and scorching will be promptly and vigorously enforced. Let a few of them stay in jail two or three days and they and all the rest of us will be the better for it."

Auto manufacturers themselves occasionally agreed that the car was far from being a perfect vehicle. Henry Ford was startled by the noise of two of his early racing models—the 999 and the Arrow. He reported that the roar of the cars was "enough to half kill a man." Questioned about the bumpy ride of one of his early cars, Ford allowed that tumbling over Niagara Falls might be somewhat smoother than riding in the car.

Motoring discomfort wasn't due only to the design of the cars, however. Most country roads of the time were better suited for covered wagons than for automobiles. The all-dirt roads were dangerously dusty during dry weather and treacherously muddy after heavy rains. Crews repaired major ones each spring by shoveling roadside dirt into the ruts and chuckholes. When rainy weather began, however, the first car along would sink into the poorly packed fillings, often with a jolt. Stranded drivers frequently borrowed fence rails to pry the rear wheels free of the mud—unless, of course, the jolt had broken the car's axle.

Dust posed a special problem for drivers of the 1908 Orient. Its engine was mounted low on the rear axle, and every time the car encountered loose dust—as often as every few miles—the motor stopped. The hapless driver had to remove the carburetor and clean it before he could resume his dusty drive.

Owners of the early Marions and Franklins had their own difficulties. These cars were equipped with a four-cylinder, air-cooled engine mounted transverse of the frame. The engine's forward end—shaped like a sugar scoop—would cool without difficulty, but the back side overheated constantly. Without a heat gauge a driver could tell his engine had overheated only when it began to smell.

Tires were another problem. In 1909 the life span of tires was only about 2000 miles—and they were expensive—about $50 apiece. Rarely did a driver travel over 25 miles without some tire difficulties. Because tires were made of woven canvas, the intense friction upon them produced tremendous amounts of heat.

The cautious driver carried dozens of pieces of equipment with him. He kept a sliced onion handy to clean his windshield; he also very likely carried goggles, a tow rope, compass, spotlight—and sometimes even a sleeping bag and tent in the event of a major breakdown.

One driver whose name is lost to history found that he could plug radiator leaks with oatmeal. He simply poured dry oatmeal into the radiator, and the flakes were sucked into the fissure where they expanded and plugged the leak.

Despite such ingenious solutions, even minor repairs were sometimes impossible to make. Spare parts were scarce and there was little standardization, even between simple items like nuts and bolts. Rarely would a half-inch nut from one car fit on a half-inch bolt of another.

Service stations were nonexistent so blacksmith shops and bicycle repair shops sold gasoline. In one town, the only source of gas was at the popcorn stand. No matter where gas was available, though, refueling the early cars was formidable. Gas was usually kept in a large drum and the purchaser had to strain it through a chamois to remove dirt before filling his gas tank.

And places that sold gasoline didn't stock large quantities. Often, incredibly, they would sell only a cup at a time. Desperate drivers occasionally took kerosene from roadside lamps. As long as there was gas enough to start the car, kerosene from the lamps would keep the auto running, although roughly.

Most of the old cars had to be hand-cranked, a difficult and often dangerous task, and backfiring engines broke many a cranker's arm. Owner's manuals suggested that if the motorist held his breath while cranking, he could withstand a backfire better than if he was breathing normally. Showing some selectivity over which arm they were willing to sacrifice, many right-handers turned cranks with their left hands.

Because of risks in starting automobiles and in driving out on the road, motoring in the early days was mostly a pastime for men. One outspoken male contended that women drivers were "inclined to become hysterical in the crises that can arise driving at speeds up to 20 miles per hour. In addition, their physical weakness makes it impossible for them to move the stick shift from first to intermediate." Small wonder that much of the nation was somewhat shocked when President Theodore Roosevelt's daughter Alice raced a car around the White House—at 12 miles an hour.

By 1917 U.S. automobile production had soared to nearly two million cars a year. But as the number of cars on the road increased, the problems they brought with them grew, too.

A lack of numbered highway route signs made cross-country driving difficult. Chambers of commerce painted utility poles with distinctive colors to keep motorists on course. For example, yellow pole markings led the way to Florida; a white band with a red streak in the middle showed you the way to Chicago. This system soon broke down however, when dozens of identifying colors were painted on single poles.

Cross-country driving was even riskier on roads that didn't have any poles to paint. Most notably in the West, spans of hundreds of miles were post-less, tree-less and fence-less. Thus, any object that seemed at least semi-permanent became the target of the paintbrush: anything from trash cans to buffalo skulls. One motorist starting out from Albuquerque to Los Angeles was instructed to heed these guidelines: "Follow the mountain range 80 miles south to a stick in the fork of the road with a paper tied to the top. Take the ruts that lead off to the right."

Forerunners of modern highway systems appeared when the old dirt roads started to be designated by numbers as well as by local names. Wisconsin started using numbers for major roads in 1917, and the other states soon followed.

By 1920 the motor era had officially begun. That's when a Sunday School teacher completed her discussion of the Creation by asking her class if there was any animal that man could have done without. "The horse," answered the boy. For his generation, and those to follow, the automobile was here to stay.

1. In the early days of automobiles, speed limits often restricted cars to about six miles per hour because
   a. cars could go no faster.
   b. cars might frighten the horses off the road.
   c. women became hysterical at higher speeds.

2. When cars were first introduced to America, they
   a. immediately became popular with most people.
   b. caused so many problems that many people preferred horses.
   c. received the unanimous support of the newspapers.

3. Drivers traveling across the country kept on course by following
   a. utility poles painted with distinctive colorings.
   b. numbered routes.
   c. signs pointing the direction to cities.

4. The motor era had officially begun by
   a. 1880.
   b. 1900.
   c. 1920.

5. When automobiles first appeared, gasoline was usually sold at
   a. bicycle repair shops and blacksmith shops.
   b. service stations.
   c. automobile dealers.

6. Engines that backfired while motorists cranked their cars
   a. were generally harmless.
   b. made loud noises but did no damage.
   c. broke many crankers' arms.

7. At the time of the first automobiles, roads were usually
   a. paved and had two lanes for traffic.
   b. either dusty or muddy.
   c. built to withstand heavy traffic.

8. Farmers often reacted to automobile traffic by
   a. placing tools and empty bottles in the road to damage tires.
   b. standing by the side of the road and cheering the motorist on his way.
   c. racing their horses against cars.

9. Some states expressed their opposition to automobile traffic
   a. by requiring drivers to take special tests.
   b. by charging fees for traveling on their roads.
   c. by refusing to sell gasoline to out-of-state motorists.

10. The main idea of this article is that
    a. the early 1900s were "the good old days" for automobile drivers.
    b. repairs were difficult to make on early automobiles.
    c. motorists encountered many problems and frustrations when automobiles were first used.

Starting time _____

Completion time _____

Elapsed time _____

Words per minute _____

Number correct _____

Percentage of
comprehension _____

Opting for Orchids*

Dick Young

You're on a trip to sunny climes and encounter a dazzling array of orchids at a greenhouse or orchid show. The flowers are fantastic, the plants are healthy and the prices are beguilingly inexpensive.

But orchids are tough to grow, you think, and a reluctant decision is made to take home the colorful memories, not the plants. You did the best thing, right?

Wrong!

Orchids are pussycats, and even the brownest thumb can grow them and bring them to bloom. Compared to touchy African violets, for example, orchids are easy. They're tough, thrive on benign neglect, and even your Aunt Minnie, who can't successfully grow weeds, can bring them to heel.

Mention "orchid," and most plant enthusiasts not familiar with the breed visualize the large and regal cattleya, the queen-line aristocrat seen most often in corsages. But the cattleya tribe is only one of many clans in the world's largest flower family, which includes about 30,000 known species and more than 75,000 man-made hybrids. (The exact number of species and hybrids is not known.)

Among the better-known varieties, in addition to the large and spectacular cattleya, are the moth-like phalaenopsis, colorful vanda, cymbidium with cascades of blooms, oncidium "dancing ladies" wearing "ballet skirts," pansy-like miltonia and earthtone paphiopedilum—the latter also mercifully known as "lady slippers."

Orchids come in every known shade of the rainbow, and only black ones have eluded the inventive hybrid-artists creating hundreds of new crosses every year.

And orchids tease the palate as well as the eye—the vanilla used to flavor hosts of tantalizing confections and desserts comes from the vining vanilla orchid, a native of Florida, Mexico and Central America.

What makes an orchid an orchid is its flower—the most highly developed in nature. There are some species with fanciful variations, but the classic orchid sprouts sepals (the outer layers of the bud) at 8:00 A.M., noon and 4:00 P.M., and petals at ten, two and six on the dial. The six o'clock petal is the showy lip containing the highly specialized column with the plant's reproductive elements.

---

*"Opting for Orchids" by Dick Young. This article has been reprinted/republished through the courtesy of Halsey Publishing Co., publishers of *SKY* magazine.

Let's examine a few more facts and maybe you'll get up the courage to try one or two before getting into the field in a big way.

First, orchids are not parasites—they're epiphytes, and extract their food from the air around them and from the medium in which they grow. Of course, it doesn't hurt to stack the deck by lacing them periodically with a suitable fertilizer in pellet or water-soluble form.

Second, orchids are either sympodial—growing from a horizontal rhizome or creeping stem and putting up many bulbs or stems, or monopodial—growing vertically from a single stalk.

The lordly cattleya is sympodial in habit, and to have one plant is to have many. As the plant grows and blooms (usually once a year) it can be divided. And the division process can be continued as each separated plant reaches maturity and grows enough new bulbs to permit another separation.

Examples of monopodial orchids include vanda and phalaenopsis. It's relatively easy to encourage them to throw "keikis" or "pups"—baby plants which can be separated from the parent plant and potted to make it on their own.

Third, orchid flowers left on the plant stay alive and vivid for weeks, even months, and some varieties will bloom anew or stay in blossom for the most part of the year.

Some—notably the vanda—thrive in full sun. Others—among them cattleya—like lots of sun, with perhaps a little shade at midday. And still others—phalaenopsis and paphiodelium are examples—prefer shade with only a little sun. The trick is to put the plants where they want to be and leave them there.

The plants may be grown in clay or plastic pots and rooted in fir bark or tree-fern fiber; some will take kindly to merely being attached to a slab of bark. Some orchids are terrestrial—they grow in dirt—and they're accommodated by placing them in a suitable potting mixture.

Orchids are fine for you, you say; you live in the subtropics. What about those of us who live where it gets cold?

Orchids grow virtually everywhere in the world, with the exception of the arctic and antarctic regions, and if you live in a cold climate, you pick the varieties that prefer cooler temperatures and don't mind moving inside for awhile during winter or cold snaps.

How do you travel with your new-found treasures? The trick is to buy juvenile plants (or divisions) and remove the potting medium. Pack them in a wooden or cardboard box, in paper or other material, to prevent crushing.

Now that the plants are home, you should know how to take care of them. Most local libraries and book stores have some books or pamphlets on orchid culture.

But, if you want to go to the ultimate source, you should contact the fount of all knowledge—the American Orchid Society, 84 Sherman Street, Cambridge, Massachusetts 02140. Enthusiasts or would-be orchid fanciers may write to join or merely to obtain information on the care and feeding of the world's most exotic flower family.

The Society's monthly bulletin—which comes with membership—lists orchid shows, sources of plants or supplies, and is laden with articles on both common and rare species, treatment of diseases, control of insect pests, and other topics of interest to orchid fanciers.

It also maintains a book service with a ten-page catalog offering publications of interest to both beginner and expert.

There are many rewards to orchid-growing. They provide year-round glamour in the trees, or can be brought inside to add color when the plants are in bloom. Vegetative propagation is easy, but cross-breeding orchids and growing your own under the most sterile conditions from tiny seeds no larger than specks of dust is a tough proposition and is best left to experts. But after you master the fundamentals, you might become one of the experts.

Think positive. Orchids *are* pussycats!

1. The author implies that
    a. many people think orchids are easy to grow.
    b. many people think orchids are hard to grow.
    c. many people buy orchids when on trips.

2. The author believes that
    a. orchids are easy to grow.
    b. orchids are hard to grow.
    c. orchids come in very few varieties.

3. The large and regal cattleya
    a. is one of the few varieties of orchids.
    b. is known by few who are not well-acquainted with orchids.
    c. is seen often in corsages.

4. Orchids come in
    a. very few colors.
    b. every known shade of the rainbow.
    c. only purple.

5. One kind of orchid not only pleases the eye, but
    a. provides vanilla flavoring for confections and desserts.
    b. provides sweetening for confections and desserts.
    c. provides a tart flavoring for sauces.

6. Orchids are epiphytes—
   a. types of parasites.
   b. they extract their food from the air around them and the medium in which they grow.
   c. plants that grow only in the shade.

7. Terrestrial plants are
   a. ones that grow on slabs of bark.
   b. ones that grow in the air.
   c. ones that grow in soil.

8. You can grow orchids
   a. virtually anywhere in the world, with the exception of the arctic or antarctic regions.
   b. only in the subtropics.
   c. only in the Northern Hemisphere below the arctic region.

9. To travel with orchids, you should
   a. buy juvenile plants, remove the potting medium, and pack them in a box in material to avoid crushing.
   b. buy adult plants and pack them loosely in plastic bags inside large boxes.
   c. buy juvenile plants and transport them in pots containing the potting medium, without closing them into boxes.

10. The main idea of this article is that
   a. only experts can grow orchids.
   b. anyone can grow orchids if he or she chooses the appropriate variety and checks on the particular needs of that variety.
   c. orchids are difficult to grow but may be worth the extreme effort involved.

Starting time _____

Completion time _____

Elapsed time _____

Words per minute _____

Number correct _____

Percentage of
comprehension _____

It's Still Blue Hawaii*

Ruth Tabrah

I am an Islander who travels often and far. Yet each time I fly home, I feel like a first-time visitor, captivated by the spell of what Mark Twain called "the loveliest fleet of islands that lie anchored in any ocean."

The enchantment of Hawaii begins when you catch your first glimpse of it, four hours and fifty minutes after your jet leaves the Pacific Coast. After the long emptiness of the ocean, the sight of land can catch you unawares. From the lofty vantage point of an airplane, the southern islands resemble a giant set of unmatched stepping stones: Hawaii Island—we locals call it the Big Island because it is; the hourglass shape of Maui; tiny barren Kahoolawe; rural Molokai and Lanai. Each lies in view of the next, all peaks of a massive submarine mountain range pushed up by volcanic activity. Eruptions still occur on the Big Island from a rift in the floor of the Pacific.

You're headed for Honolulu's International Airport on Oahu, third largest of the 50th state's eight islands. Oahu means "the gathering place," and the name's well-deserved. The island has 80 percent of Hawaii's 800,000 population, plus industry, most of the trade, the state capital, Pearl Harbor and all the key military bases, not to mention famed Waikiki. Here, high-rise hotels tower above a long gentle curve of white sand filled with bikini-clad sunbathers, beach boys with ukuleles, senior citizens and little kids with and without parents—all enjoying the 78-degree temperature of the ocean.

Below and behind you as the plane descends into Honolulu the sea stretches vast and blue to a cloud-touched horizon. Catamarans and sailboats hover outside the break of a long sweeping surf; its powerful curl propels surfers toward the shore.

From the air, Honolulu appears tranquil. Residential neighborhoods funnel into green valleys; rainbows arch up the valley walls. As you fly in from the ocean, Honolulu Harbor, the Aloha Tower, and the heart of the city lie right of the oceanfront airport. High rises stud the tropical green coastal strip. Even here you see a broad swath of freeway. But behind them all loom rugged 4000-foot peaks of the Koolau Mountains, a wilderness spiked with mists and clouds. If you're sitting by a left window, you can look out across the lochs of Pearl Harbor to the leeward suburbs around Pearl City, the cane fields of Ewa Plantation, and another lonely, rugged 4000-foot mountain range: the Waianae.

*Ruth Tabrah, "It's Still Blue Hawaii," reprinted by permission from *Odyssey*, November–December, 1973, pp. 25–30.

As you deplane the first thing you notice is the air. It seems to embrace you—incredibly soft, balmy, bearing the faint scent of flowers. The prevailing northeasterly trade winds—Hawaii's natural air conditioning—tousle the hair, lift skirts and whip the fronds on the coconut palms. You are in the subtropical latitudes of the 20th parallel where no matter what time of year it is, the temperature is going to be in the 70s and 80s. Should you happen to arrive late at night in the middle of winter, you may see a few of us locals shivering because it's 65 degrees.

If you're met by friends or are part of a tour, you'll probably be greeted Hawaiian style with a lei of orchids, or fragrant plumeria (frangipani) or a great ruff of red, pink, or white carnations. It goes over your neck accompanied by a smile, a kiss of welcome, and "Aloha!"

Aloha is a uniquely expressive Hawaiian word. It's a greeting, and it also means "I love you!" It expresses a people-to-people attitude, an open relaxed state of mind. Aloha *is* the Hawaiian experience, a one-word evocation of how and why these islands have been charming visitors for years.

The islands were settled by Polynesians in sailing canoes from Tahiti and the Marquesas some time before 700 A.D. When the English explorer Captain James Cook discovered Hawaii in 1778, the islands were ruled separately by Polynesian chiefs. Soon after Cook's voyage, Big Island Chief Kamehameha I conquered Maui, Oahu, Molokai, Kahoolawe and Lanai and made peace with the rulers of Kauai and Niihau. This made him the first chief to rule all eight islands. His statue—feather-cloaked and feather-helmeted—stands across from Iolani Palace, one of the landmarks you can look for on the drive from the airport to Waikiki.

Near the palace you see a compound, the Mission Houses Museum, built by the first missionaries who came to Hawaii in 1820 from New England. They tried to discourage the hula and the casual Hawaiian life style, but they didn't succeed and it's still all here.

Some of the descendants of these missionaries and their allies staged an armed insurrection in 1889 against King Kalakaua, the builder of the palace, and continued to agitate for independence after his sister Queen Liliuokalani succeeded him. The gracious queen who wrote *Aloha Oe* was deposed in the bloodless revolution of 1893, and a provisional government established the Republic of Hawaii. The U.S. Congress approved annexation in 1898, and the Territory of Hawaii was established in June, 1900. Statehood for these distant islands was another matter. Beginning in 1903, the Congress repeatedly ignored or turned down positions for statehood. Alaska gained entry into the Union in 1958, and in 1959—after 22 unsuccessful attempts to achieve statehood—Hawaii became the nation's 50th state. The handsome state capitol behind Iolani Palace was completed in 1968.

You are now more than halfway to Waikiki and you'll probably have noticed something strange and different, something you're going to notice all over this island, and on every island in this state: there are no billboards, no outdoor advertising of any kind—it's against the law.

Less surprising but equally striking to mainlanders is the large number of American citizens who look like "foreigners." As a traveler you can't fail to notice them: Filipino taxi drivers, Samoan tour guides, Hawaiian desk clerks, lovely, long-haired Japanese-American hostesses. Some of them speak an English that doesn't sound quite like English—it's a pidgin as colorful in its way as are the Southern accent of Texans and the nasal 'r' of New Englanders. Let them introduce you to the cosmopolitan East-West culture of Hawaii. They'll serve you a luau, show you a Bon Dance, entertain you for

Chinese New Year Chinese style, give you the big city excitement of Honolulu, or entice you to unwind in the immense quiet of the lonely, wild places on the outer islands. . . .

Most visitors enjoy Maui, largely for one or all of its three resort areas. At the base of the rugged west Maui mountains are the beach resorts of Napili, Kaanapali and Lahaina, an old whaling town. All have interesting shops, a range of excellent restaurants, some night life and good snorkeling and skin diving. . . .

In the center of Maui, twin towns of Wailuku and Kahului combine beach resort hotels and the island's center of business and county government. Haleakala, Maui's 10,000-foot-high extinct volcano, is a national park. The crater is a vast expanse of cinders, rare silversword plants and scenery that reminds you of pictures taken on the moon. Try to drive up Haleakala in time to see the sunrise from the crater rim. . . .

Among the rain forests and waterfalls below Haleakala's southern slopes is Hana, with good horseback riding and hiking, and body surfing off a black sand beach. There are small motels near Hana, including the Hana-Maui, a quietly elegant place with a Polynesian atmosphere. . . .

Whatever you do, don't miss Hawaii Volcanoes National Park. It's a 30-mile drive from Hilo and a cool (and sometimes wet) 4000 feet high. The park's Kilauea is not only one of the world's most active volcanoes; it's also a drive-in volcano. A network of good roads and hiking trails connects the main crater (caldera) to the adjacent chain of craters. One of these, Mauna Ulu, has erupted almost continuously for two years. The best time to volcano-watch is at night when the lava flows in patterns of shifting fiery red lace against the black landscape. The ground rumbles beneath your feet; the night resounds with a roaring, bubbling sound; the air wafts hot drafts and sulphur fumes past your nose. But you won't mind. Along with hundreds of Islanders whose favorite spectator sport is watching volcanic eruptions, you'll be too busy marveling (from a safe distance) at the fountains of molten lava that spew from 50 to 1900 feet into the air.

But even if you don't see a live volcano, you'll probably fall in love with Hawaii anyway. It's still a romantic special kind of place, a place where you can come on a budget with a knock-down bicycle and a knapsack; take the once-in-a-lifetime trip first class all the way; bring the whole family and give the kids a firsthand lesson in natural history, skin diving and cross-cultural living; or take a second honeymoon. Like the ads say, Hawaii is exotic America. Still the loveliest fleet of islands that lie anchored in any ocean. Still blue Hawaii.

1. This article is written
   a. by an islander for a visitor.
   b. by a tourist for other tourists.
   c. by a visitor for the Hawaiian people.

2. The fiftieth state of Hawaii is
   a. a single large island.
   b. composed of three islands.
   c. a string of eight islands.

3. The first missionaries who came to Hawaii
    a. quickly adapted to Hawaiian living.
    b. succeeded in changing the Hawaiian life style.
    c. tried unsuccessfully to discourage Hawaiian customs.

4. Hawaii's population consists
    a. primarily of people from the mainland of the United States.
    b. of many nationalities.
    c. primarily of Europeans.

5. On the Hawaiian islands there
    a. are no active volcanoes remaining.
    b. are only empty volcanic craters of cinders.
    c. is at least one volcano which erupts frequently.

6. The temperature in Hawaii
    a. usually is in the 70s and 80s.
    b. averages 65 degrees year around.
    c. averages 90 degrees.

7. The Hawaiian word "Aloha!"
    a. is reserved for greeting close relatives.
    b. is a greeting that expresses love and openness.
    c. is seldom used on the islands.

8. Hawaii entered the Union
    a. the year before Alaska became a state.
    b. when it first applied for statehood.
    c. after 22 unsuccessful attempts.

9. The islands were originally settled by
    a. English explorers.
    b. Polynesians.
    c. American missionaries.

10. The main idea of this article is that
    a. Hawaii is still an island paradise of tropical flowers and easy living.
    b. snorkeling, skin diving, and surfing are popular sports among Hawaiians.
    c. Hawaii has been spoiled by high rises, commercialism, and an influx of tourists.

Starting time _____

Completion time _____

Elapsed time _____

Words per minute _____

Number correct _____

Percentage of
comprehension _____

"Findit"*

Robert W. Gruetter

"On behalf of the Director, Mr. Gene McEathron, and the entire staff, I would like to welcome you to the U.S Customs Canine Enforcement Officer Training Center."

And so it begins for Class 37 as it has for the past 18 years as four new canine enforcement officers (CEO's) enter training at the Customs Service Canine Enforcement Training Center located at Front Royal, Virginia.

For the next 14 weeks, candidates, both two-legged and four-legged, will train together striving to become a canine team; but as in every class, new students are about to learn just what it takes to reach the point where man and animal interact in one fluid motion, giving the appearance that the job is no more difficult than playing with the family pet.

The first two weeks are deceiving. The new students are in the classroom. Here they are given courses directly related to specific tasks and the skills required to perform the canine officer position.

The students are taught the mission of the Customs Service, its organizational structure, narcotics and smuggling techniques, courtesy, firearms training, enforcement of Customs laws and those of other agencies, TECS—the Treasury Enforcement Communications System, courtroom demeanor, search and seizure procedures, methods of apprehension and restraint, and the theory of detector dog training and employment along with how to care for their animals.

Written tests follow closely. Each student is required to pass with a minimum qualifying score of 70 percent.

In addition to the Basic Narcotic Detector Course #50008, which is also made available to state and local police agencies and foreign governments, the Training Center has developed and offers a variety of other specialized courses. A 16-week course has been developed to meet the needs of the Saudi Arabian Government. It stems from the basic 12-week Narcotic Detection Course and includes an additional four weeks devoted to establishing an explosive/weapons detection capability. . . .

For the new CEO trainee, the work has yet to begin. Throughout the tedious hours in the classroom, each student has been anxiously waiting to find out which dogs have been assigned to him.

Each student will enter training with two dogs. In the event one dog is medically

*"Findit," excerpted from *Customs Today*, U.S. Customs Service, Fall, 1988.

unable to continue training or fails to progress satisfactorily, the student will always have one dog available to him.

The majority of dogs used are Labrador retrievers, golden retrievers, German short hair pointers, German shepherds and others of questionable background. But they all have one thing in common—an intense desire to retreive a thrown object. For this is the basis from which all detector dog training is derived.

After man meets animal, the students are allowed to take their dogs out of the kennel for the first time, under the watchful eye of their instructor, a man of immense patience but slightly reminiscent of a military drill instructor.

For the next three weeks of training, it will seem to some of these students that this is the roughest training since boot camp. The student will find a new definition to the word "tired," for these three weeks of training are devoted almost solely to field work which establishes scent association for the animal, develops the dog's stamina and teaches the handlers to execute point-to-point and quartering search patterns.

The gentle slopes of the Blue Ridge Mountains will seem like the Rockies. It will appear that the instructor knows only one direction—up; that the dogs know only one speed—fast; exhaustion will seem constant; smokers will vow to quit.

For some who are physically unable to withstand the pace, it will mean an acknowledgment that there is more to the job than they had indeed realized. For others, it will mean a look inside themselves to find the determination to continue. At the end of the third week, students must pass a written test and go through a practical evaluation with their dogs.

Later in training, at the end of the ninth and twelfth weeks, the student will undergo another series of evaluations and tests. These, too, must be passed before the team is certified in narcotic detection.

The first nine weeks are devoted to marijuana and hashish detection. The use of these narcotic odors makes it easier to establish proper search patterns for both dog and handler. The last three weeks of training are used to enhance the dog's capability to detect heroin and cocaine, but for those students who have made it past their third week, there is still much to do.

It does not seem possible, but from the fourth week to the ninth the pace of training will pick up even more. Now dogs and handlers must learn the proper methods of searching buildings, vehicles, mail, freight, luggage, aircraft (both commercial and private) and vessels.

After each successful exercise, the inevitable "tug of war game" between man and animal is conducted. For this is the only reward the animal receives. A playful tug on a rolled terrycloth towel and praise from his handler are all that motivate the animal to search.

For the handler, the reward is the satisfaction that comes from seeing his hard work and effort pay off as his dog's performance steadily improves—that and perhaps a "well done" from instructors whose compliments seem few and far between.

In the ninth week, the training takes on a new seriousness. Up until now if the dog accidentally bit into a marijuana or hashish training aid, the effect on the animal's health was minimal.

Now the training takes on a deadly urgency. The handler must not allow his animal to come in contact with the heroin or cocaine training aids for the purity is such that if even a small amount is ingested, it could prove fatal. In addition, the odor levels of these substances are much lower.

Teamwork between man and animal becomes essential if the detection capability of each dog is to be developed to its fullest potential.

By now, the search patterns have been established, the proper sequences performed time and time again.

Introduction of the new odors of heroin and cocaine means back out into the field, but this time for only a few days. Through the use of synthetic substances, pseudo-heroin and pseudo-cocaine, scent association is established quickly. Gradually the artificial substances are replaced with real narcotics and the search patterns and sequences repeated and the new odors firmly established.

At the twelfth week comes the final and most critical evaluation. There is no more time. Both dog and handler must pass if they are to become a certified narcotic detector dog team.

For the student, success means the culmination of 12 weeks of hard work and the pride and satisfaction of having trained his own dog. Only one more obstacle remains before he can become a canine enforcement officer—firearms training.

At the Training Center's pistol and shotgun ranges, the students are taught firearms safety, deadly-force policy, care and maintenance of weapons and the essentials of shooting with the Basic Marksmanship Course.

After demonstrating proficiency with the weapon in the basic course, students move on to the Practical Pistol Course (PPC), where they are taught to draw, fire and reload the weapons against time and turning targets. Here on this course the students must qualify with a minimum score of 240 out of 300 to successfully complete training.

As in all areas of training, students having difficulty are afforded the opportunity of remedial training, but now 12 weeks of work rides on this crucial ability to qualify with a firearm.

After qualification on the PPC course, a stress course with friend and foe targets and nightfire follow, along with the Shotgun Course.

And finally it is over—the words of welcome 14 weeks ago are replaced with congratulations, a handshake and a gold shield that says "Canine Enforcement Officer."

Is all this time and training and investment paying off? The bottom line on the success of this particular program is being written day-in and day-out by the men and women of the Canine Program. The field handlers, through their hard work and dedication, have compiled a record of seizures of which they can be justifiably proud. . . .

1. In this article CEO stands for
   a. Chief Executive Officer.
   b. Canine Enforcement Officer.
   c. College Enrollment Officer.

2. The first part of the training is
   a. training with a dog.
   b. firearms training.
   c. coursework.

3. The CEO program is sponsored by the
   a. U.S. Customs.
   b. Federal Bureau of Investigation.
   c. U.S. Army.

4. The dog's reward for a successful exercise is
   a. a playful "tug of war game."
   b. a steak.
   c. a break in the work schedule.
5. All dogs accepted for training must have
   a. a pedigree.
   b. an intense desire to retrieve a thrown object.
   c. loyalty to one trainer.
6. Dog training begins with
   a. explosive/weapons detection.
   b. heroin/cocaine detection.
   c. marijuana/hashish detection.
7. Each student who enters training is given
   a. one dog.
   b. three dogs.
   c. two dogs.
8. The pace of training is
   a. relaxed.
   b. strenuous.
   c. flexible.
9. Seizures of drugs and currency from canine enforcement teams
   a. have been disappointingly small.
   b. are hard to determine because no records are kept.
   c. have been large enough to make the field handlers justifiably proud.
10. This article is mainly about
    a. training for canine teams.
    b. making drug seizures with dogs.
    c. why people shouldn't use drugs.

Starting time _____

Completion time _____

Elapsed time _____

Words per minute _____

Number correct _____

Percentage of
comprehension _____

Mountain Flying: For Adults Only*

Richard L. Collins

There is something about mountains that makes the flatland pilot's heart thump. The Appalachians can do this and even the little Bostons and Ouachitas in the middle of the country can make a pilot twitch under certain conditions. The big mountains in the West are the ones we flatlanders are most apprehensive about, though—the beautiful but hostile Rockies. Our apprehension seems justified when we consider that almost half the airplanes lost in the big mountains are flown by pilots from flat country.

I'll tell you something though: We *can* fly in the mountains, and if we don't we are missing some of the finest flying there is. You don't really appreciate what an airplane can do for you until you slip down a valley in the cool of the morning, land on a little Forest Service strip and listen to the coyote in the snowcapped mountains surrounding the area. There were probably elk in the meadows you passed on the way in, too. Then walk down the path to the beautifully clear river, breathing the pure mountain air all the way. The delicate scent is hard to describe. So is the feeling you get flying over countryside of awesome beauty, and the realization that few humans have ever really seen that country: some Forest Service people, a few hearty campers and hikers, no

doubt some Indians and explorers in times long past, and those fortunate enough to fly low over it in a light airplane.

When you contemplate your airplane sitting peacefully on a strip like Spotted Bear or Meadow Creek, Montana, think about what you have seen, and take another breath of that air you'd like to bottle and take home, you know that the bird has asserted itself as the finest machine in the world.

The flatland pilot flying the mountains really needs only an extra measure of two virtues: patience and understanding. Those are the things that experienced mountain flyers use, and you'll see this if you are ever fortunate enough to head for the hills with an experienced mountaineer, as was I recently, with Jeff Morrison, who operates Morrison's Flying Service, in Helena, Montana. The Morrisons have been in the FBO business in Helena since 1931, and Jeff, a fellow second-generation aviator, has been doing business with the mountains for 18 years.

Our intent was to fly northwest of Helena, into the Bob Marshall Wilderness Area, and along the valley of the South Fork of the Flathead River. The weather was less than ideal: An upslope condition—an easterly flow over the rising plains and against the eastern slopes of the Rockies—was creating the

*"Reprinted from the April, 1972 issue of *Flying Magazine*, a publication of the Ziff-Davis Aviation Division."

problem. In textbook fashion, the upslope movement was producing cooling and condensation, which meant clouds and precipitation. Helena, in a large natural bowl, was good enough, with 3,000 overcast and unlimited visibility, but things were socked in just to the east of the mountains, and every ridge we could see from the coffee shop was obscured. Jeff apologized for the weather, but I was looking forward to the opportunity of watching him deal with it. . . .

Jeff was flying from the right seat as we moved over toward Mullan Pass, and things looked questionable. He made an early decision, abandoned that course miles before we got into higher terrain, and went over to have a look at McDonald Pass, where a highway crosses the Continental Divide. Even though it is a bit higher, he said it was sometimes in better shape than Mullan. It wasn't, and again he turned away early, before getting close.

We headed south instead, following a railroad and highway with excellent visibility ahead, and with obscured mountains to either side. About 20 or 25 miles south of Helena, we could see through a gap in the higher mountains to the right, and into a northwest-bound valley we could follow to where we wanted to go. It was a comfortably wide gap, and the nose of the airplane was finally pointed in the proper direction.

Patience? We flew an extra 50 miles to stay in better weather over lower terrain. . . .

Our point of first landing, Seely Lake, showed up soon. It is an excellent airport with 3,600 feet of smooth runway at an elevation of 4,037 feet, and with good approaches. I was flying, and Jeff said to allow for a long final approach and to fly the airplane at the best rate-of-climb speed at the maximum-lift flap setting until fairly close to the end of the runway. He added that it was good to use a little power, but not too much. The airplane was thus at maximum advantage for a getaway all the way in, in case a landing turned out to be a bad deal. In close, when the landing looked really good, I went on to full flaps and slowed to the normal approach speed. A go-around would have been simple at Seely Lake, even using sea-level flat-country procedures, but I could tell Morrison was leading up to some airports where real mountain procedures would be advisable. . . .

After our takeoff at Seely Lake, Jeff said he wanted to get over into the next valley, along the South Fork of the Flathead, but that this wouldn't be possible yet because of clouds, so we'd go northwest along the Swan River Valley until a good spot to cross over appeared.

We were flying at 6,500 feet, with the 9,000-plus mountains to either side obscured by cloud. I could look in the desired direction and occasionally see what might be a spot to slip through. Jeff knew them all, though, and knew that in this area, there would be about 20 miles of high ridge country between us and the next valley. I might be peering into a pass that appeared open, but that would only lead to a dead end. This was obvious on the chart, too, as long as I knew precisely where we were on the chart. . . .

The unpredictable nature of the wind is such that many mountain strips have two wind socks—one at each end. The smaller strips in the narrow valleys, in fact, can be assumed to be pretty hostile to strangers in any wind condition of consequence.

Meadow Creek was our next airport. After casing it, I was ready to go somewhere else for lunch. The approach would have to have a bend at the last minute, the strip looked smaller than its actual length. . . .

Jeff said it looked good to start an approach to the south, though, and after carefully explaining that I am a devout coward but trusted his judgment, I started working on that long and, of necessity, slightly bent final approach to Meadow Creek. It worked nicely, but the consequences of going at a mountain strip haphazardly were very apparent at this airport.

The first thing to do at a mountain strip is to carefully determine the best way to approach it, and then make some decisions in advance. At Meadow Creek, we decided to land south, and to watch for any drafts around a bluff at the north end of the strip. It was also obvious that I shouldn't slow to normal approach speed until I was very sure of the landing; once slowed and once down between the trees (it's surrounded), there would be no go-around.

Go-arounds have mastered many a pilot in the mountains. Come in too high and too fast, possibly roll the wheels a little, see that it will be impossible to stop within the confines of the strip, and then try to make a getaway. The moment the pilot makes the decision to go, the airplane is often as good as wiped out. Many mountain airports simply don't include provisions for a go-around; the air is full of rocks and trees. This is another example of patience: Fool with it until it is just right before going to a point from which no alteration in plan is possible. . . .

After a stroll around Meadow Creek, and a walk to look at the river, we took off and flew down the valley and over the wilderness area, where nothing with an engine is allowed (on the ground). Then, as the end of the valley neared, Jeff started working our way out.

The peaks on both sides had been well obscured all the way down the valley, and it had been rather like flying in a big, beautiful room. I had wondered aloud where the door would be, and Jeff said we'd look at the south end and see if it would be possible to get out. If not, we'd fly back to the north end (70 miles) and go out that way. If that didn't work, I guess we would have landed at Spotted Bear or Meadow Creek and fished awhile. Mountaineer's patience again.

Watching Jeff work his way from the valley through the mountains and into the bowl at Helena was fascinating. The key was his knowledge of exactly where we were and exactly what was ahead at all times. He also kept a downhill path toward which to turn ready all the time, and made decisions from a distance about which passes were open. No sneaking up close for a wishful look. . . .

Mountains deserve your strictest attention, and pilots who don't pay attention have done quite a job of littering our scenic hillsides with scrap aluminum. The lower elevation of Eastern mountains does modify many of the special cautions applicable to the Rockies. . . .

Remember that even though there's a bit more to flying in the mountains than to flying in flat country, there is a lot more to see.

1. Most flatland pilots
   a. are confident about flying in mountainous territory.
   b. fear the Appalachians more than the Rockies.
   c. are fearful of flying in mountainous country.

2. This writer feels that flatland pilots
   a. should avoid flying in mountainous country.
   b. should learn how to fly in mountainous country.
   c. instinctively know how to fly in mountainous country.

3. The writer believes that mountain flying
   a. is too hazardous for flatland pilots.
   b. offers pilots an opportunity to appreciate the natural scenic beauty of the mountains.
   c. should never be undertaken when the weather is cloudy.

4. Flatland pilots in mountainous regions need
   a. an extra amount of patience.
   b. airplanes capable of high speeds.
   c. the experience of flatland flying.

5. The weather on the day the writer flew over the mountains with Jeff was
   a. clear and sunny.
   b. cloudy with some rain.
   c. cold with snow flurries.

6. Making his first landing at Seely Lake, the author
   a. slowed to the normal approach speed.
   b. made a quick get-away when conditions appeared unfavorable.
   c. made a go-around at the last minute.

7. The airport at Meadow Creek
   a. was too obscured by clouds for landing.
   b. had a long, smooth runway.
   c. had a bend at the end of the approach.

8. In his statement "pilots who don't pay attention have done quite a job of littering our scenic hillsides with scrap aluminum," the writer means that
   a. many airplanes have crashed because of the pilots' carelessness.
   b. pilots have dropped aluminum cans from their airplanes.
   c. airplanes flying over wilderness areas detract from the natural beauty of the land.

9. In mountain flying, weather and wind
   a. pose no problem as long as the plane is structurally sound.
   b. can create serious problems because they are unpredictable.
   c. should never interfere with a pilot's flight plan.

10. The main idea of this article is that
    a. mountain flying can be a rewarding experience for the flatland pilot.
    b. many lives have been lost by pilots flying over mountainous country.
    c. flatland pilots should fly only where the land is flat.

Starting time _____

Completion time _____

Elapsed time _____

Words per minute _____

Number correct _____

Percentage of
comprehension _____

Albuquerque—The West's Winter Oasis*

William E. Pauli

A few winters ago most people looked at New Mexico as part of a four-lane corridor that led from Texas to the west coast. A stopover in Albuquerque was scheduled only to fill radiators and waterbags before speeding on through Arizona and the waiting desert.

Today, for an increasing number of off-season vacationers, Interstate 40 ends in Albuquerque. Almost overnight this city of 325,000 has blossomed into a winter oasis.

Albuquerque has always been a summer watering hole for tourists. They stop over to visit nearby reservations, explore ghost towns, poke around old Spanish ruins, hike in the mountains, play tennis and golf, shop in Old Town and camp out in nearby state parks.

Suddenly people are discovering they can do these things year around. And each November, the winter sports-minded can add another half dozen outdoor activities to their agenda.

For instance, Albuquerque has solved a major problem faced by skiers everywhere: how to arrive on top of the mountain without spending a day getting there.

Home of the Sandia Peak Tramway, the city provides doorstep skiing for residents and does almost as well for out-of-towners. Skiers from Chicago can fly here nonstop in two and a half hours. The city is only two hours from San Francisco and an hour and a half from Dallas. A skier in a real rush can be pushing powder in the Sandias 30 minutes after his plane touches down.

The Sandia Mountains, which sit almost in Albuquerque's backyard, have been the area's main attraction longer than anyone can remember. Spring, summer and fall the mountains, part of the Cibola National Forest, are crowded with hikers, backpackers, naturalists, picnickers, bird-watchers, Boy Scouts and other outdoor types. But the first snow of November used to shut most people out.

Downhill ski buffs and cross-country skiers could drive half way up the east side of the mountain (the only half good for skiing) and catch two chairlifts, two pomas and a pony to four novice, nine intermediate and two expert trails. But for everyone else the mountains were closed for the winter.

An Albuquerque ski enthusiast, Bob Nordhaus, helped change all that in 1966 when he opened the Sandia Peak Tramway. North America's longest tram, it carries

*William E. Pauli, "Albuquerque—The West's Winter Oasis," reprinted by permission from *Ford Times*, January, 1974, pp. 8–14.

anyone who buys a ticket three miles up-slope and a mile high in 18 minutes. Built at a cost of nearly $2 million the tram has changed the entire pattern of skiing in New Mexico. Not only do jet setters fly in for a day on the slopes, but local housewives often drop youngsters off at the tram's base early in the morning, spend the day shopping downtown, then retrieve the kids in time to be home to fix supper.

For skiers it's a short walk to the ski area from which many trails zigzag down the eastern slopes to the base lodge on State Road 44. There's plenty of powder to schuss in, too—the average snowfall is 111 inches a year, and it often packs waist deep.

Nonskiers who aren't in a hurry to get back down the mountain should stop at the Four Seasons Visitors' Center. In addition to getting a rundown on the Cibola National Forest and the wild creatures that live there, they can sign up for a snowshoe hike.

All of Albuquerque's winter sports, covering everything from bobsledding to ice-fishing, aren't a mile high. Back down the mountain duffers can tee off on any of a half dozen public links or have their home town country club cards honored at five clubs in the city. And if they're handy with a racket, tennis players need not grow rusty in winter. Four large outdoor courts stay open and busy all 12 months.

For those who look at such strenuous exercise as so much nonsense, Albuquerque offers a wide variety of slower-paced activities. There's year-round camping at Coronado State Park 20 miles north. This ancient Indian pueblo, where Coronado camped in 1541 while searching for the fabled seven cities of gold, has outstanding facilities.

The western edge of the city abounds with petroglyphs—prehistoric Indian drawings in volcanic rock. The Indians weren't the only ones to leave their mark on the land. El Morro National Monument, or Inscription Rock, is one and a half hours away. The largest piece of graffiti anywhere, the rock was first signed by the explorer Onate in 1605. After that it appears as if everyone who passed stopped to scratch his name. Today, the rock stands as a huge tablet of America's westward expansion. Although visitors can no longer sign the rock, there is a giant sandstone at the monument's entrance, placed there for those with a yen to pen their names.

If Indians interest you there are plenty of reservations around Albuquerque. However, Jack Smith, tourist director of the Albuquerque Chamber of Commerce, cautions to call ahead. "Most reservations welcome outsiders," he says. "But it's a good idea to know the ground rules before you go." In December there are Christmas Eve dances in mission churches in the Acoma, Laguna and Isleta pueblos. And on New Year's Eve, the Sandia pueblo just north of the city holds its annual deer dance.

A lot of Indians aren't on reservations, however. On most days, those who carry on the old crafts can be seen in Old Town. Site of original Albuquerque, Old Town was founded in 1706 by Don Francisco Cuervo y Valdez. Along its wide sidewalks Zuni and Navaho display handmade jewelry and rugs. Inside adobe shops tourists can watch as craftsmen hammer out intricate silver and turquoise squash blossom necklaces. Handmade clay pots, straw baskets, leather sandals and other handicrafts are also sold in a dozen shops and boutiques that line the gaslit plaza.

One of Old Town's original structures, the San Felipe de Neri Church, still opens its doors daily to the faithful. Except for minor alterations and a remodeled facade, the adobe building, with windows 20 feet above the ground and walls seven feet thick, is the same as it was over 250 years ago. . . .

Albuquerque residents are so certain of their fair weather city that for the past six years they've held a tennis-ski, golf-ski meet the first weekend in March.

"Tennis and golf get underway at 8 A.M.," says Smith. "Then the ski race, a giant slalom, starts at two in the afternoon.

"It's a one-day event we guarantee you won't soon forget."

1. One reason for Albuquerque's rapidly increasing popularity among vacationers is its
   a. nearby reservations.
   b. Sandia Peak Tramway.
   c. Spanish ruins.

2. In former years tourists
   a. rarely stopped at Albuquerque.
   b. usually visited Albuquerque only in the summer.
   c. usually visited Albuquerque only in the winter.

3. The Sandia Mountains are used for skiing by
   a. local townspeople.
   b. the jet set and tourists.
   c. both a. and b.

4. Petroglyphs are
   a. prehistoric Indian drawings in rock.
   b. the remains of a petrified forest.
   c. dances held in the pueblos.

5. According to the article, Indians who are not on reservations can be seen
   a. skiing down the east side of the mountain.
   b. working at and displaying their crafts in Old Town.
   c. among the Spanish ruins and in the ghost towns.

6. El Morro Monument is a huge rock that
   a. explorers signed on their way westward.
   b. tourists are encouraged to sign.
   c. is inscribed with witty remarks.

7. Albuquerque is
   a. a modern planned community.
   b. nothing more than a stopover when traveling from Texas to the west coast.
   c. a sporting and historical center.

8. The Sandia Peak Tramway
   a. carries people three miles up the mountain slope for skiing.
   b. transports people across the mountains when roads are closed due to snow.
   c. takes people from the airport directly to the ski slopes.

9. The snow in the ski areas of the Sandia Mountains is
   a. mostly made by machines.
   b. plentiful with both powder and base.
   c. mostly powder since it is too warm for base to accumulate.

10. The main idea of this article is that
    a. Albuquerque has always offered the summer visitor many opportunities for sightseeing.
    b. the Sandia Mountains, on the fringe of Albuquerque, provide an excellent area for skiing.
    c. Albuquerque has recently become a winter oasis.

Starting time _____   Number correct _____

Completion time _____   Percentage of
comprehension _____
Elapsed time _____

Words per minute _____

Animal Aliens*

Gary Turbak

Across the borders these aliens come. Some sneak in, undetected, on their own. Others are aided by profiteers. They carry neither passports nor visas, and virtually no nation is immune to their infiltration. Who are these unauthorized immigrants? The international animal invaders, a truly worldwide problem.

From New Zealand to Florida, U.S.A., to Czechoslovakia, animal immigrants have been surprising, infuriating, outsmarting, and—occasionally—pleasing mankind since antiquity. Wherever man has settled, creatures from foreign lands have come to dwell with him.

Rats, it seems, have always hidden in the holds of ships, scampering ashore wherever voyagers docked. Traded grain and fruit and livestock have aways carried insect pests to new frontiers. And often, man has intentionally taken animals to a new land.

Frequently, these animal invaders upset the bestial order in their new homes. Without natural enemies to hold their populations in check, the newcomers may multiply prodigiously and soon outstrip their food supply. Faced with a new environment, they may alter their habits and become destructive. Or, they may compete with native creatures, driving them out of existence. Introduction of new species has been—at best—a risky venture.

The classic case of an invading animal is the story of the lowly rabbit in Australia. In 1859, Thomas Austin brought to his Victoria ranch 12 pairs of European rabbits from England. In six years, the 24 bunnies became 30,000, and they no longer restricted themselves to Austin's land. The wool and mutton industries suffered greatly, since every five rabbits consumed the forage needed by one sheep. Spreading like a furry plague, the rabbit horde made extensive wastelands of formerly green pastures.

With clubs, traps, poisons, and their bare hands, the Australian ranchers fought back. In a single year they killed 20 million rabbits, but still the horde hopped on. They erected 3,200 kilometres (2,000 miles) of rabbit-proof fence in an attempt to halt the creatures, but the fence only slowed the march of the hares.

Finally, scientists introduced a virus (toxic only to rabbits) into the teeming herds. The pests perished in great numbers, and the land once again became fit for livestock grazing.

---

*Gary Turbak, "Animal Aliens," reprinted by permission from *The Rotarian*, November, 1982, pp. 22–24.

Ironically, the saving virus was itself an international traveler: it had been imported from Brazil.

Australia's experience was a tragic accident, but other animal invaders have proliferated with man's blessing. The earliest visitors to Jamaica brought black rats with them. The rodents took a liking to the sweet sugar cane of the island and soon began devouring the crops. When bounties and poisons failed to limit the rat population, cane farmers imported a solution.

The weasel-like mongoose, a native of India, had earned a worldwide reputation as a bloodthirsty hunter. Surely this crafty carnivore will do away with the rats, thought Jamaican plantation owners. So they acquired several pairs and turned them loose in the cane fields.

The rat population plummeted and the mongooses prospered. Soon, mongooses, not rats, roamed the entire island. Eager cane farmers in Cuba and Puerto Rico followed the example of their Jamaican counterparts.

But one important factor had been overlooked: rats are nocturnal creatures, while the mongoose prefers to hunt during the day. When the sugar cane fields teemed with rats, this situation was not a problem. But as the dwindling number of rodents became more difficult to find during the day, the mongoose appetite changed. Rather than hunt all day for a hard-to-find rat, the imported predators went after easier fare: poultry, young pigs, lambs, puppies, and a variety of cultivated fruits and vegetables.

Soon, the mongoose was a bigger pest than the rats had ever been. Just 11 years after its welcome as a hero, a bounty was placed on the mongoose's head and its further importation to Jamaica forbidden.

Occasionally, the string of ill-advised imports seems to lead on and on. Rabbits, brought to Macquarie Island (southeast of Australia) to provide food for the inhabitants, began to compete with sheep for the available grass. So, the farmers imported cats to eat the rabbits, but the felines took to dining on birds. The people saw this as a threat to the bird eggs they loved to eat, so they brought in dogs to get rid of the cats. The dogs, however, much preferred to eat seals, and this angered inhabitants even more because seal meat was considered a human delicacy. The entire matter was left in this unresolved state, perhaps after some die-hard suggested importing bears to get rid of the dogs.

Another animal invader that succeeded too well is the muskrat. Native only to North America, this rodent caught the fancy of European furriers. In 1905, Prince Colleredo-Mannsfield turned loose a few of the aquatic creatures near Prague, Czechoslovakia. At a rate of 64.3 kilometres (40 miles) per year, the muskrat then extended its range through Germany, Rumania, Poland, and France.

When Europe's marshes could no longer contain the proliferating muskrats, the rodents took to the fields and canals. Here they fed on agricultural crops and acquired the nasty habit of tunneling into drainage ditches, railroad embankments, and dikes. In Holland, especially, the muskrats' tunnels wreaked havoc by confounding flood control efforts. Only England has been able to keep the muskrats out, and most Europeans likely wish they had never laid eyes on this diminutive American invader.

England, however, was the recipient of another animal alien from the U.S.A. In 1890, the British Duke of Bedford let loose 10

American gray squirrels near Woburn. The grays have now spread throughout much of England, replacing as they go the gentler native red squirrel.

And, for some unexplained reason, the gray squirrels shipped to England significantly altered their eating habits. In the United States, they had subsisted mainly on nuts. Across the Atlantic, however, they acquired a keen taste for tree bark, a preference which has led to the destruction of large forests of slow-growing hardwood trees.

The U.S., too, has had its share of invaders. Early colonists brought along such unloved creatures as the common clothes moth and the pigeon. Later, homesick Englishmen imported the house sparrow, and the pesky bird now occupies every corner of the country.

In 1891, a New York City drug manufacturer and Shakespeare devotee named Eugene Scheifflin concluded that U.S. culture would be greatly advanced if that country were to become home to every bird mentioned by the famous bard. He noted in the play "Henry IV" the line: "Nay, I'll have a starling shall be taught to speak nothing but 'Mortimer.'" Scheifflin imported a few starlings and loosed them in New York's Central Park. Soon the strutting, obnoxious birds spread across the country.

While the starling is an old pest in a new land, other invaders are almost fantastic enough to defy belief. On the evening of 25 May 1968, a night watchman near Boca Raton, Florida, came to see what was causing his dog's insistent barking. The man rounded a corner of a building and stopped dead in his tracks. His eyes refused to accept what they saw. The object of his dog's wrath was a fish—a fish that was calmly *walking* across the bare ground.

This creature, a walking catfish from Thailand, had been imported by tropical fish dealers, and a few had escaped into the warm Florida waters. The quarrelsome, 51-centimetre (20-inch) fish can breathe air for hours and can walk on its spiny fins for long distances. It multiplies rapidly and is driving out such preferred species as bass and bluegills.

The watchman alerted authorities, but efforts to eliminate the walking catfish have proved futile. "How do you kill a fish that simply walks away when you poison its pond?" ask wildlife officials. The peripatetic piscean pilgrim has already trekked into neighboring states, and is still strolling.

Over the past two centuries, New Zealand has provided a virtual blank canvas for those interested in painting their own wildlife panorama. For 70 million years, New Zealand's two major islands lay isolated from the rest of the world. Their lush habitat supported birds, snakes, frogs, and fish . . . but there were no mammals (except for two species of bats). No deer, fox, rodents, goats, or cattle lived on the islands.

When white men arrived in 1773, they set about rectifying the situation. All manner of creatures flooded onto the islands: moose from the U.S.A., deer from Japan, mynah birds from India, hedgehogs from England, opossums from Australia, geese from Canada, and hundreds more. In all, 207 new vertebrate species were released . . . and at least 29 eventually became "problem" animals. Too many deer ruined the grasslands. Opossums fed on fruit and killed the trees. Geese devastated grain fields. And on and on. The painting was definitely not a masterpiece.

Occasionally, however, an animal importation is successful. The brown trout from Germany provides worldwide angling pleasure, and a few introduced insects have proved beneficial. But the best success story is that of the Chinese ringnecked pheasant in the U.S.A.

In 1882, an Oregon judge turned 28 Shanghai pheasants loose near Portland. In one decade they became popular game birds, with Oregon hunters bagging 50,000 in 1891. Other states got on the pheasant bandwagon, and the Chinese immigrant quickly shot toward the top of the game bird list. What's more . . . they ate no one out of house and home, carried no exotic diseases, did not drive out native birds, and were beautiful to look at. Sportsmen now take millions of pheasants annually, and the bird's future in the United States appears secure.

But the pheasant's successful invasion is not easily duplicated. Again and again, alien animals have proved destructive, unpredictable, overly competitive, too prolific, dangerous, or simply hard to manage.

"Too often," says wildlife expert George Laycock, "we are inclined to see the world of nature as modeling clay and man as the sculptor. This is just not true. The only safe way to approach the whole question of exotics is to leave animals where they occur naturally."

After all, it has not been long since man himself was, in nearly all areas, an alien species.

1. An animal alien is
   a. an unfriendly animal.
   b. an animal from another country.
   c. an endangered species.

2. The rabbit population in Australia was finally brought under control by
   a. erecting 2,000 miles of rabbit-proof fence.
   b. introducing a virus that was toxic only to rabbits.
   c. using clubs, traps, and bare hands.

3. Jamaicans tried to reduce the number of black rats by importing
   a. weasels.
   b. mongooses.
   c. snakes.

4. Muskrats were imported to Europe because
   a. their fur was desirable.
   b. they helped control floods by digging tunnels into dikes and embankments.
   c. they ate the rodents that inhabited the marsh lands.

5. Introducing the gray squirrel to England resulted in
   a. the consumption of vast quantities of nuts.
   b. the devastation of agricultural crops.
   c. the destruction of large forests of slow-growing trees.

6. An example of a successful animal importation is the
   a. pheasant.
   b. mongoose.
   c. muskrat.
7. A fish that can walk is
   a. the brown trout.
   b. a kind of catfish.
   c. the rainbow trout.
8. A country that contained very few mammals until 1773 is
   a. Antarctica.
   b. Samoa.
   c. New Zealand.
9. George Laycock, a wildlife expert, recommends that
   a. animals should be left where they occur naturally.
   b. animals should be carefully introduced in limited quantities to various regions of the world.
   c. animals should be sent in large quantities to those countries where people believe they can solve problems.
10. The main idea of this article is that
    a. man himself is an alien species.
    b. some animal aliens are successful.
    c. the introduction of new species of animals is a risky venture.

Starting time _____

Completion time _____

Elapsed time _____

Words per minute _____

Number correct _____

Percentage of
comprehension _____

The Essential New Orleans*

Marcelle Bienvenu

Here in the delta country, the livin's still easy. There's the bounce and the beat of jazz tunes in a crowded club; a quiet, flower-filled courtyard in the French Quarter; afternoon tea under a moss-covered oak in the Garden District; flamboyant Mardi Gras; the ballyhoo of the Sugar Bowl Parade, and the big game itself; spicy red beans and rice for lunch; delicate coq au vin by candlelight for dinner; the clang of the St. Charles Avenue Streetcar . . .; the fragrance of Confederate jasmine; magnolia blossoms; French bread, fresh and hot; steaming crawfish; chicory coffee and *beignets.*

These are but a few elements of the essential New Orleans, mostly the same today as they were years ago. To be sure, the city has changed, and continues to change, as old structures give way reluctantly to new high rises. But the traditions of New Orleans change little.

Begin back in 1718 when there were only the river and the bayous and the delta interspersed by small areas of high ground. John Law, who held a charter from the king of France, and Jean Baptiste Le Moyne, Sieur de Bienville, the area's first governor, came upriver from their Gulf Coast colony seeking a site for a new territorial capital. They se-lected a high area on the east bank of the Mississippi some 40 miles inland from the Gulf. The village grew to 100 homes and 500 inhabitants by 1722, when Law and Bienville named it *La Nouvelle Orleans* to honor Philip II, Duke of Orleans and brother of King Louis XIV. They also named the streets: Rue Orleans for the duke, Rue St. Louis for the king, Rue Du Maine and Rue Toulouse for his illegitimate sons, Rue Bourbon for the Duke of Bourbon, and so on. During the same year, a hurricane destroyed some 30 of the village's 100 homes (most other original wooden buildings were lost in fires of 1788 and 1794). The original village remained under French rule till 1763 when King Louis XV deeded New Orleans and other territory to his cousin, King Charles III of Spain. French control resumed in 1800, and in 1803 France sold New Orleans to the United States as part of the massive Louisiana Purchase.

During the 19th century, New Orleans grew rapidly both in numbers of people and in commerce. The population more than doubled between 1803 and 1810, as a veritable tide of immigrants, many of them slaves, arrived from Cuba and other points in the West Indies. The city was assured a dominant role as a shipping center in 1812

*Marcelle Bienvenu, "The Essential New Orleans," reprinted by permission from *Odyssey*, November–December, 1973, pp. 4–9.

when the steamboat era began. Many Irish, Italian and other immigrants from Europe came to work in the prospering port during the 1800s, and New Orleans now ranks second to New York among the nation's ports.

It's always well to start an expedition of New Orleans (*Noo Aw'lins* to the residents) at the French Quarter, the oldest part of the city, where things have changed and yet haven't changed, where the Old World charm persists adjacent to the international river port and gleaming high-rise office buildings. One of the best ways to tour the area is to hire a horse and buggy at Jackson Square and let the driver describe the sights as his horse clip-clops through the old city. Another tack: be your own guide and stroll through the Quarter. . . .

For more than 200 years farmers of southern Louisiana have brought their fresh produce to sell at the river-front French Market, always a joy to visit in the daytime. And at night after a Mardi Gras ball or the opera, it's not uncommon for ladies and gentlemen in evening attire to join longshoremen and laborers at the market's Cafe Du Monde and Morning Call. Revelers and workers alike stop in at all hours for delicious chicory coffee and sugar-coated *beignets,* those tasty square-shaped doughnuts so unique to the area.

As you tour the French Quarter, known also as the *Vieux Carre* (Old Square), you pass quaint, colorful cottages set right on the sidewalks. Wrought-iron gates guard cool patios and courtyards lush with semi-tropical plants. A French Quarter resident of many years says, ''the great mystery here is what's behind those gates.''

But the French Quarter isn't all of New Orleans. You're well advised to cross Canal Street and pass through the business district to what is generally referred to as Uptown or the Garden District. This area was developed after Spanish and French rule had ended and the city was expanded to accommodate westward-migrating Americans. The Americans and the Creoles were of different cultures, so the newcomers chose to live separately. They liked the openness above Canal Street and established there a lovely residential area of graceful avenues lined with magnolias and crape myrtles.

Their expensive and expansive raised cottages were built with the living area on the second floor while the first was used for storage and protection from high water. Covered porches for shade, high ceilings, tall windows, and wide halls to let breezes pass through were in vogue. Many of these spacious homes, set among oak trees and surrounded by beautiful gardens, are visible from the streets and some of them are opened to the public during the two-week Spring Fiesta, beginning the first Friday after Easter.

Americans who settled in the Garden District helped set the pattern for the grand and glorious Mardi Gras celebrated today. Happy-go-lucky Frenchmen of early New Orleans celebrated Mardi Gras with masking and small street parades and lively parties and balls in their homes.

Later, the Spanish commissioners banned street masking because the revelers allegedly engaged in fights and ''general wickedness.'' But the French continued their annual parties in their homes, inviting only individuals they knew and trusted. Out of this secrecy developed closed organizations known as *krewes* that exist to this day.

The Americans did little to encourage openness among the Creoles, but the new residents organized their own ''closed society.'' Soon general masking in the streets was revived and in 1838 a formal parade brought an atmosphere of public merriment to the city once more. It wasn't till 1857, however, that a city-wide Mardi Gras took place and the Mystick Krew of Comus appeared in a night parade.

Today the carnival season begins on the 6th of January and continues through Shrove Tuesday, the day before Lent. That final week's called a time of ''merriment, frivolity and madness'' when there are parades, balls, masking in the streets and when any old reason at all is a good excuse for a party.

Mardi Gras reflects only one of the moods of New Orleans. Jazz, fondly called "head music" by the old musicians, permeates the city any day of the year. And for that we must thank the black New Orleanians who express music from their hearts and souls. Jazz is like a musical gumbo, blending sounds borrowed from the French, Spanish, Africans, Cubans, and Americans. It's a blend the blacks have brought together since the turn of the century in honky-tonks, jazz halls and on the streets—wherever they can blow their horns, beat their drums and pluck their banjos.

Jelly Roll Morton, called the first "hot" piano player, Buddy Bolden on trumpet and Papa Tio, an ace on the clarinet, introduced the new rhythms that were to flow freely up the river to St. Louis and to Chicago—later to Hollywood, New York and Paris; and thanks to Louis Armstrong, all over the world.

Here in New Orleans you can still witness a traditional jazz funeral. A band, such as the Eureka Jazz Band, plays an oh-so mournful tune as the procession makes its way to the cemetery. Then, after the burial, the band blares forth:
Didn't he ramble?
He rambled.
Rambled all around,
In and out the town.
Didn't he ramble?
He rambled.
He rambled till the butchers cut him down. . . .

Well there *is* something else to the essential New Orleans: "You know, the two things people here talk about most are food and fun, and to them they're one and the same." So said a recent visitor and who can dispute it? To most New Orleanians food's a preoccupation.

Creole cuisine—the mainstay of New Orleans dining—is cooking that's indigenous to the area. It's not only French and Spanish, but also German, Italian, Indian, African, West Indian and American. (However, the term *Creole* as applied to people in New Orleans simply denotes French or Spanish colonists and their descendants, especially those who are maintaining Old World customs and language.)

Just as the colonists used what was available to build their home, so did they use what was at hand in preparing meals: seafood and wild game, native herbs, and later, sugar cane, rice and other crops from the plantations. The result: exciting dishes not duplicated anywhere. . . .

Yes, way down here in New Orleans there's a feeling for things. Although its huge port gives New Orleans a big-city atmosphere, the livin' stays pretty easy. There are always plenty of people who take time to go fishing and crabbing along the river or the bayous. . . .

And always the people of all backgrounds to listen to, to talk with, or just to look at. As a new resident said: "This is where you want to get in close with the people and touch their way of life. They seem to know what life is all about.". . .

1. The traditions of New Orleans
   a. are changing rapidly.
   b. change more rapidly than the buildings.
   c. change little.
2. New Orleans ranks _____ among the nation's ports.
   a. first
   b. second
   c. third

3. The oldest part of the city, where Old World charm persists adjacent to the river port and office buildings, is called
   a. the Italian Quarter.
   b. the Spanish Quarter.
   c. the French Quarter.

4. The Uptown or Garden District is
   a. a lovely residential area composed of graceful avenues and raised cottages.
   b. houses with wrought-iron gates set right on the street.
   c. modern high-rise apartments surrounded by parks.

5. The Mardi Gras has been celebrated in New Orleans
   a. since the French first settled there in the 1700s.
   b. for over a century.
   c. for nearly fifty years.

6. The style of music that prevails in New Orleans is
   a. rock.
   b. classical.
   c. jazz.

7. According to this article, funeral processions in New Orleans are unusual because
   a. they are accompanied by band music.
   b. they are followed by feasting.
   c. the people attending wear masks.

8. The mainstay of New Orleans cooking, according to the article, is
   a. delectable French pastries.
   b. Spanish omelets.
   c. Creole cuisine.

9. New Orleans was originally composed mainly of people of
   a. German and Italian descent.
   b. French and Spanish descent.
   c. West Indian and African descent.

10. The main idea of this article is that
    a. New Orleans is a large seaport with the hustle and bustle of a big city.
    b. New Orleans is a fun-filled city, rich in tradition and atmosphere.
    c. immigrants from many parts of the world came to New Orleans to make their homes.

Starting time _____

Completion time _____

Elapsed time _____

Words per minute _____

Number correct _____

Percentage of
comprehension _____

Daydream Your Way to Success*

Eugene Raudsepp

Daydreaming or fantasy-making was long considered either a waste of time or a symptom of maladjustment. Most psychologists and psychiatrists branded habitual daydreaming as evidence of neurotic tendencies, or an escape from the responsibilities and realities of the workaday world. They warned that continued daydreaming would eventually alienate a person from society and reduce his effectiveness in coping with everyday problems. Even more indulgent behavioral scientists considered daydreaming a childish or adolescent habit, causing students to get bad grades, and adults to fail at their jobs.

As with anything carried to excess, daydreaming can be harmful. There *are* those who substitute a fantasy life for the rewards of activity in the real world. And, when the fantasy-addict withdraws from people, when he can no longer cope with reality, his psychological health is impaired.

But these situations are rare indeed. The truth is that most people suffer from a *lack* of fantasy-making, rather than an *excess* of it. We now know how valuable daydreaming really is. There is a growing realization that if we were completely prevented from daydreaming, our emotional balance would be rendered precarious. Not only would we be less able to deal with the pressures of day-to-day existence, but our control and direction over our lives would be in danger.

Attitudes toward daydreaming have been, in a sense, much like the attitudes toward dreaming in our sleep. Night-dreaming was once thought to interfere with normal sleep and rob us of necessary rest. Recent experiments, however, have indicated that dreams are a normal part of the process of sleep, and are vital to mental health.

Dr. William Dement is conducting research on the significance of dreaming at Mount Sinai Hospital in New York. He reports that subjects whose dreams are interrupted regularly exhibit such emotional disturbances as hypertension, anxiety, irritability, and difficulty in concentrating. "One of the subjects," Dr. Dement reported, "quit the study in apparent panic, and two others insisted on stopping, presumably because the stress was too great."

Experiments in Edinburgh, Scotland, have supported these findings. Volunteers who were kept awake as much as 108 hours at a stretch dreamed considerably more than usual when finally permitted to sleep. "It is as though a pressure to dream builds up with the accruing dream deficit during successive

*Excerpted from *The Rotarian*, April 1983, pp. 29–31. Reprinted by permission.

dream-deprivation nights," says Dr. Dement. "If dream suppression were carried on long enough, the result would be a serious disruption of the personality."

In a similar fashion, prolonged daydream deprivation results in mounting anxiety and tension. Finally, many people find that the need can no longer be suppressed, and daydreaming erupts spontaneously.

During times of stress, daydreaming erects for our nervous systems a temporary shelter to shield us from the "icy winds" of reality, much in the same way that building a house protects our bodies from the elements. Both may be seen as forms of "escapism," but no sane man or woman wants to spend his or her life in an unrelieved battle for survival. Recent research on daydreaming indicates that it is an intrinsic part of daily life and that a certain amount of daydreaming each day is essential for relaxation.

But the beneficial effects of daydreaming go beyond relaxation and the reduction of tension. According to experiments conducted by Dr. Joan T. Freyberg, a New York City-based psychotherapist, daydreaming improves one's learning ability, concentration, attention span, and ability to interact with others. She also discovered that patients who easily engage in fantasy-making usually respond more quickly to treatment and are better able to cope with life's frustrations and crises.

Psychologist Dr. Sara Similansky, in private practice in New York City, has discovered that individuals who are taught how to daydream significantly improve their language and other skills. And Dr. Jerome L. Singer at Yale University finds that daydreaming results in improved self-control and enhances creative thinking. Dr. Singer also points out that daydreaming is a way to improve upon reality, and that it helps a person to cope with delay, frustration, and deprivation. It frequently helps us to change difficult situations into more manageable ones and it gives impetus to sounder future planning. . . .

Many famous scientists and inventors have taken full advantage of the relaxed moments of daydreaming. Their biographies reveal that the best ideas occurred to them when they were relaxing and daydreaming. It is well known that Newton solved many of his most difficult problems when his attention was waylaid by private musings and fantasies. Thomas Edison also knew the value of "half-waking" states, and whenever confronted with a seemingly insurmountable hitch that defied all his conscious efforts, he would stretch out on his couch in his workshop—brought there for just this reason—and let fantasies flood his mind.

Creative artists, writers, and composers have always drawn heavily upon their inner fantasies and reveries. Many of them have special ways with which they trigger their inner fantasy-pictures into motion. Debussy, for example, used to gaze at the river Seine and the playful golden reflections of the setting sun on its waves, to establish an atmosphere for creative daydreaming. Schiller kept rotten apples in his desk drawer. Their aroma helped him to evoke a mood of reverie. Dostoevsky found that he could best brood and dream up his moving stories and psychologically profound characters while pen-drawing and doodling. Brahms discovered that ideas came to him effortlessly only when he approached the state of deep daydreaming.

Daydreaming does not have to pursue the impossible, the will-o'-the-wisp. On the contrary, for many people a passive retreat into the private world of reverie is their "royal road" to making reality more real. Daydreaming helps them in self-discovery, in finding out what they really want to do. They use daydreaming as "a blind date with their deeper selves," as a means for self-study, for canvassing alternatives, for discovering fresh directions to serve as a directional guide for future actions.

Even our best-laid plans and objectives frequently change or get lost behind the haze and hurry of practical concerns. Daily life with its constant happenings and changes tends to modify our situations, and the only way we can retain a leverage on our goals and objectives, and pry them loose for examination and reassessment is to retreat back into ourselves to "mull things over." Daydreaming helps us to become more attentive to our inner selves. It helps us to repel as foreign stuff the excess baggage of irrelevant concerns that frequently block action on our more fundamental goals. Daydreaming helps us to put our true concerns, the things that are really relevant to us, into sharper focus. And in this way, we can actually improve the quality of our lives.

Many successful people actually daydream their future successes and achievements. Daydreaming for them bears a direct relationship to its expression in overt behavior.

Former pole vaulting champion John Uelses made use of deliberate, programmed daydreaming. Before each meet he vividly pictured himself clearing the bar at a certain height. He repeatedly visualized not only all the minute details of the "act of winning," but actually "saw" the stadium, the throngs of spectators, and "smelled" the grass and the earth.

Jack Nicklaus daydreams before each tournament to attain what he calls "the winning feeling." This feeling, as he puts it, "gives me a line to the cup just as clearly as if it is tattooed on my brain. With that feeling all I have to do is swing the clubs and let nature take its course."

Jim Thorpe, considered one of the greatest athletes of all time, utilized strong mental imagery to picture success before each sporting event. Author Lew Miller relates a story about Thorpe aboard a ship headed for the Olympics: "Other stars were running around the deck or exercising vigorously. The track coach spotted Thorpe, his decathlon entrant, sitting propped against a cabin with his eyes closed. 'What do you think you're doing?' the coach demanded. 'Just practicing,' replied Jim. He then explained that while relaxing he was seeing himself successfully competing in his specialty. History has recorded his legendary athletic feats and record-breaking performances. Jim Thorpe knew instinctively how mental images work to improve performance." . . .

Several clinics specializing in the treatment of alcoholism make use of the technique of daydreaming to cure alcoholics. Dr. Edward McGoldrick, whose "Bridge House" in New York has a high record of recoveries from alcohol addiction, incorporated daydreaming into his daily treatment modality. Every day his patients are trained to relax, to close their eyes and deliberately picture themselves as sober, responsible, and successful persons, enjoying life to the hilt without the "crutch" of liquor. After a few weeks of this fantasy-therapy, many patients not only attain sobriety, but a new, more positive and courageous outlook on life.

Why does a vivid projection of success help to bring the success about? "Your nervous system cannot tell the difference between an *imagined* experience and a *real* experience," says surgeon and author Dr. Maxwell Maltz. "In either case, it reacts automatically to information which you give to it from your forebrain. Your nervous system reacts appropriately to what you think or imagine to be true."

In order to "engineer" your future, you should picture yourself—as vividly as possible—as you want to be or become, or what you want to have or attain. The important thing to remember is that you have to picture these desired objectives *as if you had already attained them.* Go over several times the details of these highly pleasant fantasy pictures. This procedure will indelibly impress them upon your memory. And these memory traces, or "engrams," as they are also called, will soon start influencing your everyday behavior toward the attainment of the pictured goal.

While visualizing this way, you should be alone and completely undisturbed. Close your eyes, for this helps your imagination soar without inhibition. Many people find they obtain better results if they imagine themselves sitting before a large, blank screen—and project onto it the desired picture of themselves. Visual imagery is the predominant modality for daydreaming, and you have to make sure that your imagery is clear and sharp.

Some people first mentally relive some successful experience of the past, in order to attain a positive, facilitative mood for daydreaming. When a mood of confidence and optimism has been attained, they then, so to speak, "cloak" it around whatever they want to accomplish or become. Again, the important thing to remember is that the picture or imagining of desired things must be done as if they were already successfully achieved.

Lew Miller advises that you should build your scenario according to some *immediate* goal. "Whatever it is, you write the script as it progresses, projecting yourself actively into as many successful, triumphant scenes as your imagination permits. Concentrate on it with burning desire. Then, turn off the mental imagery and begin to act in daily life as if you already had achieved that goal." . . .

A life lived without fantasy and daydream is a seriously impoverished life. Each of us should put aside a few minutes each day and daydream, as if we were taking a ten- or fifteen-minute vacation. It is highly beneficial to your physical and mental well-being. This modest investment in time will add up to a more creative and imaginative, a more satisfied and more self-fulfilled you in a relatively short time. . . .

1. The author thinks that daydreaming
    a. is basically harmful to most people because they substitute a fantasy life for the real world.
    b. impairs the psychological health of most people.
    c. is valuable for maintaining our emotional balance.

2. Recent experiments have indicated that nightdreaming
    a. interferes with normal sleep and robs us of necessary rest.
    b. is vital to mental health.
    c. causes anxiety.

3. When people are kept awake for long periods of time,
    a. they dream more than usual when finally permitted to sleep.
    b. they daydream to make up for not sleeping.
    c. they fail to dream when they are allowed to sleep.

4. During times of stress, daydreaming
    a. disappears from a person's life.
    b. erects a temporary shelter from reality for our nervous systems.
    c. makes us even more nervous and upset.

5. Another effect of daydreaming is
    a. improvement of one's learning ability.
    b. reduced attention span.
    c. slow response to psychotherapeutic treatment.

6. Debussy triggered his inner fantasies by
    a. lying on a couch.
    b. smelling rotten apples.
    c. gazing at the river Seine and the reflections of the setting sun on the waves.

7. Another thing that daydreaming does is
    a. help us put our true concerns into sharper focus.
    b. divert us from practical accomplishments.
    c. make us less creative.

8. Many successful people
    a. daydream very little, because they are achievement oriented.
    b. daydream about their future successes and achievements.
    c. daydream about their past accomplishments.

9. Jim Thorpe found out that
    a. mental images could work to improve his performance in the decathlon.
    b. daydreaming relaxed him.
    c. daydreaming took valuable time from his exercise program.

10. The main idea of this article is that
    a. daydreaming is good for athletes.
    b. daydreaming is common among successful people.
    c. daydreaming is highly beneficial to both physical and mental well-being.

Reading Rate Chart

Find the column at the top of the chart which corresponds closest to your reading time. Then find the row at the left which comes nearest to the number of words in the article. The number at which the row and column intersect is the number of words per minute.

Reading Time in Minutes and Seconds

Number of Words	1	1-30	2	2-30	3	3-30	4	4-30	5	5-30	6	6-30	7	7-30	8	8-30	9	9-30	10	10-30	11	11-30	12	12-30
1000	1000	667	500	400	333	286	250	222	200	182	167	154	143	133	125	118	111	105	100	95	91	87	83	80
1050	1050	700	525	420	350	300	262	233	210	191	175	162	150	140	131	124	117	111	105	100	95	91	88	84
1100	1100	733	550	440	367	314	275	244	220	200	183	169	157	147	138	129	122	116	110	105	100	96	92	88
1150	1150	767	575	460	383	329	288	256	230	209	192	177	164	153	144	135	128	121	115	110	105	100	96	92
1200	1200	800	600	480	400	343	300	267	240	218	200	185	171	160	150	141	133	126	120	114	109	104	100	96
1250	1250	833	625	500	417	357	312	278	250	227	208	192	179	167	156	147	139	132	125	119	114	109	104	100
1300	1300	867	650	520	433	371	325	289	260	236	217	200	186	173	162	153	144	137	130	124	118	113	108	104
1350	1350	900	675	540	450	386	338	300	270	245	225	208	193	180	169	159	150	142	135	129	124	117	112	108
1400	1400	933	700	560	467	400	350	311	280	255	233	215	200	187	175	165	156	147	140	133	127	122	117	112
1450	1450	967	725	580	483	414	362	322	290	264	242	223	207	193	181	171	161	153	145	138	132	126	121	116
1500	1500	1000	750	600	500	429	375	333	300	273	250	231	214	200	188	176	167	158	150	143	136	130	125	120
1550	1550	1033	775	620	517	443	388	344	310	282	258	238	221	207	194	182	172	163	155	148	141	135	129	124
1600	1600	1067	800	640	533	457	400	356	320	291	267	246	229	213	200	188	178	168	160	152	145	139	133	128
1650	1650	1100	825	660	550	471	412	367	330	300	275	254	236	220	206	194	183	174	165	157	150	143	138	132
1700	1700	1133	850	680	567	485	425	378	340	309	283	262	243	227	212	200	189	179	170	162	155	148	142	136
1750	1750	1167	875	700	583	500	438	389	350	318	292	269	250	233	219	206	194	184	175	167	159	152	146	140
1800	1800	1200	900	720	600	514	450	400	360	327	300	277	257	240	225	212	200	189	180	171	164	157	150	144
1850	1850	1233	925	740	617	529	462	411	370	336	308	285	264	247	231	218	206	195	185	176	168	161	154	148
1900	1900	1267	950	760	633	543	475	422	380	345	317	292	271	253	238	224	211	200	190	181	173	165	158	152

Reading Rate Chart

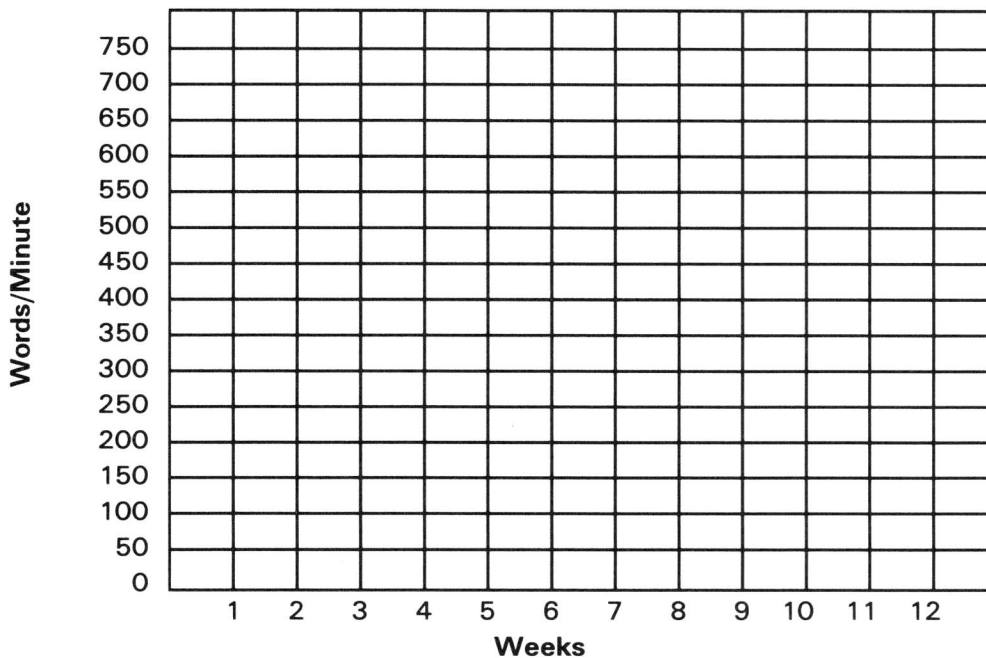

Words/Minute

750
700
650
600
550
500
450
400
350
300
250
200
150
100
50
0

1 2 3 4 5 6 7 8 9 10 11 12

Weeks

Reading Comprehension Chart

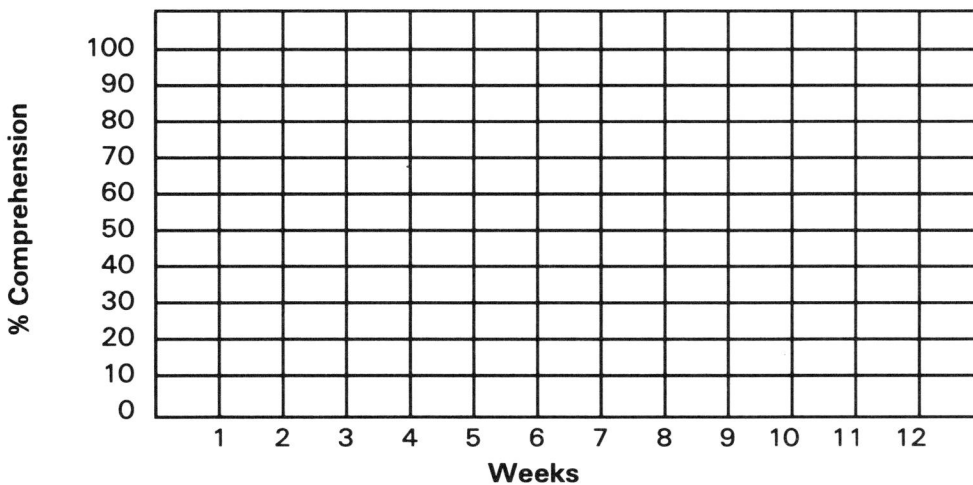

% Comprehension

100
90
80
70
60
50
40
30
20
10
0

1 2 3 4 5 6 7 8 9 10 11 12

Weeks

INDEX

H

Health
    comprehension strategies applied to, 250–61
    vocabulary, 206–9
History, specialized vocabulary for, 196–98
Homographs, 87–92
Homonyms, 86
Humor to reduce stress, 10
Hyperboles, 93

I

Ideas
    arranging, in sequence, 130–35
    main, locating. *See* Main idea
Idiomatic expressions, 93–98
Importance or sequence, clue words or phrases to
    show relative, 142
Index cards of words to memorize, 51
Index of a book, 22–23
Inferences
    drawing, 144–53, 155–56
    false, 145
Information, extracting pertinent, 296, 299–303
Interruptions, reducing, 13
Introduction
    of a book, 22
    paragraph, 105
    of selection to express main idea, 116
Irregular verbs, principal parts of, 76
"It's Still Blue Hawaii," 377–79

K

Knowledge
    associating new material with existing, 36
    ways people acquire, 7

L

Language, figurative, 93–98, 150–53
Latitude, parallels of, 210
Learning style, 7
    inventory, 7–9
    planning study sessions according to your, 13
Legends on maps, 210

Library, features to know about, 24, 312
Listening as a study skill, 34–35
Lists
    memory aids for recalling, 36, 37
    of words to improve spelling, 39
    of words to improve vocabulary, 50–52
Logic
    of author's arguments, 163
    faulty, awareness of, 185–88
Logical sequence, 130
Longitude, meridians of, 210

M

Magazines
    subscribing to, 312
    types of, 313
Main idea
    of an article or selection, finding, 116–23, 154
    of a paragraph in first or topic sentence, 116–23
"Man Under Machine," 369–71
Map reading, 210–16, 325–26
Mathematics vocabulary, 201–6
Meaning
    observing clues to, 141–44
    units of, 102–12
Meanings of word, choosing among multiple
    dictionary, 72
Memorization, 35
Message
    in a business letter, readiness for, 339
    understanding the writer's, 162, 334–38
Metacognition
    use in evaluating understanding and recall of, 36
    use in reading of, 5
Metaphors, 93
Metric units, 202–3
Mnemonic devices to recall lists, 36–37
"Mountain Flying: For Adults Only," 385–87

N

Name calling, 190
Natural science
    comprehension strategies applied to, 245–50
    vocabulary, 198–201
"New Flying Saucer Story, The," 346–48
News stories, structure and function of, 304–5